Tony Abbott and the Times of Revolution

Gerard Charles Wilson

Gerard Charles Wilson Publisher

Tony Abbott and the Times of Revolution

Copyright © 2021 Gerard Charles Wilson

Gerard Charles Wilson Publisher

Mount Martha VIC

Australia

Email: gerard.wilson1@bigpond.com

website: https://author.gerardcharleswilson.com/

ISBN 978 1 876262 24 2   paperback

ISBN 978 1 876262 30 3   ebook

Cover illustration: Temel Pixabay

Dedication

To those dedicated nuns, brothers, and priests who gave me an excellent
education and a love of reading

Also By Gerard Charles Wilson

FICTION

Sixties Series

Times of Distress (Book 1)
In This Vale of Tears (Book 2)
Counterculture Dreams (Book 3) 2024
The Counterculture Goddess (Book 4) 2025
Love in the Counterculture (Book 5) due 2025
Dreams to Nightmare (Book 6) due 2025
The Castle of Heavenly Bliss (Book 7)
A Sense of Loss (Book 8) due 2026

Bitter in Love
Seeking the Divine Spark: A Satire in the Style of Evelyn Waugh

NON-FICTION

Social History Series

Contents

INTRODUCTION

ON THE MORNING of 23 June 2010, the Australian Labor Party (ALP) began tearing itself apart. Julia Gillard had awoken to some disagreeable news and decided she had had enough of her prime minister. Later in the day, she told Prime Minister Kevin Rudd he was up for a challenge. Our television viewing was disrupted that evening, and we were taken to Canberra, where a hand-wringing Rudd faced the cameras in a darkened forecourt. Camera flashes exposed the solemn faces behind him. Baffled by the unexpected cross, I could not help fixing on Rudd's twisted expression. The short address was something about remaining prime minister no matter who said what. It didn't take long to understand. 'You idiots! You can't be serious!' I shouted. During the rest of the evening, I kept muttering, 'morons', 'idiots', 'you're out of your minds' whenever developments flashed across the screen. The following morning the Labor Party elected Julia Gillard leader. Her torment had begun.[1]

Gillard's clinical removal of Kevin Rudd may have impressed her socialist left colleagues, but for many Australians ignorant of the machinations behind the scenes, the feeling reigned that the rules of the game had been subverted. That game was our brittle system of democracy. Backstabbing a prime minister is an act of treachery nearly impossible to justify for ordinary people, no matter how strenuously the assassins work at it – as Julia Gillard does in her book *My Story*. The first blows within days of her ascendancy proved perhaps the most fatal. Typically, they came from veteran Canberra reporter Laurie Oakes who repackaged two leaks that could have come from only one source. They cut Prime Minister Gillard's feet from under her. What might have been had she not let that rush of emotion overcome her that morning and followed the accepted route to party leader?

In a move which surprised everyone – shocked many – the Liberal Party opposition had elected Tony Abbott leader in 2009.[2] An open dispute about climate change precipitated a spill during which a flukish set of circumstances gifted him the leadership. Some appalled colleagues whispered their despair to their favourite gallery hack. The media was full of mockery and forecasts of disaster. 'Captain Catholic' and the 'Mad Monk' were the common coin in the currency of abuse. But, undaunted, Abbott set to work. Despite the forecasts and the unrelenting attempts to destroy him, inside and outside the Liberal Party, Abbott proved an extremely effective opposition leader. He was tough, verbally brutal without resorting to abuse, and determined. He was the torment Gillard's treachery had earned.

Two seats deprived him of securing minority government in 2010. Labor lost eleven seats, and the Coalition gained seven. Two independents betraying their conservative rural constituencies kept the Coalition from government. It would not be close in the 2013 federal election. The Coalition swept to government with a gain of eighteen seats. Labor under a second Rudd leadership lost eleven seats. In the meantime, Rudd had returned the favour and booted Gillard, restoring party equilibrium for many Labor people. Despite the handsome win, Abbott faced mountainous obstacles. He was saddled with the most incompetent Senate in Australia's history. An ignorant amateurish minority in the Senate blocked every attempt to pass vital budgetary legislation. The Senate was no longer a house of review, acknowledging the mandate given by the electorate. That the Labor Party and the Greens would frustrate Abbott at every turn was to be expected. The ignorance, perversity, self-aggrandisement, and in one case, vulgarity of the backbench amateurs were not. It was constitutional sabotage.

Amid the cussedness and abandonment of principle in the Senate, Abbott's army of enemies on the left, in and outside the mainstream media, was pitiless. They jumped on him for every stumble, whether trivial or significant. High-profile 'respectable' journalists abandoned their duty as journalists and behaved as partisan political operators. A few media commentators who describe themselves as conservative joined the battering, occasionally displaying an ignorance of conservatism as a political philosophy and the reasoning flowing from conservatism's philosophical presuppositions. Some Liberal MPs openly criticised Abbott and backgrounded the media. Talk of a leadership challenge grew, promoted by the media who smelt blood. Abbott survived one leadership challenge, but it did not take long for the backroom campaign to bear fruit. Despite warnings from the Liberal Party base, Communications Minister Malcolm Turnbull mounted a successful coup. The extent of the conspiracy and treachery unfolded over the following months.

The dyed-in-the-wool, the rusted-on, the salt of the conservative earth, the people who had sought their political security in Robert Menzies' party were appalled. How could it have happened? How could Liberal MPs get it into their heads to backstab a first-term prime minister elected to government with a handsome majority? Were they suffering from amnesia? Did they not see what Julia Gillard had done to the Labor Party? It was delusional. It was insane. The Liberal Party was in tear-apart mode until Menzian conservatives restored order by booting interloper Turnbull in September 2018 and sending him to sulk in his million-dollar apartment overlooking New York's Central Park.

Abbott's critics may think his defeat in the 2019 federal election was just retribution for his alleged role in Turnbull's expulsion and a sign Australians want none of his type. Scott Morrison's victory contradicted this claim. Prime Minister Morrison was a conservative Pentecostal Christian, hardly an improvement on Abbott's religious deficits. The real message in Abbott's defeat in 2019 is the ascendance of the college-educated and what

Abbott calls 'millionaire lefties' who are an increasing part of the Labor Party's constituency. But that is an issue outside my purpose.

FOUR BOOKS appeared on the Abbott Government. The authors were on the leftist spectrum, keen to feed their political class. And it was just the ideological aspect that has always drawn my attention. Central was a clash of worldviews Abbott's enemies wanted to subsume under the guise of a battle for a 'compassionate, diverse, inclusive, democratic' government. Tony Abbott, they said, was a throwback to the 1950s, a time in Australia's history when racism, exclusion, and all manner of prejudice reigned. Abbott could never be a legitimate leader of the country, no matter how many people voted for him. There was a broader warning. Nobody of Abbott's conservative views and makeup could be a legitimate leader.

Fearful that Abbott was heading for the prime ministership in the 2013 federal election, prominent feminist Susan Mitchell and author and gay activist David Marr argued a desperate case for his disqualification. In her book *Tony Abbott: A Man's Man* (2011),[3] Mitchell strove in the obsessive prose of the extreme left to persuade women Abbott personified the male's inherent toxicity, hated women, and, above all, was a slave to an irrational sexist religion. In a word, Abbott was 'dangerous'. In far more accomplished prose, David Marr entertained us with a postmodernist fantasy about Abbott that won him the 2013 John Button prize for writing on public policy and politics. In his Quarterly Essay *Political Animal: The Making of Tony Abbott*, Marr gave free rein to his imagination to conjure a schizophrenic conflict between 'values' Abbott and 'political' Abbott. In the end, Abbott would surrender to the brutish side of his psychopathology. Marr showed he had no idea of conservatism as a political philosophy. Nor did he show any acquaintance with the schools of political thought that are the background to the discourse about political principles and policy. These philosophical aspects so often mark Abbott's formal writing and speeches. Marr's and Mitchell's manic efforts were crying out for a response.

I had long considered writing an analysis of Tony Abbott's philosophical ideas and motivations to correct the misrepresentations of his enemies and the misapprehensions of ordinary Australians. In explaining his ideas, I would be deploying mine. Many of his critics blame Catholicism for his beliefs and actions. The criticism often degenerates into crude anti-Catholic sectarianism, as in the cases of Mitchell and Marr. What they miss is the natural law component in Tony Abbott's thinking. Among his strongest intellectual influences are conservative philosophers Edmund Burke, Roger Scruton, and Michael Oakeshott.[4] I will argue that the natural law interpretation of Edmund Burke's political philosophy is the primary driver in Abbott's political action. Mitchell's and Marr's books consolidated the plan, and the books about the Abbott Government gave me the impetus. So I began planning a book about the Abbott prime ministership.

Because my core theme would be the ideological clash, I had to go back to the beginning to trace Abbott's intellectual influences, including the revolutionary 1960s and his years at Sydney University. Marr and Mitchell covered his time at school and university. As my research passed from school to student politics, I discovered a fascinating story of right-left political warfare in the pages of Sydney University's student newspaper *Honi Soit*. It was illuminating. Here was a separate story that paralleled Abbott's time as opposition leader and prime minister and exemplified the misrepresentations. With the same purpose, I decided to concentrate on Tony Abbott's actions in the vicious, uncompromising warfare at Sydney University and leave his prime ministership for a second book.

In David Marr's 2012 Quarterly Essay, one comes across the incendiary passage below. It was July 1977. Barbara Ramjan had just been elected President of Sydney University's Students' Representative Council (SRC), beating Tony Abbott:

'[Tony Abbott] approached Ramjan. She thought he was coming over to congratulate her. 'But no, that's not what he wanted', she recalls. 'He came up to within an inch of my nose and punched the wall on either side of my head'. Thirty-five years later, she recalls with cold disdain what he did. 'It was done to intimidate'. Abbott tells me he has no recollection of the incident: "It would be profoundly out of character had it occurred".'5

The uproar this passage provoked went on for weeks. The media piled in, ecstatic to have such unassailable evidence to confirm their worst opinions of Abbott. Michelle Grattan, the doyenne of political commentators with *The Age*, deliriously churned out a batch of pieces all flailing Abbott without mercy. Ramjan received support from David Patch, 'a barrister and a former Judicial Registrar of the Industrial Relations Court and of the Federal Court of Australia' and 'Ms Ramjan's [student] campaign manager in 1977'.

In my journey through student politics at Sydney University from 1973 to 1980, I discovered that close colleagues David Patch and Barbara Ramjan played starring roles as members of the far left. They were bitter implacable adversaries of Tony Abbott's, seeking to destroy him at every turn. Ramjan's feeding her story of the alleged punches to Marr merged Abbott of the 1970s with contemporary Abbott. Ramjan and Patch have extended the political arena of their unrelenting hatred for him from the present to the 1970s. They burn as much as they did then with the purpose of political liquidation. I undertake a detailed analysis of Ramjan's accusations in chapter fourteen and find holes through which a herd of elephants could be driven.

I draw on many sources, the main ones being the pages of Sydney University's student newspaper *Honi Soit* and Alan Barcan's excellent

From New Left to Factional Left: Fifty Years of Student Activism at Sydney University.[6] Critical findings in Gerard Henderson's 'Media Watch Dog' about David Marr's punch allegations appear in chapters 2, 8 and 14. But I also draw deeply on my memories and experiences of the times. Indeed, this book is as much about me and the revolutionary upheaval I lived through as about Tony Abbott. While reading and responding to the radicals' writings in *Honi Soit*, I had the unnerving feeling that I was back in those turbulent times. Tony Abbott became a vehicle through which I could express my criticisms of leftist thought and the student rebellion of the 1960s and 1970s. Three themes are intertwined: The character of Tony Abbott as displayed in his clash with Sydney University's radicals, what it means to be a conservative in a leftist world, and my critique of the student and sexual revolution.

Part One

The ideological Prelude

Chapter 1

The School Years

TONY ABBOTT WAS born in London on 4 November 1957. His father, Dick Abbott, born in England in 1924, came to Australia with his parents at sixteen. At the end of the Second World War, he studied dentistry at Sydney University. After graduation, he returned to England to gain specialist qualifications. There he met Fay Peters, a dietitian and science graduate of Sydney University, on a working holiday. She had grown up in the southern beach suburb of Bronte. They married in 1957 and returned to Australia in 1960. Tony Abbott was two years and ten months when they arrived back in Sydney. They lived a year at Bronte with Fay Abbott's parents and then moved to Chatswood, where Dick Abbott established a successful orthodontic practice.

In 1971, the family, now with three girls, moved to Killara, a smart suburb further up the North Shore (train) line. Tony attended Holy Family convent at Lindfield until second class (1965). He completed his primary education at St. Aloysius Milsons Point (1966-1969). For his secondary education, he moved to St Ignatius Riverview (1970-1975). He excelled at sport and study, often topping his year. He was first in the external exam in his final year. He pursued tertiary studies in economics and law at Sydney University. He was a voracious reader with a liking for books on history. From his extensive reading, he said, 'I became an admirer of parliamentary democracy, freedom under the law, and liberal institutions. As these were

largely made in England (although often improved elsewhere), I also became an incorrigible Anglophile'. He was awarded a Rhodes scholarship to
attend Oxford University in 1980.[7] He described his feelings on returning
to the place of his birth:

'When I eventually went back to England as a student, I didn't feel that I
was visiting a foreign country, despite the passport queues at Heathrow
airport. As I flew over the city of London, it felt like more than a home-
coming. The metropolis was not just the inspiration for a Monopoly board
but the chief source of the language I spoke, the centre of the system of law
I lived under and the fountain of the democracy I cherished. It belonged
to me as much as to any Briton. 'Beating the Poms' is as important to
me as to any other Australian, but it's like wanting New South Wales to
beat Queensland in the rugby league state of origin series. Only on the
sports field are the British an alien tribe. Indeed, it would be a very rare
Australian, I suspect, who feels like a stranger in any English-speaking
country regardless of disagreements that might exist between governments
or about policy.'[8]

Abbott's extensive reading had given his contemplative mind a keen sense
of culture and national identity. For him, one cannot be complete without
a deep understanding and an unbroken consciousness of one's cultural an-
tecedents. Without this knowledge, one cannot understand Tony Abbott,
the real person. Many Australians share this sense of cultural identity and
understand the significance of the historical links to the British Isles.

'Apart from my parents,' Abbott wrote in *Battlelines*, 'the church was
the biggest influence on my early life'. As with most Catholics in those
years, his religious education was centred on the family and the Catholic
school. The parental commitment to religious education may have di-
ffered from family to family, but the school commitment was extensive
and uniform. Because the media class entertains fantastic views about that

education, it is necessary to what follows to review what young Tony and his Catholic contemporaries like me experienced at school.

When Abbott began attending the Holy Family convent school in 1963, the Second Vatican Council (1962-1965) was already four months underway. There would be no wholesale changes in the Church until 1969, when the Novus Ordo Mass (the New Mass) was promulgated. The dark forces unleashed by the Council would not manifest themselves until some years later, around the time he finished school. Therefore, the school regime and ethos during Abbott's school years were, pre-Vatican II, little changed from the previous fifty years.

The pre-Vatican II school was not a school with religious lessons tacked on, as it often seems to be today. The spirit of the Gospels and Church teaching pervaded all aspects of the school. In addition to the classes devoted to religion, there were prayers before and after classes. At midday, there was the Angelus, the prayer celebrating the Incarnation, and there were visits to the church nearby for Confession, Mass, and prayer. Classes on religion were about the Bible (Old and New Testaments), Church teaching, the heroic lives of the saints, and devotions students could follow, the rosary, for example. The spirit of the Gospels was to motivate students. Nuns, brothers or priests oversaw the student's behaviour in class and at play and meted out punishment for failures to live up to the mark.

Such a school regime is likely to confirm the view of the Church's critics that it subjected its pupils to a process of indoctrination. If they were right, what were the content and orientation of the alleged indoctrination which young Tony Abbott enjoyed at such an impressionable age? And what would make the Catholic educational regime indoctrination and the secular school system doctrine free? After all, the Catholic school followed the same curriculum and sat the same external examinations as the state schools. The short answer is, of course, the religious content, which for my purposes, needs explanation. I will leave aside the unexamined ideological content permeating the state school system.

The study of the Old Testament began with the Fall, the expulsion of the human race's first parents, Adam and Eve, from the Garden of Eden for a fundamental act of disobedience. They wanted to be like God – an ambition that found fertile ground in the 20th century. Original Sin is the name of that act whose effects have marked Adam and Eve's descendants. The idea of Original Sin is a vital concept in modern political philosophy, although it is called something else, depending on the context. That man is a flawed and fallible being capable of great virtue and great vice is argued against those convinced man is perfectible and can reason himself to a utopian condition.

The pupils heard the stories of the Tower of Babel, Sodom and Gomorrah, and Noah's Ark that told of the disasters precipitated by turning away from God's law. The stories of Job, Abraham and Isaac, Daniel in the Lions' den exemplified God's protection and rewards to those faithful to Him and his ordinances. There was the great epic of Moses leading the Israelites out of Egyptian oppression to their promised land. Once again, despite rescue and redemption, man continually murmured and turned away from God, calling down severe punishment. During the journey to the Promised Land, Moses received the tablets etched with the Ten Commandments. God made clear what reason could have recognised. If these stories are not always factual, they form instructive allegories for life in the 21st century. In all this, the school pupil learned about God's omnipotence, man's utter dependence on God, man's propensity to sin and the punishments earned for transgressing God's laws, and the rewards and protection for remaining faithful. Above all this was the promise of redemption.

The New Testament ushered in a new dispensation. In the person of Jesus Christ, God became man to redeem his people from their sins. There is no change to God's laws in the Old Testament. Indeed, Jesus said himself that he did not 'come to destroy the law and the prophets ... but to fulfil' them (Matt. 5:17). But there was a dramatic change of emphasis, and it is explicit in a few core verses of Matthew's Gospel. When one of the Pharisees, always keen to trap Jesus in his words, asked what 'the great commandment in the law' was, Jesus answered:

Thou shalt love the Lord thy God with thy whole heart, and with thy whole soul, and with thy whole mind.
This is the greatest and the first commandment.
And the second is like to this: Thou shalt love thy neighbour as thyself.
On these two commandments dependeth the whole law and the prophets.

The New Testament several times repeats the commandment that you treat others as you treat yourself, stressing its centrality in the message of the Gospels (e.g. Luke 6:31, Matt: 7.12). It also accords with unaided reason. A key feature of German philosopher Immanuel Kant's moral philosophy that one must never treat people as a means to an end but always as an end in themselves echoes what other cultures call the Golden Rule. Finally, one can express the dependence of 'the whole law and the prophets' on the two supreme laws in a valid conditional argument: if you love your neighbour as yourself, then you won't harm your neighbour. In all this, Revelation complements reason.

If the question now arose about who one's neighbour was, the Pharisees and teachers of the law, never giving up, made another attempt to trap Jesus. They asked who one's neighbour was. Jesus responded with a parable in twelve masterly verses paradigmatic of Christian ethics and at the heart of Western Civilization in its laws, government and art. The story of the Good Samaritan (Luke 10:25-37) is one of the few Biblical stories still widely known in our de-Christianized society. Those few verses are about a Samaritan, a foe of the Jews, who stopped to help a man lying injured by the side of the road after being robbed. A priest and a Levite had passed the injured man before the Samaritan, taking pity on him, took him up and organised his care. When Jesus asked which of the three was a neighbour to the distressed man, the teacher of the law had no choice but to say the Samaritan. But the law of charity, love for one's fellow man, went beyond t his.

Jesus's instruction to his disciples was not only to love your friends. That was easy. No, one was to love one's enemies and to do good to those who harmed you. In answer to the question about how many times one must forgive those who harm you, Jesus answered, times without end. Forgive and no grudges. There is one more crucial instruction in the New Testament related to Tony Abbott's religious 'indoctrination' and the influence it exerted on his adult life – as much influence as the law of charity did. It is about authority. In brief, those with authority, said Jesus, were servants to those over whom they exercised authority (Matt. 20:25-27). The supreme example in the Church is that one of the pope's titles is 'Servant of Servants of God' (*Servus Servorum Dei*).

The lessons of the New Testament were at the core of the lessons in religion and the whole Catholic school ethos. The New Testament was the hinge on which all other aspects of the Catholic faith hung. The doctrine became progressively more demanding as the student rose through secondary school and was always linked to the Scriptures. The heroic lives of the saints, which inspired so many young Catholics of Abbott's and my generation, were about the uncompromised practice of the Gospel's law of charity. One of the more inspiring saints was St Ignatius Loyola, founder of the Jesuit order of priests who exercised such a decisive influence on schoolboy Tony. The law of charity was eminently reasonable. It motivated an extensive complex of hospitals, schools, and charitable institutions the atheist will find listed in the pages of the telephone directory. The ethos of the Catholic school, based on the law of charity, was, and is, a potent preparation for a career serving one's fellow man, not only in politics. It explains why so many Catholics, practising or lapsed, work in the service professions. Tony Abbott is one among many. It is curious that some sections of the media have singled him out for their obsessive anti-Catholic abuse.

Turning now to the other influence on Tony Abbott's formation, we read in *Battlelines* that his 'parents had two messages for their children: first, "be as good as you can be at whatever you do", and second, "we love you whatever happens"'. This was pretty much the attitude of my devout Catholic parents. Being a good person is more important than being successful. Abbott confessed he sometimes failed the lessons, but in doing so, he 'never had the impression that my parents were mad at me rather than about my (fairly frequent) misdeeds'. Again, that is my experience. My parents distinguished between the sin and the sinner, reflecting the key Christian doctrine of original sin and a sympathetic non-ideological view of human nature. When Tony Abbott began the daily trip to St Aloysius' College in 1966, he experienced an intimacy with his father that reinforced his parental instruction:

'For several years of my childhood, every weekday, I walked the couple of kilometres or so from home to Chatswood railway station with my dad before the train ride to school. I can only remember the odd snatch of conversation, which, I'm sure, would have been about trivia as well as the things that were going on in my life. I do very clearly recall, though, Dad's insistence that it was better to be a good man than a successful one.'[9]

He finishes by paying tribute to the influence of both parents:

'Both my parents taught by example. From Mum, I learned that the ideal home welcomes people and makes them feel part of the family. From Dad, I learned that you should always look for the best in others and try to be for them what you would have them be for you ... I could not have asked for a better start and for more ongoing encouragement. Mum and Dad were the best type of parents, nearly always thinking well of their children, sometimes to the point of imagining that we're better than we really are.'[10]

It is no fluke or coincidence I could say the same about my parents. The moral and religious education my parents gave me contradicts the image of the bible-bashing, heartless, finger-wagging Catholic parents of the sectarian fantasies. Like Abbott's parents, they taught by example. That train ride from Chatswood to Milsons Point not only furthered Abbott's general religious education but it heralded the start of a particular Catholic education. From 1966 to 1969 (school years 4-6), he attended St Aloysius' College, Milsons Point, whose motto was 'born for higher things'. From 1970 to 1975 (school years 7-12), he attended St Ignatius, Riverview, whose motto was '(roughly translated) "do as much as you can"'. The two mottos, he says, 'give a good idea of the Jesuit ethos at that time, which I thoroughly assimilated, sometimes to my masters' annoyance'. What, indeed, did student Tony assimilate between 1966 and 1975?

During my childhood and youth, the Jesuit schools were renowned for the rigour, extent and depth of their education, an education applauded or execrated depending on one's religious and political outlook. My father, who came from a poor but genteel Catholic background of tradesmen, was in awe of the Jesuits. He always regretted his parents, who had lost everything in the Great Depression, never had the means to send him to a Jesuit school. They considered the Jesuits the great bulwark of the faith. It was his pride and joy that he could send me to St Ignatius Riverview for the last year of my schooling in 1963. Riverview was the Jesuit school he idealised. By the time Abbott attended Riverview, the 'Spirit of Vatican II' had made deep inroads into the Jesuit order. In other words, they were 'liberalising'.

In *Battlelines*, Abbott shows he is aware of the charge of liberalism, even of heresy, by some orthodox Catholics. In defending the Jesuits and the education they gave him, he is defending the Jesuits as he knew them during those years under their tutelage. Perhaps it's truer to say he defends those Jesuits he admired and was close to. That defence is crucial to understanding the cast of mind that would forever determine his behaviour:

'The Jesuits who taught me wanted to bring out the very best in their students but didn't expect them to be saints. They weren't disloyal to the Pope or subversive of the church but often seemed impatient with the 'scold' side to religious teaching. 'Don't bother giving up chocolates for Lent', Father Emmet Costello used to advise, 'but do something positive like going to Mass more often'. 'We are all the products of those who have loved us or failed to love us', he often observed ... For me, the message was that God preferred big-hearted people who might sometimes make mistakes rather than robotic rule worshippers.'[11]

These are the words not of the dogmatist who has no regard for human frailty but of the person who understands the father's love and forgiveness in Jesus' parable of the Prodigal Son, the best-known parable after the parable of the Good Samaritan. They reflect the love and forgiveness Jesus displayed in absolving the woman caught in adultery whom the Pharisees wanted to stone. Abbott draws out the central role of the law of charity in his faith by referring to those scriptural verses I have already discussed:

'Even though the Jesuits weren't much fussed about rote learning the catechism, at least in those days, their charges mostly seemed to assimilate the greatest Christian truths: to love God with your whole heart and to love your neighbour as you love yourself. This second commandment is rightly the whole basis of human ethics. 'What would you want if the boot was on the other foot?' provides the best answer to so many moral dilemmas. The social teaching stemming from this reflected, it has always seemed to me, not some Vatican diktat but the best human instinct.'[12]

It may pass notice, but the contrast Abbott makes between an imagined

'Vatican Diktat' and 'the best human instinct' is the same contrast that Edmund Burke made between prescription based on rigid abstract theory and decisions determined by natural moral feeling. I make this point because Tony Abbott is a Burkean conservative. Edmund Burke (1730-1797) is considered the father of modern conservatism. I mean conservatism considered as a political philosophy. Abbott's Burkean conservatism governs his political decisions far more than Catholic dogma. His religious education and repeated views of how he sees his Catholic faith do not support the image of him as a drooling, breast-beating dogmatist that many frontline media celebrities energetically propagate.

Michael Duffy attributes to Abbott a sense of entitlement.[13] I rather think the evidence suggests a sense of destiny. That sense of destiny, a call to leadership, was integral to his character from the earliest age. He said of himself in *Battlelines*:

'As best I can remember, my interest in public life first stirred as a child reading the Ladybird books that my Mum brought home. These usually turned out to be about great figures in history: Julius Caesar, Francis Drake and Henry V are three that I seem to recall. The lesson, invariably, was that duty and honour carried the day. They were caricatures, of course, as I was to discover over time, but uplifting ones. In the real world, good doesn't always triumph, and justice doesn't always prevail. Even the best turn out to have their flaws. Despite that, ideals don't cease to matter because they're never perfectly achieved or because their adherents are compromised.'[14]

It was not an ambitious warrior's military and political success that impressed him. The leader whose talents, sense of duty, and honour prevailed in the frequent struggle of life was young Tony's model of righteous action. The honour and justice of the cause called out those qualities in the awe-inspiring leader. Later, the lessons of human frailty tempered his concept of moral heroism. Enduring ideals and principles, whatever the failures of circumstances and character, were to govern the concrete action. This is a profoundly conservative outlook. Abbott's character and sense of destiny made it inevitable that someone would notice more than his cleverness, outspokenness and energy.

Father Emmett Costello, Riverview's chaplain with extensive contacts in politics and high society, was 'struck by [the schoolboy's] combination of intelligence, ability to talk, arrogance, and a sense of entitlement'.[15] In 1973, he took Tony under his wing. He prompted him to ponder the nature of leadership, encouraged his sense of duty, and broadened his understanding of the political world, but endeavoured at the same time to moderate what some saw as arrogance and brashness.

The spark of Tony Abbott's interest in the duties of public life would grow into a flame. In 1972, aged fifteen and in Year 9, he experienced 'the first stirring of a political commitment'. His history teacher set the class the task of examining the policies of the political parties in that year's election – and unwittingly steered young Tony into a political course that has lasted until this day. It was the epoch-making election that brought the Labor Party into government under the erratic leadership of the suave Gough Whitlam who had his seat among the battlers of Western Sydney. Tony watched the campaign launch of the major parties, but it was the launch of the conservative Democratic Labor Party (DLP) that grabbed his attention. Fifteen-year-old Tony 'liked [its] support for traditional values and support for workers in a market economy.'[16] His reaction was purely conservative. There were school principals in those days, Abbott wrote, who

'still sympathised with the work of [well-known political and religious conservative] B.A. Santamaria. Some used to suggest the names of school leavers to be invited to conferences about university life. When a school friend received an invitation, I was only too happy to provide him with company. That conference helped to channel my Jesuit-inculcated desire to be 'a man for others' into an immediate political outlet. It was a thrill to meet people of influence and authority in public life. Most of all, it was good to learn that there was a way to get involved immediately through joining the Sydney University Democratic Club. This was the successor to the former DLP club and was supported and sustained by Santamaria's National Civic Council.'[17]

In December 1975, at the end of his school days, the political ideas of 18-year-old Tony Abbott were settled. He had completed the full course of the indoctrination to which the Catholic school subjects its captive students. When his critics refer to his Catholic beliefs and upbringing, they use a shorthand way of dismissing him and his beliefs as having no basis in reason. But, apart from the elementary fallacy in the argument that someone's views are irrational because they are Catholic, are there any grounds for the claim that Catholic teaching is based on unreason? Susan Mitchell's book *Tony Abbott: A Man's Man* is a tedious, repetitive catalogue of Abbott's alleged 'dangerous' views, indictable influences, and character traits. Her project of destroying Abbott relies heavily on the claim that his thinking is irrational because Catholic belief is irrational. The question seems mad and unnecessary given both St Aloysius and St Ignatius's colleges are schools of high repute to which professional parents and leading members of the business community have sent their sons for over a century – and paid heaps of money for doing so.

As I have described it, the law of charity hardly qualifies as irrational – forget about its Scriptural context. The injunction to love one's fellow man as one loves oneself is eminently reasonable. Unaided reason, reason independent of Revelation, discovers this central teaching of Christianity. You don't have to be an orthodox Christian to judge it true as a moral injunction. Moreover, you don't have to be a Christian to accept that if you love your fellow man, you would not kill him, lie to him, steal from him, commit adultery with his wife and turn a covetous eye on his property.

These deductions hang on the law of charity. The law of charity has both a biblical basis and a basis in unaided reasoning. This is essential Catholic teaching which distinguishes between faith and reason. The teachings that draw attention in politics are usually about moral issues. With many moral questions that arise in contemporary politics, one can reason without reference to Scripture and stay consistent with Catholic teaching.

When I deduced objective moral positions above from the law of charity, I took for granted love constitutes the human person. The human person's nature is to love his own and, by extension, his fellow man, despite the depths of vice to which he can descend. To talk about the nature of the human person is to talk about an ordered world of which that nature is a part. And here, we lead into the secular moral philosophy the Catholic Church developed and applied. It is the natural law. Natural law philosophy has been the most enduring moral philosophy in Western Civilization. It informed all moral, legal, and political discourse until the period of the 'Enlightenment' and is still the moral philosophy that makes the most sense for many people, quite apart from those in the Catholic Church.

Edmund Burke's political philosophy presupposes an idea of natural law that developed from Plato (424-348 BC) and Aristotle (384-323 BC) through the Roman Stoics to its fullest expression in the writings of St Thomas Aquinas. It is the form of natural law Tony Abbott's moral and political discourse presupposes. Abbott never invokes Catholic dogma to argue his moral and political views. It is always a natural law argument incorporating Edmund Burke's ideas about the operation of prudence. Abbott's adherence to natural law moral philosophy reflects his deep consciousness of Western civilisation's history and Australia's place in it through our Anglo-Celtic heritage. There are thus two essential parts of the education Tony Abbott – indeed, all students at Catholic schools – underwent. The first is Scripture's law of charity and what it means. The second is the objective nature of moral truth argued through the natural law. Parents and teachers thought their children and students were well-armed with this education to go into the wider community. Abbott took this moral armament onto the campus of Sydney University in 1976.

Susan Mitchell had quite another view of the dimensions of Abbott's mind in 1976, and she strains in her book to conjure a picture of him, the opposite of the one I have sketched. At the time of her writing (2011), she said, there was no 'full-length political and personal analysis of Tony Abbott'. There was only Abbott's brief account of his school and university time in *Battlelines* and Duffy's limited *Latham and Abbott*. Mitchell thought it urgent to correct this dangerous lack in the marketplace of ideas. She follows Abbott's life and deeds up to around the halfway point of Julia Gillard's term as prime minister (2010-2013), leaving it to the media to propagate and expand her findings. She does not mince words about Abbott and the goal of her book. Her judgment is heralded in the title and detailed in the introduction. The conclusion is first, and the evidence and argument follow for what they're worth. Talk about Abbott as a 'man's man' suggests she thinks there is something bad about being a man. The first page of the book makes the thought explicit:

'Of all the men who have held or sought to hold the office of prime minister, I believe he is the most dangerous. This is not just because of his retrogressive attitudes and beliefs regarding women and their role in the world, but more generally because his ideological framework is so narrow. The man, his values, and his beliefs have been created and nurtured by men from another era — men whose ideas are rooted in the past.'

Narrowness of thought and proposing different (retrogressive) ideas about women makes Abbott dangerous as a prime minister – dangerous presumably to Australia and Australians, not only women. This is an extravagant claim, one warranting clinching evidence and overpowering argument – you would think. Unfortunately, this passage's two points of evidence do not bode well. The first claim, in line with the book's title, is that men created dangerous Abbott. That what men do is bad because men as men are bad is unadulterated prejudice. She develops this unabashed prejudice throughout the book into full fly-blown misandry.

The second is that ideas of the past are necessarily dangerous because they are ideas of the past. That does not follow, of course. The naked claim ideas are wrong or harmful because they are of the past is intellectually crude, hardly worthy of a daydreaming schoolgirl. Apart from the question of logical coherence, whether past ideas are good or bad rests on the empirical evidence of their effects. Mitchell adds 'age' to her prejudice against men. Abbott has been 'educated and mentored by older men'. She repeats this claim *ad nauseam*. We have pure prejudice again, now about age. All governments and local state authorities make it a priority to take measures against discrimination based on age. For Mitchell, one can jettison those measures with Catholic Abbott.

Abbott, Mitchell continues, has 'rarely worked outside institutions created and run by men', which she describes as a 'narrow world'. On the same argument, girls educated in an all-girl environment would be similarly narrow in their thinking. Not only is the assertion fallacious in both cases, but those feminists who think girls do better in an all-female environment have to reassess their views. If Mitchell's argument is consistently applied, then some highly respected girls' schools, jealously protected by their female guardians, would have to be shut down. But that won't happen because Mitchell's claim about Abbott's narrowness is just as silly as her other claims. Because of these deficiencies, she claims, Abbott cannot understand women. Now Abbott may or may not understand women, but one must investigate the reasons for either case. The empirical evidence reveals that women are far from disliking Tony Abbott, let alone seeing him as a danger to them and society. Only a rigid, unthinking ideologue would hold onto such ill-considered fallacious views.

Added to Abbott's severe handicaps in coming under the tutelage of older males in an all-male environment is something a good deal worse.

The mentors, tutors, and clergy right up to the pope are all Catholic! The Catholic badness is something that Mitchell hammers to death, especially in the school period I have already covered. I have already offered a response to the charge of unreason levelled at people of faith, not only Catholics. So I need not repeat it except to say in convicting and disqualifying Abbott from political life in Australia, Mitchell also disqualifies a significant section of the Australian community. But that's of no account for Mitchell who certifies for citizenship only those that fall in line with her Marxist feminism. The rest are outsiders who suffer a 'benign' disenfranchisement. So doing, she is carrying on the heritage of the Orangemen of the Protestant Ascendancy who doggedly worked to keep Catholics in their outsider place in Australia's colonial society.

Mitchell's coverage of Abbott and his school years is all condemnation. She is unrelenting in her effort to find bad in everything about him and his background, right down to his parents and their boasting of his objectionable qualities. He lacks empathy, is dominated by a snooty 'North Shore upbringing', has a woman problem, has no 'genuine belief in separation of Church and state', sees 'no room any more for a reasoned discussion of policy differences', 'treats complex problems in a manner that frightens people', sees governing as 'giving glory to God', he dumbs down democracy, 'adores' John Wayne movies, and so on it goes to extreme tedium.

These accusations are without evidence or sustained argument and are clearly meant to draw their force from the not-too-subtle associations her constituency will mindlessly make. In the long run, Mitchell argues two contradictory interpretations of Abbott. He is either slavishly under the influence of older male mentors and their evil ideas, or as an exemplary male, he has, from the beginning, cunningly manipulated them for his nefarious designs. Either way, Tony Abbott can't win. Mitchell's arguments against Abbott can be reduced to the existential badness of maleness and the badness of the Catholic religion. In both these elements of badness, Tony Abbott excels. The irony is that Mitchell's obsessive hatred of Tony

Abbott causes her book to degenerate into unreason. Later, however, when I came to revise this chapter, I realised it was likely Mitchell was not at all concerned with problems of logic and evidence in her attack on Abbott. Her object was not the truth but the destruction of Abbott as a political force. In recent years, high-profile feminists, inside and outside the media, have used the same tactic to destroy other men of conservative values. In some cases, they have been stunningly successful, leaving the object of their attack utterly destroyed, in one case, fearful of appearing in public.

Chapter 2

The cancerous counterculture

WHEN 18-YEAR-OLD Tony Abbott began his first day of lectures in 1976, Sydney University, one of Sydney's most prestigious educational institutions, was tapering off from a period of wild revolutionary unrest. Student activism had shaken the university to its foundations. The action had been part of a worldwide social and political upheaval. I turned thirty in 1976. I witnessed that turmoil, sometimes close-up, in Australia and later in Holland. The phase of activism that led to the explosion of the student rebellion at Sydney University roughly between 1967 and 1974 had its seed in the early 1960s. I was never a part of it and far less of a supporter. I was like most of my contemporaries who began at Sydney University in 1964 – an innocent 17-year-old from a sheltered middle-class background and in awe of my surroundings, including the relatively small, sophisticated group I came to know as the 'student radicals'. I was present at probably the first major anti-American demonstration in Australia. It was outside the American Consulate in Sydney on 6 May 1964. I had gone there with friends in all innocence, not knowing what it was about or what to expect. Until then, the political activities of the small group of leftist agitators were at a distance. I had more than enough to do, trying to order myself and adjust to my new circumstances.

When we arrived in Wynard Place, opposite Wynard Park, where the American Consulate was, a vast crowd was already there, surging this way and that amid a tumult of shouting. A haze of smoke hung over the area from a burning cross placed in a drum emblazoned with KKK. Smouldering strips of blackened rag hung from the cross or lay around on the ground. The police, some on horseback, tried to contain the crowd surging to and fro as if possessed by some spirit. Brawls erupted, bringing a rush of police with more shouting. The whole happening unnerved me, especially the recklessness of the small number taunting those we had always taken as symbols of authority. The demonstration was over civil rights and the American presence in Vietnam. Fourteen activists were arrested for brawling. As young and green as I was and thoroughly unnerved by the time we hurried away from the tumult, I experienced a political awakening that day. My background and temperament later came into play, and I formed a view that strengthened as I grew older and understood the concrete issues.

What stands out in my memory from when I first set foot on the grounds of Sydney University in 1964 were two connected campaigns: the overthrow of 'illegitimate' authority and the Vietnam War. A bunch of youths were out to defy and destroy all authority they considered illegitimate. These youths fresh from the school classroom judged no authority legitimate unless the tribunal of their considerable reasoning powers gave it their passport. They scorned the authority of custom, convention, and Church as having no 'rational' basis. Custom, convention, and the Church were thus in the front row for overthrow.

The student newspaper was one of the chief instruments for propagating radical student views. The Sydney University student newspaper was (and still is) *Honi Soit*, the editors of which were predominately libertarian in the early stages of the New Left activism. The Marxists would come not long after. Some well-known names were editors of *Honi Soit* around this time, including Richard Walsh, Laurie Oakes, Bob Ellis, and Clive James, all of whom could be described as libertarian. But Richard Neville, the 1962 editor of *Tharunka*, the student newspaper of the University of New South Wales, was the real star and force behind the radical movement to bring obscenity in all its forms into the family lounge room. Neville, later euphemistically describing himself as 'counterculture', joined with Richard Walsh and artist Martin Sharp to produce Oz, a 'magazine of dissent' – again a nice euphemism. Neville waged a cultural war against his (bourgeois) society and 'the weapons of revolution [were] obscenity, blasphemy and drugs'.[18] Their efforts brought them twice before the courts on the charge of producing an obscene publication. They were convicted but later acquitted on appeal.

The pieces of obscenity for which Walsh, Neville and Sharp were charged were rather trifling attempts to bring down the censorship laws, though a step in that direction. Behind these attempts was Neville's political program to indiscriminately 'root' as many 'birds' as possible, including his mates' girlfriends. He dressed up his anarchic sexual drive in the tatty, rat-gnawed clothes of a 'non-ideological' ideology he called 'Play Power'. Clive James somewhere makes the wry comment that his libertarian friends were keen to swap their girlfriends. With this sort of libertarian trade in female flesh, it is no wonder the feminist movement took hold among Neville's female counterculture companions within a few years. In 1966, having led the charge to collapse bourgeois morality, Neville moved to the UK, where he, Sharp, and Jim Anderson, another similarly committed Australian, produced a London version of *Oz*. Their *Oz No.28*, 'The *Oz* School Kids Issue' brought Neville, Anderson and 'working class' Brit Felix Dennis before the English courts charged with obscenity and 'a conspiracy to corrupt public morals'.

Schoolkids Oz featured a cartoon of a favourite children's comic strip character, Rupert, the Bear, 'in an explicitly sexual situation'.[19] Anderson, one of the editors of the School Kids edition, proudly described the cartoon thus: 'Basically, it had Rupert with a whopping big dick getting it on with an old granny'.[20] *The Rupert Bear Annual* was one of my favourite children's books when I, as an innocent 8-year-old, was in Second Class at the local convent school. Wikipedia has a rather anodyne entry for Neville, except for one sentence about Neville's boast of 'fucking' a 14-year-old from a London comprehensive school.[21] The *Oz* School Kids Issue was an expression of Neville's anti-authoritarian political outlook and unsated sexual ambitions. Indeed, Neville's 'fucking' an underage schoolgirl should be seen in his libertarian/power play crusade as a brave revolutionary act on behalf of everyman's freedom – the tearing away of the shackles of the middle class's repressive sexual morality.

The London Oz trial (1971) was one of the longest obscenity trials in English history. Well-known lawyer John Mortimer QC, assisted by junior counsel Geoffrey Robertson, defended Neville, Anderson, and Dennis. Ubiquitous Robertson has become a sparkling expatriate celebrity with a constant flow of human rights guff. A star graduate of Sydney University, Robertson grew up in Sydney in middle-class Eastwood and attended Epping High School, both a few miles from where I grew up in Lane Cove. He was active in left-wing student politics while at Sydney University. After a stint on a Rhodes Scholarship at Oxford University, he settled in the UK, where he acquired a dual passport and honed an already pompous accent into upper-class acceptability. He has mastered the rhetoric of his political class. Since that class is our Western Society's dominant class, his intellectual windbaggery is seldom challenged in the media – or anywhere else, for that matter.

In a curious coincidence, the news of Neville's death resulting from Alzheimer's disease came through just as I finished writing the above. Here was the great courageous knight of the counterculture striking down Christian Civilization with the revolutionary weapons of 'obscenity, blasphemy and drugs' reduced to drooling mental and physical impotence. His wife wrote on Facebook that 'our wonderful Richard has gone on to his next adventure'.[22] Mrs Neville must fervently hope the Marxists were right about Christianity being part of the phantom superstructure of the capitalist oppressors and the opiate of the working class. Otherwise, that new adventure may not be all that comfortable – though Catholic teaching tells us a chance of repentance exists to the last instant of life.

Nobody should have been surprised to find Neville's friends flying to his defence across the media with gorgeous speeches about his charm, his revolutionary courage, and his sticking it to the hypocritical conservative society of Australia's first one hundred and seventy-four years. His mate and collaborator on the Australian Oz, Richard Walsh, dreamily reminisced in a piece titled, 'Richard Neville, an ebullient, mischievous charmer'.

'[He] was the most charming man I ever met ... When I first met him, his charm and his raw, visceral appeal combined to make him a legendary babe-magnet ... He sat at the epicentre of a vast network of male and female friends, many of whom remained close to him all his life ... Both Richard and Martin reigned as rock stars in a world of drugs, free love, and psychedelic art.'[23]

Similar syrupy declarations came from past associates like Germaine Greer and Marsha Rowe, the latter co-founder of *Spare Rib*, a second-wave feminist magazine, but it was left to lawyer Geoffrey Robertson to go right over the top. In a choice of media instruments appropriate to his celebrity, Robertson cast Neville in the royal robes of a noble warrior for truth and justice and the *Oz* as a 'work of morality' unrobing the moral hypocrisy of middle-class society, both in Australia and Britain. In the *Guardian*, he gushed that Neville's and his entourage's activities, especially in the *Oz*, demonstrated a 'commitment to sexual equality, rock 'n' roll and human rights', that he argued 'for the rights of oppressed groups – women, black people, gay people and school-children', and that in the kids edition of *Oz*, 'they railed against paedophile teachers'. Neville and his team did this while the *Oz* School Kids edition 'mischievously depicted Rupert Bear with a truly bear-sized erection' rooting 'an old granny'.[24]

Robertson could not let an opportunity go by where he could demonstrate his erudition to those overcome by his brilliance. So, what the ordinary untutored person in Australia and Britain regarded as a nasty grubby rag tossed together by a bunch of spoilt middle-class snotnoses unable to break free from their self-centred adolescent fantasies, Robertson depicted as an unsullied instrument of justice – an instrument to change and improve:

'The trial was a chance to challenge the whole censorship apparatus in Britain, which was based on the notion that there was only one moral standard – what Bernard Shaw derided as 'middle-class morality ...'

But it also carried an opportunity to demonstrate that hypocritical English morality could not be enforced by criminal law.

The strategy we'd devised was to bring the modern science of the mind to bear on the traditional assumptions of the law. We called psychiatrists and psychologists as well as artists, entertainers, and prominent media critics to give evidence. We even recruited Ronald Dworkin and Richard Wollheim, two leading moral philosophers, to testify that Oz was a moral work.'[25]

Robertson breezes over the hard-fought and far-from-decided issues of moral relativism and goes for a favourite target of the left – the middle-class morality of Marxism's bourgeoisie. The phrase slips off his tongue without a hint of what, for the contemplative conservative, stands behind it: the complementarity of natural law and Christianity, the prescriptive customs, manners and conventions formed over centuries, and indeed the English Common Law. He invokes the contentious 'modern science of the mind' to beat down 'the traditional assumptions of the law' – whatever he means precisely by that woolly expression. He has no taste to commit to the wearisome task of explaining his references, whose mention anyhow is just to show what a brilliant fellow he is. We can safely assume the posse of entertainers, artists etc. are all purveyors of the same sort of libertarianism that drives Robertson. Finally, he goes in for the big hit with Wollheim and Dworkin, safe in the knowledge that few of those reading the 'Story of Oz' would have heard of them, let alone have any idea of what they believed as 'leading moral philosophers'.

Wollheim, for many years the Grote Professor of Mind and Logic at University College London (1963-1982), was known for his work on the mind and emotions and the philosophy of art. His best-known work was *Art and its Objects*. It is difficult to see how Robertson derives 'moral philosopher' from the work that qualifies Wollheim rather as a philosopher of aesthetics. On the other hand, the appeal to Ronald Dworkin's authority would seem appropriate, but not as a moral philosopher, which is odd. Odd because Dworkin was a celebrated professor of Jurisprudence known for his academic work on the philosophy of law. His best-known work, a legal bible for many human rights lawyers, is *Taking Rights Seriously*. Indications are that human rights lawyer Geoffrey Robertson and his colleagues at Doughty Street Chambers would be slavish disciples of Dworkin, who at times was Professor of Jurisprudence at University College London and Oxford University. So where does Robertson get Dworkin as a moral philosopher from? Perhaps it is just the citing of an illustrious intellectual that is his purpose – to set his narrative ablaze with the glow of intellectual profundity.

It is curious he should cite Dworkin in 2016 for the defence of the school kids' edition of Oz. In 2015, Roger Scruton, the world's leading conservative philosopher, released his book *Fools, Frauds and Firebrands: Thinkers of the New Left*. One of the fools, frauds and firebrands Scruton hammers is Ronald Dworkin.[26] If one reads a few chapters of Scruton's devastation of the New Left to understand his categories, one would slot Dworkin into the category of the fraud. Rehearsing Scruton's analysis of Dworkin's work in a few sentences is not possible, but the conclusions of Scruton's analysis will clarify where Robertson was coming from in citing the support of Dworkin.

Among the causes Dworkin staunchly defended and promoted, writes Scruton, were civil disobedience, reverse discrimination, sexual liberation, feminism, 'abortion rights', and pornography. In a nutshell, 'if conservatives were against it, he was for it'. In defending the liberal causes and thrashing conservatives over their defence of traditional society, he 'provided intellectual fireworks, patrician disdain, and cosmopolitan mockery in prolonged flourish'.[27] Dworkin claimed he argued from principle but, says Scruton, 'when the discussion enters the higher realm of philosophy, we need to know how those principles are justified. And this is a question from which he flees'.[28] Scruton's refrain is that the New Left theorists evade a sustained philosophical defence of their views. His conclusion at the end of his analysis of Dworkin's influential work on jurisprudence is: 'And here, I think, is where we see the profound weakness of Dworkin's way of arguing. It is the way of the barrister, snatching whatever useful trick is to hand, but not the way of the philosopher, with an eye for universal truth'.[29]

Dworkin's promotion of the causes of sexual liberation and pornography shows Robertson's attraction to Dworkin's work. Dworkin is right in there with Robertson's and Neville's right to obscenity, blasphemy, drugs, rock 'n' roll, and free love, as expressed in the *Oz*. Free love means the right to treat all females as sexual objects or, in the vernacular of the 1960s, to root any bird that takes your fancy. The retelling of the fun of Neville's libertarian agenda may bring a warm glow and misty eyes to the ageing libertarian of the Sixties now paying for his excesses. But neither they nor the younger defenders of Neville and his activities have mentioned two incidents that resulted from the logic of Neville's social and political dogma. Gerard Henderson of the spoiled the fun by having the nerve to bring them up in an article in the *Australian*,[30] clearly as a counter to the effusions of Robertson and Co. First, Henderson wrote of Neville's having sex with a 'cherubic' 14-year-old:

'The fact is that Neville, for all his charm, was a self-confessed pedophile. I became aware of this when I read his book Play Power in 1970 ... In Play Power, Neville boasted of having a 'hurricane f..k' with a 'moderately attractive, intelligent, cherubic, 14-year-old girl from a nearby London comprehensive school'.

Henderson points out that at the time of this hurricane root, Neville was 'about twice the age of the girl', thus in a power position over the girl. If it were not Neville, a guru of the counterculture Movement, but a member of the Catholic clergy abusing that girl, then we know that the frenzied indignation of the left and the call for punitive measures would have been uncontainable. If the exploitation of his power over the minor is not enough, Neville plays up the delight of enjoying the girl's innocence while displaying upper-class contempt for a dispensable person. Neville's act is the playing out of the logic of his counterculture philosophy, and it is this logic that Geoffrey Robertson defends. That Robertson does not mention the abuse of the 14-year-old in his many articles and interviews about Neville's death raises serious questions. The full passage, which Henderson abbreviated, appears in the chapter 'Group Grope' of *Play Power* in which Neville describes the driving principles of the Sexual Revolution:

'I meet a moderately attractive, intelligent, cherubic 14-year-old girl from a nearby London comprehensive school. I ask her home, she rolls a joint and we begin to watch the midday TV movie. It is The Woman of the Year, and Spencer Tracy, almost against his will, finds himself in Katharine Hepburn's apartment. (He kisses her, flashes his look of 'there's a volcano bubbling inside me' and hurriedly leaves.) Comes the Heinz Souperday commercial, a hurricane fuck, another joint. No feigned love or hollow promises. (Tracy, at work the next morning, reads a note from Katherine: 'You left your hat. What's the hurry? He smiles, and the wheels of matrimony grind into operation.) A farewell kiss, and the girl rushes off to finish her homework.'[31]

Neville contrasts the repressive middle-class culture of Western society with an attitude to sexual activity as an appetite that one satisfies when one is so inclined – like eating when one is hungry. No need for all the bullshit about courting and false respect for the other, the other being the female. There's no power position involved. Age has nothing to do with it, as Neville makes clear in the core chapter of the book, 'The Politics of Play'. Underground sexual morality is direct, he says, 'if a couple like each other, they make love'.[32] He mocks magazines like Hugh Hefner's *Playboy* as a flagship of the sexual revolution. I'll show you a real sexual revolution, says Neville. The terms 'seduction' and 'surrender' (again referring to the female) are 'obsolete'. Feel like it, do it.

At a point in the same chapter, Neville declares in a flight of profound enlightenment, 'It could be just possible that the sexual candour of the radical generation is indicative of a healthier, more honest overall relationship ... It's groovy to be carnal. And there's nothing more carnal than the Underground ...' Buoyed by this soaring enlightenment, he continues to give examples of unashamed rooting in all manner of public places where no one who has experienced the enlightenment of the counterculture turns a hair. Then in the transport of his numinous meditation, Neville talks of 'the occasional gang bang', citing a newspaper account of a naked 'young long-haired girl' dancing in the rain in Central Park. A 'dozen young men' seized and gangbanged her while 'her friends stood by' and 'no one helped her, no one cared'.[33] Why should anyone care about such a natural expression of sexual freedom? He follows a few paragraphs further on with, 'While everyone has his own idea of what constitutes sexual fitness, many believe that the Underground freedom from inhibition is the first step *en route* to a new freer and happier civilisation'.

Although the goal of throwing off all the restrictions of Western bourgeois society on sexual activity was central to the Underground movement,
there was more to it. Neville declared the Underground or counterculture
was non-ideological, but he made his non-ideology into a distinct ideology,
and his Play Power was its manifesto. The 'Movement' incorporated three
'divisions' that were 'broadly consistent'. Neville names them as the New
Left, the Underground, and the militant poor. The Underground 'em-
braces hippies, beats, mystics, mad-men, freaks, yippies, crazies, crackpots,
communards and anyone who rejects rigid political ideology (it's a brain
disease)'. Those with the brain disease of ideology were the Marxists and
New Left student associations. He describes how these divisions cooperated, and according to my observations at the time, he was right. Sometimes
they overlapped in their actions, and sometimes they were in conflict. But
more often, there was a different mixture of the protest ingredients. That
the Underground and the New Left were not as separate or distinct as
Neville claims or that one was not much more ideological than the other
is suggested in his grand statement of the essential political thrust of the
'Movement' – and the point of his book:

'There is one quality which enlivens both the political and cultural dom-
inations of youth protest; which provides its most important innovation;
which has the greatest relevance for the future; which is the funniest,
freakiest, and the most effective. This is the element of play, and it will be
examined more specifically in the final chapter.'[34]

The intervening chapters are a tedious account of the actions to 'fuck the
system' and revolt 'against the assumed conformities, bland hypocrisies
and comfortable conceits of modern [bourgeois] society'. The imperative
was to build an

'alien culture – a culture that is destined to create a new kind of man

... outwardly by their appearance, inwardly by blasting their minds with drugs, rock and roll and communal sex; by abolishing families, nationalities, money and status, those of the new generation are disqualifying themselves from becoming somnambulating flunkeys of the power structure'.[35]

No respectable Marxists could take exception to this aim, as will be seen in the following chapter. Pursuing these aims unleashed 'uncontrolled student demonstrations', occupation of empty properties and sit-ins in university buildings, 'massive pop-music freak-outs [and] freak shows of anarchists'. The following evidence will show that Neville was right, but the Marxists carried them out at Sydney University, not the counterculture freaks who rarely featured in *Honi Soit*.

During this time, that glorious highpoint of the counterculture, Woodstock, happened on a dairy farm in New York State over three days from 15 to 17 August 1969. Around 400,000 semi-naked girls and boys experienced an ecstatic outbreak of love, peace, and flower power. In Neville's terms, this meant a great deal of spontaneous rooting. On the other side of the continent, on the West Coast in Benedict Canyon near Hollywood, hardly a week before Woodstock, there was another memorable freak-out enjoyed by a gang of dropouts: the Manson Family. The Manson gang, too, enjoyed themselves over three days from 8 to 10 August 1969. Neville's final chapter presents the denouement of his laboured narrative. The ideological-laden title is 'The Politics of Play'.

Neville provides a long list of the many wacky characters of the Underground that fill the preceding chapters. Significant is the 'Hitch-hiking Honeybunch Kaminskis ("aged thirteen – what a little yummy")'. Honcy Bunch Kaminski was a comic character created by underground artist Robert Crumb. There is a famous (and now expensive) poster of the character made from an illustration in one of Crumb's comics (Snatch Comics #1). The poster was an insert in *OZ Magazine* 24. It depicts Honey Bunch Kaminski as a buxom underage girl naked from the waist up, sporting large breasts with large erect nipples. The tag at the top says, 'Jail bait of the month'. Underneath is the caption '"Honey Bunch" Kaminski, 13 of LA What a little yummy!' In another illustration, she is 'America's favourite teenybopper'. There can be no doubt that Honey Bunch Kaminski is a paedophile character. It is no accident she appears in Neville's list with her title of 'little yummy'.

After providing the list, Neville asks what all these people have in common. His answer is 'their attitude to work. They don't'. The movement's ethic is 'anti-work, pro-play'. This is its essence. He contrasts the movement's 'laughing, loving, lazy, fun-powder plotters' with 'the sober, violent, puritan, Left extremists'.[36] Neville's concept of 'play-power' is where the overlap with the left finishes. It won't be the agitation of the left with their 'grubby' leaflets and tired rhetoric that will defeat the capitalist bourgeois class. 'It will be an irresistible, fun-possessed, playpower counterculture' with its pop groups, dancing, rooting, and drugs that will 'put an end to toil'.[37]

According to the core principles of his play power manifesto, members of the Underground will: '1. Transform Work (i.e. Work = Play); 2. Sow their own wild oats; 3. Fuck the system'. The formula for turning work into fun is simple. You take a healthy, well-run organisation and apply strategies the very opposite of those that made the organisation successful.[38] This transformation of work is linked to the third article of 'fucking the system'. Once you have caused the collapse of the organisation that enables you to pay your way in society, you plan strategies for getting whatever can be got free. Collapsing the system is further linked to 'Sowing Wild Oats – and other goodies'.[39]

Neville tells us that the 'protest generation not only changed politics but altered their relationship to one another'. The pursuit of fun results, he says, in the tying of relationships that create communes. This is how it works. In pursuing the fun activities of sit-ins, occupations, protests, producing porn, and so on, one spends time with others of the same spirit. Delighting in this new camaraderie, one naturally likes to 'extend it in time' and 'consolidate it in space'. In such a way, communes are created with the result that 'the commune movement has spread across the world'.[40] These communes manifest a new political organisation replacing corrupt bourgeois society that rests on an 'outmoded family structure'. In the communes, the people live together, sharing everything, including the children. The children belong to all in the commune. This structure, says Neville, is 'a true sense of the people'. In a manner reminiscent of a faithful Marxist, he continues in his peculiar idiom:

'The new communalism reacts against Western style family 'units' and their seedy inventions of old people's homes, mother-in-law hatred, baby sitters and baby bashers. The bank manager's ideal family isolates one from another, ill-preparing its offspring for relating to the outside world. Love they neighbour – so long as he is safely ensconced within his capsule. The primary importance of the commune movement lies in these efforts to reinterpret the family role as well as the determination to minimise the significance of money, if not of chocolate biscuits.'[41]

The communal system eases the discomfort of dropping out. In a group, one has more success in stealing or cadging the necessities of life and sharing them. For the particularly slothful dropout, there is access to 'free clothes ... free accommodation, free dope, free love, and free money'. Pursuing the theme of sponging on the part of society that is productive, Neville looks into the future and concludes that technology will take over the labour of the ordinary worker. The state, presumably the working and productive part, will then have to sustain those in pursuit of fun, that is, in pursuit of drugs, pornography, freak-outs, rooting, dancing, music and so on. Satisfied he had turned bourgeois ideas about the family on their head, Neville returns to his favourite topic of sex, that is, sex and having plenty of it. Infants, he asserts for our edification, are fully operative sexual beings whose drive is to be admired, copied, and partaken of. There can be no other reading of the following introduced under the heading 'Sex is Pure When it's Playful':

'Infants get the most out of their sex life. They play with themselves unashamedly, anarchistically, freely, and solely for the purpose of grati-fication. As they grow up, their sexuality becomes repressed, neurotic, perverted. In his Life against Death Norman O. Brown stresses that 'Freud's definition of sexuality entails the proposition that infants have a richer sexual life than adults...Children explore in indiscriminate and anarchistic fashion all the erotic potentialities of the human body'. Sounds like the Underground, which is still, like children, narcissistic and guiltless.'[42]

If children explore their erotic potentialities in an indiscriminate and an-archistic fashion, then what is to stop someone with a perverted bourgeois attitude to sexual activity from joining them to purify themselves of their perversion? Indeed, it is a moral prescription. Neville lectures the left that bourgeois sexual inhibition 'paralyses the instinct to rebel... again the instrument of repression is the family, a mini-government'. Presumably, submitting themselves to the sexual tuition of infants will obliterate the bourgeois family and cure them of the neurosis suffered.

Neville wraps up his manifesto under the heading 'Play Culture is Com-ing Back'. He bases this claim on the spreading activities of the Under-ground and the example they are setting for the rest of the dull popu-lace. He repeats the examples already repeated *ad nauseam* with much optimism but deflates that optimism by admitting that 'for every Wood-stock, there's a private Altamont'. Few people today would know what he is referring to. The Altamont counterculture rock concert (6 December 1969) was a Woodstock-style happening that went wrong. It was anything but a breakout of love, peace, harmony and understanding. Among much violence was a murder close by the stage while the Rolling Stones were performing. There is dramatic vision of a gun drawn and the stabbing in response. Mick Jagger is lucky a crazed, drugged maniac rushing the stage with a drawn revolver did not shoot him dead. An internet search will uncover all the details I need not dwell on to make the point. The point is the social disintegration Neville's counterculture unleashed.

The Manson murders, a series of hippie dropout murders that shocked the world, was an even more graphic illustration. *Play Power* was published in 1970. The grisly Manson murders were committed in August 1969. By December, the world knew about the heartless cruelty and diabolical violence to which the members of the Manson family subjected their victims. Neville knew about them but, it seems, ignored the obvious link between the Manson Family and the counterculture he so fervently promoted. For all his preaching about new and healthy ways of living, overlooking the Manson murders was a gigantic cop-out. But there is more to the Manson murders than the diabolical violence, and I will return to it in the next chapter.

The second incident to which Gerard Henderson referred occurred in 1975 when Neville was back in Australia. Neville now felt confident enough to spread the wings of his brand of libertarianism to sell his idea of an enlightened future to the masses – at least to those who listen to the Australian Broadcasting Corporation. Now working as a reporter on ABC radio, Neville slotted in well. On 14 July 1975, six months before Tony Abbott arrived on campus, Neville entertained his audience on 'Lateline' with a program titled 'Pederasty'. Henderson:

'ABC publicity described the program in the following terms: 'Pederasty, as defined by the Penguin English Dictionary, is the homosexual relationship of a man with a boy. The subject usually creates feelings of revulsion and disgust with most people. The issues raised by such relationships are discussed by three pederasts'.

Neville invited the men — two of whom were friends — into the ABC Sydney studio to discuss their sex lives. As The National Times reported on 21 July, 1975: 'During an episode of Lateline ... three men described with relish their sexual relationships with teenage boys and a teenage boy described his relations with an older man'. According to contemporary reports, when the boy detailed his first experience with a man, one of the pederasts was heard to moan with delight.'

Given the preaching in *Play Power*, it is no surprise that Neville's circle of friends included pederasts. The program caused disgust and consternation outside, but the defence of Neville and his program came from the highest level of the ABC. The then chairman of the ABC Richard Downing 'told the *Herald* that "in general, men will sleep with young boys"'. He also wrote a letter to the newspaper on 19 July 1975, calling on Australians to "understand" the urges of pederasts'. Neville's special program and its defence by the ABC Chairman were not isolated occasions of the apparent condoning of paedophilia. Neville had a nose for where society was going, the direction of which he had a lot to do with, and media organisations paid him for his prognostications. It was difficult to tell whether they were prognostications or barefaced promotions. Whatever the case, he gave voice to efforts to radically extend the traditional boundaries of sexual activity – and who was fair game in that activity. Henderson wrote in the article of 15 March 2014:

'In an article in the September 1984 issue of *Quadrant* magazine entitled 'Paedophile Liberation and the Radical Homosexuals', writer Andrew Lansdown documented how pederasty had become fashionable within sections of the Australian Left in the 1970s and 80s. He quoted an article in OutRage magazine ['for lesbians and gay men'] which declared its 'defence of the civil liberties of paedophiles'... Lansdown documented the existence in Australia at the time of a Paedophile Support Group.'

I have said enough to make my case about the destructive influence Richard Neville's ideological activities had on his 1960s generation and their success in collapsing vital features of Western civilisation, and how well Nevillism went hand-in-hand with the Marxist agenda. It was a prelude to Abbott's political responses at Sydney University. But I must briefly mention another Australian who was just as eccentric with her own unique brand of libertarianism. Her influence was worldwide. I could be speaking of no one else but of 'our' Germaine Greer, a close mate of Neville's and a leader in the sexual revolution.

After graduating from Melbourne University in 1959, Greer moved north to pursue her studies at Sydney University, where she became a senior tutor. She joined the Libertarian movement known as the Sydney 'Push'. In the 1950s, the Push grew out of 'the radical but anti-authoritarian Freethought Society, acolytes of the former communist, former Trotskyist, now libertarian philosophy professor [of Sydney University], John Anderson'.[43] The libertarians were active on campus and at pubs in the city centre, attracting a motley bunch of students, bohemians, and sundry hangers-on. So profoundly did she absorb the Push ethos that she would spectacularly 'out-libertarian' her fellow members. She graduated from Sydney University in 1963 with a first-class Master of Arts degree. She then took off to Cambridge University, where she delighted in spraying (and appalling) all and sundry in her 'strong Australian accent'. Of less importance, she tossed together a brilliant thesis and received her doctorate in 1969. By this time, she was deep into the counterculture. More than this, she was its outstanding example and tenacious promoter. She contributed to Neville's Oz, among other counterculture instruments.

From May 1971 to December 1973, I lived in Holland with my Dutch wife. I worked at a Dutch bank in the middle of Amsterdam. Often at lunchtime, I would take a walk from where the bank was on Rembrandtplein along the busy Kalverstraat to Damplein and back again. One day in 1972, on my way back to the office, I stopped at a little kiosk that sold newspapers, books and magazines, including all manner of pornography. By 1972, pornography was everywhere in Holland. I picked up a newspaper called *Suck*. The title and page design called up associations. It turned out that *Suck* was a collaboration between Greer and three entrepreneurs of pornography, among whom was Heathcote Williams, supermodel Jean Shrimpton's lover. I opened its pages to be confronted by a full-page photo of Germaine Greer displaying her private parts in grisly close-up. Christine Wallace, in her unauthorised biography of Greer, describes Greer's pose:

'[It] was a shot taken in a pose worthy of an advanced yoga practitioner or circus contortionist. Greer's buttocks and vagina loom graphically as, legs in the air and head sticking out between them, she grins cheerfully at the camera.'[44]

This wasn't a photo to arouse the animal. On the contrary, as one of the paper's writers remarked in admiration, it was a revolutionary act. *Suck* and Greer were 'all about the sexual revolution and through it spiritual revolution'.[45] Greer was journeying to the spiritual through unrestrained copulating. I would not describe Greer's grin as cheerful. It was instead a mixture of defiance, contempt and sneer expressing Greer's utter rejection of bourgeois morality.

She and Neville were among the standard-bearers of the worldwide youth rebellion. But we can clearly distinguish between the two. While Greer's sexual preaching and example aimed to make women more assertive, independent, and free from male domination, Neville sought to collapse masculinity, destroy what it meant in the culture to be male, and enslave men to their basest inclinations. For a thousand years up to the second half of the 1960s, the Code of Chivalry influenced men to a greater or a lesser extent. At its lowest level of operation, one could summarise it thus: protect the weak, pay your debts and keep your promises. The Code was all about self-control, self-discipline, fairness, honesty, and courage in the face of evil. Neville's code for men was drugs, alcohol, and pornography – and plenty of it. His prescription was to turn their spine into jelly and indulge their appetites, whatever the cost to others, particularly to females. Neville's bequest to society is the destruction of maleness and masculinity.

Chapter 3

The Marxist maggot

THE STUDENT ACTIVISTS' political agitation and violent demonstrations from the mid-1960s were the vehicles on which an enormous
social and political change was rammed through western society. By 1970,
a social fissure had opened, and Australian society underwent a rejigging
during which many of its beliefs and rules were upended and its history
revised. But, if my judgment sounds a little exaggerated, Alan Barcan, in
his *From New Left to Factional Left: Fifty Years of Student Activism at
Sydney University*, goes well beyond it:

'The transformation of western society in the late 1960s and early 1970s
was a major turning point in the history of civilisation. The cultural revolution or the cultural collapse were comparable, for instance, with the
transition in ancient Greece of the fourth century BC from the Classical
to the Hellenistic age. The student revolt was an initial element in the
transformation of modern civilisation.'[46]

Barcan, a communist in his student days, provides an enthralling account
of the New Left's leading role in the explosive political action that gripped
Sydney University between 1967 and 1974. He divides the Left's influence
in Australia to the 1970s into three phases. There was the Old Left from
1921 to 1970, followed by the first phase of the New Left from 1956 to

1967, which was consolidated by the second phase of the New Left from 1967 to 1974. The Old Left and the first New Left (1956-67) would save civilisation from capitalism. 'The second New Left of the 1970s', he writes, 'sought to destroy traditional western culture and the capitalist ethos'.[47] He goes into much detail about the New Left's activities at Sydney University during those years. For my purpose, I will highlight a few aspects of his story, at the same time, drawing on my own experience.

The catalyst for the rise of the New Left was the Soviet invasion of Hungary in 1956. The Soviet invasion of a communist client state caused an intellectual and ideological crisis that precipitated an exodus of intellectuals and students from the old communist parties in the West. New communist parties formed. Some maintained an adherence to the Soviet model. Others, calling themselves Trotskyists, followed Leon Trotsky and formed a Trotskyist party. Still others created a grouping based on Maoism, the teaching of the Chinese communist leader Mao Zedong. In addition to the split of communist parties into a revised form of Marxism, New Left theorists and movements proliferated around the West in a broad political movement. The neo-Marxist theorists became a crucial and enduring influence in the New Left. They included the Frankfurt School, Antonio Gramsci, Georg Lukacs, and Louis Althusser, the last exercising influence at Sydney University.

The appearance of Trotskyists and Maoists in student activity heralded the first consolidation of the New Left at Sydney University. A pro-Chinese faction within the CPA had broken away and established the Communist Party of Australia (Marxist-Leninist) in March 1964. In the same year, a Trotskyist faction formed. Because Trotskyists manoeuvred to take a leading role in student activism after 1967, a basic understanding of Marxism is necessary to follow the events. Without that understanding, it will be difficult to comprehend what motivated Tony Abbott and other conservative students in their fight with the radicals. It is a sad irony that those most critical of Marxism, those for whom most is at stake, often have a poor understanding of Marxism as a theory.[48] As some readers may already have a basic understanding, I have provided a brief explanation in Appendix I for those who have not.

The essential points are that Marx turned Georg Hegel's idealist dialectic into a materialist dialectic. Whereas Hegel spoke of the clash of ideas resulting in a higher understanding, Marx spoke of the clash of (economic) classes, of the oppressor and oppressed. The clash of classes would proceed in the form of thesis-anthesis-thesis until the end stage of the socialist state. Key concepts in the unfolding of the materialist dialectic were the 'means of production' which determined the 'production relationships' and 'superstructure' (of laws, government, morality art and so on). The hand mill (the means of production) gave rise to feudalism and its superstructure; the steam engine gave rise to capitalism (ownership of the means of production) and its supporting superstructure. The capitalist class is in an oppressive struggle with the workers (the proletariat). That struggle will inevitably lead to a socialist society of the free and equal. So far, communism (the implementation of Marxist theory) has not turned out that way. Indeed, it has been a cruel and inhuman system in all cases.

No one represented the radical leftist student more than the ridiculous Trotskyist Hall Greenland at Sydney University. Greenland was primed for his life's vocation before he arrived at Sydney University to develop the well-tutored political orientation of his thought. His mother worked for a 'Stalinist-led trade union, was secretary of the Vietnam Action Campaign, assisted Bob Gould, and was also in the Labor Party'.[49] He burst onto campus in 1962 at the tender age of seventeen 'in pursuit of existentialism and Marxism – and girls'.[50] I suggest Nevillism was a strong motivation. And no doubt he connected Sartre's support for the French communists with the Trotskyist doctrine spooned into him from an early age.

Bob Gould was a leading Trotskyist and bookseller who entertained the full range of demented leftists at his various bookselling establishments. Greenland and Gould were members of a small group of hyperactive

Marxists who strove to wreck Australian society. It was a glorious work that has left Australian society, the society our self-sacrificing colonial ancestors built, almost fatally broken. It is a measure of his undisguised war against Australian society and its people that he has never taken much trouble to hide his support for Trotskyist Marxism and its totalitarian aims. Tracking Greenland's representative career will convey the rich flavour of the chaos and wreckage those middle-class Marxists wrought during those years.

By 1966, Greenland had ascended to a position where he could unleash his Trotskyist urge to promote permanent worldwide revolution. He was president of Sydney University's ALP Club and, in the second half of the year, appointed the editor of the university's student newspaper *Honi Soit*. If the general population in Australia were solidly behind Prime Minister Menzies and his support of the United States to counter the progress of the worldwide Marxist revolution on the Vietnamese front, Greenland and his Trotskyist companions were feverishly planning to change and defeat the wishes of the people. In October of that year, President Lyndon Johnson scheduled a visit to Australia to thank Prime Minister Menzies and the Australian people for their much-appreciated support. The planned visit must have caused orgiastic anticipation in the now 21-year-old postgraduate history student. Greenland put his head down and produced a bumper issue of *Honi Soit* on the Vietnam War. He incited his teenage readership with 'a front-page article by Jean-Paul Sartre calling for Russian counter-escalation in Vietnam and a back-page collage of Vietnam atrocity photographs'.[51]

While he produced his bumper issue of *Honi Soit*, he and a motley bunch of radicals were planning a demonstration to make President Johnson's visit unforgettably painful. In Greenland's words: 'The three main protest organisers in Sydney at that time were Bob Gould's Vietnam Action Campaign, the Communist Party, and the Youth Campaign Against Conscription'. He describes Bob Gould as 'a Trotskyist activist who had almost single-handedly launched the anti-war movement in Australia'.

These quotations were not from Greenland the student of fifty years ago but from Greenland the white-haired 72-year-old unreformed, un-reconstructed Trotskyist in October 2016. Yes, Greenland, preserving his malignant 17-year-old Trotskyist fantasies, is still at it.

He maintains a blog called 'Watermelon Papers'.[52] The 'Watermelon' references are unmistakable. He boasts, 'in the 1980s I was among the founders of The Greens ... For the past two years, I have been the convenor of the Greens in New South Wales'. He took the title from the blog of a fellow Green fanatic who explained that 'Watermelon is a political blog: an assertion of a leftist perspective within and alongside Green politics. And the colours are not just red and green, but also black – the seeds of libertarianism throughout'. A nod to Nevillism.

In October 2016, Greenland celebrated the fiftieth anniversary of the triumphant 1966 Sydney demonstration. His misty-eyed, almost artless account of the happening supports my claims about who was driving the student rebellion. I have lucid memories of the event as reported in the media, particularly of New South Wales Premier Bob Askin's reaction to Greenland and his fellow demonstrators' lying on the road and preventing the passage of President Johnson's motorcade. 'Run over the bastards!' Premier Askin is reported to have shouted. It was an instinctive outburst most Australians cheered.

President Johnson's visit to Australia in October 1966 was the first by an American President. Most Australians greeted the visit with pleasure and pride. The organisers put together a program that enabled them to give the president a hearty welcome. In Sydney, a motorcade would take him from Mascot airport through the city to the Art Gallery of New South Wales, where a luncheon reception awaited him. A million people waving flags and throwing streamers lined the streets on 22 October to cheer the president. It was a festive affair – or was meant to be. Among the million people, a group of hard-bitten, far-left protesters gathered. Greenland continues with his adolescent enthusiasm:

'The anti-war protesters, a few hundred strong and most of them students and activists like me, were waiting further down [from Oxford Street], opposite Hyde Park, and as the cavalcade approached, the booing began, and the stop-the-war placards shot up. A dozen or so of us readied ourselves for a more direct action ...

'As the thin blue line opened up, the rest of us saw our opportunity. We ducked under the barriers and sat down in the middle of the road ...

'The crowd's chanting of 'Stop the War' throttled up. The motorcade stopped dead. The NSW Premier Sir Robin Askin, riding with LBJ and the First Lady (Ladybird Johnson), put his head out the car window to find out what the trouble was. Seeing a tangle of protesters lying down in the presidential pathway he lost it, yelling 'drive over the bastards' to the cars in front.'

Jean Curthoys, now a retired academic but then a rebellious 18-year-old from a well-known communist party family, recalls determinedly pitching herself onto the road three or four times. 'Police picked me up and dumped me by the side of the road, so I just jumped up and ran back.'

'I took my place in the middle of the road next to my ALP comrade Aiden Foy, but I wasn't there for long. Seeing the stationary press bus 10 metres away, I made a dash for it. I'd like to say it was a reasoned move because I was editor of *Honi Soit*, the student newspaper at Sydney Uni, but in truth, it was just an impulse to jump on board. Fronting a bus full of what appeared to be startled American reporters – judging by their crew-cuts, sports jackets and the button-downed collars of their striped shirts – I announced the bleeding obvious, that this was an anti-war protest. The longer speech I would have liked to deliver to this captive audience was cut short as the bus began to move. I threw in a couple of chants and jumped off.'

So, there you have it. 'A dozen or so' far-left fanatics stole the show with their carefully planned action. Not surprisingly, the newspapers had space only for sensationalised reports of the sit-down and photos of what looked like wild brawling between police, officials, and the demonstrators on the road. Greenland gleefully notes that 'Monday's *Sydney Morning Herald* was not pleased, editorialising: "The point is not that the demonstrators won a victory – as they undoubtedly did ... it is that they were allowed to win it [sic]. Those who deserve to have the vials of wrath emptied on them are those in charge of security arrangements"'. *The Sydney Morning Herald*, a very different newspaper in 1966, was spot on. The demonstration and sit-down were not just a failure of the security people. It was more a failure of the authority where the buck could not be passed. Greenland was all smugness:

'The real plotters behind the sit-down [sic] were only revealed weeks later when the Commonwealth Police named me as the chief culprit. In their version, I had 'apparently' convened the meeting at the University of Sydney of radical students and the Sydney Libertarians which had planned the sit-down. The crucial meeting in fact had taken place in a downtown pub which was logical enough as the Sydney Libertarians were a group of anarchist punters who met regularly in pubs and were in the process of turning their attention from the races at Randwick to the war in Vietnam.'

With justifiable pride, Greenland finishes his celebratory post with the comment 'in retrospect, it was amazing that we were able to carry out the plan ... I am astonished at our audacity in daring to sit down in front of the motorcade, in "disrespecting" the great United States president. In a small way, however, we were part of a historical turning point'.[53] Indeed, they were. But it was more the playing of a treacherous subversive role in turning the Western World's centuries-old moral and political make-up on its head, precipitating a steep moral, social and political decline. That is an astonishing boast for the socially and morally backward group that lay on the road in Liverpool Street in 1966. It might cause Greenland to beam. The ordinary Australian could not deplore it too much.

Few people at the time knew anything about Marxist theory, especially its prescription to manipulate and subvert the minds of 'the people'. Most understood the malignancy of Marxism through the proven disaster of communism as an economic theory and the barbarism of the communist leadership class in its conquered territories. They were unaware that the Marxists' public disrespect to the leader of the free world was a conscious and fundamental act to demoralise them and corrupt their attitude to authority. Most Australians born after 1970 would have little idea of the ordinary person's respect for authority before the student rebellion and how much the prevailing cohesiveness of Australian society depended on the community's respect for properly constituted authority and for the people of proven character who filled society's most important offices of authority. Greenland and his Marxist mates' deliberate disrespecting act shocked most Australians on 22 October 1966.

I remember the first time I witnessed a public act of student disrespecting. It happened during a meeting between several student leaders and the University of New South Wales authorities. The meeting was to conciliate student demands. Primetime news bulletins showed the event. But, unfortunately, conciliation was as far from the students' minds as the prisoners of the Soviet Gulags. That little group of radicals began shouting abuse in the faces of the authorities, including the Vice-Chancellor, giving them no chance to answer. I was shocked and embarrassed to see the authorities cowering before the abusive onslaught. It was not too long before such unabashed disrespect that disobedience to a teacher might have earned you six cuts of the strap. This prescribed penalty punished a social transgression while asserting the properly constituted authority of the teacher. The unrestrained goal-driven ideological action of the student radicals showed how vulnerable a liberal-democratic society dependent on accepted rules, traditions and conventions developed over time was to people sworn to destroy that society. These people put no moral restraints on the means.

Barcan writes that the '*The Bulletin* blamed [Greenland's] edition [of *Honi Soit*] for much of the protest against the Australian visit of US President Johnson and called for a public inquiry into universities. The Senate considered a censure against Greenland but dropped it as his first term of office had ended'.[54] It would be the first of a series of spineless cop-outs granting the adolescent Marxists freedom of the city. Greenland's editorship of *Honi Soit* may have ended but spurred on by his success and the caving in of the university authorities, he continued to throw himself into his work of subversion.

He and fellow radical Rowan Cahill, another leading activist, used the *Student's Handbook* for the 1967 academic year to preach to the unsuspecting 17-year-olds arriving on campus. Greenland is introduced as 'the controversial ex-editor of *Honi Soit* and one of the few campus radicals'. In his piece 'Trainers and the Trained', Greenland, always solicitous about the bourgeois indoctrination of his fellow students, criticised the prevailing hierarchical structure of the academic-student relationship. To insist that the teacher appointed to pass on knowledge and expertise to the pupil should stand above and direct the student in the teaching activity was similarly anathema. Such an oppressive bourgeois relationship, according to Greenland, sprang from 'vocationalism', the idea that the content of the curriculum should be governed by its occupational or industrial utility and marketability as human capital. Setting up a course in economics or psychology or engineering, for example, so that the successful student could lead a fruitful working life and earn a wage to support him and his family was undemocratic for Trotskyist Greenland. His solution to vocationalism: 'students should share power and responsibility with academics in developing the university'. The departments of philosophy and economics would feel the white-hot rod of this Trotskyist madness.

Cahill's piece supported a central contention in my account of the student rebellion. In 'Student Life', Cahill asserted that 'the student body as a whole' was not the author or instigator of any particular happening on campus. He wrote, 'It is rather the work of "a minority", the term the newspaper editorials use, or "elite", which is the term I use. Left or right-wing, Catholic or Anglican religiously; atheist, free thinker, libertarian, etc., etc. – it all boils down to a fraction of the student population"'.[55] Just so. It was always an unconscionable minority that drove the political action. It is ironic, considering the present worldwide political atmosphere, that Cahill preferred to describe himself and his fellow radicals as an 'elite'. Of course, it is disingenuous of Cahill to name his opponents as if there were a touch-and-go struggle on campus.

The record shows that the radical Left took all before it, battering all opposition off campus. The ferrets and weasel took Toad Hall without much of a fight. Tony Abbott was among the few offering determined resistance. Cahill was also eager to instruct the fresh-faced first-year students, particularly those from private girls' schools, that 'sex is to the university student as water is to the duck'.[56] You were not part of the university community if you didn't screw at random, in particular with dashing student leaders. Nevillism was entrenched.

Barcan marks April 1967 as the start of the radicalism that shook Sydney University. The first disruption occurred in response to an increase in library fines by Fisher Library. Max Humphreys had the good fortune to secure an appointment as a part-time tutor in psychology. To celebrate the honour of an academic appointment, he organised an after-hours sit-in in Fisher Library with a small group of like-minded radical students to protest the increased fines. No doubt, Humphreys was invigorated by his recent arrest for a one-man demonstration against the visit of President Ky of Vietnam. The University police kicked them out. Undaunted, Humphreys issued a pamphlet urging another sit-in, an action that brought him before the Vice-Chancellor to receive a warning.

A sit-in followed on 10 April, earning him a suspension from his Master of Science candidature for a year. This was the signal for the radicals to whip up a lunchtime meeting on the university's front lawn. A protest committee was elected followed the next day by 'a huge lunch-hour meeting of 1,000 students in the Quadrangle ... addressed by the ubiquitous activist, Hall Greenland'.[57] To show how ubiquitous he could be, Greenland dashed to the airport to take the next plane to Paris on the break-out of the student revolution in Paris in 1968. No way would he miss out on that historic freak-out.

The rolling sit-ins and occupations proceeded through 1968 with some 'moderation'. Roy Smee, a former communist and at this time Registrar for National Service, told Barcan that the early actions were 'good-natured events under the rowdy surface'. The change came with the takeover of the demonstrations by the American import Students for a Democratic Society (SDS), a loose organisation that claimed to be promoters of democracy of the participatory sort. When the Left use the word 'participatory,' they mean a system of direct democracy that tears apart established arrangements. After the SDS democratists took over, said Smee, 'the protests were not only more violent, but threats were made to my family'.[58] 'Yet after the SDS collapsed,' adds Barcan, 'the Far Left intensified the level of violence.'

Greenland, his revolutionary fervour undiminished, was back in Sydney by 1970 to take a leading role in the Victoria Lee ruckus. Lee was a Macquarie University student who wanted admission to Sydney University to study Anthropology. On refusal, 'a group of students' took up her cause. After much harassment by the students, Professor Taylor, Chairman of the Professorial Board, agreed to meet them in Wallace [lecture] Theatre, but when the group switched the meeting to the front lawn, he refused to go. If you ever attended a student meeting on the front lawn of Sydney University around this time, you would have understood why. Professor Taylor's attendance at the proposed meeting would have been like submitting oneself to the stocks and having rotten vegetables and fruit thrown at you. The year before (1969), the State Governor, Sir Roden Cutler, was 'spattered' by two tomatoes thrown during a brawl outside the Great Hall. The brawl was linked to a front lawn meeting at which 2,500 students were present. Professor Taylor would not have any of that.

In response, Greenland, channelling the spirit of the 1968 Paris mobs, led a contingent of around 500 students from the front lawn and took over the administration offices.[59] They set fire to parts of the offices, causing the closure of the University administration for a week. The university resorted to the sensible action of seeking an injunction in the Supreme Court against the ringleaders. With a poignant demonstration of where the law was in protecting our democratic society, Justice Street dismissed the case.[60] About mid-year, the University authorities mustered the gumption and expelled Greenland. At the start of 1971, the Senate did the usual cave-in and readmitted him 'after an examination of 15 minutes'. The nuttiest of the Sydney University far-left radicals triumphed once again over the battered authorities. During his suspension, Greenland applied for a position as 'Administrative Trainee' (you've got to laugh) with the Commonwealth government. The Public Service Board asked ASIO to check Greenland's record. In a highly illegal action, someone sympathetic to Greenland hijacked ASIO's report and handed it to *Honi Soit* for the scoop of the year. ASIO reported 'Greenland is unfavourably known to ASIO' and that 'Mr Greenland is a self-confessed Marxist'.[61] You don't say.

Enough has been said to create the scene of chaos, violence and decay engineered by Greenland and his juvenile but devastatingly effective Marxist mates. I will, however, suffice with one more spectacular Greenland action. The occasion was the '24 June 1971 demo in support of the Vietnamese National Liberation Front at SU'. In a rambling pamphlet (June 2000), Bob Gould fondly reminisced about Greenland's impressive audacity:

'The star speaker at this meeting was the First Secretary of the South

Vietnamese Embassy. He was heckled rather vigorously by most of the audience and, after he had finished speaking, your then colleague, Hall Greenland, grabbed the microphone from the chairman, Professor David Armstrong, and started putting to the meeting the point of view opposed to the war, and got rapturous applause. Armstrong rushed forward and, after colliding awkwardly with Lyn Regan, took a spectacular swing in the direction of his student opponents with his fist, which they managed to evade. In the middle of this melee, Rowan Cahill climbed up on a desk and addressed the thousand students cramming the auditorium.'[62]

A *Sydney Morning Herald* photographer snapped a sensational photo of Professor Armstrong trying to hang one or two on Greenland and Cahill. You've got to hand it to Greenland. Not a jot of respect for anyone who did not fall into line with his rigid Marxist ideology. As expected, the Left used the photo as a source of mockery, dubbing Armstrong henceforth as the 'Beast'.

The application to join the public service was an aberration because Greenland left university to carry on as a committed Trotskyist determined to break bourgeois society. His work seems to have been in journalism and local council politics. He is still hammering away at the keyboard, never for one second giving up hope he will achieve his life's aim of subjecting the Australian people to the proven nightmare of his Trotskyist delusions. In the meantime, he lives off its benefits. The question of pathological delusion is pertinent. A speech by Trotskyist figurehead Bob Gould at Greenland's sixtieth birthday in 2004 shows how eternally deluded the far left is.[63] There were eighty people present in Greenland's backyard. This is how Gould describes the assembly:

'The people at Hall's 60th ... were a rather more diverse group than those who attend Socialist Alliance events. They included Hall's associates over

arrived, a demeaning death considering his heroic status in the wreck-
ing-left and the gale of praise that followed. Gould was seventy-four. Eulo-
gising obituaries appeared in all manner of media instruments, all warmly
acknowledging his unfailing adherence to Trotskyism. A report in the *Sydney Morning Herald* (23 May) revealed that his daughter, Natalie, claimed
'her father was first and last a Trotskyist, yet his hero was Lenin'. Greenland
penned a somewhat restrained piece highlighting Gould's Trotskyism and
his role in the student radicalisation of the 1960s. A crowd of 'over 500
people' turned up at the funeral. Labor Party members in federal and state
parliaments heaped praise on him.[64] It seems the eulogies might have gone
on until dark had the organisers not put a stop to the outpouring of grief
and adulation.

AS INFORMATIVE, as Barcan's book is about student activism, he does
not come to a definitive assessment of the period and its actors. He appears
to leave it to the reader. In their book *Seizures of Youth: The Sixties and
Australia*, Robin Gerster and Jan Bassett do not hesitate to assert one
outcome of the student rebellion at which I have hinted. 'Many young
Australians', they wrote, 'began to practise a brand of experiential, indi-
vidualised politics which played with allied notions of revolutionary Marxism and uninhibited sexual expression'. Their attitude 'had been given
intellectual sanction by [neo-Marxist Herbert] Marcuse, who advocated
a seductive combination of political and erotic protest, an unleashing of
energies both social and sexual'.[65] They relate the famous incident of a
naked youth wearing a gorilla mask gate-crashing a formal occasion in
Sydney University's Great Hall during Orientation Week in 1969. The
youth had 'the words "The more I make love, the more I make revolution"
emblazoned on his chest'.[66]

This action was a more elaborate expression of the cry 'Make Love, not War' that rang throughout the halls and lecture theatres of the university right into the school playground. Gerster and Bassett relate an incident at Mordialloc High School in Melbourne in November 1970. The students went on strike, protesting the suspension of three boys for wearing their hair too long. They rallied at lunchtime under a National Liberation Front flag hoisted on the school's flagpole and sang 'We Shall Not Be Moved'. 'The influences of the university-inspired anti-war movement', Gerster and Bassett wrote, 'could hardly be more patent'. 'Spurious ideological credibility' clothed typical teenage discontent and defiance of authority. A photo shows the three long-haired boys outside the school fence chucking a victory or peace sign ('it did not matter' which) to an 'adoring audience' among whom 'some girls ... look suitably impressed'.

With good reason, Gerster and Bassett suggest 'male vanity, vainglory and the desire to defy authority' were at the heart of the action.[67] They might have added the influence of Nevillism. Where was this male vanity and vainglory leading? Were the girls following Neville's prescriptions with the same enthusiasm as the boys? Neville gave the impression women could not possibly resist the power of his non-ideological ideology. Gerster and Bassett made the connection Barcan avoided – or at least downplayed. Former hippie Robin Morgan dismissed 'male radicalism as "counterfeit" and male radicals as defenders of "cock privilege"'. She urged 'women to seize control of the Left'. [68] It turned out the sex revolution came at a cost for women. A fact of nature that men and women are different in critical ways asserted itself.

The radical feminist literature flew across the Pacific to be taken up by feminists like Anne Summers, who encouraged women 'to leave the sexual merry-go-round'. In 1970, Morgan added that 'the "theory" of "free sexuality" meant "sex on demand for males"'. There may be some exaggeration in Morgan's claim, but the expectation did exist even if not always fulfilled. Richard Neville and Germaine Greer had succeeded in entrenching cock privilege without responsibility, and it was the female who was left with the baby, so to speak. Worse, Gerster and Bassett make a compelling case for connecting Nevillism with the Manson murders:

'To women like Morgan, the grisly Tate-La Bianca murders that rocked California in 1969, orchestrated by a megalomaniac hippie ... seemed to clarify the perniciously masculinist tendency of the entire counter-cultural experiment ... Manson collected human refuse thrown up by the social upheavals of the decade. In particular, he gathered around him a harem of adoring hatchet-women, disaffected young refugees from the middle-class ... women who, according to Morgan, fulfilled in extreme form 'the normal American male's fantasy' by doing 'all the shitwork, from raising babies and cooking and hustling to killing people on order'... The Tate-La Bianca slayings constitute a patently sixties 'happening', featuring a messianic male figurehead, hippies, Hollywood, sex and drugs and rock 'n' roll. And death. Death executed in order ...'to instil fear ... into the Establishment'.[69']

Is this a suitable epitaph for the sixties sexual revolution that 'fucked the system' and the women who succumbed to cock privilege? Leaving aside the Nevillites, the Greer adulators, and the Marxists and their project to free us from bourgeois sexual morality, those conservative males who blame feminism for destroying the natural relationship between men and women should examine their conscience about first causes. Feminists may have wielded the sword, but men who succumbed to Nevillism gave them the weapon. How conscious was any male at the time that each heedless sexual act was also a heedless act against the system (our age-old system of customs, traditions and conventions) and that most males were complicit in creating a weapon that would deprive them of what feminists call male privilege? Whatever male privileges there were, males had a duty by nature. Increasingly men ignored this duty. Gerster and Bassett's epitaph is no less damning about that other instrument of play power:

'Drugs, one of the 'weapons of revolution' celebrated by Richard Neville, have ushered in unstoppable waves of crime and degradation. The dealer, once glamourised by Timothy Leary as a 'spiritual guerrilla' involved in 'the noblest of all human professions', is now widely despised as a merchant of death.'[70]

By 1974, the flame of youthful rebellion had faded. At least, it seemed so. The mammoth anti-war demonstrations no longer flooded the inner-city streets of Australia's capital cities. Victory was going to the Vietcong and North Vietnam government. The occupations and sit-ins, so devastatingly effective, were sporadic. The likes of Hall Greenland were forced off campus to con a living in bourgeois society. There was some peace on campus – at least to the casual observer. Gerster and Bassett end their book with the chapter 'Revolution? What Revolution?' In his final chapter, Barcan asks, 'Was There a New Left?' Alas, there was still an old and new left, fat from gorging on the entrails of Australian culture and society. Conservatives were premature in cheering the perceived collapse of the New Left and the restoration of Australian social and political society.

The Left gave up the idea of the violent overthrow of capitalist society. Instead, they integrated into mainstream society and politics, succumbing to one or other theory in the smorgasbord of New Left theories. They would work at subverting traditional Australian society from within to achieve their idea of a 'just' and 'equal' society. Barcan names many student radicals who went on to fill prominent positions in the media, government, the public service and education. They produced the progeny that kept the cause alive. Gerster and Bassett offer this sorry conclusion to their book:

'That the phenomenon of sixties radicalism, so much the product of youthful hostility to the middle class, made its greatest impact when it itself became 'embourgeoised' is a paradoxical outcome from a decade of contradictions.'[71]

They make a convincing point by characterising the outcome of the radical's political action as a self-serving, subversive, hypocritical alignment with the society they were determined to sweep away. The judgment is not severe enough. I prefer the image of the maggot feeding on the rotting flesh of a bloated, diseased body.

Part Two

Sydney University 1973-1975

Chapter 4

1973 – Politics and Pornography

MY COMMENTARY on student politics at Sydney University begins in 1973 and goes on to 1980, when Tony Abbott finished his undergraduate studies. Tony enrolled in January 1976, but I start with 1973 for four reasons. First, the political struggle in which he was a leading player began around mid-1973 when the latest leftist clique conceived a campaign to gain control of student affairs. Most students saw the SRC (The Students' Representative Council) as an irrelevance. That had to change. The second reason was that women's studies in the Philosophy Department and political economy in the Economics Department became the focus of the radicals' activity. The third reason was that many of Abbott's bitter adversaries began university around this time. David Patch, who despised everything about Abbott, had enrolled in 1972 and, during 1973, was in the lead group of radicals determined to 'reform' the SRC. Barbara Ramjan, his intimate protégé and ally, enrolled the year after. Finally, I wanted to show comprehensively how student politics works, who most often prevails, and the tactics they employ to prevail.

Student politics parallels politics at the federal level with similar characters, manoeuvrings, manipulations, assassinations, lies, deviousness, betrayals, and, above all else, unbending ideological fundamentalism. The student newspaper records most of the action where the raw words and emotions of the leading players echo. The pages of *Honi Soit* were the rough equivalent of parliament – a parliament like that of contending factions in a tribal conflict where no binding authority exists to enforce the rules. Those who manoeuvred to gain political ascendancy called the shots, some with a poorly disguised pretence of following the rules. Some factions were more ruthless and unconscionable than others, as they are in federal politics.

Three factions were vying for control of student politics in 1973: the conservative 'Liberal-NCC (National Civic Council) alliance, Labor Left, and the hard Left'. Labor Left and the hard Left could cooperate – there was overlap in ideas and aims – but they were implacably opposed to the Liberal-NCC alliance. Although the leftists scorned the Liberal-NCC alliance as 'far right' (allegedly) dominated by the 'Catholic fanatic' B.A. Santamaria, the alliance was the home for social and political conservatives who represented the general community. Most in the alliance were members of the Democratic Club. Not all members of the Democratic Club were religious, let alone Catholic. There was a Liberal Club, but as we shall see, it hardly qualified as conservative. During 1973, the conservative voice was mute in the pages of *Honi Soit*. That would change in the second half of 1974. *Honi Soit* covered all issues dear to the heart of the radical, but in 1973 there were five fixations: censorship and pornography; the radical Left's campaign to 'democratize' the university's faculties and change the method of subject assessment; establishing a women's study course; establishing a department of political economy; and the reform of the Students' Representative Council.

BY THE early 1970s, the student rebellion, though running out of puff, was far from finished. Barcan writes that 'as their support amongst the wider student community evaporated, the Far Left turned their attention to a body they had ignored, the Students' Representative Council [SRC]. They now sought to alter its structure'.[72] The widespread dissatisfaction with the SRC became an opportunistic vehicle.

In his fourth and final year in 1973, Chris Sidoti was SRC President. He was also president in 1972, a tribute to his popularity and political competence. Sidoti was not your usual student leader. He was in the vanguard of what could be called the Catholic leftist movement. He was educated at Christian Brothers St Patrick's at Strathfield. He joined the Liberal Party in 1969 but became 'disillusioned with conservative politics and ideology'. His changing political perspective became visible when he fed a story to *Honi* editor Matthew Peacock in 1972 that 'unmasked' the National Civic Council's role in the establishment of a campus peace group (a brilliant Peacock scoop). Following that bit of untrustworthy action, he paid a visit to Cardinal Freeman to urge him to stop the NCC's recruitment of students in Catholic Schools. Presumably, it was preferable to allow far-left people to recruit in Catholic schools than have the disgusting ultramontanes from the NCC wandering unchecked among the young and impressionable.

In the 4th edition of *Honi Soit* (21 March),[73] Sidoti tried to broach SRC reform from a neutral position. Everybody agreed, he said, the SRC needed 'reform and complete restructuring'. As 'an organization [it] was discredited and largely moribund'. The ordinary student was not interested. A lot of chatter had gone on, but now was the time for action. He warned that 'any restructuring is doomed to failure unless it comes from the students and satisfies student demands'. He called for a 'Reform Programme [that] involves a series of Faculty meetings to discuss the aims and goals of a students' organization and how these can be attained'. He proposed a 'committee open to all students' that would consider the proposals.

Meetings would follow, during which proposals would be considered. This would lead to a referendum for students to vote on the proposals. All this sounds fair enough. Sidoti then asked rhetorically why there should be a Students' Representative Council anyhow. His answer:

'I believe that there is a need and a role for a students' association. Increasingly, the individual student is a voiceless number in the bureaucracy of the University and Society. An organization of our own is needed to give us an effective voice, needed to look after the problems we encounter as a group or as individuals, needed to press for reform in both the University and Society. A students' organization also has the job of arranging social functions for students as a whole, for providing an information centre that students can use.'

On the face of it, it was a moderate idea of a students' representative body. Even the notion of reform need not be a problem for conservative students. It depended on the reform. Edmund Burke said a society could not conserve itself without having the means for change. But then he (Sidoti) quoted from the existing constitution: 'the aims of the SRC [were] to promote the interests and maintain the traditions of the Student Body and of the University'. This statement gives a different perspective to Sidoti's vision. Promoting the 'interests and traditions' of the students and university administration is conservative. The maintenance of university traditions and cooperation with the university's authority does not gel with Sidoti's stated form for the SRC. Quoting from the constitution was evidently a ploy to allay the fears of conservative students. Of course, the last thing radicals had in mind was maintaining bourgeois traditions linking students with the authorities. Sidoti's proposal was of the soft Left, a ploy to keep the radicals from going feral before he could forward his plans for a sensible reconstitution of the SRC.

Under the heading of 'Progressive Movement' in the same issue, an unidentified writer harangued the reader about the failures of 'student government' because of people seeking 'self-aggrandizement or furtherance of their own selfish interests'. These named people comprised two groups representing 'nothing more than a choice between two evils', presumably the dark forces of the 'far right' and the less than ideologically pure. So 'to combat this selfish opportunism the PROGRESSIVE MOVEMENT has gathered together a group of people ready to work on behalf of the best interests of the student body...This year THE PROGRESSIVE MOVEMENT will concentrate on the Union and the SRC'. There followed an appeal to come to a meeting and 'put the student back in student government'. [74]

On the same page under 'Briefings' was a warning headed 'NCC PLOT'. The innocent student is urged to beware of 'an impeccably dressed, but dark and evil-smelling young man' who wants to waylay you with 'an offer of a free weekend at an Economics-cum-Political Science Conference AND/OR an invitation to a free slap-up dinner'. This person was a far-right Catholic operative bent on inviting you to 'an interminable harangue from a varied line-up of Peace With Freedom and NCC freaks followed by a free introduction session of yellow peril aversion therapy!' The spectre of Catholic ensnarement was lurking in every crack on campus.

A response to the appeal of the Progressive Movement was not lacking. In H5 (28 March), Jack H. Herman, a long-term student and flamboyant activist with a long rap sheet, let fly with much sneering and name-calling. *Honi* had shamelessly stooped 'so low as to publish the puerile rantings of petty politicians and fresh-faced first years'. Behind it all was a bunch of 'SRC-ALP hacks ... malevolent muckrakers [and] armchair pseudo-revolutionaries' whose aim was 'to establish themselves before the students so that when a viable SRC structure emerges, they can pull it into the same mire through which the present Council is wading'. One may wonder who the 'fresh-faced first years' were. More than a hint was to come.

Sidoti's attempt to establish a moderate SRC, one that would appeal to the bulk of students, failed. The gap between the Liberal NCC alliance, the Labor Left, and the hard Left was too wide. The SRC became chaotic and dysfunctional. *Honi* printed nothing from the Liberal-NCC alliance, and it defies belief the conservatives had nothing to say. Resignations followed. Sidoti saw it was pointless to persevere and resigned as president. His resignation loosened the last restraints on the Far Left's virulent anti-Catholic bigotry. For the rest of the year, there would be sniping in *Honi* at Sidoti's imagined far-right Catholic attitudes and allegiances, all this when he displayed an outspoken moderate-left approach to reforming the SRC. Sidoti was not without support.

Malcolm Turnbull (yes, *that* Malcolm Turnbull) arrived on campus at Sydney University in March 1973 as a 'fresh-faced first year'. He came from the competitive schoolyard of exclusive Sydney Grammar School, where he excelled in learning and leadership. He had won the Lawrence Campbell Oratory Competition, a competition in impromptu public speaking between representatives of Australia's foremost schools. Alas, Malcolm's first steps in public debate were not reflective of his schoolboy academic and public speaking fame. Nevertheless, those first efforts are of interest. After all, Tony Abbott's student utterances were brought up years later, notably by Turnbull himself. In H9 (2 May), Malcolm broke from the pack in a letter to the *Honi* editors:

'I have read *Honi* this term with great interest. Apart from your articles re pornography and censorship the main item covered seems to be the SRC and its bankrupt leadership.

'If the SRC is indeed as bereft of real leadership as it appears, I feel you must take a great deal of credit for it. I have had some little dealings with student politicians and indeed sponsored an attempt to set up (once again) a new 'Progressive' movement.

'Naturally, the egocentric politicians on this campus were too busy stabbing each others' backs to try and cooperate for the common good. These student 'Machiavellis' are so petty and childish that they have driven people like Sidoti out of the SRC by frustrating every attempt to get something done or to find a real role for the SRC. Now instead of Chris Sidoti, who I feel was trying to do something positive, we have that blustering bag of wind Jack Herman whose chief claim to fame is his mastering of the petty technicalities he bores people with on Wednesday nights.

'You have attacked Robyn Tupman – to what end? Under the charming title of 'Flog of the Week' we see yet another potential leader condemned. When will you, Matthew Peacock, do something constructive, when will you suggest a role, a *raison d'etre* for the SRC instead of abusing those who have failed to find one.

'I have no political interests on this campus, no aspirations to the SRC – for I, unlike Sidoti, am not willing to break my heart fighting pettiness, ignorance, arrogance and the greatest product of all these three – *Honi Soit*:'

The irony now drips from this letter. Editors Chris Kiely and Barry Peak, one or two years ahead of Fresher Turnbull, could not contain their scorn:

'Now here is a person accusing us of arrogance. You just broke all records for arrogance, hypocrisy, bullshitting and insincerity, Malcolm.

'First of all, your little 'Progressive Movement'. You who have no 'political interests on this campus, no aspirations to the SRC' organized a 'Progressive' ticket and got your beloved Robyn Tupman, whom we have grievously maligned as a flog, as patron. Needless to say, the movement fell flat on its face.

'Also, Jack Herman does not bore people on Wednesday nights with his petty technicalities. He bores them on Friday nights when SRC meetings have always been held. You should turn up sometime.'

The scorn of mere student editors did not perturb Turnbull. In H11 (14 June), he raised his sights. This time he aimed his considerable oratorical artillery at Professor Jones, president of the Union, over a trivial matter. It would not be the last time he made an injudicious political decision with such flare:

'Once again, the Union puritans have thrown their collective wet blankets on students trying to use their Union for their own enjoyment. One of the oldest clubs in the University, the Rugby Football Club, will this year have to use the facilities at the UNSW for their Annual Ball as the Union Board does not rent halls to its members on Saturday nights – not even the Union's City Road answer to the Opera House. This is not only another example of President Jones' duplicity but a thing of terrible shame to all Union members that the most successful of all the university's sporting clubs must go begging to Kensington to find a hall.

'If the Union can't provide basic services to its own clubs, to its own members, then the gang of sycophantic sybarites that are too cowardly to stand up for the students they represent, let alone play a game of rugby, should retire to that place where all carping pinch back would-be Caesars belong — anonymous ignominy.'

That Fresher's impertinence did not please Professor Jones. In H12 (21 June), the following grovelling apology appeared in a separate box:

'APOLOGY: I, Malcolm Turnbull, hereby retract and apologize for any distress I have caused Prof Jones in my letter to Honi last week. The letter was couched in a strident tone to arouse rather than to wound. I have great faith in Prof Jones' management of the Union.'

With Chris Sidoti's resignation, the SRC elected 'a nine man group known as the April the 7th Committee' to take over the SRC president's role. Among the nine were Bret Mattes, Jack Herman, Barry Peak, and Matt Peacock. The group of nine did not prove workable because by early May, they had elected a 'temporarily acting president'. H8 (2 May) announced the appointment under the headline 'Meet a president – Drunkards choose Herman for SRC'. Several photos of students with beer cans stuck to their mouths decorated the front page to illustrate the atmosphere of the election. Flamboyant Jack F Herman was to head 'the shattered mess we call student government'. No one else nominated because the election meant 'nothing and [the presidency] no longer carries any respect or authority'. Despite the tone of despair, the different factions embarked on composing constitutions to restructure the SRC. By late June, some proposals were ready. H13 (28 June) featured the efforts of Chris Sidoti and David Patch. Both were versions of participatory or direct democracy, Patch's being far more radical than Sidoti's,

Sidoti's constitution seemed a modest effort to reach a compromise between a representative system that included a flattened hierarchy of management with the more radical ideas of participatory democracy, like David Patch's. I include Patch's full proposal because it represents the views of his radical faction and an agenda which would dominate in the following years:

'The Philosophy behind the constitution of which I was co-writer is one of participatory democracy. This is the only viable method of real student control of their organization.

'Under this constitution the Student Body will form itself into 7 standing committees. To become a member of a committee, a member of the Student Body merely has to attend 2 of any 3 consecutive meetings of that committee. There are no elections whatsoever to these committees eliminating in one simple move the elitist, top heavy council structure that has existed up to now.

'There will be no President. Isn't it time we broke away from oppressive hierarchical systems and the notion that we need 'someone to speak for us?'

'All students, both postgraduates and undergraduates will be members of the Student Body. The membership fee will be refundable.

'Decisions of General Meetings will be binding and can therefore override all decisions of Committees and Officers of the Student Body. So control is doubly invested in the students, once by Committees open to all, and once again by all powerful General Meetings.

'Eliminate the top heavy elitist SRC and substitute participatory democracy in student Government.'

Patch did not bother to explain his system of participatory democracy. He never did. Why is hierarchy necessarily oppressive? What's a top-heavy council structure? Why have committees if a General Meeting can override their decisions willy-nilly? He ignored the openness to abuse and manipulation of committees and general meetings – for self-serving reasons. How does a small general meeting – it can happen – express the wishes of thousands of students? The truth is that Patch held his views about participatory democracy dogmatically and expected his fellow students to do the same. Patch was in his second year of university, barely two years out of school. Presumably, he was nineteen. Where did he get his radical ideas? Three of Patch's factional and ideological mates presented as candidates to represent the student body in the Senate, the governing arm of the university. The election was to take place on 25 September. Those mates were Paul Roberts, Tutor in the Department of Economics, Jean Curthoys and David McKnight (Arts III). Curthoys displayed her considerable Marxist credentials in the campaign to establish a women's studies department (see below), McKnight was a member of the CPA (Communist Party of Australia), and Roberts was in the frontline of the campaign to introduce Marxist economics in the Economics Department.

In H18 (6 September), Roberts, Curthoys, and McKnight warned that the proposed reorganization of the University's Senate was not to give students more say – the declared aim – but to centralize the Senate's power. It was 'to accentuate Professorial control, by making it extremely difficult to win staff-student control in departments and placing in the hands of a small body of professors, some staff and token students, the power to decide not only staff appointments as now but also to have the final decision on course content for the whole university'. We couldn't have professors, qualified, experienced professionals, deciding staff appointments and course content, could we? The proposed reorganization amounted to a blatant 'increase in authoritarianism'. The professors were reacting 'to the movement for democratization in departments and the wish of students to have some control over the courses they do and the exams for which they sit'. Students with the correct vision needed to hold the bourgeois-stacked Senate to account. The trio prescribed how the university should be governed. The plan complemented and filled out Patch's vision:

'Instead of the proposed centralization of decision-making, we propose total decentralization of authority, giving democratic departments with full staff and student participation the right to determine their own direction ... Basically, students should have as much say as possible in their education ... Here then is a double solution to one of our most pressing problems with courses.

'Interrelated with the powerlessness of students is the educational philosophy that permeates this university. The students' role is to sit and scribble notes quietly in lectures, fill out the required number of words in exams and essays, play the game of impressing the tutor – they are passive recipients of dead knowledge.

The lack of acknowledgement given to students in university deci-sion-making is also a function of this philosophy. We believe the best way to break this down and make the university a stimulating and egalitarian experience is to begin by staff and students having formal power to shape their own courses, choose the way they are to be examined, etc.'

Like Patch, our Marxist trio evaded the task of explaining the key features of their idea of democratization and philosophy of learning. What did they mean, for example, by the students being the passive recipients of dead knowledge? What was live knowledge in contrast? How could first-year students construct the course they're enrolled in? You would think two doctoral students functioning as tutors would be aware of the need for explanation. Were their doctoral theses to be polemical rants? They seemed guilty of the failings of which they accused the Senate. They expected their devoted audience to lap up their ideas without asking any questions. But there is more to this than the objections the ordinary person outside the walls of Sydney University would raise. Let me set up a simple analogy.

In sending their son to a technical college to be a carpenter or elec-trician, the ordinary parent in 1973 would expect their sons' teachers to be experienced in their field, to have a thorough technical knowledge of their trade, and to be practised teachers. The state had to oversee the courses and competence of the teachers in such important trades, not least for community safety. The young fellow coming direct from school had nothing to say about the staff and course content. To suggest to the parent there was something fatefully flawed in their son having to passively receive a bunch of dead knowledge from a hierarchy of teachers or being disadvantaged by the lack of democratic staff-student control would have brought wide-eyed, open-mouthed bemusement. If their son expected to be a 'passive recipient' of the course material and not be attentive to his lessons, the parent would warn that such an attitude would likely bring failure – and a loss of financial support.

To everyone not subjected to the Marxist opiate, successfully following a course in any particular field is an active process without which one cannot master the course material or acquire the skills for which one attends the course. One has one's own evidence. You follow a course because you are interested, and being interested, your intellect processes the material. If you are passive, you are passive for different reasons: you don't like the course, you are not interested, you have been forced to take the course, and so on. In these cases, the problem is you, not the course or the philosophy of learning behind the course.

Why then would these smart doctoral students express views about courses and learning that defy the ordinary person's commonsense? Well, the answer is that Marxism operates more like a drug than intellectual illumination, and Marxist theory, in particular, the Marxist dialectic, is behind the Marxist trio's counter-intuitive claims. Marxism is rooted in German philosophy from the great Immanuel Kant to Georg Hegel, whose idealist dialectic had a critical influence on Marx's materialist dialectic. It is difficult to understand the theory without knowing this philosophical lead-in. Understanding Marxist beliefs about knowledge and knowledge acquisition is necessary. Leading Marxist scholar Robert L. Heilbroner writes in *Marxism: For and Against* that Marxism's attitude to knowledge is 'activist':

'A Marxian approach to philosophy stresses the production, rather than the passive receipt of knowledge – the involvement of the act of inquiry in shaping, as well as in discovering, knowledge ... Marxian dialectics maintains that knowledge is not bestowed but won ... [Dialectics insists] that 'philosophizing' can only be vindicated and validated by some kind of activity and that reality is not merely what 'is,' but what we make it.'[75]

Not only does this view of activist knowing raise serious epistemological questions and contradict the ordinary person's understanding, but it dismisses the whole content and enterprise of university departments as they have existed for centuries. If students are engaged in shaping their knowledge and reality, the rest is irrelevant. The professors, with their years of research and intellectual contemplation, are nothing. They might as well leave the students each to their process of winning knowledge and reality making and repair to the professorial bar. One can now understand the crazy idea (to ordinary people) of student self-assessment, on which many of the radicals insisted. If you shape your knowledge and create your reality, who else can correct it? With the political onslaught of Marxists like our clever trio of Curthoys, Roberts and McKnight, departments were in a continual struggle to fight off chaos and disintegration. One final point about the Roberts-Curthoys-McKnight piece is the not-too-subtle warning that attempts at centralization in the face of 'democratization' of departments would be met with strikes. Did not the authorities know the recent strikes had been a resounding success? The authorities had to eat dirt in all cases. As ever, the radicals reduced all disputes between the authorities and the students to power – the naked power of a small, determined minority. Curthoys was the only one of the Marxist three to be elected.

In early September, the SRC elections took place. Bret Mattes came from behind to win the president's position. Editor Chris Kiely (H20, 20 September) dropped his usual facetiousness saying the hardly visible Mattes was seen 'as the only person likely to be able to lift the SRC from its present moribund state, back to its old prominence as a welfare/activity oriented cooperative'. He was upbeat about Mattes' ability to 'dissociate himself from the petty arguments that are sure to develop on the new council'. Except for David Patch, elected Arts Representative Men full-time, and Geoff Windon, Arts Men part-time, it appeared none of the visible radicals was elected faculty representatives. But what about the constitutions to be written and voted on in July? I found no mention of them after Patch had entertained the reader with his blueprint for participatory democracy.

The inaugural meeting of the 46th Students' Representative Council, 'mainly concerned with the election of officers for 1974', took place on Wednesday, 10 October. Editors Chris Kiely and Barry Peak were up-beat in their report on 'A New Deal' for students (H28, 18 October). 'The general tenor of the meeting', they wrote, 'was one of goodwill and cooperation. In a radical departure from past form, the council did not divide up into opposed political factions and managed to agree that its function was primarily in welfare education and student involvement in university decision making'. Was there any reason to think this ominous? Perhaps the cooperation and goodwill were due to the appointment of like-minded mates as SRC officers. The editors noted that David Patch, a 'prominent figure in the philosophy dispute, was unopposed as Welfar e Officer' (see below). Nobody was more radical than Patch in their plans for the coming year.

IN H5 (28 March), a feature article appeared under the heading 'Stron-garm Tactics?' The first sentence read, 'Well-known member of Peace With Freedom and Cultural Freedom, Professor Armstrong, has again had a run-in at the Philosophy Dept'. What had Challis Professor David Arm-strong of Sydney University's Philosophy Department done to deserve this crude sarcasm? He had vetoed a course designed and to be run by two female graduate students. The unnamed article writer provided a lengthy account of the episode, one favourable to the student course designers and unfavourable to Armstrong.

On one side were the two doctoral students, Elizabeth Jacka and Jean Curthoys. An apparent majority of the staff and students of the Philoso-phy Department backed them. Late in 1972, the democratization of the department had so advanced as to include all students, even first years, in its administration. First-year students, along with their professors and teachers, could vote on all matters about administration, courses, and lecturers. I say an 'apparent majority' because only those that turned up at meetings could vote. This was the trick of leftist democratization. Such 'open' meetings enabled the radicals to stack them and manipulate the students who did turn up.

The meeting to consider the course proposal took place the previous month (February). The unnamed writer of the *Honi* article wrote, 'At a departmental meeting, a 29 to 6 vote was recorded for the course. Five of the six were permanent staff, including Armstrong, who said he would oppose it at Dean level. Twelve of the twenty-nine were students and postgrads'. According to Peter Westmore in his *Quadrant* article of the July-August 1973 issue, 'Of the majority of 30 who voted for the course, only six were permanent members of staff. Those who voted against the course included the four senior members of the Department – Professor Nerlich, Professor Armstrong, and Associate Professors Rose and Campbell'. Associate Professor Rose was the acting head of the department.

The partly qualified or not qualified at all voted down the qualified and experienced, upending the procedures for department administration and course setting that had endured in universities for centuries. David Armstrong, a philosopher of international repute, was told to shut up and take his directions from a political cadre that included first-year students. What was the dispute over, besides a proposal for two students to design, run and examine a full-year course never given before? Their course entitled 'The Politics of Oppression' would cover 'liberal democratic theories of women's rights', 'general theories of oppression', 'theories of internalization', and theories of sexual oppression'. Some of the philosophers studied would include Marx, Engels, Satre, de Beauvoir, Marcuse and Greer. The course had a Marxist orientation, and in an interview with the ABC radio program 'PM,' Jacka and Curthoys revealed how radical its content was. Westmore quoted the sections of interest:

'INTERVIEWER: Well, Elizabeth Jacka, what does your course involve?

MISS JACKA: Our course will start from an examination of women's consciousness of their own oppression in history and at the present time. Then it will go on to discuss the economic basis and origins of this oppression, and finally, we hope to discuss how women may liberate themselves. Whether it will be by conventional, political action, by raising their consciousness or by other methods, including revolution.

INTERVIEWER: Is it a political propaganda course, then?

MISS JACKA: Not necessarily. We don't pretend to be neutral. We are committed to women's liberation. But we hope to maintain objectivity and philosophical rigour in our discussion.

INTERVIEWER: Jean, is this the new phase in the women's lib. Movement?

MISS CURTHOYS: In my personal opinion, yes. I think that up until now, although women's liberation has been very effective, that it has suffered from a lack of theory and, in a sense, a lack of direction. I hope that our course will help remedy this. I personally think that the future of the women's lib. Movement lies in tying itself up with Marxist movements. This is something that is now happening in Britain, and I hope to see it happen in Australia.'

And towards the end of the interview:

'INTERVIEWER: . . . couldn't you allow some other male [teacher] ... to teach it?

MISS CURTHOYS: We could, but this is quite contradictory to the very aim of the course. Our position is that women being the oppressed people are the only ones who are able to come to a proper understanding at this stage of how and why they're oppressed. The oppressor simply can't understand the nature of the oppression.'

The unnamed article writer of H5 was more precise about the disqualification of men and male thinking as necessary for the integrity of the course:

'Western culture and, in particular, the intellectual tradition has been almost exclusively the product of men, and that there has been no special study of the nature, experience and aspirations of women clearly poses a problem for those who wish to study questions relating to women, since the only theory available in which to do so is just that arising from this male-dominated intellectual tradition.'

These views were a departure from the philosophical enterprise of strict reasoning to principles understood by all. The disqualification of men, branded as the oppressor, from understanding women's supposed oppression signalled that the course described variously as 'The Politics of Sexual Oppression' and 'Philosophical Issues in Feminist Thought' amounted to a year-long course in Marxist dogmatics, akin to a Catholic seminary's course in dogmatics. Catholic dogmatics are not neutral – they draw from the Scriptures – but they are argued and developed logically from their base.

To understand this, you don't have to be a philosopher with an international reputation. If faults of reasoning had been in the claimed male-dominated intellectual tradition, then those possessed of reason – that is, men and women alike – could critique the weak parts and develop theories correcting those faults – faults understood by men and women alike. The disqualification of half of humanity from having a legitimate say about a course in 'sexual oppression' was unapologetically sexist, and presumed sexual oppression only applies to women. It was unimaginable for Jacka and Curthoys and their feminist pals that a case from nature could be made about male disadvantage. Their proposed course of Marxist dogmatics was far from the philosophical tradition that the famed Professor John Anderson had established in Sydney University's Department of Philosophy. Armstrong, one of Anderson's students, did not think Marx was a significant philosopher and rebelled against the campaign to degrade the intellectual traditions of philosophy.

The Marxist faction did not accept Professor Armstrong's veto, and the agitation continued. The course supporters appealed to the Arts Faculty, and they approved the course. That was it for the supporters. All that Professor O'Neil of the Professorial Board needed do was to name the lecturers. But O'Neil, pressured by Armstrong and his supporters, got up a committee to consider the course and the appointment of Jacka and Curthoys as lecturers. The committee came back with the recommendation to accept the course if it was supervised. Professor Armstrong gave a strong presentation before the board, citing the issues of academic competence, the irregularity in establishing the course, and the appearance of radicalism. He also warned that 'given the present [democratic] structure of government in the Philosophy Department, this measure appears to be full of danger to academic standards'.[76]

The Professorial Board, the highest court of 'appeal', overruled the committee (votes 39 to 7), rejecting the course and the appointment of the two feminists – even under supervision. Westmore wrote that 'two days later, on Wednesday, 20 June, a General Meeting in the Philosophy Department, attended by about 250 of the Department's 661 students and members of staff, voted to strike until the two postgraduate students were appointed to teach the course'. *Honi* reported the same meeting with different numbers. It put the vote at 109 to 6 in favour of a strike – 115 students out of 661. This was staff-student democracy in action.

In H14 (5 July), Geoff Windon, who covered the affair for *Honi* and was likely the author of the unnamed article, enthusiastically announced that on Friday, 29 June, 'the SRC voted by more than a 2 to 1 majority to call a general strike of students in support of the widening dispute in the Philosophy Dept'. He did not mention the number who voted. Windon went on to describe the serious problems (he perceived) in the arguments for rejecting the course. On the question of competence, he said, there were other postgraduate students giving lectures. He did not name those cases. It does not follow that because a particular postgraduate student is appointed to 'lecture' in a particular course, every other postgraduate student is qualified to lecture in a given field. The particular circumstances of the case in hand would decide competency as it did in the philosophy case. Windon seemed ignorant of what an analogical argument was. He ridiculed the candidates' 'supposed political beliefs'. There was no 'supposition' about Jacka and Curthoys' political beliefs. They were as naked as one could wish. He then broadened his objections to cover 'two related issues'.

The first is 'the Board's misuse of its power to subvert the constitutional right of the dept to determine its courses'. This rested on the assumption that the democratization process rammed through by leftist students could be defended theoretically and in practice. Armstrong's point was that it could not be defended, and the results would be disastrous – as they were. The second was 'the employment of sexist and/or political sanction' to silence dissent from the wishes of the established authorities. On the evidence, this objection could more reasonably apply to Jacka, Curthoys and their supporters.

Having warmed to his subject, Windon made a global leap to the university's administration, whose essential quality was that nobody had elected it. 'Under the present situation', he said, 'power is concentrated in the Professorial Board and the Senate, neither of which is elected by the population of around 20,000 staff and students'. Real, genuine democracy, devoutly wished for by the pure of heart, would prevail if 20,000 students 'told by the head' submitted their vote for all positions of authority in the university. The disaster that happened to the Philosophy Department over the following years is a clear indicator of where the university would have ended if Windon and his colleague David Patch had forced their vision of direct democracy on the university.[77]

Windon, who disappeared from *Honi* pages after this matter, wrapped up his report with a cherished Marxist myth about alienation. The university's 'archaic and extremely authoritarian system', wrote Windon, promotes 'a sense of alienation and extreme loneliness ... forcing large numbers of students to drop out or miss out on so much the university has to offer'. No evidence is offered for this supposed alienation. There was no necessary logical connection between the university's structure of authority in 1973 and a sense of alienation and loneliness. Such an assertion is decided empirically. My experience attending university in the 1960s and again in the 1970s and 1980s at three different universities speaks against the claim. An atmosphere of diligence and dedication prevailed among my fellow students to the learning enterprise. But being called on to match experience with the theory is an inconvenience, as Roger Scruton puts it, the leftists did not want to face.

Nothing is more exciting for the leftist student than a bit of strike action that shuts down long-established systems and proven ways of dealing with everyday life. The subsidized left-wing student is unlike the young plumber or carpenter learning his trade. The budding plumber and carpenter must follow established methods and learn strictly defined skills. Entertaining ideas about direct democracy would have them booted from technical college and their apprenticeship. With state money stuffing their pockets, the leftist student and the well-paid junior staff, increasing numbers of whom were the graduates from the 1960s madness, could go the whole hog. A 'women's embassy' was set up on the main Quadrangle. After a meeting of 'between 700 and 800 staff and students', 300 students 'peacefully' invaded the building where the Professorial Board was meeting. Other Arts Faculty departments joined the strike. Windon could not name the support of science and applied science faculties, nor did he supply the *for* and *against* votes. The SRC declared a general strike of students.

Because of the disruption, the Professorial Board began negotiating with the students and staff. In other words, they entered a phase of capitulation. A bit of pushing and shoving followed, but a month after the strike, the board, the students, and the staff agreed to a compromise. Jacka and Curthoys would be allowed 'to teach "The Philosophical Aspects of Feminist Thought" in consultation with John Burnheim, a permanent [leftist] member of the philosophy staff. He will have only an advisory status'. Marxists Jacka and Curthoys were under no restraint. The students crowed that they had won – with good reason – and David Armstrong and the other department senior members had to eat dirt. He had earlier spoken of the dilemma they faced:

'As large street demonstrations became rare after 1971, leftist agitation concentrated on smaller and more focused campaigns. As long as the Left could keep small numbers of committed students 'confronting' authority, university administrations were faced with the dilemma of failing to react, leading to contempt for their gutlessness and to further demands, or reacting firmly, causing radicalization of a wider body of students.'[78]

Armstrong had a point, and one can sympathize with the members of the Professorial Board. Most of them were in their positions because of their academic status and not the management of a mob of unscrupulous Marxists who put no limits on political activities so long as it promoted the Marxist project. Nevertheless, with no less than Western culture at stake, you would think a few had the backbone to stand up to the leftist bullying. Instead, with long faces, they had to watch from the Gothic windows of their professorial apartments the mocking jubilation of the students celebrating their famous victory. James Franklin reported one visitor's description of the celebrations:

'They were singing sentimental Irish songs under the banner 'Philosophers hitherto have only interpreted the world – the point now is to change it'. [A Marxist reference.] They had two four-gallon casks of wine – which is counter-culturally acceptable alcohol; spirits and beer are frowned upon, spirits because of their upper-income connotations and beer because it is associated with the worst kinds of Australian male behaviour. We talked briefly with George Molnar, a lecturer in philosophy who had been centrally active in the strike. He was making the "goodies" in the kitchen (not savouries). "Tomorrow the world", he said.'[79]

It was entirely proper for the victorious students to consume marijuana and yell Marxist slogans. Later that year, in October, Vice-Chancellor Bruce Williams, sick to death of the dispute, announced splitting the Philosophy Department into 'radical' and 'orthodox' philosophy. Five senior members of the department, including David Armstrong, felt the conflict had been too rough to entertain any cooperation with the radicals. They insisted the two new departments function separately, and students could only take subjects from the department they enrolled in.

Jean Curthoys bemoaned the split in an article on the front page of H27 (4 October), making the obvious point that such a split was not in the spirit of philosophy, a subject all about reasoned argument. That was a bit rich coming from a champion of Marxism, a body of doctrinal claims accepted in the long run on faith. She deplored circumstances in which the orthodox students could not sup from the dish of Marxist porridge. There was a long road ahead for Sydney University's Philosophy Department before it vaporized. The *Honi Soit* editors paid tribute in their final issue to David Patch as a 'prominent figure in the philosophy dispute'.

Mid-year, following the exhilarating success of the radicals in the Philosophy Department, those in the Economics Department were emboldened to gear up their 5-year campaign of forcing democratization and the introduction of 'political economy', that is, Marxist economics. The campaign ran in tandem with the 'renewal' going on in the SRC. The proponents of political economy blamed the troubles in the Economics Department on the arrival of Professors Warren Hogan and Colin Simkin in 1968 and 1969.

Hogan and Simkin, according to Richard Fields (H15, 12 July), were guilty of the 'streamlining of the [economics] course involving greater stress on the technical aspects of the subject and an increased workload, at the expense of the philosophical and ideological aspects; and further, denying much time or opportunity for critical appraisal or genuine thought. Teaching has in large measure degenerated to the nature of indoctrination'. Instead of the indoctrination in courses like quantitative economics and econometrics, the new indoctrination was to be in Marxist dogma. Fields called a meeting of students and staff for Tuesday, 10 July, to discuss and vote on six demands. Those demands were to be 'presented to Professors Simkin and Hogan, backed up by a threat of strike action if the demands are not quickly met to a reasonable degree'. Once again, the authorities, those qualified and professional, had to bow – or else. Field's six demands were about democratization, 'the Head should be elected', 'no recriminations against staff and students' for behaving like a Stalinist rabble, examinations to be no more than 50% of the marks, no compulsory maths, more options, all courses optional constructed 'with specific student objectives in mind'.

In contrast with the philosophy affair, Professors Hogan and Simkin held their ground no matter how fierce the student bullying. At least they had the support of Vice-Chancellor Bruce Williams, also a conservative economist. Hogan and Simkin's refusal to give in provoked a 'Day of Protest'. Fields again reported the day and its happenings in H18 (2 August). Because they didn't achieve their aims, Fields coloured his report with much mockery and sneering at Hogan and Simkin, and grovelling reverence for the staff members who actively participated in the protest. An alternative lecture program by the radicals followed the regular lecture schedule. Dr Frank Stilwell, an influential figure in Australia's New Left, regaled his radical audience with his leftist erudition, but the main event was Communist Associate Professor Ted Wheelwright's paper 'Criticism of New-Classical Economics'. Wheelwright had been an economic advisor to the Marxist government of Chile. A most enjoyable day was had by all, according to Fields.

The inspiring lectures by the adored Marxists contrasted unfavourably with Professor Simkin's effort to give his regular 10 a.m. lecture to a class of third-year honours students. A student who wanted the lecture given 'over for discussion of departmental problems' interrupted the lecture. When Simkin reprimanded the student for his impertinence and refused to acknowledge him, the lecture deteriorated into 'paper darts and some rather bold heckling'. Fields had much fun mocking Simkin and his dealings with the 'imaginary student' of the first question. However, Simkin did not budge and so earned Fields' description as 'one of the most autocratic (even despotic) and obstructionist professors in the University'.

In a courageous gesture, Simkin agreed to a student interview. He must have realized *Honi* was never going to make him look good. Although the unnamed interviewer's leading questions squeezed Simkin into a corner to make him look like an autocratic despot worthy of everyone's contempt, he did have the chance to state truths with which most people outside the university walls would have had sympathy. He explained the Economics Department taught more than neo-classical economics, and 'Marxist theory can't be taken seriously today because it does not apply to any real economic situation'. In response to the claims of student participation in decision-making, he said, 'It's true that Professor Hogan and I are in charge of and responsible for the department, but the department does have a large amount of machinery for cooperation with staff and students... You can't run a place like this without a large amount of consensus, but I believe the traditions of this university – that it is here to transmit knowledge – are of primary importance. This university is not primarily a democracy'. All very sensible for ordinary people but not for 19-year-olds breathing in the opiate clouds of Marxism. In the 'Briefings' rubric, an unnamed writer commented on an Economics Faculty meeting in which Professor Simkin not only put everyone to sleep but 'undaunted the turd spoke on and eventually put himself to sleep'.

David Patch provided a report (in the third person) about his starring role in a meeting to discuss the dispute in the Economics Faculty between a group representing the Faculty and some 'Administration heavies'. The heavies were 'Prof Taylor (Head of Prof Board), Prof Williams (Vice-Chancellor), Prof O'Neil (Deputy VC), Prof Leonie Kramer, Prof Birch, Hugh McCredie, Harold Maze, Mr Fisher'. Patch:

'The representatives from Economics pointed out that only the neo-classical approach to Economics theory was taught in the Dept, and that all attempts to introduce either an institutional approach or a Marxist approach had been blocked by Professors Simkin and Hogan. In other words, these two professors were enforcing their own narrow beliefs on an entire Department – despite worldwide questioning of the neoclassical approach. All attempts to make changes had been and were continuing to be frustrated by an autocratic Professorial veto ...

'David Patch asked the Vice-Chancellor whether or not it was Senate policy to demand that a clause be inserted in any proposed new Student Body Constitution, giving the Senate a veto power over amendments to that constitution. Prof Williams' reply was (surprise) 'yes', and he went further and said that if this was not done, the university would refuse to collect SRC fees. Such an ultimatum is nothing short of political blackmail and demonstrates the arrogant attitude of the Vice-Chancellor. On present indications, the students will never allow the Senate to exercise control over the affairs of the Student Body, and Williams will find himself stumped if he tries to instigate it.'

Patch, whose arrogance had puffed him up to the size of the Hindenburg, was not above behaving like an angry despot with his own fixated narrowness of thinking. In H18 (6 September), a long, turgid Marxist 'Critique' of neo-classical economics followed Patch's report, presumably to give substance to the youthful radicals whose knowledge of Marxism could never be more than the surface claims propagated by hardened Marxists.

Marxist martyr Bill Waters was the author of the critique. In 1970, Waters was a department tutor in the vanguard of the agitation to introduce the subject of political economy. His contract was not renewed at the end of the year. From a business point of view, the termination of his contract was reasonable, quite apart from the issue of academic competence. A business could not tolerate someone working against its ideas and goals, a principle understood in the general community. Waters' critique is nothing more than a long one-sided explanation – sometimes little more than a rant – of key Marxist ideas on capitalism with frequent appeals to Marxist authorities, including a sycophantic appeal to Wheelwright. There is no defence of the shaky foundations of Marxism (dialectical materialism), and no coverage of possible objections. Curiously, one of the authorities Waters appeals to is a highly respected Marxist scholar, Robert L. Heilbroner, from whose book *Marxism: For and Against* (1979) I draw for criticism of Marxism, notably of the dialectics.

In H19 (13 September) was a report about another meeting between the student radicals and one of the 'heavies', this time Professor Hogan. There is no need for the details. The meeting takes the same form to which the professors subjected themselves. The only position understood and tolerated was that of participatory democracy and Marxist economics. Contempt and ridicule greeted any resistance by the teaching authorities and the administration. This was the repetitive form of student combat.

THE EDITORSHIP of *Honi Soit* was a commanding position in the SRC hierarchy. A talented editor, or an editorial collective, could wield enough power to unseat the president and other members of the council. The SRC had appointed Matthew Peacock editor for 1973. In the third edition (H3, 14 March), Peacock revealed what was on his mind. An illustration of a man dressed in clothes men in the public service wore in the first half of the 20th century was on the back page. But the man had no pants. The caption named him a 'slightly obscure gentleman fighting to preserve what he termed the community's "commonly accepted standards of decency"'. This man 'worked in an undercover capacity (complete with trench coat, no trousers, leather gloves and a bag of boiled lollies)'. You get the picture. Peacock and his editorial support staff saluted this ridiculous, sexually disturbed man with 'Hail Mr Griffiths, the new Chief Secretary!' Around the Chief Secretary was a series of Patrick Cook cartoons depicting various sorts of sexual activity considered at the time pornographic and utterly tasteless. Peacock's aim was obviously to offend the general community's sensitivities to the full extent of his powers. In this exhibition of Nevillism, he succeeded gloriously.

No doubt, Peacock and his smug pals in the SRC got an immediate reaction, but it was not until two issues later (H5, 28 March) that Peacock reported on it. On 'The Self-Abuse Page' under the headline 'No More Fucking Pornography' Peacock sneered that around a 'dozen morally a-ffronted' students, mainly of the Evangelical Union, visited the *Honi* office to denounce Peacock's promotion of pornography. According to Peacock, their principal objection to his rampant Nevillism 'was that it was against God's will'. Peacock announced in a comment soaked with sarcasm that he recognized 'these people' as 'sensible, worthwhile [with] a sincere concern for the moral welfare of the community'. But he added, 'we have no hesitation in printing their letters and saying PISS OFF, FUCKWITS!'

Later in H5, Peacock put aside his contempt and abuse and undertook a 'serious' analysis of the proposed Act to defend 'commonly accepted standards of decency', words Peacock attributes to the NSW Chief Secretary Ian Ross Griffith. Griffith was a minister in the Askin Liberal Government. He had served in the Royal Australian Navy during the Second World War and reached the rank of lieutenant. It was Griffith that Patrick Cook sketched as the man 'complete with trench coat, no trousers, leather gloves and a bag of boiled lollies'. Griffith proposed the Indecent and Restricted Publications Act, which aimed to maintain and protect 'commonly accepted standards of decency', an idea that copped more sneering. Legislation to protect the ideas, standards and feelings of the general community seems to me one of the essential responsibilities of democratic government. The Coalition Government's Act intended to do that – obey the will of the community. Peacock and his editorial staff saw the Act's intentions in a reverse light:

'In fact, the Act contains in it some of the most repressive and totalitarian legislation which Australia has seen or is likely to see. Police powers are widened to a frightening degree, and freedom of speech is effectively wiped out. Taken in a favourable light, the Act would seem to be a rather severe regression; taken unfavourably, it is open to unlimited abuse.'

Peacock ran a series of hypothetical cases to demonstrate his claims. Speculative or abstract reasoning can lead to all sorts of outrageous conclusions as a first-year philosophy student quickly learns. Peacock introduced all his examples with the singular 'you' as in imagine you happened to be in the wrong place at the wrong time, and the police caught you. In such circumstances, you risked being locked up. Abstractly speaking, it is true that even the most upright person in the community could be in a position where a policeman who just happens to be standing next to him finds pornographic material in his hands. There is no logical contradiction here. But it is not an abstract matter. It is an empirical matter. The community is not an abstract thing or a hypothetical case. The community is a particular concrete entity made up of real people in a real society with a range of particular customs, traditions, conventions, laws, and so on. The unwritten but understood laws and rules of manners, customs and conventions circumscribe legislation which should reflect those unwritten prescriptions found in every society – even in those without a democratic form of government. The NSW police in 1973 could not arbitrarily arrest and confiscate the property of an individual. The individual in our once healthy liberal-democratic society had recourse to various people and departments in and out of government and the public service – not just to po lice.

There were, however, other concrete circumstances that justified Griffith's Indecent and Restricted Publications Act. Peacock and his editorial staff were not promoting pornography for the hell of it or just to give the finger to bourgeois society, particularly to World War II veterans like Ian Griffith, for whom they had a lazy contempt. No, they took their lead from Richard Neville, who had shown the way in *Oz* and *Play Power* to bring obscenities into Australia's lounge rooms, promote child sex and gangbangs, and generally to 'fuck [the bourgeois] system'. The erasure of the censorship laws was an integral part of SRC renewal.

The community was appalled at the actions of a small group of adolescent fanatics who seemed to have free rein in their destructive political campaigns. They were screaming for the authorities to take drastic action. But by 1973, it was too late. Griffith's plan was too late. Those with the power and authority to stop the degradation were caught like bunnies in the glare of the headlights. Men like my father and Ian Griffith, proud of their war service, could never have imagined in 1943, during a respite from the roar of war, what would happen twenty years later to the nation and society for which they were ready to give their lives. Griffith's proposed Act was already a dead letter when he penned it. Within a few years, such legislation as it existed would be repealed, resulting in open slather. Pornography is the internet's biggest earner. Most children have been exposed to graphic pornography by the time they turn twelve. Men exercising their right to be free of censorship are regularly caught with thousands of photos of child pornography on their computers.

Peacock did not rest with exhibiting his anti-Christian bigotry and providing a self-serving analysis of the proposed Act. In the same issue, he introduced a new rubric on '*Honi*'s first Tasteless Page'. The new rubric explained what the editor sought under the heading 'Eating a Turd'. The criteria would not be artistic or literary qualities. Instead, the degree of tastelessness would decide the drawing's or article's merit. He urged students to send in their best 'animal' stories. A preoccupation with vomit featured. Its best expression was in a new comic strip called *Vomit Man*. Needless to say, vomit and other such bodily fluids spewed from the page. All very funny, of course. The *Vomit Man* comic strip would appear until the end of the year. H6 (4 April) was a bumper issue on pornography hilariously titled 'PORNUCOPIA!' CBK (presumably Chris Kiely) treated us to an account of a pornography rally on the front lawn. This exciting festival of pornography, indecency and tastelessness heralded the start of like-festivals to denounce Griffith's 'scurrilous legislation...oozing its way through State Parliament'. Jim Staples of the Council for Civil Liberties and Wendy Bacon addressed the rally. Germaine Greer turned up to sing 'a very pleasant Blues song about fucking'. Other activities appropriate to the festival were rampant among the sweaty, unwashed throng of pornography connoisseurs.

There were co-editors for H6: Chris Kiely, Matthew Peacock and Barry Peak. Kiely and Peak had been promoted from staff support. Was there any significance in this change as there may have been in the SRC forcing the *Honi* team to apologize to members of the Evangelical Union? The apology was implied, not written, and the editors added, '*Honi* will not be dictated to by extremists of the right or left'. The last issue in which Peacock was one of the co-editors was H8 (2 May). Was it a coincidence that the *Honi* prize for virulent anti-Christian bigotry had to go to 'the jesus christ column' in this issue? You could scarcely have a more spectacular example of anti-Christian bigotry.

What happened to Matthew Peacock? Why did he cease to make any contribution to *Honi Soit* after May? Peacock was dragged before the courts in 1974 for his hand in H3, but he had handy connections. Jim Staples, ideological mate, barrister, and a former member of the Communist Party of Australia, convinced the judge to dismiss the case.[80] It would be understandable if Peacock kept his head down when legal action loomed. An additional reason may have been that Australia's most powerful media instrument, the government-owned and funded Australian Broadcasting Corporation (ABC), had recognized Peacock's talents in his wonderful pieces on pornography and religion. The ABC had a place for 21-year-old Matt.

The pornography coverage died down to *Honi*'s usual level of grossness after May, except for one blaze of pornographic glory in H11 (14 June). The influence of Nevillism was evident in a new comic strip titled *Little Orphan Amphetamine, The Freak Brothers' favourite 14-year-old runaway.* Kiely and Peak unashamedly ripped off Robert Crumb's creation of 'Honeybunch Kaminski, 13 of L.A. what a little yummy' that featured in Snatch Comics and was a favourite of Neville's. Little Orphan Amphetamine is a Little Orphan Annie look-alike. Orphan Annie is famous for her cuteness and innocence, the reason the look-alike was obviously chosen to be portrayed as a 14-year-old runaway, blasé about being raped by a gorilla and gangbanged by a mob of ugly drugged degenerates. You get the picture. This was the only appearance of *Little Orphan Amphetamine* in support of free speech in 1973 *Honi Soit*. One can understand the reasons.

Honi's editors boasted they were 'attacked from all sides' and were 'labelled bigoted, atheistic, tasteless and unfair', all of which was correct. They gave the finger to the 'fuckwits' whose letters they generously printed but made it plain those defending community decency would not cow them. Things did not always go their way, though. In H7 (18 April), they reported some persons had gotten away with 5,000 copies of the Pornucopia issue. They said, 'the reason for the theft is unclear'. Really? They added, 'a number of members of EU (the Evangelical Union) were at two of the sites of the thefts, however [sic] they had seen no one acting suspiciously'. Kiely and Peak could be as unsubtle as they liked, but they had to cop it sweet. If that wasn't enough, they reported two months later under the heading 'Piddling Turds' (H12, 21 June) that 'a group of women burned approximately 2,000 copies of *Honi* outside Fisher [Library] and the Refectory. Following this, 10 women demanded to see the Sexist Honi Editors.' When told the editors were unavailable, they trashed the office causing $110 in damage – a fair sum in 1973. The reason for the trashing was a quote from Mao Tse-Tung in the Little Orphan-Amphetamine comic strip: 'Genuine equality between the sexes can only be realized in the process of the socialist transformation of society as a whole'. There was no limit to the Left's wackiness.

Kiely and Peak had to confess that persons unknown purloined a further 5,000 copies of *Honi*, making the total 7,000 copies of that issue gone. Add the 5,000 copies from two months earlier, then the SRC suffered a loss of 12,000 copies. Another demonstration of the Left's financial delinquency. Kiely and Peak's whingeing about 'selfish behaviour and gross overreaction' showed yet again bullies can't take their own medicine. The 1973 academic year ended with renewed enthusiasm and determination. The groundwork for the major far-left campaigns had been laid. David Patch's best times were ahead of him.

Chapter 5

1974 – political economy now!

WITH THEIR PLANS established, the far left got off to a brilliant start when the new editors for *Honi Soit*, Marxists Simon Grose and David Margan, began their term in January 1974. However, the force behind the articulate Grose and Margan was the clever, even more articulate David McKnight of the Communist Party of Australia (CPA). Grose and Margan referred to Comrade Dave as the 'Archangel', no doubt with the cosmic rebel Lucifer in mind. They ran *Honi* on a committee basis. Like all leftist groups, a small vanguard group of which Dave was the guiding light, ran the show. Along with Grose, Margan, and McKnight, the names of far-left Chips Mackinolty and manic Craig Johnston cropped up in the credits. Others of like-minded outlook contributed irregularly, including eccentric grandiloquent Herman K. Herman. The far left, having captured *Honi*, were thus well placed for the year. The first edition of *Honi* was already blazing away with propaganda.

In '"STUDENT POWER" or a weekend away in the country', Comrade Dave McKnight presented the student body with a manifesto to democratise university departments and to introduce 'radical educational reform' of a 'learning process in which [students] are essentially powerless'. To promote the manifesto, Dave and a bunch of far-left mates formed

an organisation called 'Student Action Movement'. The manifesto was:
'1. For a struggle for staff-student control of education through open
action committees of students in departments and faculties. 2. Against
the examination system. 3. Against lectures as a learning method. 4. For
a university that is critical: i.e. we will fight for courses that cease to serve
capitalist corporations or government bureaucracies rather than human
needs; we will oppose course content that reinforces values where male
supremacy, racism, the exploitation of workers and authoritarian personal
relations are taken for granted'. Comrade Dave's program, then, was to
reorganise university departments, so they had no lectures, no exams, and
were to be governed by the votes, or raised hands, of a random number
of 'staff' and 'students' told by the head. Then, in apparent contradiction,
they were to decide how individually they shaped reality and 'won' their
knowledge.

Comrade Craig, totally lacking the Archangel's finesse, furiously supported Comrade Dave's call to arms in his Student Action Movement
(SAM) manifesto. Craig was all for shooting and asking questions later.
With much delight, he recounted in the *Honi* rubric 'Glimpses' how he
and fellow SAM members gave the Enrolments Director the finger. He
told him to get lost when he ordered the removal of their SAM propaganda table from the entrance to the Great Hall during Orientation
Week. Johnston and his mates did not have permission to be there (no
other club or association had set themselves up there), and the material
they handed out about courses slandered some lecturers, among other
things, calling them 'lousy'. The lecturers were lousy not because they
were ignorant and incompetent but because they did not teach the Marxist
dogma second-year Arts student Johnston prescribed. Comrade Craig was
ideologically unflinching. 'The present alienating, conformist, pro-status
quo university, controlled by people like the Enrolments Director' justified
the SAM action. Johnston and his SAM mates refused to move.

The Assistant-Registrar suffered the same treatment when she arrived to order their removal. What did the Assistant-Registrar do when Comrade Craig told her to bugger off? She caved in. With good reason, Johnston was all triumph. He scoffed at the authorities, who in the end were 'paper tigers ... like all reactionaries'. Johnston was there to undeceive students about the paper-tiger authorities who depended on capitalist conditioning (family, religion, school, etc.) to ensure community obedience. Johnston and his far-left mates wouldn't for one moment tolerate that. The Student Action Movement wanted 'staff-student control of the whole university', and they would have it.

Comrade McKnight enlightened his readers with a review (H2) of *Communes* by I. V. Greenburg & D. D'aprano, which was an analysis of living in a commune in a capitalist society. Dave had seized the chance to display his understanding of Marxist theory. He maintained coherence when he deployed his ideas about democracy, however challengeable those ideas were. It was downhill from there, though. He enthusiastically surveyed the authors' thoughts on the problems the nuclear family (allegedly) causes, not just for living in a commune but for our lives as autonomous people.

In brief, for Dave, a nuclear family upbringing 'leads to the creation of crippled human beings' who (allegedly) do not have the skills to cooperate in communal living. You know, the child has everything done for him – clothed, fed, mollycoddled, etc. – without inquiring where all the sustenance comes from. He wrote, 'young people not having participated in their own upbringing simply didn't know the costs involved in accommodation, conveniences, and their own sustenance'. The pitiable victim in the crippling of young lives is the mother, the downtrodden slave to all the children's whimsies. Dave approvingly quoted the remedy the authors prescribed to correct these social deficiencies:

'Our early sexist and emotional dependency conditioning, together with the capitalist system makes all attempts of living together *ad hoc* solutions until such time as society is changed to one where each person participates as fully as possible in their own and other peoples' socialising process.'

There is no necessary connection between being brought up in a nuclear family and being a 'crippled human'. The empirical evidence does not appear to give much support, either. It is an observable fact that children, by being children, need education, support, and correction. One may observe many a young person socially immature when leaving school. But the reasons are manifold due to character, ability, family environment, and other factors. My experience was that most of my classmates were well-adjusted, independent people when they left school. Comrade Dave's colleagues in the SRC were more mature than many of their fellow students regarding independence. Their Marxist delusions were about something other than immaturity.

The empirical evidence for the claim that the alleged conditioning of bourgeois capitalist society makes attempts at 'living together *ad hoc* solutions' is also lacking. Western Society is precisely made up of traditions, conventions, and economic, social and political arrangements that have stood the test of time. This would be the opposite of *ad hoc* arrangements. CPA Dave showed gaps in his theoretical understanding when he tackled the concepts of 'alienated work' and 'commodity fetishism'. Let me take the concept of commodity fetishism:

'Quite clearly one of the things many people wish to escape by living communally is what Marx called 'commodity fetishism': the attempt to realise oneself and to gain status by the accumulation of property. One cannot of course, escape this 'consumerism' simply by changing (superficially) lifestyles, (to Glebe from Artarmon) since the ideology of 'consumerism' is carried round in all our head — no matter what lifestyle.'

This is a crude comment about commodity fetishism which Dave seems to equate with consumerism. They are not the same. Consumerism has various meanings, all of which cannot be called Marxist. On the other hand, commodity fetishism is a vital concept in Marx's analysis of capitalism. It refers to the inclination to give life to objects. The capitalist, claimed Marx, talks about Land, Capital and Labor as if they have a life. It is precisely the dialectical method that takes the socioanalysis past the surface of the fetishised object to the reality of the capitalist order and the realm of the unity of opposites and Marx's notion of 'contradiction'. But what did Comrade Dave care if he entertained a faulty idea of commodity fetishism? Most of his student audience, including his far-left mates, hadn't a clue about the materialist dialectic.

The editors complained there were no letters for issue H2 and made an appeal. The appeal fell flat because H3 also had no letters. What could have been the reason? Perhaps it may have occurred to the editors that many of the articles had little appeal to most students. Articles on the socialist struggles around the world (Chile, Africa, Palestine, etc.), the environment and local issues were not guaranteed to excite interest, no matter the degree of ideological fidelity. David Patch was preoccupied with Sydney University's encroachment on the communities surrounding the university, and he wrote long boring articles that could not arouse interest. The student parliament got going when an issue arose that was immediate and drew in most students. McKnight and his fellow radicals continued to think they had one with the Political Economy affair.

In H3, we find a whole page devoted to political economy under the title 'AS A MATTER OF URGENT NECESSITY'. The unattributed article is a long indignant rage with many block paragraphs in upper condemning intransigent Professors Hogan and Simkin for resisting the wishes of most staff and students. The history of the affair is repeated yet again, and Hogan and Simkin cast abusively as mindless agents of reaction. H4 (April) failed to keep up the fury. The edition appeared sloppy and hastily thrown together. The editors printed a handwritten piece admitting their disorganisation and appealing for contributions.

In one of three letters, John Oliphont (Arts) gave a return serve. He attacked the poor quality of writing and the bias of the articles. There were, he wrote, 'Robespierres among us ... with their verbal guillotines', propagandising 'for what is called 'Staff-Student Control''. Their writing lacked argument and was full of abuse. 'Can the "Student Action Movement" and the other advocates of "Staff-Student Control'", he continued, 'do no better than this? If not, they should display the same moral rectitude which they indulge so fondly and often, by leaving university'. Good point. Referring to Craig Johnston's adolescent mockery of the Assistant Registrar, Oliphont rightly characterised it as juvenile insolence. He pointed out the nonsense of judging courses by popularity instead of content and deplored the insolence and familiarity expressed towards 'a professor of great integrity'. This is all pretty much the view of the average citizen. He ended his letter thus:

'None of this nonsense would be worth a single word of comment did not its perpetrators take themselves so seriously and did not their noisy and ill-mannered antics embarrass the civilised amongst us. Scores of little Robespierres dreaming of their very own Committees of Public Safety; little Lenins longing for another Bolshevik revolution. There are those of us who – given a choice of evils – would much prefer Napoleon.

H5 was not much of an improvement. There were three letters. Judith Mackinolty complained about the male animals on the pink cover of H2. 'Is this an example of male chauvinism?' she asked. 'Or should I be more charitable and interpret the cover to mean that it is only males who adopt this "follow the leader", unthinking and unimaginative conformism?' Two letters appeared in H6, causing the editors to cry: 'There are 22,000 of you out there, 17,000 students and 5,000 staff – and you're all slack. Write to us'. It seemed not to penetrate the editorial group that the flood of leftist scribbling led by clever Comrade Dave was boring.

With a sizeable budget, the SRC had to run like an ordinary bourgeois business, a responsibility many of the core group, as it turned out, did not understand. 'Commem Day' (Commemoration Day) was one of the events for which they were administratively and financially responsible. For years it had been a day of harmless student hijinks and the occasion to collect charity money from selling a special fun edition of *Honi Soit*. There was a dress-up procession into the city and later a pub crawl along George Street, in the city centre, among other activities. By 1974, the colour of the *Commem Honi* was not only leftist but offensively and tastelessly leftist. Called the Sydney Morning Harold, it mocked everything traditional, conservative and Christian, which meant the majority of the community was its target. For example, the article 'WAR! DEMANDS RSL' begins:

'The President of the NSW RSL, Colonel Fred Fascist, today called on the Federal government to declare war on Chile or New Zealand or Brazil or anyone. Speaking on the eve of Anzac Day, Fascist pointed out that the number of Returned Servicemen marching this year would be our lowest ever because there was [sic] no wars to provide new recruits. 'In the good, old days,' he stated, "we had regular big wars whether we needed them or not! Remember the days when young people respected their parents. The good old days of the Sudan, Boer War, the Great War, World War II – the big one, Korea and Malaya..."'

Depicting returned soldiers from the First and Second World Wars as mindless drunken warmongers and rapists would not enhance the reputation of students whom many ordinary citizens of the Depression and World War II generation regarded as 'educated ratbags'. Commem Day did not rate a mention in the following *Honi* (H8). Nor in H9 (May). But there was a report with a connection to Commem Day. On page three, a thick black headline screamed: 'SRC ROBBED!' In a style mimicking a melodramatic police report, editors Margan and Grose wrote that David Patch and Colin Menzies (Education Officer) arrived on Monday, 29 April, to find that someone had stolen the money ($420) out of the cash tin in the SRC secretary's office. The police were called. As Margan and Grose reported, the mystery was how the thieves got into the building. There was no sign of forced entry which suggested someone with a key got into the building and then into the secretary's office. Margan and Grose, treating the affair as an opportunity to have fun, ended their report with an offer to take people on a guided tour of the crime scene – $20 for the public and $1 for students.

In H10 (Jun), SRC President Bret Mattes finally found his voice and demanded those with permits to sell Commemoration Day *Honi* and had not returned the sales money and the unsold papers to do so immediately. Their names, he advised, were with the University administration and the NSW police. The burgled office affair came up for review in H15 (July). The money stolen in the office burglary was adjusted to $490. In the meantime, *Honi* reported someone had run off with $490 from the cash register, money paid for ball tickets and sundry front counter transactions. Police concluded that 'both thefts were carried out by a person or persons familiar with the offices of the SRC'. If that wasn't enough, a discrepancy was found in the 'AUS Friendly Society accounts amounting to $1,074'. The AUS money was for membership in their health scheme. Police suspected someone sneakily removed completed membership forms to the value of $1074. It looked like an inside job.

The theft and disorganisation reached calamitous levels. 'Anything between 2,000 and 6,000 dollars' was lost through the 'poor organisation' of the sales returns of *Commem Honi*. Rumours alleged 'that a certain proportion of the missing money was collected from Wynyard Station by some unknown person who has since disappeared'. To cap it all off, 'a smaller amount, some $300, consisting of cheques for unspecified purposes including the hire of an Avis Rent A Car for two weeks and five days also remains to be settled'. The Commemoration Day organiser had rented a car and kept it for personal use.

The SRC confessed they 'must share some responsibility for the events that occurred'. What? Some? If the SRC had instituted the standard security and financial recording measures, none of it would have happened. The report ended with a whinge that the attempt by the conservative Democrat (4 July) 'to label [the SRC] entire membership as corrupt ... [and an] attempt to gain cheap political capital from what is a serious matter', something, of course, to which Comrade Dave and his Marxist pals would never stoop. Martin Wallace, defending the Democrat, asked, 'if the Democrat had not reported the scandal – for such it is – then who would have? *Honi* Soit, perhaps?' *Honi* had admitted they kept the thefts quiet while the police investigated. Wallace pointed out that a group so fixated on direct democracy should have let students know where their money went. Interestingly, something that *Honi* did not report, Wallace accused the SRC leadership of making inoffensive side-lined Bret Mattes the scapegoat. The SRC should have taken responsibility. A fair point. It was left to the Archangel to conjure a report (H16, July) of a 'special SRC meeting' under the heading 'Commem Ballsup' to discuss the affair.

De facto President Comrade Dave owned up to the charge of culpable disorganisation in the SRC. Hiring a car for more than two weeks by the Commem Convenor was considered beyond the pale, and 'a motion censuring him and asking for his resignation was passed'. Most alarming, though, was the 'pitifully low' return of money for the sale of Commem *Honi*. He offered two explanations. First, the sellers did not return the total revenue amount. Very perceptive. Second, the money 'went astray after Honi sellers handed it in'. Went astray? Dave sank into euphemisms when the Left were in the dock. Those looking for a scapegoat brought a second motion to censure the invisible Bret Mattes. The motion failed. Dave and Chris Sidoti told the meeting that kicking the Commem Convenor was an effort to divert the attention from 'the real issue of the missing money'. Really? Instead of discussing the real issue, Dave diverted attention to 'the far-right forces' that were guilty of 'concocting' the amount stolen. It was $2,800, not $5,000 'as reported in the Herald'.

He went on to utter two logical howlers. 'The money taken in robberies,' he said, 'cannot be blamed on the SRC – would the Chemistry Department, for example, be responsible if it was broken into and robbed?' First, the Chemistry Department would be responsible for the theft of equipment or money left in unsecured rooms that were the responsibility of the Chemistry Department – an exact parallel with the SRC negligence. Second, the analogical argument is so weak as to make it invalid. The business of a chemistry department is not like the business of the SRC. Then in a comment approaching a contradiction, clever, articulate Dave said, 'the police and many people on the SRC believe the robberies were the work of people associated with the SRC'. More than associated with the SRC, I would conclude on the evidence. To top things off in this process of evasion, Dave complained, 'Perhaps the greatest "crim[e]" of the SRC as a whole is its trusting and naive attitude'. His efforts to evade or shift the blame for the appalling cock-up of Commem Day were entirely unconvincing. The thefts resulted from negligence and a base ignorance of standard administrative procedures. What would one expect from a bunch of smartarses who were busy creating reality and winning knowledge while they strove to destroy the university's entire establishment?

Few would be surprised to hear that the university discontinued Commem Day to prevent a repeat of the fiasco. Sarah Sheehan (Med II), a devotee of Dave's, announced its demise in a facetious report a few months later (H26, Oct). Alas, Ms Sheehan's efforts at ridicule were well below the subtlety of her admired leader. She acknowledged that the once acceptable Commem Day practical jokes eventually turned people off 'because of mismanagement and the total irresponsibility displayed by many of the participants'. The favoured charity refused to be associated with the day.

Ordinary students refused to act as sellers. Then she added irrelevantly and unconsciously what was a deep dig at her male colleagues. 'Consider Commem Honi', she wrote. 'People only buy it because they expect it to be "dirty" – read racist, sexist and full of white bourgeois heterosexual male humour'. Her target was presumably those non-university white male slobs – Dave's constituency of labourers, tradesmen and the like – at loose in the city.

Exclusive Abbotsleigh educated Sarah seemed to forget the racist, sexist, white bourgeois heterosexual male humour in *Honi* emanated from the revolutionary minds of her far-left colleagues. I note here that anti-white racism, flowering so colourfully in the second decade of the 21st century, was alive and well in 1974. Sarah had not finished with her odd comments. In reporting the SRC's decision to discontinue Commem Day, she added that people in the city would no longer 'be subjected to a form of armed thuggery'. The editor could not help interposing, 'What?' She finished her report with the equally mystifying, 'Goodbye Commem, Goodbye Schooldays!'

ALTHOUGH there were articles in *Honi* on all manner of topics close to the leftist heart (many from outside the student body), the major causes for the student parliament through 1974 continued to be staff-student democratisation, a thorough overhaul of subject assessment, and the establishment of a Department of Political Economy. The arguments for these causes were continually repeated, both in articles and in the letters section. Comrade McKnight best presented those for democratisation and student self-assessment. I need not repeat them here, except that the Marxist interpretation defending them was that of the Communist Party of Australia to the glory of which Comrade Dave had devoted his not inconsiderable talents. Dave did not venture into a theoretical defence of his brand of Marxism. His less disciplined colleague Craig Johnston did that for us in a misty-eyed confessional piece in H8 (April) under the heading 'Appeal to the Left', that is, to those who were with him in the leftist campaigns. His confession is intriguing for the insight it gives into the far-left mind.

Like the lapsed Catholic who was suddenly 'born again' and joined a fundamentalist Protestant sect, Comrade Johnston confessed that however active he had been in the campaigns of recent years, he had been in a state of self-deception. In a moment of self-reflection, he found himself in 'the world of Left sects' and was brought to consider 'whether social-democracy was, in fact, the heir of Marx... so I decided to read Marx and Lenin and Trotsky to give myself some overall perspective. Meanwhile, I kept my membership of the Labor Party, justified by the Trotskyist line of "entrism"'. Entrism (also entryism) is the tactic of entering an organisation to subvert it. Johnston did not understand he had made a barefaced admission of the Left's integral tactics of subversion and sabotage. The upshot of this reflection was the realisation that 'the mindless euphoric of the "New Left" period was over and that I would have to seriously consider what being a radical meant'. This enlightenment process pushed him to conclude that the Communist Party (of Australia) embodied the true radical doctrine. Two overriding considerations gave him no choice but to join the Communist Party:

'First, its working-class base. I know that only the vast majority of the people can bring about a revolution, and the working class is the backbone of that majority: so this class has to be won over ... Second, self-management. When Australia's Communists rejected the Stalinist model of socialism, the clear alternative was self-management ... As the Communist Party sees it, it is the 'exercise of decisive political, economic and social power by the people thru a system of workers' and community councils subject to recall and direct democratic processes'... And if this is what your concept of socialism is, then how you get it is obviously also going to be thru encouraging the initiative and self-action of 'little people' and making sure The Party never substitutes itself for the masses... Or, at the same time as campaigning for the defeat of the obstructionist conservatives and the re-election of the Labor government, you could present the total alternative to the political/social system. This is what the Communist Party is doing.

Comrade Johnston's heartfelt appeal was to those on the Left to undergo the same enlightenment to arrive at the same purity of doctrine. Despite his emphasis on the working class and the 'little people' as the basis of worldwide revolution, Comrade Johnston, as well as Comrade McKnight, proposed a form of Trotskyism as the highest enlightenment. Leon Trotsky believed in worldwide revolution led by an enlightened vanguard. The little people could not destroy capitalism and achieve socialism on their own. The enlightened ones had to be the guiding light. Comrade Craig displayed the fervour of one making the way straight for the enlightened one. The contradiction was ignored.

THERE WAS little challenge to the Trotskyist hegemony in the SRC in the first half of the year, but the conservatives mounted a counterattack in the second half. The challenge came mostly from three members of the Democratic Club: Jeff Phillips Arts-Law II, Frank Lane-Mullins Economics II and Aavo Karulin Science III. Aavo's mastery of the detail was a match for Comrade Dave even if he lacked the same sparkling style. Jeff, Frank and Aavo copped a lot of mockery and ridicule, but Dave deigned to take them on. One battle was over the war in Vietnam, which had not yet reached its denouement. In H5, Dave contributed a lengthy article under the heading 'Vietnam: The war drags on'. Dave believed the PRG (the Provisional Revolutionary Government) representing the 'peasants' of South Vietnam had won the war. But the filthy capitalists were too cussed to admit it and, contrary to their undertakings in Paris Peace Accords, were still propping up President Thieu's corrupt, unrepresentative Saigon government with men, equipment and funding. It would all be in vain, couldn't the Americans see?

We were witnessing, he wrote, 'the final act in the drama of the liberation of South Vietnam ... we see a movement among the peasants that has faced the most brutal bombardment in history and has then been able to stand up and thrash half a million American troops'. How could the peasants 'take on the most technologically advanced power in the capitalist world and beat them to the negotiating table and then force them to withdraw?' Well, said Dave, it was because the peasants, promised 'democracy and land by the National Liberation Front', raced to support the kind Vietcong with all they needed to sustain the struggle. It was not 'because they [were] manipulated [and] duped by the communists' who would have shot them in the head if they had not cooperated. Oh no, not that, not action in line with the actions of the North Vietnamese army when it overran the South, causing pandemonium among the masses desperate to get out of the country. Dave was only repeating the rhetoric and propaganda (very eloquently, mind you) of the very effective Western supporters of the Communist North without whom the forces of Marxism would not have defeated the Americans. The promise of democracy to the peasants? Don't make me laugh.

Michael Slattery Arts/Law III gave a scornful reply (H9, May). Opening with 'David McKnight's rhetoric has waltzed him into a corner', he wrote. If it were true the peasants had thrashed 'half a million troops', then 'Thieu would be a minor obstacle. Yet in dealing with him, the PRG [Provisional Revolutionary Government], with "the support of the people", has lost its thrashpower, for he still rules'. A logical point. In fact, the PRG lacks the "support of the people", who prefer a Thieu (with all his faults) to government by the North'.

A reply, equally scornful, was not lacking. Comrade Dave acknowledged Slattery's point that he 'appeared to contradict [him]self'. But did he have an explanation? No, he resorted to a common tactic of the Left. When you face an unanswerable argument, ignore it. So, Dave accused Slattery of missing the article's point, and he repeated his evidence for America's continuing 'illegitimate' support for Thieu and the South Vietnamese government. Dave didn't mention like-support from the Soviet Union and Communist China for the communist North's campaign. Whether or not Slattery missed the point (he did not), Comrade Dave did not answer the 'apparent' contradiction. He then dealt with 'the old red herring that government by the Vietcong – now the Provisional Revolutionary Government, (PRG) – would in fact amount to the control by "the North" – I take it he means the Democratic Republic of Vietnam'. Well, yes, he meant the communist government of the North established by Ho Chi Minh, who brought his heavy load of radical European political theory got up in Paris and the Soviet Union back to Hanoi to impose on the indigenous people of Vietnam. Dave then repeated the most favoured leftist myth of the time. The Vietnam War was not about the invasion by the communist North as a step in worldwide communist revolution. It was rather 'an indigenous war of national liberation against colonialism and its local henchmen'.

In 1966, as an immature disorganised student, I thought that was rubbish. In 1974 when married with two children and in my first job with an educational publisher where an American colleague denounced my views about the Vietnam War as 'corrupt', I still thought that rubbish. In 2023, in a retirement devoted to my writing, I still think that rubbish. And I have never seen any evidence or argument to change my mind. Take Vietnam today. There is no North or South Vietnam. The army of the Communist North overran the South in 1975 and established a Marxist-Leninist one-party socialist state to govern a 'reunified' Vietnam from Hanoi, now known as the Socialist Republic of Vietnam. Even if there was no evidence of mass executions, hundreds of thousands were sent to re-education camps to learn the dogma of the political theory imported from Manchester. Many succumbed to torture, hard labour, starvation and disease. Comrade Dave's indigenous people of the south exchanged the yoke of (alleged) imperialism and colonisation for the yoke of a mass campaign of farm collectivisation. As with all Marxist economic experiments, this resulted in economic chaos causing the Marxist-Leninist government to depend even more on Soviet economic and military aid. With whose views does the history of Vietnam since the 1960s accord – mine or the Archangel's?

For my parents' generation, who had reached their forties and fifties in the 1960s, the anti-Vietnam War protests were incomprehensible. How could these young people with the privilege of a good education and experiencing nothing like the upheavals of the first half of the 20th century take the side of an atheistic enemy bent on destroying their democratic Christian society? My mother and father's generation, who lived through the Great Depression and the Second World War, had known severe economic hardship and the fear of war with the loss of family members. They had persevered, and just when the society they were building promised to deliver well-being and material security for all, these young people took the side of an enemy who wanted to wreck it all and bind them with the chains of a cruel totalitarian government. How could it be? Who could explain it to people who had suffered the deprivation of war and backbreaking labour to survive?

The dislocating changes in society tormented my father terribly. He understood evil and evil people existed. What he could not understand was that young people with all the advantages he and most of his generation never had were at war with his society and, second, that society's leaders did nothing about it. How could those leaders stand by and watch the sabotage of their society? Let's be clear about this. The anti-Vietnam War protests were not just about the nastiness of war, though many naive protesters falling for the unceasing leftist propaganda professed that as their motivation. The Marxist drivers of the organised protests supported the North Vietnamese and the Viet Cong against South Vietnam and its allies, Australia being one. Not a few student organisations were open about collecting money for the Vietcong enemy, thus subsidising the bullets fired at Australian troops.

It broke my father's heart to see this boisterous treason, and to see the leaders of his society cowering before it. He had served on HMAS *Sydney* in the Mediterranean. He had heard the scream of bombing aircraft and the thunder of Sydney's massive guns in response to the enemy's fire. What had he fought for? What had all those diggers now mingled with the dirt in foreign countries fought for? They had not fought to hand their country over to totalitarian oppression and moral decay. It would not be too long before those same Marxists, and their flunkeys began a campaign of mockery and denigration of World War Two veterans like my father.

❦

PAUL BURNARD complained (H12, Jun) about a meeting in which votes were manipulated and SRC funds misused to support the communists. 'The farcical nature of the meeting', he wrote, 'was reflected in the 15-minute wait to reach a quorum – eventually achieved by dragging reinforcements out of the Union'. Ethnic minorities oppressed by the forces of the South and North were deserving of support, he knew from experience. (Burnard was a Vietnam veteran.) Instead, the meeting amounted to 'the usual ideological re-hash' to justify the SRC's allocation of $200 to the North Vietnamese. 'I remain convinced', he said, 'that McKnight and Co use the conflict for the fostering of their own political ideals'. Of course, they did. Paul Burnard was too polite.

Jeff Phillips was more forthright about the bungling of SRC finances and the syphoning of funds to leftist causes. He wrote (H14, July) that in the year to date, '$1000 has been given to a South African guerrilla force, $400 has been stolen from the office, $500 has been given to the ALP... and $200 has been raked off to the North Vietnamese'. He fervently hoped the student body would remember the 'shameful record of mismanagement, broken promises and contempt for the student body...at election time when the incumbent cronies and "Machiavellis" will seek your support for another year of bungling and burglary'. Neither Comrade Dave nor the SRC reacted to Burnard's and Phillip's accusations.

For the most part, during 1974, David Patch stayed above the sweaty conflict on the floor of the student parliament. No doubt, he considered his superior legal talents more valuable at a higher level. And one must admit as SRC Welfare Officer he threw himself into the task. Even though he was not reluctant to praise himself in the third person (H17) for having been the main instrument in establishing a Legal Aid Service for students, the evidence suggests the credit was rightfully his. Similarly, his long, plodding articles on Sydney University's expansion into the surrounding suburbs of Darlington and Chippendale deployed sound arguments. The rights of the residents to maintain their way of life and the preservation of the suburbs' architectural heritage were compelling reasons to protest. From an outsider's point of view, the fault was that his activism and arguments were always filtered through his extreme left ideology.

There was never any goodwill or intention in his political opponents. On the contrary, they were authoritarian, oppressive, neglectful of the rights of the small people and so on, and so on. Worse, if Patch did not get his way, he resorted to threats of student action. For example, he had reasonable arguments against the administration's proposal to establish a new car park on the university grounds. But Patch was not content to rest on the reasonableness of his arguments. No, his opponents, notably Vice-Chancellor Bruce Rodda Williams, for whom he showed unremitting contempt, were guilty of dirty play. There could never be any question of the Vice-Chancellor having the welfare of the students in mind. Patch, therefore, warned in H16 that 'if the [Buildings and Grounds] committee behaves normally and endorses the Vice-Chancellor's action, the student body may have to take things into their own hands'.

In H9 (May), he reported his presence at a meeting where he copped some of his own medicine. The federal election of 1974 was due to take place on 18 May. Patch and a group of fellow Labor supporters 'attended Mr Snedden's [Liberal Opposition Leader] policy speech at the North Rocks Community Hall'. With burning indignation, Patch related how roughly a Labor supporter was handled when he tried to disrupt the speech – obviously, the reason Patch and his Labor cronies were there. 'Two [Labor] women were forcibly removed', and Patch himself was (horror!) 'jabbed in the stomach by a Liberal Party supporter'. An outraged Patch ended his letter with: 'Such violence by officials and supporters of any Australian political party is appalling, and should be condemned by the people of Australia'. In the same *Honi* issue, he found it necessary to tell the student body that the heavily promoted 'Exorcist Ball' had nothing to do with the SRC. The ball was 'a private profit-making enterprise', he wrote. The last thing the 1974 SRC collective would have anything to do with was a private self-funding venture making a profit. The boys and girls of the 1974 SRC had shown their contempt for the responsible accounting of the money they got from having hands deep in the students' pockets.

Despite his efforts to keep above the fray, he was occasionally prodded enough to respond to taunts in the Letters section. He hated any hint he did not conform to his carefully cultivated image of being for the little people. He was particularly sensitive to the taunt that he was 'David Patch of Turramurra' (a well-to-do northern suburb in Sydney). He always insisted that he was 'a resident of [inner-city] Chippendale and an active member of the Darlington Chippendale Resident Action Group'. Turramurra was only a temporary residence, he claimed.

In H18 (Aug), he batted away the Turramurra sneer in a Democrat article before dealing with questions (again) about his part in the allocation of SRC funds to leftist causes, in this case, $500 to the ALP's 1974 election campaign and $100 to the Communist Party. Feeling he had adequately corrected any misapprehension by 'the reactionaries in the Democratic Club' about the allocated funds, he addressed the claim he 'was nominated by David McKnight of the Communist Club' for SRC President in the approaching SRC Annual Elections. He made a distinction that hardly made a difference to the Democratic Club's point. 'This is not true', he wrote, 'although he [McKnight] is supporting me for SRC President'. His attempts to stay at arm's length from the communists and other radicals fooled no one close to the action. Nor did his underhanded political manoeuvring appear anything else but that.

A flare-up between the Democratic Club and the Liberal Club gave a fascinating glimpse into the manoeuvring in student politics. The dispute also sheds light on Tony Abbott's intervention in the Liberal Club in 1977, an intervention that had an echo forty-odd years later. The dispute began in H14 (July) when G.K. Burton (Arts/Law I) accused the Liberal Club of 'conducting an act of piracy aimed at producing the ALP Club's propaganda for them...and happily destroying their own movements' philosophical foundations and political reputation'. A haughty reply came (H15, July) from 'Derek Culey (Secretary) and Ian Wisken (President)' of the Liberal Club. They always signed their letters as a duo. They begged Burton to be cognizant of the fact that the 'Liberal Club is NOT affiliated in any way with the Young Liberals (and never will be) and is independent from the Liberal Party'. The 'basic philosophy' of the Sydney University Liberal Club (SULC) was 'one of small "l" liberalism'. Until the Liberal Party conformed to the SULC's ideals, it would not have their support. So there.

Aavo Karulin accused the Liberals of losing their way (H17, July). 'Weak, weak liberal minds', he wrote, 'fearing to go against the "grain" of the university built by the vocal pro-Communist left-wing, have decided to go AP or ALP and become uncontroversial, fitting into fashion'. He claimed the collapse of liberalism in the SU Liberal Club was reflected in the federal Liberal Party with their adoption of Labor policies. He suspected the *Honi* editors would mock him for his stand (they always did), but that would 'only enhance my mental hardening for entry into politics outside the university, to fight for democracy and the downfall of Communist slavery'. Culey and Wisken were ready with a sniffy reply (H18, Aug). They resorted to the overworked 'reds under the bed' evasion when anyone points to the many self-declared Marxists and their very visible organisations.

'The reds are under bed', they wrote, 'Gough Whitlam's a communist, and the Liberal Club has turned ALP, and Mr Aavo Karulin lives in fairy-land'. Did it not occur to Mr Karulin, they went on, that the lefties he was talking about 'just may have some liberal policies too?' To search out that possibility, the SULC met with people of various ideologies, including 'Mr Red' himself, Jack Mundey. Meeting such people was surely a sign of 'some progressive inclinations'. Indeed, could the Liberal Party not 'learn some-thing from those propounding different ideologies and even occasionally agree with them'. Marx's sneer about 'useful idiots' and 'fellow travellers' comes to mind. And Aavo must have thought himself vindicated. Culey and Wisken's sniffiness did not impress Warren Richardson (Arch. I). He wrote (H19):

'Although I did not accept at first Mr Karulin's assertion that the SU Liberal Club has gone AP or ALP, the SU Liberal Club's reply to Mr Karulin has convinced me. The SULC's 'reds under the bed' and 'Gough Whitlam is a Communist' is a miserable pseudo-slanderous attempt to discredit. The 'reds under the bed' stance belongs solely to the AP and the

ALP and now also apparently to the SULC. '

Liberals had no business consorting with the likes of unionist Jack Mundey. It would 'only encourage Mundey "types" to continue their anti-democratic activities'. He ended his letter by saying he did 'not believe there is any "Communist conspiracy" but only that the SU Liberal Club is fucked!' In the same issue, 'GB' wrote that Culey and Wisken were wrong about 'reds under the beds'. It was rather that 'Derek and Ian and other "rich radicals" have REDS IN THEIR BEDS after making ALP propaganda'. Just so. Aavo Karulin criticised Culey and Wisken for their misconceptions and shallow thinking. He accused the Liberal Party of compromising their principles to attract the votes of the young and the SULC of succumbing to 'trendiness'. He pointed to the empirical evidence of communist regimes to refute his supposed paranoia about reds under the bed. Finally, if Culey and Wisken entertained replying, they should 'try to construct a rational argument without the necessity to resort to worn-out cliches to make up for intellectual deficiencies'. Culey and Wisken remained aloof.

THE ISSUES of democratisation, exams and assessment, and political economy continued to dominate the discourse in the second half of 1974. Most contributions to *Honi Soit* were from the Left. Any dissent from the leftist view was unmercifully ridiculed. The one-sided 'debate' was often couched in the issues of SRC administration and who would control it. This emphasis was because the SRC Annual Elections were scheduled to take place in early September, surprisingly late. In the years I am covering, they usually were in late July or early August. The lateness hinted at the ongoing disorganisation. David Patch and a cohort of his leftist mates, including Comrade McKnight, contributed (H17, July) what was virtually a manifesto for the 1975 SRC administration. Although a group of fourteen, which included the faction controlling the SRC, signed the manifesto, it was clearly in Patch's trainee-lawyer style – dry and plodding. None of the flair, articulation, and sparkle of the Archangel. It surprises me that Dave put his name to it, though I suppose he had no choice for reasons of solidarity. He would have his opportunity later.

Patch & Co deplored (yet again) the lack of interest in the body that represents all students. They confessed the SRC was to blame. The trouble was that Patch & Co talked about the SRC in the third person when they should have used the first person. The SRC had a 'lack of purpose and direction ... it patently does not represent students. Plagued by an almost pathological preoccupation with itself, with petty personal politics of division of spoils of office and budgetary allocations, the SRC makes no real attempt to involve itself with the needs and problems of varying individual students, student groups or the surrounding community'. This public self-incrimination did not prevent them from offering themselves as the corrective to their incompetence, neglect and abuse of authority. The same rhetoric about democratisation, new teaching methods and 'support [for] the struggle in the Economics Dept' followed.

PATCH & Co's manifesto did its work – or at least did not harm their campaigning. The annual elections took place without much fanfare in Honi, awarding the SRC presidency to John McGrath, a moderate rarely mentioned in *Honi*. It was a surprising result. The first meeting of the 47th SRC took place on 27 September. A report of the meeting appeared in H23 (Oct) 'written by Simon Grose' [with] 'additional inspiration supplied by the Archangel David'. It was a lively, well-written piece covering serious matters, backed by much fun, satire, ridicule, nastiness (towards the non-left infidels), and caricature of friend and foe. I would guess the Archangel contributed more than inspiration, but that might be unfair to Grose. In any case, it was one of the best-written pieces of the year.

I will leave out most of the fun, ridicule and caricature and concentrate on the material that concerns me. Grose (and Dave) opened up (yet again) with the admission that the students were 'apathetic' towards the SRC. But did he shoulder the blame? Not on your life. He and his far-left mates were 'caught up in inner wrangles ... mainly as a result of the cancerous work of the DLP' – meaning those miserable Catholics. So, the incompetency, bungling administration, negligent (even illicit) use of funds and so on were all the fault of scheming Catholics. The evidence does not support the charges. They were, of course, talking about the Democratic Club. The gnawing nuisance for Grose and McKnight was the reasonable, justified, and rightful intervention by conservatives in the running of the SRC. But redemption was at hand.

The far-left cabal scored most of the SRC officer positions, including Patch for Welfare, Craig Johnston for Education, and Sarah Sheehan as AUS Secretary. The faction also got the Orientation Week Handbook, marvellous for propagandising, in addition to the vital *Honi Soit* editorship under Dave McKnight, Paula Taylor and Chris Mackinolty. The 'progressives' had every reason to be jubilant. Their members in the 1975 SRC Council could pack down in a formidable political scrum. Even those elected outside the far-left pack, 'the Innocuous Upper-Class Twits', were not entirely unfavourable to them. The rolling political mauls would bring them along. However, an ominous note sounded for John McGrath, the new SRC President.

McGrath, wrote Grose, was 'nervous in his new post [and] his performance was tentative'. If he was not up to dealing with 'an impatient radical council...they will eventually stampede over him'. McGrath should work with the radical faction – or else. Coupled with the threat to conform or else was the ridicule meant to disable the conservative enemy. The mockery of Jeff Phillips was unceasing. They mocked his candidature for Education Officer lampooning his speech as something heard in a Country Party meeting. Whenever *Honi* printed a letter of Jeff's, the editors would place a mocking title above it. Some of the headings were (often in upper case): BARK BARK, WOW! HUMPH! Drivel, GROWL, JEFF'S WRONG, JEFF'S STUPID, JEFF'S FUCKED, JEFF'S GALVINISED.

Comrade McKnight and his fellow Marxists never presented Phillips as someone you could take seriously. It was not because Jeff had nothing to say or could not argue his point. It was because the SRC far-left clique thought that mocking him was enough. They could not allow any of his interventions to seem sensible. Aavo Karulin was a more serious case, though. He wrote long letters against McKnight & Co full of argument and evidence. They had to bring in heavy artillery to deal with him. Grose (or Comrade Dave) in fine style:

'Aavo Karulin...There he was, the Gormless Goth, sitting at the end of the table like a dyspeptic teddy bear, taking up his post as intellectual stormtrooper for the forces of papal indignation. The refugee mentality, Estonian widows and ancestries of terrible persecutions, Stalin was a communist and thus all communists are Stalins, it's an onerous burden for anyone to carry.

Can he shrug it off, or will he sit there all year, immoveable and preposterous, growing more and more fearful of that which he sees as madness and chaos as it careers around his head? It is an onerous burden and it feeds upon persecution, but all things are possible, and Aavo's enlightenment would be an enjoyable achievement. If he remains intractable and incapable of appreciating anything new he will at least be the source of humour throughout the year, even if it is a bit pathetic ...'

Clever and amusing. Amusing bigotry towards Catholics, refugees, Baltic

Sea people, and mental illness. No need for me to comment. Aavo could answer for himself. And he did so in H24 after the meeting. He acknowledged he was the butt of their sneering and ridicule, but Grose's (or Dave's) effort 'really outdid all expectations'. If students wondered why he was given such a 'heavy going over' and called 'Gormless Goth' and 'intellectual stormtrooper for the forces of papal indignation', it was because of his success 'which the left-wing detests!' He then countered the charges, pointing out how he had left enlightened Craig Johnston babbling incoherently in their exchange during the meeting. However, he was most vigorous in putting down the bigotry of his sneerers and defending the capitalist system.

Talk about his being a tool of the Vatican was nonsense because he was not Catholic. It would be odd if the Democratic Club were a DLP front because 'card-carrying members' of the Liberal and Labor parties were members. The charge was nonsense. As for the refugee insult, he was 'derived from East European political refugees', but that put him 'in a unique position to understand Communism'. Establishing a dictatorship is easier when the economy and other governmental instruments are under the government's control. The capitalist system with the right to private property is stable and far more successful in providing prosperity. In response to the sneer that all communists are Stalins, he said, 'What my knowledge of the USSR tells me [is] how easy it is for a small clique to propagate terror and obedience over a large population'. Just so.

WARREN Richardson (Arch. 1) was back in H22 (Sept), claiming that 'the SULC's "progressive inclinations" became apparent in the SRC and *Honi* editor elections, with Liberal Club endorsement of left-winger David Patch of the ALP for SRC President and the Communist trio for *Honi* editorship'. McKnight & Co would inject 'liberal' values into *Honi Soit* by swelling the pages with their 'Marxist doctrine'. It was tough that Patch, with his liberal ideas, failed to gain the presidency. And wasn't it too bad that despite the SULC's support for Patch, McKnight & Co, nobody liked them? Perhaps, he suggested, if they changed 'liberal' to 'liberation' in their name, they would have a better chance of attracting the radicals.

Others lined up to bash the SULC. Karin S wrote (H25, Oct) that the 'SULC has, in my opinion, been given the caning it thoroughly deserves' and that they were 'dabbling in political perversion in an intellectual vacuum'. But that was not her primary concern. She had learned that 'the last edition of *Pundit* [the SULC's periodical] was rolled off the press by [far-left] Chips Mackinolty. I wonder who wrote it. Could it be that the communists produced *Pundit* to try to pull off votes from the liberals – and with Wisken's approval!' A heavy accusation, indeed. If that accusation was not severe enough, Michael J. Carruthers came up with an even more inflammatory charge. Why would the SULC support Patch, he asked? Patch had nothing to offer the SULC. He had nothing to offer anyone. The explanation, according to rumours, was that 'the people responsible for the writing and production of that *Pundit* had made a private deal with Patch and Co. Patch and his friends were to support the political interests of certain SULC committee members in return for *Pundit* support. Ian Wisken wrote the *Pundit*'.

During the exchanges over the SULC, Aavo Karulin duelled with Comrade McKnight over a range of issues besides the SULC. Dave did not get the better of him which caused David Patch to send a one-sentence letter to H25: 'Aavo Karulin's letters give me the shits!' Aavo was not the only one to give Patch the shits. In a very shitty mood, Patch replied to Carruthers' charges. He deplored the spreading of concocted rumours during election time. As a candidate for the SRC presidency, he naturally came in for 'a good deal comment' in the 'plethora of political rags' peddling their propaganda. 'One of these rags was the SU Liberal Club broadsheet, *Pun-*

dit. This publication supported me for SRC President'. That he should corruptly support the interests of particular SULC members in return for their support was an outrageous slander:

'AT NO TIME HAVE I EVER MADE A DEAL WITH THE LIBERAL CLUB OR ANY INDIVIDUALS ASSOCIATED WITH IT.'

If this were true, how did he explain the outspoken support for a member of the radical Left by a small 'l' liberal club whose foundations were the ideas of that execrable bourgeois John Stuart Mill? Simple really:

'The real reason for *Pundit*'s support was, as far as I have been able to ascertain, that the Liberal Club made an objective assessment of the ability and activity of the candidates, and supported the one, who, in their opinion, would be best able to further the interests of the student body.'

You've got to laugh. When Patch reported on himself, he was as pure as the angels and as mighty as Caesar. What was the truth? Was there a secret Labor-type deal between Patch and the snooty leaders of the SULC? I leave it to the reader to judge whether such a deal was consistent with the evidence and character of the players. Curly and Wisken remained above the sweaty rabble and did not deign to answer the charges. Less than eighteen months later, they would have no choice. The reason would be Tony Abbott.

The question of student funding was of the utmost importance for those keen to hand out SRC funds to their favoured campaigns and organisations. It would become the core issue – the do-or-die struggle – between Tony Abbott and the far left. It now became a crucial post-election question. The group controlling the 47th SRC, of which Patch was a leading heavy, wanted an increase in the student levy. The conservatives of the Democratic Club opposed the increase until the SRC showed they could handle the money responsibly. In H26 (Oct), the yes and no cases were presented. The 'Case for Yes' was presented by SRC President John McGrath, Dale Haskell, David Patch, Rod Pickette, Louise Redmond, Jack R. Herman, and Chips MacKinolty. Apart from McGrath, it was the usual stack of far-left activists. Patch & Co were motivated, they wrote, by the increase of votes in the SRC elections – 2,800 up from 1,600 (out of a student body of 16,000). Is it shamelessness or sheer delusion that Patch & Co could then come up with the following as the preamble to their case?

'The elections, probably as a result of increased interest and participation, saw the return of an almost entirely new body of representatives. This is in contrast to some years of an apathetic and demoralised SRC obsessively preoccupied with itself, easy prey to dishonesty and corruption. Such is now not the case. The present Council is committed to action – much of it long overdue – not apathy; to an expansion of SRC activities.'

At least half the elected positions went to far-left members long active in the SRC – Patch, Pickette, Sheehan, Crisp, Bishop, among them – and the SRC executive and its officers turned out to be even more weighted to the far-left. Patch & Co owned up to being 'obsessively preoccupied with [themselves], easy prey to dishonesty and corruption'. Under normal administrations, the admission of such a record would disqualify them at once. But, no, Patch & Co were experts at playing the charade.

The tactic of stacking a meeting with leftist mates was not the only way to manipulate an outcome. One could avoid stacking altogether. 'WANDI the Poet' reported (H25, Oct) that he and about thirty students were hanging around on the front lawn waiting to buy tickets for a Bo Diddley concert when David Patch, 'secretary of the all-powerful Kuringai branch of the ALP', addressed them through a megaphone. Did they want 'to be a General Meeting of the SRC and vote $100 towards the Labour Party?' Patch 'was promptly told to get fucked', an invitation others, it seems, issued to him. You would have to have a hide two inches thick to try to rope in a random group of students for your political purposes. Patch did not get his General Meeting.

AAVO Karulin did not receive a reply to his response to Simon Grose's ridicule in H23. In H26, he complained he did not attend the second meeting of the 47th SRC because the notice arrived late. After a thorough investigation, he concluded 'that there is here a case of extreme negligence on the part of SRC employees or a deliberate attempt to withhold notice of meeting'. On consulting fellow students, he learnt that others had experienced the same 'neglect' and 'you had to be wise to it'. The 'withholding of notices of meetings', he wrote, 'may constitute a left-wing conspiracy to at least create a nuisance to non-Left SRC members and at most to aid leftist hopes of minimising opposition to leftist motions'.

On this occasion, no smartarse comments adorned Aavo's complaint, nor did he receive a response. In the final year's edition (H27), a letter appeared from Aavo under the heading, 'Goodbye Aavo'. It opens with, 'Although one might explain such errors from just negligence, it has nonetheless previously been the case that my letters have been deliberately altered'. The rest of the letter is garbled. The editorial collective had done their work.

A surrogate reply appeared from sweet upper-class Sarah Sheehan, a former pupil of Abbotsleigh, a very (very) smart girls' school in the premier northern suburb of Wahroonga. Here it is exactly as it appeared, including the question mark:

?

Dear Simon and David.

Heres cheers for Aavo Karulin, famous reader of tea leaves and weather-vanes, for his long awaited finale Aavo broke all previous records. Yes indeed folks, those nasq [*sic*] little Red devils are at it again. This time they've infiltrated the SRC front office. The Coms, anarchists, procommie ALP and Sydney Uni Liberal Club Trendies have all climbed in, on, or under the Bed (together$) and conspired to subvert the SRC staff, (psst! Any 'defectors' to the FO .see Dave McKnight at midnight. I can't give you the place because Aavo also thinks (0) *Honi* often deliberately SABOTAGES such details.)

In appreciation of Honisoit 1974.

Sarah Sheehan.

PS Dear Santa, bring Aavo The Crusible.

In H23 (Oct), 'Disgusted Engineer' wrote, 'I regrettably had the misfortune to stray through the SRC offices the other day on my way home and was disgusted with the new interior decorations. Such sights as sandwich crusts, empty beer cans, a dead cockroach, unfiled papers littered the corridor and especially that cesspool the AUS office. All I hope is that the SRC activities are cleaner than their shithouse offices'. David McKnight was the hero of the academic year 1974. The depth of the admiration earned him the title of 'Archangel'. I wonder whether Archangel Dave, spurred on by enlightened Nevillism, ever had the occasional midnight tumble among the sandwich crusts, empty beer cans, dead cockroaches, and unfiled papers of the SRC premises.

Chapter 6

1975 – David Patch rising

DAVE MCKNIGHT and his comrades had manipulated and manoeuvred in the student parliament. If he had gone for a percentage success, the usual hope in political activity, he could have been satisfied it had gone so much better. His hard work had borne abundant fruit. He now had a broad platform on which to deploy his considerable abilities. But did it occur to him while he and his comrades were busily preparing the first edition of *Honi* for 1975 that less might be more?

During 1975, *Honi Soit,* with a much-improved layout and format (an altogether more professional product), bulged with articles on the full range of leftist issues. Favourable articles by specialist authors appeared on feminism, gay rights, abortion, Aboriginals and drugs. Every oppressed people around the world in their struggle against authoritarian capitalist governments seemed to have a turn: Cambodia, Vietnam, Timor, Palestine, South Africa, Spain, Portugal, Chile, and more. The oppressive authoritarian governments of Singapore, Malaysia, and Israel came in for heavy stick. Dave took a keen interest in the plight of the inmates of Australia's prison system, focusing on Bathurst jail, where the bourgeois authorities perpetrated great injustice on the crooks and murderers who could not help being crooks and murderers.

In contrast with 1974 *Honi,* in which Dave had churned out articles and commentaries at will, he hardly contributed to *Honi* 1975. When he did, it was about SRC matters. His editorial plans and duties evidently took up his time. Nor was there much from his Marxist colleagues. Contributions from David Patch were surprisingly few, although he was feverishly working behind the scenes, as became evident later in the year. The only 1974 contributor to boost their output was Sarah Sheehan, who had become part of Dave's inner circle.

The one issue run hard was the Political Economy Affair. Here, too much was never enough. It was not in the Letters section where it received the most coverage. The editorial collective worked the affair to a fever pitch and maintained the fury of a disturbed hornets' nest until late in the year. After every *Honi* issue, I thought Vice-Chancellor Bruce Williams and Professor Hogan of the Economics Department would capitulate and grant the Marxists' demand for a separate department with its own chair. But no, they faced down the students. During 1975, the argument turned not so much around economic theory (Marxist economics vs neoclassical economics) or staff-student democracy. The supporters of political economy seemed to think they had won those battles. What enraged them was the wretched Vice-Chancellor's veto of the decisions of those tribunals responsible for determining whether a separate department could be justified. On every appeal, to whatever tribunal, it was decided that it could.

The first issue of *Honi* (24 Feb) opened with a letter from John Burgess and an article by John Collins, both tutors in the Department of Economics. John Burgess deplored 'the archaic employment standards which are tolerated within this institution'. The reference was to Paul Roberts, a fellow tutor in the Department of Economics who would not have his contract renewed for 1976. It was an outrage that the professor had the authority to employ tutors, allocate duties, and end contracts when it suited him. He could even terminate a contract late in the year! The tutor then had to seek a position under a cloud of suspicion. Burgess suggested that it may not be coincidental that Roberts was actively opposed to Hogan's departmental plans. Well seen.

John Collins took up Hogan's sordid 'discriminatory' action in more detail, providing some history about the conflict that had raged for years. By the end of 1974, the supporters of political economy had gained the Professorial Board's approval for a first-year political economy course and a second-year conversion course (Economics 1(P) and 11(P)). Why the hell, then, did Williams refuse to create a separate department, they all wanted to know? Was he stupid or something? To emphasise the obduracy of the Vice-Chancellor, Collins then explained the theoretical background to the conflict, an explanation endlessly repeated. There was a 'worldwide crisis in economic theory', he claimed. 'Distinguished economists...have become outspokenly critical of mainstream economics', meaning neo-classical economics. Moreover, there were 'two insuperable problems' with neo-classical economics.

For a start, there was its 'internal logical inapplicability'. It appears that Collins was referring to Marx's materialist dialectic. You would think that having referred to the foundation of Marx's philosophy, Collins would have tried to explain Marx's ideas about capitalism's internal 'contradictions'. 'Contradiction' has a precise technical meaning in the materialist dialectic. An explanation would have given some idea about why he claimed the 'internal logical inapplicability' was 'the inability of mainstream economics to explain the real world because of its role as an ideological justification of the capitalist system'. Because he skipped the epistemological and the metaphysical aspect of the dialectic, pinched from Georg Hegel, he lapsed into question-begging Marxist rhetoric. To compound the question-begging rhetoric further, he claimed 'mainstream economics' can't answer 'the major economic problems of poverty, unemployment, racism, sexism, underdevelopment, imperialism'. Apart from the assumed Marxist meaning of these terms, the empirical evidence has demonstrated that a capitalist market economy has been far more successful in alleviating poverty, unemployment, and underdevelopment – in brief, of giving a far higher standard of living than socialist countries. Marxist economics has been a disaster wherever it has been imposed.

Collins and his colleagues celebrated the 'resurgence in political economy; of Marxism, of radical economics, by overseas economists'. And here we have a hint of the real issue for Vice-Chancellor Williams and Professors Hogan and Simkin. Political Economy, meaning Marxist economics, was not one subject among others – to be studied critically beside other major economic theories. That would be a reasonable proposal. But, no, the supporters of political economy wanted Marxism to supplant any course in which they detected the poison of capitalism. The Department of Economics at Sydney University was to become a school of Marxist dogmatics. Others had caved in. Williams and Hogan appeared ready to fight to the end.

The notification that Collins's contract would terminate at the end of the year riled the political economy supporters. They demanded the reinstatement of Collins and Roberts. Marxist Professor Wheelwright and Dr Stilwell deplored the intransigence of Professor Hogan. They charged him with being 'avowedly antipathetic to courses in Political Economy' and with retaining 'absolute power in respect of staff appointments'. Well seen. They expected him to 'systematically undermine the new courses by exercising this power – and he has already begun to do so; and the Vice-Chancellor, by inference, concurs'. They weren't far off the mark. But they stopped short of threats of disruption. They would leave such action to the more rabid among the radicals. And so it happened. A meeting of political economy agitators (H4,17 Mar.) decided to present a list of their demands to Vice-Chancellor Williams. Having drawn up the list, they marched in a group of around 250 to the administration 'to present the demands in person to the lovely Bruce'. There Hugh McCredie, University Secretary, obviously on guard, told them the Vice-Chancellor 'was not available and would not be available'. The pack hung around for around thirty minutes before deciding 'to strike at a more visible target – Professor

Hogan...conducting a lecture on the other side of the campus'. But it was not Professor Hogan giving the lecture. Guest lecturer Professor Eckstein was on the rostrum. When the students appeared, Hogan stopped the lecture and led Eckstein away.

Four students, though supporters of political economy, deplored (H4) the 'invasion' and disruption of the lecture given by 'a well-known authority about Chinese Economic [sic]'. The action by a minority trashed their rights and was a 'gross insult on our guest lecturer [sic]'. The *Honi* report acknowledged the 'hostile reception from several quarters' and the students' 'shouts of "piss off," "selfish bastards" etc ... hurled by many people'. The radicals were unrepentant. The attempt by Williams, Hogan and Simkin to frustrate the plans for a department of Marxist economic theory justified the violent action. Leaders of the radicals, Mike Brezniak and Rod O'Donnell, wrote to Professor Eckstein 'on behalf of the Movement for Political Economy' to apologise for the disruption. Recognising Professor Eckstein's interests lie in the 'very sort of economics that we have been struggling' to implement, they perversely subjected him and *Honi* readers to another boring repetition of the arguments. The central point of the hollow apology was that, given their lofty aims, they had no choice but to disrupt his lecture – and any other occasion that did not suit their radical plans.

If the repetition had not bored the student body witless, the *Honi* collective (H5, 25 Mar) seemed bent on reducing them to a catatonic state. That edition was devoted entirely to the political economy affair. What could clever Comrade Dave have been thinking? The feature of the edition was the Vice-Chancellor's suspension of just one student (Mike Brezniak) out of around fifteen who invaded the lecture. Was this a tactical mistake? On the surface, it seemed so. The agitators quickly seized on the move, demanding to know why the Vice-Chancellor was singling out poor Mike Brezniak with his Afro. Shouts of victimisation! Intimidation! The agitators were jubilant when Williams said, 'Brezniak was the only student known, and that if he received statutory declarations from other students saying that they had been involved, he would suspend them also'. The agitators rallied around and presented more than thirty signed statutory declarations to Hugh McCredie. Williams lifted Brezniak's suspension and charged him before the Proctorial Board, the tribunal for such disciplinary matters. The agitators thought they had not only Williams in a corner but the university's processes of justice. But had the Vice-Chancellor acted tactically in keeping the hornets preoccupied with a side issue?

The Vice-Chancellor and Professors Hogan and Simkin had their supporters. Jane Seymour (Ecs. III) wrote (H6, 2 Apr) that Brezniak and his fellow agitators had 'no right to burst in on any lecture being given at the university, let alone one at which a guest was speaking'. The students could have approached Professor Hogan at another time. The reason for the invasion was, of course, tactical. She then made the obvious point about the number of agitators:

'But, how many students in the Faculty of Economics are in support of Political Economy? There were relatively few who disrupted the lecture compared to the number who attended the lecture to hear Professor Eckstein speak. I would say this is indicative of the support for Political Economy. Those who supported it are a vocal minority, and they consider their views on the teaching of Economics to be superior to those of all other students.'

Just so. Peter Taylor (Arts III) made a stronger point (H7, 7 Apr). 'All this bullshit about Political Economy,' he wrote, 'is with us again.' And again, and again, I would have added. He was amazed that many students had no idea 'they've had the wool pulled over their eyes'. Political economy, he claimed, 'is not economics, nor a near-alternative... And what about Dip. Eds who want to teach economics and are doing PE [Political Economy]? And what sort of help is PE if you're doing accounting? The fact is that PE is as related to Economics as Whitlam is to Fraser'. Peter Taylor was obviously in need of re-education. Mike Brezniak submitted (H9,14 Apr) an article in which he regurgitated the history of the dispute, self-righteously wriggled his way out of the charges of disrupting Professor Eckstein's lecture, and condemned the university's justice processes. The only exciting part of the article was the accompanying photo of Mike in his ostentatious Afro.

The report in H9 under the heading 'A Right Panic' about the 'the non-appointment of Associate Professor Wheelwright' to the third chair in the Economics Department broke out another front of buzzing hornet fury that would carry on for weeks. To state the obvious, Wheelwright was an incorrigible Marxist directly opposed to Hogan and Simkin. Hogan and Vice-Chancellor Williams would not want Wheelwright in such an influential position. The skilful propagandists of political economy cast this as the opposition between enlightenment and 'ossified' authoritarian conservatism. Indeed, the leading members of the PE Movement appeared to be far better propagandists and manipulators than economists. The author of the unattributed report issued the usual warning that action would be taken and 'such action should make this unacceptable decision as uncomfortable as possible for the forces behind the decision'. In other words, violence was up ahead for Williams and Hogan.

The editorial collective allowed SRC President John McGrath to make a rare intervention (H10, 24 Apr). He wrote, 'this decision [to reject Wheelwright] represents the most despicable and blatant act of personal and political prejudice by our University administrators that I have witnessed'. The rage over Wheelwright's rejection and the appointment of Professor Mills of Kent University (UK), deemed unqualified for the position, and the Brezniak affair continued through to July. David Patch submitted one of his few comments for the year (H14, 25 Jun) in which we are treated to the 'Student Senator's' swelling opinion of himself and his brand of logic. At the last meeting of the Senate he 'asked the VC why he had suspended

Brezniak and strongly criticised him for so doing'. Williams replied that the evidence of witnesses justified the suspension. Patch commented that Williams 'gave the impression that he had suspended Brezniak as a sort of punishment'. Then we have this from the trainee lawyer:

'However, Chapter VIII A, 3(l)(b) of the By-Laws says, 'The Vice-Chancellor may for the purpose of maintaining good order, suspend any student etc...' Quite clearly, the VC has no power to suspend a student as 'punishment', but only 'for the purpose of maintaining good order.' I will be obtaining legal advice about this, and if my opinion is correct, will bring the matter up at the next meeting of the Senate.'

Patch has slid easily from impression to fact. He will have to do a lot better when he goes to the bar. What a purgatory it must have been for Vice-Chancellor Williams to deal with the likes of Patch. No wonder he had to take sick leave towards the end of 1974.

Patch's arrogant letter was an introduction to a PE bumper issue of *Honi*. Seven broadsheet pages of twenty (including the cover) were devoted to inciting the student body to rise against the properly constituted authority of the Department of Economics. It was a paradigm case of leftist manipulation ending in violence. The history, the arguments, the name-calling, the slander, the distortion, and the misrepresentation were all regurgitated as a prelude to the call for student action. Wednesday, 2 July, was named 'D-Day for decision making'. Under the leadership of Comrade Dave, *Honi* called out a 'uniwide stoppage/teach-in'. Students were urged to 'turn your classes over to a discussion of student participation and political economy', to gather on the front lawn to demonstrate their 'dissatisfaction with this reactionary remote control', and 'to sign a petition for an independent enquiry'. An independent enquiry was one that would decide in favour of the radicals. They would call it until the tribunal got it right.

The radicals invaded and occupied the Vice-Chancellor's office. There was, as usual, no regard for the administrative employees, ordinary people seeking to do their work. They were the necessary collateral of violent student action. Sarah Sheehan wrote up an account of the occupation (H15, 9 Jul). Its tone is sneering, facetious and self-righteous – with a break-down in logic clever Dave would never be guilty of. Five hundred students (out of 16,000) gathered to pass motions in line with their repeated demands and in contradiction of the policies of the Vice-Chancellor and Professor Hogan. In a throwback to a primitive religious ritual, they burnt 'an effigy of Professorial arrogance', after which 'some 200 students marched to the VC's office to present the demands'. They found the Vice-Chancellor's office closed and the Vice-Chancellor absent. 'Six years of working', wrote Sarah, 'via the "legal" channels, letters, petitions, protests, leaflets, appeals, etc., all to no avail, gave the students greater determination on Wednesday. The occupation was on'. The mob barged in and crammed one hundred sweaty, hairy, dishevelled bodies into Williams' office while the rest waited in solidarity outside. Bruce Williams returned at 4 pm and, refusing to discuss the matter, ordered the students out.

The police were called, and 'nine paddy wagons containing some 60 cops, backed up by plainclothes men plus Special Branch' police arrived. The 'notorious' Summary Offences Act was read to the accompaniment outside of 'Cops off Campus', which was amended to 'Pigs off Campus' when the students slunk away at around 5 pm, leaving the administration staff to give the office a thorough airing. 'We then gathered',' Sarah continued, 'in the middle of the Quad in the evening gloom to burn a second professorial effigy, to chants of "Student-Staff Control", "Political Economy Now"; etc.'. No doubt such a scene was to be witnessed regularly five thousand years ago deep in the forests of Germany. Alas, in her pleasurable reminiscing of the fiery gloom, Sarah wandered in her reasoning. If the students had been guilty of violence – invading the Vice-Chancellor's office and holding the staff at bay – so were the Vice-Chancellor and

Professor Hogan:

'It seems to me that political sackings are violent actions, the more so because they are covert. Bill Waters, Dave Hill, Paul Roberts and Jock Collins
have all been sacked. Arbitrary suspension of a student is a violent action,
designed to intimidate other activists – Mike Brezniak was suspended
without reason as the Proctorial Board report made clear. Under-staffing
of political economy courses is violence against both students and staff.'

If 'political sackings' (contract terminations) are violent, more so when
they are covert, then violence is a way of life in any organisation. When
Sarah Sheehan wrote this, she was a third-year medical student. If she
were to reach a position of authority in the medical field, then meting out
violence would be part of her work. Jeff Phillips' letter in the same *Honi*
issue brought balance to Sheehan's fantasy. It had become crystal clear, he
wrote with caution, that 'the Movement for Political Economy is prepared
to use physical force in order to communicate its argument... To stoop so
low' would only damage their cause. He provided information Sheehan
had omitted and drew an obvious conclusion. The Movement for Political
Economy had

'disrupted a lecture given by an eminent visiting economist, Professor Eckstein, jostled and punched members of the Senate, including the Chancellor, Sir Herman Black and a Supreme Court judge, forced entry into
the Vice-Chancellors office by busting through locked doors and breaking
windows. An action which regrettably compelled the calling of police onto
the campus ... Indiscriminately daubed slogans in paint over university
buildings.'

Nobody could defend 'this history of assault and vandalism'. It was 'high
time the Vice-Chancellor realised the small band of bashers and smashers

are not needed in the university community'. In the meantime, the Proctorial Board dismissed the charges against Mike Brezniak. Understandably, members of the Senate, the Professorial Board and the Administration were livered. Brezniak had admitted to disrupting the lecture. Students had testified and objected to the wilful, planned disruption. It was an open and shut case for the ordinary person not under the duress of political standover. The Proctorial Board had added itself to the list of authorities caving in to the far left. Chips Mackinolty, one of the *Honi* far-left editors, was full of contempt for those criticising the Board and accused Williams & Co of a 'secretive' and 'underhanded' attack on people who had 'no redress'. The leftist mind knows no shame.

David Patch commented on the Brezniak case and the recent occupation of the Vice-Chancellor's office in his report of the recent Senate meeting (H16, 16 Jul). Curiously, he repeated the Vice-Chancellor's vivid description of the occupation as 'a breaking and entering ... in a commando-style operation' with 'great force'. Presumably, he thought a legitimate protest 'against the autocratic university government' counter-balanced the violent occupation. When the Senate put up a motion justifying calling in the police, he voted against it. 'I took the view', he wrote, 'that the use of police, so often a method of repression of political dissent, was absolutely unjustifiable'. He did not bother to explain why calling the police, in this case, was unjustified. No doubt, saying the use of police was a method of repression of political dissent – like their use in the Soviet Union – was enough for the half-baked lawyer.

He was amazed 'the University authorities have tried to discredit the Board's report'. He added as if there was some double standard or inconsistency, 'imagine how different their reaction would have been if Brezniak had been found guilty'. Well, of course, their reaction would have been different. The authorities thought they had sound reason to criticise the Board's dismissal of the charges. He then related how during the Senate meeting of 9 May he had got up to leave on hearing the announcement of

Professor Gordon Mill's appointment to 'the vacant chair of Economics in preference to Ted Wheelwright'. He wanted to whip away 'to announce this decision to a group of students outside the room'. The Vice-Chancellor challenged him based on an 'an archaic and elitist' convention that 'appointments to Chairs are considered confidential'. Patch gave the finger to that convention. After a 'very tense interchange between [him] and the Chancellor', he left to carry out his mission. Patch seemed surprised that he was censured by the meeting he had just attended, relating that 'personal abuse and vituperation [came] from all sides'. I wonder it did not occur to him that many found him an objectionable shit.

The lecture invasion and the office occupation appeared counter-productive. The agitation dropped off considerably after the radicals left the Vice-Chancellor's office to the childish chant of 'Pigs off campus!' The Brezniak acquittal, though a triumph, was a warning the authorities would not easily give in. The referral of the office occupation to the police caused the radicals to hesitate. Interminable legal action in the past had followed such stunts. The announcement in June for the SRC annual elections must have been a relief for many on campus. So, with the occupation behind them, the radicals turned their attention to electioneering. The record of the current SRC was significant to all those in election mode. So how did the SRC executive and Comrade Dave and his editorial collective do? Did the executive control Dave, or did Dave control the executive? Did the election of John McGrath as SRC president in 1974 amount to a charade?

❧

Honi came to life in late February 1975 fully matured, a worthy competitor to the communist Tribune. No tentative, amateurish feeling about it. It was a tribute to the new editors Chips Mackinolty, Paula Taylor and Dave

McKnight. The editors would operate as a collective and make the 'internal matters' of the university a priority. They outlined the responsibilities of the SRC to make clear that a rise in the student fee was necessary. Dave was keen to present the SRC as a vehicle of urgent reform. That reform consisted of 'the struggle for staff-student control of courses and the departments' so they could 'decide the important things that affect [the student body], rather than having fossilised professors, businessmen, government bureaucrats, "prominent citizens" and professional bodies making all the important decisions'. The campaign of reform also included tackling 'constitutional and regulations changes', and 'deletion of sexist terminology'. Dave and his collective had set the standards and were all revved up to go. What happened?

Honi from that point, as I have said, bulged with long articles by specialists on the issues occupying the Left that few were interested in. There was hardly an average student contribution to be found. The priority of 'internal matters' disappeared. Students didn't hear from the editorial collective on SRC concerns until H6 (2 Apr), in which they expressed outrage that thousands of copies [of the bumper *Honi* issue on political economy] had been stolen. 'We believe,' they wrote, 'it is quite clear that groups of the political right were responsible ... We warn our thieves on campus that we will physically defend freedom of the press'. When it came to free speech Jeff Phillips and Frank Lane-Mullins had plenty to say. They bickered with Jane Rawlings over *Honi*'s censorship of conservative contributions, the loss of submitted articles, and their barefaced anti-Catholic bigotry. *Honi* announced (11 Jun) a front lawn meeting to discuss an 'SRC fee rise'. The collective listed all those you-beaut services the SRC offers. But inflation was devaluing the disposable funds. The fee rise was justified if the students just wanted the services kept up. The editorial collective lost. The student body voted it down. In the meantime, the SRC elections were announced (H13, 18 Jun).

In the light of the fee rise defeat and the start of electioneering, Glenda Travers (Arts/Law IV) took a big stick to the Left (H14A, 2 Jul). Under the heading of 'The desperation shuffle', Glenda warned that the defeat of the fee rise campaign was 'a severe blow for the SRC'. The outcome should give pause to the SRC 'heavies'. The students, she wrote, 'are cheesed-off, pissed-off and fed-up with student bodies...who couldn't give a stuff about student opinion so long as they extract their supporting votes and their money from them'. Some students care more about what they can do for students rather than playing politics. 'But invariably it's the usual group of ratbags', she continued, 'who monopolise the SRC's time and money for political and ideological ends, and who as a result just stultify the rest of the council members into disbelief, amazement, frustration and finally non-attendance'. Maybe the defeat will force the radicals to think again. The rest of the students should make sure the radicals are voted out. Without the radicals, the ordinary student may consider supporting a fee rise.

The same issue reported on the last meeting of the 47th SRC. The barely visible president John McGrath announced the candidates for the SRC presidency. We had heard nothing from Malcolm Turnbull in *Honi* to that point. But there he was on the list of six candidates, described as 'an elected member of the Union Board' and having failed 'in his bid last year for the editorship of *Honi Soit*'. The others were Michael Hintze (present SRC Secretary/Treasurer), Richard Wilson (Gay Liberation), David Patch (Welfare Officer and second go at the presidency), Craig Gibbons (Engineering and 'far-right'), and Jeff Phillips (second go at the presidency and 'associated' with the Democrat). Dave and his collective ranked the candidates according to their politics. From right to left they were: Phillips, Gibbons, Turnbull, Hintze, Patch and Wilson. Note that conservative Jeff Phillips was placed before genuinely far-right Gibbons. Comrade Dave couldn't help himself, could he? The only team presenting for the editorship of *Honi* was the far-left trio Jane Rawlings, Faye Westwood and

Michael Gormley. They could be confident of success. Jane had put in sterling work for her group.

The rough and tumble of student electioneering soon showed its ugly side. For *Honi*, the crude and unjust always came from the right. Two letters from members of Gay Liberation appeared complaining about 'queerbaiting' (H16, 16 Jul). Under 'Fowl Fighting', Ken Davis denounced the tactic of the 'extreme right-wing forces' and warned the 'insult to the many hundreds of homosexual women and men on this campus' was counter-productive. The extreme right were oppressors 'and should be treated as such'. The second letter was from candidate Richard Wilson who complained about a 'pamphlet called the SRC Form Guide'. The guide compared the candidates as racehorses. Richard was described as 'gay Wilson...a gelding running in the RED colours [who] should be put out to stud'. As Phillips did not reject such crude 'poofter-bashing', one could conclude he found it 'acceptable'. Indeed, Phillips, Richard charged, had a record of 'poofter and commie bashing'. He had appeared on television criticising the 'homosexual content of television programming'. He had also argued against a grant to Sydney University feminists because they were 'just a bunch of lesbians anyway'. Phillips and his poofter-bashing mates could throw as much mud as they liked, but Richard was 'proud to stand on [his] record as a socialist and as a long-time homosexual activist'. There was no response from Jeff Phillips. At least none was printed in *Honi*.

A long comment on the elections amounting to a critique of the Right followed the two gay liberation letters. As there was no byline, one presumes it was the work of Comrade Dave and his collective – more the tone and thought of Dave than his collective mates. The report's central theme was a 'push' from the Right to drain money from the SRC and cut funding to *Honi*, though not exactly in those words. The tactic was to work on 'traditional student cynicism about the SRC' to remove the leftist incumbents who misused its power. The report approves of the Right's plan to give more money to the faculty societies. That was good in itself, but it was a tactic 'to dismember the SRC' and reduce its activity. In brief, the idea, never wholly formed, seems to have been that if the Right could not dislodge the Left from the power positions of the SRC, they would render it impotent by depriving it of funds. As smart as Dave was, he seemed not to see the full implications.

The election results for the 48th SRC were known by the end of July and reviewed by Jane Rawlings (H18, 30 July). Jane did not serve up the tedious prose of a David Patch. Her commentary was colourful, facetious, entertaining and satirical – not all at once, of course. One feels the atmosphere of the political contest where ideas and personalities rub against one another. It was one of the best pieces in the oh-so-serious *Honi* of 1975. The headline was 'Election Results – The Left Take to the Hills'. She began with the students nervously lined up in the corridors awaiting the results, the left overtaken by 'profound gloom'. She then made an incriminating admission. The 'anger at the present SRC' had motivated the Right to run candidates in all Council positions. They ran a better campaign while the Left were 'fragmented'. This 'gave them the election'. There had been 'a right-wing drift among the student body ... as a reaction to what has been a very radical SRC'. As a result, 'four Right candidates were elected unopposed'. She added, 'the rest was almost downhill.'

After 'wading through the chewed off fingernails' while awaiting the results for the presidency, she rejoiced the far right was unsuccessful. Its traditional 'joke candidate' and the candidate of the far left were gone. 'Malcolm Turnbull, rather better known for his activities on the Union Board than for his involvement in the SRC went next'. Now David Patch sinks into paranoia and wonders whether 'to hire a van or use a car to remove his files from the Welfare office'. Jeff Phillips is a 'picture of innocent joy'. He is catching up to Patch. Finally, the last vote is counted, and Patch is triumphant. He only has to move across the hall. Then it was Jane's turn to contribute to the 'ever growing pile of nail chewings'.

She could relax. Her team won *Honi* for 1976. She ran through the other results observing that left-wing women seemed to do better than the men. Jeff Phillips had not done as well as he had hoped, but he clinched one of the Arts Men positions. Patch took the other. Jane's final judgement was that 'this Council then is predominantly Right with a sprinkling of moderates, lefties and political unknowns. It has a Marxist president and an *Honi* editorship that refuses to take sides'. She correctly painted Patch as a Marxist. It would be a miracle if *Honi* did not take sides.

It did not take long for the new 'Right' SRC to receive a patronising lecture about their duties. You would expect from the Left the hypocritical demand that the 48th SRC not indulge in partisan politics, discrimination against all things left, sound financial management, fair distribution of funds, etc. etc. In a word, the right-wing SRC was not expected to carry out all those abhorrent practices of which the previous radical left SRC were guilty. And so, it came in a letter headed 'An Open Letter to the New SRC' (H19, 3 Sep). But strangely, the letter was unsigned. Whether the author wanted to remain unnamed or the editorial collective (they were in the job until the end of the year) was showing some spite is not apparent. The style of the letter and a careless sentence, however, gave the author away.

The letter opened with the claim the 'right-wing' had control of the Council 'by virtue of monumental student apathy', their good organisation, and the bad organisation of the left. A 'grave responsibility' rested on the shoulders of those right-wingers most of whom were 'members of the Democratic Club which stands well to the right of student opinion, such as it is'. This last is nonsense, of course. It shows the author, then as now, had little idea of conservatism as a political philosophy. As they appeared in Honi, all the signs were that the Democratic Club was a club of conservative-minded people representing community standards. On the surface, it would seem the author contradicted himself by acknowledging the Right won the vote but did not represent most students. But, no, the students were apathetic, presumably meaning the bulk did not vote, and if they had voted, the result would have been in favour of the 'moderates', moderates as understood by the author then as now. Furthermore, Jeff Phillips had engineered a 'shift of centre votes' to himself by fooling students into thinking he was a 'moderate'. The author was clearly suffering from the same sort of delusion then as now.

He then spent several paragraphs lecturing the Right about their responsibility to be scrupulously fair politically and financially. Above all, '*Honi* must be the forum for ALL students'. Contributions were to be accepted 'from all sides' and judged on their 'literary or stylistic features'. No doubt the author thought he was giving an example of the literary and stylistic requirements. If this SRC indulged in 'political censorship or manipulation of *HONI*, it would be branded 'as the worst the University has ever seen'. On Malcolm's standards (the author is clearly Malcolm Turnbull), I would have thought the 47th SRC hard to beat as the worst. Malcolm expressed dismay on hearing a whisper of the Right's plans to take 'as much power as they possibly can away from the new President, David Patch'. But they should think again. The Right may have 'won a majority on the Council', but (this is where Malcolm gives himself away) 'in the only clearly defined ideological contest of the election, David Patch, of the Left, defeated not only Jeff Phillips, of the Right, but other centrist candidates like myself and Michael Hintze'. Malcolm wanted David Patch to be allowed what he (Patch) would not allow his opponents – to fulfil his duties unhindered. Any attempt to the contrary would be 'petty, vicious and an unprincipled rejection of the students' vote'.

Malcolm need not have worried. Patch had shown he could mix it with the best (or worst) of them. They would have to get up pretty early to outwit David Patch, trainee lawyer, fixated radical, and manipulator without peer on campus. Plodding Patch would not make the same mistakes as Comrade Dave. Perhaps that's why he kept *Honi* at arm's length but worked independently behind the scenes to secure the SRC presidency. It

was now time to see how he would fare after gaining his object. We have a
big hint in an interview with 'New El Presidente' Patch in H18 (30 Jul). It
was revealing, displaying more than a little hubris. I suspect the Spanish
title, with its hint of Spanish or South American tin-pot dictators, was
deliberate, showing the spiteful hand of his editorial detractors.

We hear that Patch was born in 1953, attended exclusive The Armidale
School, and scored a scholarship to university in 1972. He began in Science
but switched to Arts/Law after a year. He was embarrassingly open in reply
to the interviewer's suggestion that his victory was 'hollow' because the
Right had control of the SRC. Well, the victory may seem hollow, he said,

'But I don't take office until 1 Dec, and by that time, the Left will have
regained control. I think this for two reasons: first, the Right's interest in
the day to day work of the SRC has always lapsed very quickly and second,
the officers (e.g. Education, Environment, Welfare, etc.) elected at the New
Council's first meeting will probably not do a very good job and if so, will
need to be replaced at the beginning of next year.'

His reply was not only embarrassingly open. It also displayed jaw-dropping
arrogance. Here he was already firm in his plans to void the elections and
manipulate the SRC according to his ideological projects. In reply to the
suggestion that the Right were 'more ideological and determined' this time
around, Patch dismissed them as few and only successful 'by roping in
people who have had little or no previous interest in politics, let alone the
SRC'. Asked about his influences, he said,

'Basically, when I was at school, I became peripherally involved in the
anti-Vietnam and anti-apartheid movements. I used to distribute 'National U' around school and organise seminars on Vietnam and apartheid. A
few times, I was beaten up for my troubles. The ultimate reason, I guess,
was in reaction to the authoritarian school atmosphere. When I came to

uni, I naturally involved myself with the radical sections of political life.'

Questioned about his membership in the ALP, he confirmed what was evident in his actions and words. 'I'm a socialist', he said. The Labor Party was the party of 'most worker activists'. Then he pointed out a crucial difference in approach from Communist Party member Dave McKnight. The Labor Party was 'the only realistic way of making Australia a socialist society'. In answer to the proposition that Australia was already 'well on the way to being "socialist" because of the Labor Government', he denied the ALP was socialist as yet. The Labor Party was misguided in 'its aim ... to make Australian capitalism more humane and efficient'. The ALP needed radical internal change. This was all copybook Trotskyist. Patch dismissed the claim the SRC was 'non-political' and had no business giving money to 'outside' bodies. Quite the opposite. 'The SRC', he said, 'has always been a political organisation [and] students have traditionally been a political force in society'. Political organisations cooperate with other political organisations 'which sometimes includes financial assistance to them'. That was his justification for distributing student money to those leftist causes and organisations he favoured over anything or anyone with the slightest whiff of conservatism.

When asked about the university's encroachment on the surrounding community, he voiced his determination to 'oppose any further University expansion'. There were sound reasons for opposition, as I have said. But you don't have to be of the radical Left to support the community against government threats to your well-being. He freely admitted he photostated the Senate minutes dealing with the issue and sent a copy to South Sydney Council. At the very least, his action was highly irregular. At worst, it was an unconscionable breach of confidentiality. Patch showed, and would continue to show, he had no regard for business etiquette or confidentiality when it was at odds with his ideology. Asked about the women's movement and homosexuals, he gave the Left's stock reasons for his support.

Finally, he said the occupation of the Vice-Chancellor's office was entirely justified. His reasons amounted to the Vice-Chancellor's failure to fit in with the ideological schemes of 22-year-old David Patch.

A report appeared of the first meeting of the 48th SRC in H19 (3 Sep). The author was 'Dale' who had not appeared before, though obviously belonging to the excitable extreme Left. Like Jane Rawlings, Dale wrote an entertaining piece giving the flavour and smell of sweaty unwashed student politics. However, unlike Jane, who tempered her report, he shamelessly cheered for the extreme Left during the election of the SRC executive and deplored the success of the 'extreme right'. The report had the heading 'Night of the Long Knives' suggesting that his side's defeat was the result of the Right's malevolent manipulation.

The evening began, he wrote, with much (childish) mocking of the Vice-Chancellor, after which the 'collection of time wearied and eager, fresh-faced reps [sitting] around the central tables, with a host of onlookers and "interested parties" filling the remaining breathing space', got down to business. The election officers, 'amidst growing tension and oxygen short-age', supervised the first contest between Gay Liberation Angelo Rozas of the Socialist Youth Alliance and has-been conservative Tony Renshaw. Rozas got up. Rising Law School personality Irving Wallach beat off 'moderate' Michael Hintze and conservative Frank Lane-Mullins for AUS officer. Child Care Officer went to leftist Billee Ayling. But then things went haywire. Let's go to Dale's description:

'And then the tide began to turn with the election of education offi-cer – the Right were by then anxious and began to mobilise as Frank [Lane-Mullins] and the gang oscillated around the table conferring and issuing stern over-the-shoulder 'advice' – delegations to parts unknown outside the room became crassly and obviously frequent. They arrived expecting, perhaps a landslide of victories. Things had not been going to plan, though, and so they were suitably freaked out.'

They needn't have been. First-year Alan McIntosh, allegedly along for the right-wing ride, beat out John Cozijn, 'an activist for student participation and control, in the English department'. Now there was cause for panic. Alan McIntosh's success meant 'the Right had control of one of the actual offices within the Wentworth/SRC complex. Redecorations are now taking place'. Things went from bad to worse. 'The rest of the evening saw a succession of electoral fiascos as the right tightened their grip and the last remnants of objective appraisal of candidates faded into obscurity'. Martin Wallace, another hopelessly inexperienced right-winger, stood against experienced Julian Holland for Environment Officer:

'To the amazement of horrified onlookers, Wallace took the position. One could picture Frank and Co pissing themselves in glee. They were playing the numbers games skilfully aborting any pretence of rationality in the process. To many, the night was as good as over with such calculated opposition speeches and other 'democratic' observances to be dispensed with and no difference noticeable. Many participants, embittered not merely by the power of the Right, but by the blatant persuasion and manipulation of certain individuals, retired in disgust.'

When conservatives play the numbers game that the Left are so skilled at, they are irrational. The horror continued when Joe Bullock was elected as Director of Student Publications and Marcus Weyland as Race Relations officer, both defeating opponents with vastly more experience. Dale continued:

'The elections of Wallace and Weyland in particular, are a stunning indictment of the right on council – of their dangerous and manipulative potential, of their subjugation of real needs of social change and awareness for pure and undeniable political muzzling and deception. By this stage of the meeting, and already it was close to early morning, my departure became physically necessary ... the tone of the meeting was one of political squalor heralding a year of stultification and bitterness within and without the SRC.'

This entertaining but hysterical account was an example of the squealing that goes on when the opposition adopts far-left tactics. The democratic process is not to be endured when the Left don't succeed in slotting their candidates into the desired positions. If Jeff Phillips and Frank Lane-Mullins had not detected a hidden threat here, they were naïve. Even more so when hard-left Angela Nanson (Welfare Officer) and Clive Hamilton (Economics Representative) were immediately off the mark circulating a slander sheet ripping apart the conservative members of SRC. They weren't the only ones off the mark. The Left collective wasted no time in bombing conservative efforts to make the new administration work.

Frank Lane-Mullins (H20, 10 Sep) was frustrated by the 'singular unwillingness of the hard-left members of the SRC to work with their fellow representatives in the interests of the student body at large'. Of course, they were never going to cooperate with the conservatives. He noted that five SRC representatives out of eighteen voted against the motion, 'that the SRC reaffirms its support for the Political Economy Movement, but abhors any violence used for their cause'. Two of the five were Nanson and Hamilton. Two rules of the Left are demonstrated here: violence must always be an option, and a conservative regime, no matter how democratically elected, is never to be endured. Subversion, sabotage and undermining will be the order of the day. Another warning came when Education Officer Alan McIntosh, so viciously mocked when elected, organised a committee meeting. Marcus Weyland wrote (H22, 20 Sep) 'it was stacked by a large group of radicals who ignored him, ran the meeting by their own schedule, and passed motions in the name of the SRC education committee'. The bullying and undermining continued, and conservatives responded with politeness, appealing to the sense of fair play they imagined in their adversaries.

Skirmishes continued in *Honi* between the disgruntled, defeated left and the new right-wing SRC. The themes the left promoted were that the Right were (apart from their theoretical and moral error) incompetent and neglectful of their tasks. The implication was they were unsuited to their task, and the sooner they could be got rid of, the better. Far-left John Cozijn pursued the proposition (H23) that the contest was not between Left and Right, but between those 'who want to get on with the job in hand and those who are opposed to ALL forms of positive action. It is between those who want to use the SRC to further the interests of students and those who would seek to paralyse and destroy it'.

Comrade Dave, who must have been in a severe state of depression by this time, gave in to his worst side. He lashed out with an exhibition of extreme anti-Christian bigotry. In H19 (3 Sep), Dave and his collective used an illustration depicting the crucifixion of Christ to promote advertising in *Honi*. A speech bubble coming from the mouth of Christ says, 'Don't get hung up by advertising! Try *Honi*'. Clever Dave had gone to the outer boundaries of offensiveness for Christians. He could pat himself on the back. As expected, a letter appeared (H21, 17 Sep) complaining about the 'advertising gimmick using the Crucifixion of Christ'. Dave appeared delighted. The collective attached to the letter, 'We have reprinted the offending advertising gimmick on the right. Let's see how many more wraths we can incur'. The illustration was larger and thus more graphic. Letters flowed in from offended Christians, compensating Dave for the political rout and the consequent depression. But Dave was heartily sick of it all. Poor Dave – and he had so laboured to produce a first-class quality student newspaper. What a kick in the teeth that he had to make do with a miserable unsatisfying go at defenceless Christians.

The *Honi* editors said goodbye to their task in H27 (29 Oct), the last issue of the year. Not surprisingly – at least for me – they headed their goodbye with '*Honi* Soit: We're Glad to See the Backside of It.' They began with, 'Well, that was the year that was: *Honi* 1975. After having suffered with a bunch of commos, pinkos and petit bourgeois spontenaists [*sic*] for the last three terms, we're on our way out'. If there were 'petit bourgeois spontenaists' beavering away in *Honi*, there was no evidence of it, as far as I could detect – except perhaps for the sports section and the advertising. Apart from that, it was end-to-end commies and pinkos. Oh, yes, there was the indulgence of a few articles from Jeff Phillips and Frank Lane-Mullins, which provided the chance to mock them about their imagined religious affiliations. Otherwise, it was a product to do the communist Tribune out of its readership. But let me not be too severe about this final hurrah in which Dave, Jane and Paula tried to present a frank assessment of their success and failures. Indeed, the intriguing part of *Honi Soit* 1975 was the more in-depth look into the workings and contests within SRC, including *Honi*.

Surprisingly, *Honi* 1975 was well managed financially in contrast to the financial delinquency of the 1974 SRC. New equipment had been installed, and efficiencies in organisation achieved. Dave and his colleagues could be proud they brought in the year's production well under budget. The expenditure was the same as the previous year's *Honi*, a very inferior product. An excellent result. What an irony that CPA Dave McKnight's most significant success for the year was a capitalist success. As far as the aim to make *Honi* 1975 a 'democratic, participatory paper' went, Dave admitted it was mostly a failure. Well, of course. For those not suffering the delusions of Marxism, the empirical evidence of time out of mind is that individuals are different in all sorts of ways. Collectives don't work. They either create on-going instability leading to chaos, or a dictatorial elite takes over the group. That's the reason conservatives strive to maintain arrangements that have been proven over time. It's not difficult, merely common sense. Dave also admitted that most people contributing to *Honi* were Economics and Arts students. How democratic was that? The situation would not change. The Left would have the SRC and *Honi* by hook or by crook. The crook would come in 1976.

Part Three

Sydney University 1976-1980

Chapter 7

1976 – The White Knight arrives

IN DECEMBER 1975, Tony Abbott attended a Christmas conference at Bilgola organised by the NCC (National Civic Council) to prepare students for life at university. A friend had received an invitation to attend, and he was 'only too happy to provide him with company'. He said of the experience:

'That conference helped to channel my Jesuit-inculcated desire to be 'a man for others' into an immediate political outlet. It was a thrill to meet people of influence and authority in public life. It was exciting to think that I might be able to make a difference to the wider world. Most of all, it was good to learn that there was a way to get involved immediately through joining the Sydney University Democratic Club. This was the successor to the former DLP club and was supported and sustained by [Bob] Santamaria's National Civic Council. At that time, Santa had been a political crusader for forty years, a public intellectual much loved and greatly loathed in almost equal measure. Only in retrospect can I dimly appreciate the degree of commitment to a cause that led him to take so much trouble over potential recruits. What impressed me, even as a youth, was the courage that kept him going as an advocate for unfashionable truths. He always seemed more concerned for the cause than for himself.'[81]

Those truths were only unfashionable to a powerful minority of students and an intellectual elite in and outside the university. In 1975, they were truths most ordinary Australians held. They were the moral truths of Western Civilisation dictated by the Scriptures and discovered by unaided reason applying the norms of the natural law. They were the political and social arrangements that had stood the test of time and, for that reason, had prescriptive force. They were the customs, conventions, and traditions that formed a coherent culture in which its members invested their heart and mind. Buttressing these thoughts was a philosophical tradition (classical realism) whose pedigree flowed back through people like Edmund Burke, Thomas Aquinas, Augustine of Hippo, the Roman Stoics, to where the idea of the natural law is first found in written form in the Greeks, particularly in the writings of Aristotle and Plato. In other words, the National Civic Council and the Democratic Club were, in a philosophical sense, thoroughly conservative organisations.

For Tony Abbott, as he has shown in his talk about culture, there was more to it than a rational buttressing of a conservative outlook. The operation of the moral imagination and natural feeling was crucial in Edmund Burke's thought. Truth was to be loved, and the love of truth inspired courage and self-sacrifice to protect it – even to the point of self-annihilation. The acts of courage and self-sacrifice were to be celebrated as a memorial in dazzling colour, brilliant finery, and solemn ritual. A conservative does not forget the great occasions, the outstanding achievements, and his culture's great acts of virtue. A mind so formed about its culture and preservation was steeped in the ancient lore of Chivalry. All this, in brief, is the reason Tony speaks so feelingly about the courage and self-effacement of Bob Santamaria.

If one wants an image of Tony's appearance among his fellow students during Orientation Week in February 1976, then one can imagine a helmeted knight on a white-robed steed, his spear poised, sword by his side, and wearing an expression of quiet determination. It was an image the Left would laugh to scorn. The Left had minds purposely gutted of their cultural heritage. Whatever the social and political ideas Tony Abbott and the Democratic Club held, the far left at Sydney University, those controlling the SRC, continually abused them as far-right, fascists and Vatican stooges. They did not, and could not, see anything else. During Orientation Week, they also could not foresee the terrible torment the conservative knight would cause them.

In 1975, Greg Sheridan enrolled at Macquarie University, but dissatisfied with his choice of law and the leftist control of the student association, he switched to Sydney University in 1976, where he enrolled in the Arts Faculty.[82] Economics was one of his subjects. During the first lecture, candidates were called for the position of Economics representative on the staff-student economics faculty committee. Ignorant of the battle over the blanket democratisation of Sydney University, Sheridan volunteered. At the following lecture, he found himself up against 'a beefy fellow with [short] sandy hair and a ready grin'. Leftie-looking Sheridan with shoulder-length hair and a bushman beard put his opponent down as a 'surfer-type'. This was his first meeting with Tony Abbott. While Sheridan tried to spark his student audience with a 'plodding' speech about how he was there to serve them, Tony treated the occasion as an opportunity to be entertaining and satirical. Although he did this with 'great wit and charm' and amused his audience, he lost to the 'long-haired geek'.

Later that day, Sheridan relates, he made his way to the first meeting of the Democratic Club. He ran into the sandy-haired surfie there. 'You!' Tony shouted in a typical reaction of 'mock outrage'. Greg and Tony became firm friends, cooperating in the fierce battle of conservatives against the feverish far left. By this time, they were already a couple of weeks into the first term. Their putting their hand up for the staff-student position and their presence at the first meeting of the Democratic Club signalled they were primed to take an active part in student politics. Two or three editions of *Honi* had already appeared. H1 (23 Feb) was a bumper issue with a lavish smorgasbord of the usual leftist fare. Surprisingly, Simon Grose and David Margan, the grubs from *Honi* 1974, were among the collective. Several new names appeared for the first time, one of whom will come under David Patch's patronising tutelage. Barbara Ramjan was already in her third year of Social Work and had been an 'honorary member of the Social Work Students' Association in 1974 and 1975.

The collective outlined its agenda for the year, which was to serve all students and offer a forum for all points of view. Few would have believed it. *Honi* was full of staple-diet tiresome leftist rhetoric. The PE Movement received two full pages to propagate their cause, all from the Marxist perspective that had been thrashed to death in earlier *Honi* issues. It would be tediously repetitive to review all the causes appearing H1. As all roads lead to Rome, as the saying goes, so were the arteries of all social organs connected to the heavily pumping Marxist heart. We take that for granted. It was to be David Patch's big year. And he had a huge agenda. With some hubris, he had signalled his intentions in his interview the previous year. His first contribution to *Honi* was not as SRC President but as David Patch, Student Senator, puffed to bursting.

Patch had a full page to dazzle his fellow students with his knowledge of the Senate's work and how he cunningly schemed to undermine its standards and procedures. Under the heading 'Senate Rave from Dave', he said, 'Senate is the highest decision-making body of the University' and its meetings had a detailed agenda to get through. He was quite right. But as with all responsible bodies dealing with the ongoing issues critical to the running of an organisation, the Senate expected its members to maintain confidentiality. Their meetings were, therefore, closed. Nothing unusual for most organisations. Patch bared his bum to that. If anyone wanted to know what went on in Senate meetings, he was there to tell them. 'I am only too pleased to be a leak', he boasted. 'In fact, the closer I approach a sieve, the better'. He justified breaking confidence by saying,

'It is totally outrageous that the governing body of any organisation, let alone a University, which is supposed to consist of the more enlightened and educated sections of the community, should meet behind closed doors and make its decisions in a virtual vacuum, almost devoid of responsiveness to the wishes of those "outside".'

This is all nonsense, of course, the sneering of someone without any experience in the real world of business organisation. The true 'enlightened' and 'educated' ones for him were those who entertained his dictates about direct democracy with its roots in his garbled understanding of Marxism. The other (mature) members of the Senate understood the sensible need for confidentiality and followed long-established administrative procedures. There was no vacuum. A group of highly qualified and experienced men and women discussed the needs of the university and made decisions for which they were accountable to those who put them there. The reference to those 'outside' was to his tiny far-left clique who had even less experience about the world outside the university.

Having dazzled his Fresher audience with his adolescent bravado, he showed how brazenly he could break the confidentiality to which he subscribed by accepting a position in the Senate. He attacked the Senate for their handling eleven different issues. Underlying his criticism of the Senate was its failure in each case to follow his ideas about participatory democracy. It is unnecessary to explore each of these issues. But for their flavour, let me take one of central interest in 1976 and the years following. The Senate Finance Committee had recommended 'not to collect the SRC fee in 1976'. He did not explain the Committee's reasons but claimed the 'recommendation followed an amazing ... hotchpotch of insinuations, misunderstandings, facts that were twisted or taken grossly out of context, and plain lies, that was labelled a "report"'. What precisely these insinuations, misunderstandings and lies were, remained hidden. In truth, the finance committee recommended the measure because Patch and his clique refused to play according to the established rules.

The rules were about the SRC fee students paid under stated conditions and for stated purposes, which did not include syphoning off amounts to the far left's political campaigns. He accused the committee of a 'blatant' attack on the autonomy of a student representative body. The autonomy that Patch had awarded to the SRC ignored the reality of the SRC's subordinate position in the university's organisation. There was no SRC without the established lines of that organisation. It was an unworkable idea which presupposed all freedom and no responsibility. Experience has shown that administrative chaos follows such an idea. Patch finished by lamely accusing the administration of being driven by a 'dislike...for the political activity of the SRC'. Whatever the political allegiance of individual Senate members, it was clear Patch's antics provoked contempt for him.

An attention-catching feature among the many tired leftist articles was a two-page spread spurring the student body on to sexual abandon. On the left-hand page, under the name Jean Rhodes, was a vigorous exhortation with the satirical title, 'Superfluous Facts About Academic Eroticism Towards A Theory & Practise Thereof'. The opening paragraphs will be enough to illustrate its purpose (words in full in the original):

'Well now friends and lovers, we're all here to rock and root, and get into c..t and ass, get poked by Shakespeare, and stoked by the rules, get off on pricks and Virginia Woolf and all have a fucking orgasmic time. University is the womb which one fucks back into ... a great warm, wet, palpitating, energising environment ... seamy, sordid, incestuous ... c..t juice slipping through sticky hot sweaty fingers, sucking pseudo-semen eggs – SNARING moist pubes ... [and so on, and so on ...]'

Alan Barcan suggests 'Jean Rhodes' was a pseudonym. It was possible with the hands of the grubs Simon Grose and David Margan in the mixture. Cock privilege was just as likely the motivation for an invitation over which the parents of female students in 1976 would have despaired. The name Jean Rhodes, however, appeared continually in the editorial collective of 1976. She was the editor of the bumper homosexual edition. A photo of an attractive Miss Rhodes with long silky hair graced the pages of *Honi* later in the year. To which place were Miss Rhodes and her rocking and rooting comrades taking the students? Whatever the direction, the bourgeois despair of 1976 parents, sufferers of the Great Depression and the Second World War, would have been great fun.

Abbotsleigh girl Sarah Sheehan re-appeared (H2, 2 Mar) to correct a misapprehension of the Orientation Handbook's editors about the AUS (Australian Union of Students). 'The AUS Council', she wrote, is 'the supreme governing body of the Union' and not some little dickie organisation subsumed in lower-level student politics. She did not say that, but that was her meaning. Since her tutelage under Comrade Dave McKnight, she had risen to higher things. She signed off with, 'yours in student struggle, Sarah Sheehan, NSW Organiser, Australian Union of Students'. NSW AUS organiser was a paid position that entailed much (paid-for) travel. Had Sarah tossed in her medical ambitions for the more invigorating activity of subverting bourgeois high society from which she had sprung? Jenny Bourke followed Sheehan's letter with a fierce attack on the Orientation Handbook, venting her 'horror at that elitist obsequious, ruling class shit that filled the Orientation week handbook'. She singled out Frank Lane-Mullins' 'mediocre ... article on Political Economy'. The 'warped, megalomaniacal nature of his politics' was known ... 'so why did he write the article?' she wondered.

Related to Jenny Bourke's disgust at the audacity of Frank Lane Mullins to express his political views was the collective's editorial which devoted most of its content to mocking a handout titled 'The Marxist', apparently published by the 'Communist Studies Group'. After pointless speculation about its origin (obviously from the 'far right'), they mocked its contents as 'like the TV raves of one B.A. Santamaria' – a not-too-subtle hint at the Santamaria/Democratic Club/Vatican axis. No attempt, of course, to explain what was objectionable about the series of articles. That would be to commit to a detailed analysis instead of spouting leftist abuse. This was simply more of the same for anyone with critical faculties. Jeff Phillips and the Democratic Club should have paid close attention to the final paragraph of the editorial because it contained a warning, the full significance of which should have been plain. 'The last two meetings of the SRC have had to be abandoned because of the lack of a quorum', the collective wrote. The 'right-wing members of the council (led by one Jeff Phillips)' were absent. Their absence made the SRC unworkable. In the next issue of *Honi*, they would publish the names of 'just who's doing the work and who's sitting back on their arses'.

Joe Bullock, SRC Director of Student Publications, defended the Orientation Week Handbook (H3, 9 Mar). 'For the first time in my memory as a student and as Director of Student Publications', he wrote, 'here was an SRC publication which was not filled with revolutionary left-wing material, vicious attacks on the administration and lessons on how to become a feminist, communist or homosexual'. The information was helpful to the average student, and all organisations had space to broadcast their message. The handbook presented 'both sides of the Political Economy dispute'. Students were glad of a 'respite from the political propaganda'. It was a measured reply which provoked a long paranoid Marxist rant from far-left Garry Bennett, ever ready to spout the calcified Marxist view of bourgeois capitalist society and the evil influence of the Vatican.

The Handbook, he wrote was 'an incoherent mish-mash of elitist right-wing rubbish, having little or no relevance to students generally'. It's only redeeming quality was an article by far-left mate David Patch. That really says it all. For a flavour of the paranoia that runs through the rant, he claimed Australia's economic crisis at the time was not due to 'the shift to the left in politics'. One had to consider 'to what degree the crisis was stage-managed by multinational corporations, domestic capitalists, and the CIA'. The SRC was 'dominated by the Democratic Club, a DLP front, although many would call it a fascist front, in league with various other agents of the Vatican'. For someone who grew up under the care of responsible Catholic parents of the highest principles, this sounds like the delirium of an asylum inmate.

With all his talk about capitalism, progress, reactionaries, the middle class, and so on, Bennett showed he had swallowed the Marxist fantasy in big gulps. He knew the distinction between the (capitalist) economic base and bourgeois superstructure and that the evil capitalist base determines the corrupt superstructure of bourgeois society whose members wallow in error and deception. But like all his Marxist mates, he showed no sign of understanding the philosophy underwriting the materialist dialectic. Bennett's letter was just the start of a ferocious attack in H3 on the Right and right-wing students. The fanatical Chris Mackinolty took the baton from Bennett under a contribution titled 'A New Image for the Old Guard'. I will come back to it below.

The preamble to Mackinolty's full-frontal attack came in the editorial after a rave bordering on incoherence about their task to lay bare the corruption of capitalist society in which the fascists Prime Minister Malcolm Fraser and media baron Rupert Murdoch played malevolent roles. Catching their breath, the collective concentrated their attention on their primary 'function as an alternative to the daily press, and [Honi's] value as a critical forum on this campus'. In fulfilment of that function, they were printing 'an article about some of the behind-scenes influences on your daily life – forces that you may not have realised existed'. This said article that followed Mackinolty's raised 'many serious questions which must be answered quickly'. Despite an expected backlash, the courageous collective was prepared to suffer and do their 'duty'.

Mackinolty pushed the absurd fiction the Right had been in ascendance in SRC politics at Sydney University. In contrast to Bennett's Marxist rant, he at least tried to argue a case against the conservative enemy, however confused and deluded much of it was. He began with the tactic of attributing a view to the conservatives they did not hold. It was naïve, he wrote, to try to rid student organisations of politics. Student activity was inherently political. Of course, it was. That was not the issue for the conservative students. They wanted to rid student politics of the overwhelming leftist rhetoric and propaganda that vitiated all discussion. Mackinolty, one of Comrade Dave's triumvirate who sandblasted the campus with far-left propaganda in 1975, described student politics as 'bourgeois, tedious, alienated and irrelevant'. The backdrop of 'wider political ideologies and political practice' must be understood. Then, astoundingly, he described himself as 'left of centre' when he was at the front line of all the far-left campaigns. We must take such assertions as tactical rather than thinking Mackinolty was completely off his rocker.

As a left-of-centre student, he would do his fellow students the favour of appraising the present sorry situation of the SRC. This required some history. Determined to show he was indeed off his rocker, Mackinolty characterised student politics over the previous five or six years as a struggle by the 'left-leaning' students, often disorganised, to barely hold their own against the organised far-right forces that ever threatened the peace and tranquillity of the SRC. 'At present', he revealed to the unsuspecting student body, 'the Students' Representative Council (SRC) is in the large part dominated by members of the extreme Right'. The students had to understand how this had happened. In brief, Jeff Phillips and his far-right coterie had fooled the student body into thinking they were 'responsible', 'moderate', 'hard-working' etc. Now their actions were showing what they were really like. The reader should remember that inconsistency and contradiction are never far from the leftist discourse.

After creating a scenario of a highly organised right-wing assault that 'swept the field' and 'dominated' the SRC, Mackinolty went on to say that 'identifiable right-wing candidates captured just under half of the SRC positions'. Then he hammered the incompetence, negligence and disorganisation of the right-wing officer bearers. More than half of Mackinolty's article is a detailed exposition of how each of the right-wing office bearers was unqualified, incompetent, full of nasty political tricks, were just there for political reasons, were negligent in their duties and so on and so on. Above all, the right-wingers didn't give a fig for the students. Just like Susan Mitchell, who painted a contradictory picture of Tony Abbott, Mackinolty pushed the image of the right-wingers as cleverly organised on the one hand and negligent and incompetent on the other. It is a left-wing propagandist tactic to assert contradictory or inconsistent claims about their enemy. They do it because it often works.

All this, however, was to serve an overriding tactical purpose. It was one to which Jeff Phillips should have been a wake-up. After building up a picture of right-wing incompetence and negligence, Mackinolty pushed home his central point. The neglect of the right-wingers and their absence made the SRC 'unworkable'. Meetings could not take place 'because a large section of the SRC – the right – have failed to show up'. If the right-wingers were less than half of the SRC and some turned up, and a full complement of the left turned up, there was no reason not to proceed for want of numbers. That small point of logic, however, was of no account. The point was that the negligence of the right-wingers made the SRC unworkable. The conclusion, drawn (and proposed) by the leftist junta, was that the remedy lay in getting rid of the right-wingers. By this time, David Patch's unsubtle warning of the previous year should have been clamouring in the conservatives' ears.

Bennett's and Mackinolty's efforts were a lead-in to the blockbuster revelations the editorial collective had promised. Indeed, the article covering two full pages of *Honi* had the impressive title 'Unholy Alliances: The Operations of Right-Wing Extremists in the Universities'. A head-and-shoulders photo of a cleric in black habit leering at the reader adorned the pages. And there you have the overriding message of the author Harry Moore, who featured in *Honi* for the first time. Moore's motivation was a drooling staring anti-Catholic bigotry. He talks of extremists and social reaction, but the driver of the extremism and social reaction is unmistakably Catholics and the Catholic Church.

Moore did not indulge in a Marxist rant but kept mostly to his aim of describing the 'right-wing extremist' conspiracy afoot in student politics, particularly at Sydney University. In fact, Moore hastened to tell us, it was more than 'a carefully organised and coordinated conspiracy'. It was 'much more haphazard and of deeper causes', and more than a mere political organisation. Those desperate right-wing extremists were drawn together by 'a similarity of "worldview"'. That worldview was 'engendered through schooling and religious instruction (especially in Catholic schools)'. At this point, he slotted in one of his few references to a Marxist framework. That worldview arose out of a bourgeois mentality, that is, 'an appreciation of one's privileged economic political and social position being challenged by social reform'. Then he undermined his central thesis that the Catholic Church was behind the right-wing conspiracy. He acknowledged that communism united 'non-Catholics and even anti-Catholics' with Catholics in their battle against the communist conspiracy in the West for which there was abundant evidence and in which Moore and his far-left mates played a significant role.

After laying bare the extreme right's aims and motivation, Moore devoted the rest of his article to a lengthy account of how they organised themselves and carried out their propagandising actions. Leaders and ideological instruments, like the *Democrat*, were named, and testimony to their nefarious actions brought forward. All this was without the high emotion of those like Garry Bennett and Chips Mackinolty. As far as I can judge from my reading and experience of those times, most of Moore's account is correct about the names, actions and organisations one would call conservative – including the Catholic Church.

The irony is that Australia's conservative forces, to the extent they were organised, took their lead from the superb organisation of the myriad Marxist groups unceasingly working to undermine and destroy church and society in Australia. Bob Santamaria warned those battling the Marxist agenda they would not get anywhere unless they organised themselves as effectively as the left. When Moore spoke of National Civic Council (NCC) recruitment in schools, for example, you could match the single NCC action with a dozen leftist organisations pursuing members in schools – and probably more efficiently. The same applies to student actions, newspapers and the like. All more numerous and more efficient on the left as was demonstrated by the bumper issue of H3.[83]

How, then, did Moore convert an unexceptionable account of the conservative efforts to combat the left into propaganda for the leftist cause? He did it in ways the Left have always done. He stuck to manufacturing a dark scenario, smearing conservatives with views they didn't hold. In a flagrant denial of the evidence, he branded conservatives as 'the extreme right', conjuring up images of black-shirted Nazis and Italian fascists, while conservatism as a political philosophy is opposed as much to Nazism and fascism as it is to Marxism. Moore's conservative targets strove to maintain the beliefs and structures of their Western Society, with which most Australians were in unison.

Allied to the tactic of conjuring a sinister atmosphere around conservative organisations were the testimonies of people who had been (allegedly) subjected to the manipulation of conservatives. Here the article descended into farce. One unnamed student who witnessed the right's (alleged) manipulation told of the occasion he was invited to 'dinner-cum-meeting' in a luxurious setting with views over the Parramatta River. 'There were about 50 to 60 of us', he testified. 'We were treated to one of the best meals I've had: a great smorgasbord salad, followed by a fantastic dessert-trifle, fruit salad, watermelons, rockmelons and finally coffee and mints'. The student was staggered to find that this lavish repast was 'completely free'. How did he interpret the offer of a free meal?

Well, he thought all those luscious dishes 'very ingenious devices used by those sponsoring the meeting to make their young audience more responsive to propaganda and more likely to join the organisation'. Shouting a free meal at an occasion meant to win people to the cause is hardly ingenious. Smorgasbord dinners were popular at the time as a cheap way for hotels and other catering organisations to offer a variety of foods without a menu and cook. More importantly, an organisation was deluding itself if it thought providing a lavish meal was critical to winning people to their cause. The witness comes across as young and naïve, just the sort to succumb to the grandiose promises of Marxism. A second witness told how she unwittingly got caught up in a group of conservatives. When she understood who she was with and what they believed, she said, 'I still find it hard to comprehend that people who look normal can be like that'. Moore made no effort to lay out those ideas or to analyse them. That was beside the point. How effective his smearing and misrepresentation were, was the point. Results would testify to how effective H3 had been.

The issues of political economy and staff-student democracy simmered along. Clive Hamilton doing his best to discredit neo-classical economics, tried to explain the Marxist concept of 'contradiction' and the dialectic but produced a confused piece that would have reinforced the average student's impression that Marxism was gobbledygook. The trouble was that any such short explanations presuppose a knowledge of Hegelian concepts, a grasp of which clever Clive Hamilton seemed to lack. But all this was a sideshow because blockbuster H3 had provided the fully built platform from which David Patch could strike. Indeed, he struck with a ferocity that blinded friend and foe (H4, 16 Mar). 'In an extraordinary sequence of events', the editorial revealed, 'two representatives were recalled by petitions of their constituents, and four officers were removed by vote of Council'. It was a beautiful piece of leftist work.

Patch had dug down into the hoary depths of the student constitution and found a poisonous little provision. 'If it is believed', the editorial continued, 'that there are sufficient grounds for recalling or effecting the resignation of a representative, the SRC constitution allows for the collection of a petition among his or her electorate'. Patch had the required number. At the SRC meeting of 11 March (three days after the release of H3), Patch fatally pricked democratically elected representatives Jeff Phillips and Frank Lane-Mullins, who, in their death throes, protested fruitlessly. The editorial collective sneered about Lane-Mullins' doomed struggle, 'so much for his "regard" for constitutionality and correctness'. The meeting then voted to dismiss conservatives Alan McKintosh as Education Officer, Jeff Phillips as Vice President, Gary Osborne as Honorary Secretary-Treasurer and Martin Wallace as Environment Officer. The collective claimed the votes 'represented the opinions of left, centre and some right-wing councillors'. Pull the other one. But what a beautiful symmetrical strike. Patch had foretold what he planned the previous year (replace the democratically elected right), and he followed up with a clinical cleanness an industrial antiseptic could never achieve.

In a letter written before the coup (H4, 16 Mar), P. Sommers (Science II) noted in an apparent response to Mackinolty that Patch's victory over Jeff Phillips was narrow. So it was 'fair that Patch should be President and Phillips Vice-President'. He added, 'I am surprised that Patch got elected, knowing how many personal enemies his type of slimy politicking makes'. In another letter, moderate Michael Hintze (former SRC Hon. Sec-Treasurer) said he was 'disgusted by the present SRC administration'. After detailing the (alleged) mismanagement of the unjustified fee rise of $2.50, he accused David Patch, Jeff Phillips and Gary Osborne of 'buggering the whole show'. Patch was a 'Turramurra cocktail socialist, "please give me a

Rhodes scholarship, Mr McCredie, sir, I'd like to be just like Bob Hawke"'. Hugh McCredie was the university secretary.

Patch would not let such scurrilous attacks on his integrity and competence pass. Point-by-point, he refuted Hintze's claims, no doubt compelling for those unacquainted with the figures (H5, 23 Mar). It was up to Hintze to respond. Furthermore, he resented being called a 'Turramurra cocktail socialist', only ever lived a year in Turramurra, never asked for a Rhodes scholarship and had no desire to be like Bob Hawke. Finally, he did not want to be associated with the likes of Phillips and Osborne. 'I am', he sniffed, 'implacably opposed to their kind of reactionary views, and it was a pleasure to move the motions that dismissed such irresponsible and lazy persons as SRC officers', a self-incriminating confession he seemed unaware of.

Hintze responded (H6, 2 Apr). David Patch, he wrote, seemed 'to display a remarkable inability to grasp the facts for someone who purports to be "in touch"'. He then confidently answered some points of financial management, which at this distance cannot be verified. Of more interest, he accused Patch of being absent 'at the first four meetings of the Joint Orientation Week C'ttee which helped determine O-Week policy'. To end, he stuck him where it hurt. His description of 'Turramurra cocktail socialist' was not about Turramurra but Patch's 'elitist aspirations'. Nor was it about his attendance at an exclusive 'GPS school' (The Armidale School). 'Ask him how one day he expects to be a Federal MP. Ask him why he sought a Rhodes Scholarship. Ask him about his trips to AUS Travel Conferences on his Welfare Officer's budget'. Hintze fervently wished Patch would get to 'work for students, and not himself'.

Stung, Patch accused Hintze of knowing 'very little about the functioning of the SRC, and about myself' (H7, 6 Apr)'. He gave another point-by-point refutation of the financial issues, the accuracy of which one cannot now gauge. Then came this jaw-dropping claim: 'Hintze's final paragraph, full of vindictive lies about my so-called political ambitions and "elitist" aspirations, is the type of malicious mud-throwing that one sometimes, but rarely, sees in campus politics'. Was this a worry-causing fantasy or an example of the leftist's tactic of telling gigantic porkies? He scorned all Hintze's claims about his elitist ambitions. In particular, he 'never sought a Rhodes Scholarship'. He bitterly resented 'any slurs' that he did not work. He was on sound ground there. Patch had the commitment of a political fanatic whose output was impressive.

J. Sterns (Arts III), evidently one of Patch's 'reactionary' students, voiced his frustration (H4) that *Honi* continued to print the 'trash' it had printed in the past. Makinolty's 'article on the Democratic Club' exemplified such trash. The SRC of 1976 was inexperienced but had broad representation distinguishing it from SRCs of the past. Sterns seemed to be pleading for fair play because he added that no one would 'stand for positions' when 'exposed to the sort of scurrilous attacks seen in last week's *Honi*'. The level of debate, he concluded, would be 'more intelligent' when *Honi*'s writing was 'responsible and truthful'. The collective did not like that poke in the eye because, puffed up with self-righteousness, they challenged Sterns to show where they had lied. Sterns' reply is not recorded, but he could have said the deception was not in the detail of people and organisation but in the distortion, misrepresentation, bias and omission. Sterns' angry letter was just one expression of the fury that followed Patch's Machiavellian coup.

To calm the raw feelings, C. Tennison-Woods (Ecs. II) pointed out the lessons of Patch's glorious action (H4). He wrote that charisma and supportive friends don't win elections because if they did, 'Phillips would be SRC President and Patch would be a faceless nobody. It is organisation, dedication and hard work that wins ... Patch and his left-wing partisans excel in these three qualities ... For this reason, the Left ... control the SRC. And do they not deserve to? Last week, Patch and Co executed a bloodless "coup d'etat", purging the SRC ranks of Phillips' faction. And they did this wholly in accord with the SRC regulations and constitutional provisions.

This coup was legal'. Conservatives fail to digest the same lesson time and time again – not only in student politics. The Left may be liars, but they are superbly organised liars. 'If the Right and their moderates wish to regain an influence on the SRC', Tennison-Woods concluded, 'they must take a lesson. They must [be] disciples of the Left's mastery of political tactics. They will then one day be able to beat the Left at its own game'. All sound advice. But were the conservatives listening? Tony Abbott was.

In their editorial (H4, 16 March), the collective said that 'through the week, despite our offer of space to reply, no serious attempts have been made to answer allegations against certain members of Council'. Whom were they kidding? H3 was released on 8 March, the coup meeting was on 11 March, three days after, and the collective expected a reply to long, detailed articles before the deadline for H4? The collective knew they had to cover their backsides against their bias. In rare condescension to the conservatives, they allowed one letter and an article to prominent Democratic Club member Tony Rogers (H5, 23 Apr). Rogers said the facts *Honi* related were 'basically accurate'. The problem was the many omitted details.

For example, Frank Lane-Mullins and Jeff Phillips were removed by petitions 'whose existence they were unaware of until the day of the SRC meeting'. Patch and his far-left mate Clive Hamilton had sneaked around the classes with their allegations without giving Lane-Mullins and Phillips 'the right of reply'. One representative allegation was that Lane-Mullins had not been at the SRC offices during the holidays. The reason was straightforward. Because Lane-Mullins was not an SRC officer, he had no business there. Rogers was often at the SRC offices between January 8 and February 23. During that time, he doubted he saw more than '5 representatives' there. Left-wing officers Angelo Rosas (now resigned) and Irving Wallach, who was traipsing around the world', were no-shows. And Angela Nanson was there 'infrequently'. Lane-Mullins was not the only one to be absent. This, said Rogers, was no problem for Mackinolty because his intention was 'to discredit the right, not most deep-seated friends'. Absolutely. The tactics of Patch and his acolytes were to rush a judgment against Lane-Mullins and Phillips before they could react and regroup.

Mackinolty's article, Rogers continued, was 'mainly notable for the number of half-truths and total inaccuracies contained within it'. Of more importance, 'it dealt the cards for the removal from office of Arts representative Jeff Phillips and Economics representative Frank Lane-Mullins, so that the left-wing on campus, by use of insinuation [could regain] their "rightful" positions as the controllers of student politics'. Rogers made the obvious point that even on Mackinolty's evidence, the right did not dominate the SRC. He added there was no example of the 48th Council engaging in the activity of a 'vaguely rightest nature' and there was 'no attempt to censor the lopsidedly pro-left attitude of *Honi Soit*' which might have been the tendency of 'an extreme right' Council. And no money was diverted to right-wing causes. The financial delinquency of earlier leftist administrations was absent under the conservatives. Rogers related many ways the 48th Council was moderate because of the influence of conservatives. There were no errors of 'substance, so any attacks had to be on minor points and done with a total disregard for giving the full facts'. He spoke of the left's intimidation of those aligning themselves with the Democratic Club. As an example, he cited a 'prominent member of the CPA' threatening to give a member of the Democratic Club a 'clubbing'.

This sort of intimidation explained why conservatives were reluctant to participate in student politics. Glenda Travers had raised the problem in 1975. 'Invariably it's the usual group of ratbags', she wrote, 'who monopolise the SRC's time and money for political and ideological ends, and who as a result just stultify the rest of the council members into disbelief, amazement, frustration and finally non-attendance'. Frank Lane-Mullins (Sept 1975) cited the 'singular unwillingness of the hard-left members of the SRC to work with their fellow representatives in the interests of the student body at large'. Conservative Education Officer Alan McIntosh organised a meeting (Sept 1975) that became 'stacked by a large group of radicals who ignored him, ran the meeting by their own schedule, and passed motions in the name of the SRC education committee'. The bullying, intimidation and stacked meetings had cleared the way for Patch's manipulation of the Constitution.

Patch responded (H6, 2 Apr) to Roger's charges in *Honi* and in the *Democrat*, the latter described as 'the broadsheet of the extreme right on campus', which was nonsense, as I have already pointed out. In fact, there was no extreme right on campus. It is not a distortion to say Patch generally considered those to the right of him, of whatever degree, as 'extreme right'. Under the heading 'I Did It My Way', he pummelled those mounting 'a large scale slander campaign' against him. He facetiously acknowledged such 'gems of political insight as "Patch=Kerr", "Sack Patch", "Patch has destroyed the SRC", and many others' scrawled in chalk on the pavement and walls of the university. He was blasé about the close parallels between him and the hated fascist Malcolm Fraser, who had sacked Prime Minister Gough Whitlam just a few months before by invoking a never-before-used provision of the Constitution. The justification of his sackings, which was Patch's purpose to argue, would neutralise such ridiculous comparisons.

He would 'detail some of the things which led up to the SRC meeting on 11 March and, in so doing, refute the inaccurate charges and incorrect "facts" presented by Rogers in his letter and article in the last *Honi*'. He then launched into an account of Phillips' neglect of duty. Before considering his case against Phillips, it is pertinent to highlight Patch's conception of his role as president and the duties of the vice-president, which he explained, not in a preamble, but in the conclusion to the defence of his action. 'As President', he wrote, 'I have a primary responsibility to ensure that the SRC, its staff, its Officers, and the Representatives, are all doing their bit'. In the two months that was the time framework of Phillips' neglect (Dec-Jan), Patch was away from campus for at least four weeks – two weeks holidays, and two weeks attending the AUS Conference in Melbourne. One should also keep in mind Patch's other grave responsibility, his role as a student senator, a role into which he threw himself with an unquenchable zeal. On his own account, he had gone away and left the running of the SRC to others for at least half the period in question.

'Vice-President [Phillips] should have done a lot of work over the holidays', Patch wrote, 'preparing for the coming year, helping the various SRC officers, and assisting the President. He did none of this, never, at any time, offering to help or co-operate with me'. But Patch was absent for half the time Phillips could offer his cooperation. He expected Phillips to carry out duties he made it impossible to do – and apparently not take a holiday. As for cooperation, Patch openly swore off anything to do with reactionaries like Phillips and Co. Instead of being present to fulfil his duties as president, Patch pushed them onto someone else. For the organising of Orientation Week, which was the chief source of Patch's evidence against Phillips, he hived off his duties to Sarah Sheehan, who also attended the 1976 AUS Conference.

The Sydney University Delegation to the 1976 AUS Conference in Melbourne consisted extreme leftists closely connected with the running of the 1976 SRC, Angela Nanson (Welfare officer); Sarah Sheehan (former AUS Secretary); John Cozijn (Trainee Teachers); Richard Kuhn (SRC university government representative); Tony Press (former environment Officer) and David Patch (SRC President). Presumably, if Patch had taken two weeks holidays, one would have expected those less driven than him (the rest) to have taken more time off. Patch did not allow Phillips holidays and expected him to cooperate with people absent for much of the time. It is relevant to mention that H24 (1975) listed the Orientation Week directors as 'Hintze, Phillips, Patch and Rogers'. We must further note that Hintze accused Patch of being absent 'at the first four meetings of the Joint Orientation Week C'ttee which helped determine O-Week policy'. Patch did not reply to this accusation. Phillips was not the only one guilty of non-attendance at important meetings.

Patch began his refutation of Roger's charges by claiming he could not get a quorum together on 5 December 'to approve a 1976 budget and appoint an Orientation Week Convenor' because 'the right-wing boy-cotted the meeting'. But 5 December was surely not the only day he had to organise a quorum. A little consultation might have hit on a day when the 'right-wingers' could attend. Besides, a quorum depends on numbers, not on allegiances. Patch could have got up a quorum of his leftist mates to form a legitimate meeting. If he still lacked the numbers, the right-wing weren't the only ones to boycott the meeting. Then in contradiction, he said he had 'to hunt around' to find someone 'to accept the position of O-Week Convenor and organise Orientation Week'. It was obviously not necessary to have a meeting for that task. Why did he have to hunt around? The directors were already appointed. His first stop should have been his fellow directors, to whom he owed an apology for non-attendance.

He appeared, after all, to have no trouble contacting Phillips to ask him to be Convenor. Phillips said, 'he would think about it'. Mackinolty claimed he accepted. Rogers claimed Phillips refused. Sarah Sheehan, ap-pointed Acting President by Patch while he was on holidays, checked Phillips during Patch's holidays to see if he would take the job. Why didn't Patch pursue contact with Phillips if it was so vital? Or was he so impor-tant that his holidays could not be interrupted? Rogers claimed Phillips accepted 'on condition that it not be necessary for him to commence work until February'. Patch claimed Phillips accepted the position without conditions. Patch returned to Sydney 'around 25th January' to find the preparations for O-Week 'in chaos'. If it were true Phillips could not attend to O-Week preparations before February, then Patch logically would have found little progress. He would have known that because his lieutenant Sarah was in Melbourne with him. Whatever the case, Patch had his pretext to act. With only two weeks before the deadline to have O-Week activities organised, he sacked Phillips. That was on 27 January before Phillips, according to a friend and colleague, could be available for the job.

'I organised O-Week myself in the 2 weeks that remained', Patch boasted. 'Considering it normally takes 2 months I don't think things went too badly'. This time at least, he did not refer to himself in the third person. If it took two months to organise O-Week, and Patch had the overall authority of O-Week, it was poor organisation not to have had the preparations bedded down before he absented himself for four weeks and shunted his responsibilities onto a colleague. One could also question Sarah Sheehan's inaction as Acting President. The accusations about Phillips's inactivity as Vice-President were insubstantial apart from other considerations, as they were against Gary Osborne and Alan McIntosh. Rogers accused Patch's closest mates with neglect and non-appearance (for example, Angela Nanson, Irving Wallach and Angelo Rosas) to highlight the double standards. But, as I say, Patch had connived enough to have a pretext to get rid of Phillips.

It was a paradigm case of leftist manoeuvring, manipulation, and misprepresentation. It gave Patch the signatures for a petition based on a rarely, if ever, used provision of the SRC Constitution. As expected, Patch's far-left mates filled the positions vacated by the dismissal. He could now boast the SRC ran smoothly. He fervently hoped that 'the right-wing (don't be fooled when they call themselves "moderates") never get another foothold in the SRC'. But was Patch's coup too slick? Perhaps he showed the same hubris as Comrade Dave – with a thick crust of arrogance. Was it a case of taking a sledgehammer to crack a nut? As the editions of *Honi* rolled out, the suspicion arose that Patch was so damn tricky he even pissed off his colleagues.

The perpetually punchy Chips Mackinolty wrote a furious piece defending the girls of the editorial collective against the horrible right-wingers of the Democratic Club. He displayed his unique brand of logic by defending charges of bias against the collective's objective of promoting causes never appearing in the downtown rags. He denounced the slander that Jane and Faye (and Michael, of course) refused submissions that did not chime with their ideological views. 'The only overtly "political" article that had been rejected this year', he pointed out, 'has been by David Patch. This was because it was dull and boring and repetitive'. It was an achievement of the coup's leader that he could brown off a rigid leftie like Chips with his political prolixity.

The brilliance of the coup did not temper Michael Hintze's contempt for Patch, either. He came back with a blast against Patch's 'misinformed rave' (H8, 14 Apr). He again disputed Patch's financial figures, but the real thrust of the attack was on Patch's swollen arrogance. If Patch was (as he claimed) at work for the SRC for five hours a day, then what did he have to show for it? Hintze had already mentioned 'his failure to attend policy meetings of the Joint O-Week Committee'. Patch's 'record during O-Week' was evidence of his elitist stance. 'He flaunted [himself] at the Official Welcome and the Evening Students' Welcome', Hintze wrote. 'Yet at no stage did he get down to the nitty-gritty work that had to be done – stall staffing, leaflet distribution, gathering support for functions. I call such inaction elitism'. He repeated, 'I really do wish David would get on with the business of being SRC President and work for students and not himself'. Hintze surely had a point. What, indeed, did Patch have to show for his period as SRC President? The end of term two was approaching. The SRC elections were due in July. Electioneering would start well before that. The evidence was that Patch had spent most of his time deploying his strategy to bounce the right-wingers out of the SRC.

Patch did not reply. Unperturbed, he filled a page (H8) with a long, abusive account of the administration's warning they would call police onto the campus to deal with student violence. His piece was tricky legalistic Patch at his best. He spoke with contempt about Vice-Chancellor and the Chairman of the Academic Board Professor Ward, boasted of angry exchanges with them, and made out that their action was intimidatory, repressive, and stifling of dissent. He ended with warning those senile conservatives unwilling to 'change the system' that they would be resisted. Jane and her editorial collective supported Patch but were more explicit about the fundamental cause of student resistance. The administration 'upholds the University's function as an institution supporting and helping the capitalist economic system', and without student resistance, 'the present power structure in the University will instil capitalist ideology undisturbed'.

Far-left Craig Johnston took up the same refrain, characterising the administration's warnings about student violence as repressive, destructive of democracy, denial of rights and so on, and so on. The call went out to resist the intimidation. The intriguing part of Johnston's letter was his comment on the administration's shirtiness that 'the SRC [had] not made a submission on the report of the Academic Board's Committee on Examinations and Assessment, even though the SRC had received copies of the draft report' in 1975. This was a rather tenuous connection with the administration's warnings about student violence. It was not a tenuous connection with David Patch's responsibilities as SRC President. Surely the great defender of direct democracy and self-assessment would have exploited an official submission to the architects of student oppression. He was too busy advancing his elitist interests and kicking the democratically elected opposition out of the Students' Representative Council.

During this time, Tony Abbott settled into his room at St John's College, joined a footy team which required training twice a week, indulged in his favourite pastime of boozing with his mates, and eagerly took part in the campaigns got up by the Democratic Club. At that time, Tony Rogers was producing the *Democrat* for the Democratic Club. The *Democrat* was, according to Greg Sheridan, a modest weekly 'gestetnered newsletter printed on both sides'. No doubt, Abbott was busting to have a go at Patch and his far-left mates in the university's official student newspaper. And so, a historical moment, Tony Abbott's first public political intervention came in H9. Here is his letter in full in a tone and style that has changed little since 1976:

'The recent meeting, which supported a motion to give $300 of student funds to the ALP campaign, was a perversion of democracy. Although the motion was carried by a majority of nearly 100, a decision by 600 in a campus of nearly 20,000 can hardly purport to be active participation democracy.

'The actions of David Patch in initiating the move constitute a perversion of his position as President of the SRC. Surely the SRC should not take up a blatantly partisan political position. If it must enter wider politics, surely it should support all parties to the extent that each is supported by the student body. It is wrong for the SRC of ALL to support, to identify itself, with only one party, especially when that party is opposed by a considerable proportion of students.

'It is hard to understand the actions of Patch, which must only lead to the SRC falling further in the estimation of most. Patch should finally start to involve himself in obtaining a better deal for students on campus (which is, after all, the true function of the SRC), rather than in currying favour with the ALP. The ALP does not need Patch, the fundraiser, it has Khemlani. The ALP does not need Patch, the leader, it has Whitlam. Patch, the pseudo-socialist, the middle-class Marxist, whose delight is a cocktail party in exclusive Turramurra, seems intent on proving with student money that he really does want Labor preselection to further his own ambition.'

Tony Abbott was eighteen and four months when he submitted this balanced, well-written, carefully constructed letter. There is no loose phrasing, exaggeration or emotion that give the character of ranting to the ideological pieces of the left. He starts in a measured way detailing the facts of his case, draws damning conclusions, satirises Patch's political bias, and finishes with a personal poke. Noteworthy is the distinction Abbott makes between the satirical 'pseudo-socialist' (the pretend socialist) and the accurate middle-class Marxist. Even Patch's far-left mates recognised Patch for what he was – a middle-class Marxist snob. The editorial collective headed Tony's letter with 'PERVERSION'. I wonder whether the thought passed through their minds that they were enjoying the singular privilege of printing the first public utterance of a political player who objectified their most deep-seated political hatreds. Could they have imagined that that letter was the beginning of a long road of political torment for Australia's left, that they had taken part in a historical event?

In the meantime, David Patch had not finished eliminating the opposition. A little over a month later, his mate Garry Bennett, now Honorary Secretary-Treasurer, announced (H9, 21 Apr) that 'Section 12 of the SRC Regulations empowers the Honorary Secretary-Treasurer to dismiss from Council any Representative who fails to attend two consecutive meetings and does not give good cause for this seven days prior to the next meeting'. Because the non-attendance of some representatives prevented a quorum being formed for a meeting, and a meeting was necessary for urgent business, he had no choice but to use that power. He spent many words justifying his dismissal of the 'deadwood'. It so happened, he said, that most of the delinquents were those 'who supported the election of reactionaries to the various officer positions last year'. He listed nine representatives whom he dismissed forthwith. There are questionable points about Bennett's explanation for his action.

There were 29 members of the 1976 Council. Four had been kicked off, leaving 25. It appears half were necessary to form a quorum. Bennett named nine members who were dismissed. That left 16 members. But

Bennett said there were 18 left. He added, 'The quorum shall then be 9, easily obtainable by the dozen dependable members of Council'. But why the sackings if there were a dozen dependable (leftist) members? Patch could have formed a quorum from the 25 members, most of whom were on his side. Another aspect of the failure to form a quorum was that the responsibility lay on Patch's shoulders as SRC President. In a comparable organisation outside the university, the manager was responsible for ensuring the right staff attended crucial meetings. He had to use the organisational skills that got him to the position of manager: consultation, cooperation, fair dealing, and so on. His first resort was never job termination. The manager had to account for failing to organise essential business meetings, a failure that might have meant sacking. The truth is that Patch was never interested in consultation and cooperation with those who did not fall in behind him. Finally, Patch said (H6, 2 Apr) the affairs of the SRC were running smoothly without the four members he had sacked. Clearly, they weren't, or Patch was running a zero-sum game like the dedicated Marxist he was.

<hr>

THE FOLLOWING issue of *Honi* gave everyone a break from the sackings and the reconstitution of the SRC to satisfy Patch's ideological ambitions. The editorial collective produced a 24-page super-bumper edition entirely devoted to the apologia and promotion of homosexuality H10 (4 May). On the cover was a photo of two women in a passionate embrace under the headline 'How Dare You Presume I am a Heterosexual'. The emphasis was on the delights and power of lesbianism with as its target the corrupting influence of heterosexism in bourgeois capitalist society. The edition opened with an important 'communiqué'. It announced that 'at 4.23 a.m. on Monday, April 27, 1976, Gay liberation forces stormed

the offices of the well-known subversive news rag *Honi Soit* and com-
mandeered issue 10 for their own purposes. A number of heterosexuals
... were exterminated in the bloodbath'. The communiqué goes on to
say a few heterosexual pieces had escaped the 'faggot fires', but the gay
forces undertook to 'ruthlessly eliminate all heterosexual copy from future
issues'. Those forces further warned that 'this is just the beginning, we are
angry, proud gays on the warpath, and we are fucking pissed off with all
you liberal heterosexist deadshits who somehow think it's akin to making
a stand by being "tolerant"'. This was all very amusing, of course. Nevertheless, there was a chilling prophetic end to the communiqué:

'*Honi Soit* has fallen into our hands forever and one by one we will capture
all the other vital service of the heterosexist financial institutions, gun in
hand. Then our glorious millennium will begin, all heterosexuals being
painfully oppressed into oblivion.
Today *Honi Soit,* Tomorrow the world World!
World Homosexual Revolution! '

The homosexual edition covered as many aspects of homosexuality as
could be squeezed into 24 pages. It would be tedious and pointless to
attempt an adequate coverage. Gay ideology is now in such ascendance that
everyone knows the fundamental dogma. It is pertinent, however, given
the royal commission that focused on clerical sexual abuse of minors to
mention one article. The article by Martin Smith has the title, 'Everyone is
Naughty'. The subheading is 'Literature and Gay Expression'. The article
opens:

'PEDERASTY – boys are encouraged to read about it but not to try it.
WHY? While the world's pre-puberty boys and, to a lesser degree, male
teenagers have, for countless years, been brought up on a literary diet of
pederasty (bluntly, love of youth. But what's the word for a youth who

loves an older male? Hero worship?), if any attempt is made to turn fantasy (fantasy resulting from reading) into fact then both people involved, the youth and the older male, are in for a rude awakening. What is permitted between the covers of classics is not right in reality, at least, that's the ruling of society, and stringently enforced by those whose job it is to see rulings of society are abided by – police and judges. In passing, take a glance at TV, it is obvious the relationship between young Will and Dr Smith in 'Lost in Space', is more than filial. There are other small and large screen examples one could write about, but in this feature we will be looking at literary only.'

For a start, pederasty is not just love of youth. It is the love of youth involving sexual relations. Smith fills a page and a half of (allegedly) pederastic relationships drawn from classic works of literature. As an example, he claimed the relationships in Charles Dickens's novels between David Copperfield and Mr Wickfield (David Copperfield), Mr Brownlow and Oliver Twist (Oliver Twist), and Richard Carson and John Jarndyce (Bleak House) were all pederastic. In brief, any relationship between an older man and a boy or young man that involved hero-worship or close friendship was, according to Martin Smith, a pederastic relationship in which sexual relations implicitly took place – outside the novel's text. Smith ended his long article thus:

'Brought up on a diet of such literature, is it no wonder young boys find it natural to build up heroes among the older males they know? In this feature, I have not argued the rights or wrongs of pederasty but merely attempted to show that, as far as the writers of children's literature are concerned, strong emotional relationships between boys and men are acceptable.'

I have a two-part reply. First, Smith's readings are false if you accept the empirical evidence that no sane person has ever offered such a preposterous interpretation. Pederasty is read into the text for ideological purposes. Second, having been a boy, I feel qualified to talk about what hero worship means for most boys. Admiration and emulation of older males of proven bravery and athletic ability, especially those protective of the weak, is hard-wired in boys. The ancient code of Chivalry encapsulates those ideals and more. As a 13-year-old in the first year of secondary school, I remember how most boys in my class idolised the champions in the school's first football team. The thought of having sex with them, if it were ever suggested to us and we could think in those terms, would have made us throw up. It is unnecessary to develop this reply. The crucial point is that Martin Smith's purpose was to normalise pederasty as part of the Marxist campaign to overthrow the sexual norms and relations of Western Society. It is significant that Smith's article appeared in *Honi Soit* around the same time as Richard Neville's sympathetic interview on the ABC with two paedophiles.

During this time, the by-election to replace former Arts representatives Jeff Phillips and Frank Lane-Mullins took place. A total of 85 votes was received. Far-left Garry Bennett was elected with 40 votes, and Steve Lewis with 22 votes which was the right outcome for Patch, but on democratic principles, made the election a total farce. Of interest was that Barbara Ramjan was elected unopposed as Arts Women's Representative. Barbara was on her way, backed, no doubt, by her experienced mentor, the redoubtable David Patch. This was just a warm-up because the nominations would shortly be called for the 49th SRC, with voting in late July.

Jack Goodacre (Science III) complained (H11, 8 Jun) that the previous *Honi* was 'the worst I have read in three years of University'. Because the homosexual population of the university was 'less than 5%', most students would have had no interest. That conclusion does not follow. He should have offered testable evidence for his claim. He was on firmer ground when he said *Honi* should spend its $20,000 grant on subjects that had wider appeal. If the editorial collective catered for the majority, he added, '*Honi Soit* will be called *Honi Soit* and not Honi Shit'. With its shaky arguments, the editors would not let Goodacre's letter pass. Jean Rhodes, 'saddened' by Goodacre's criticism, justifiably nailed him for his faulty logic. On that point, she was right. The shameless bias, the narrow point of view, and the political promotion were another issue. Tony Abbott took them up in his second public letter (12A, 22 Jun). The editors gave it the heading 'OUR FIRST POISON PEN LETTER'. Here's the letter in full:

'The derisive and scornful comment ['Kritical Korn'] with which you prefaced the letter of Jack Goodacre is typical of *Honi Soit*'s attitude towards anyone who refuses to conform to your stereotype of the trendy radical student. While not necessarily wishing to support his figure of 5% being homosexuals, I wonder whether any more than a microscopic minority really sympathises with *Honi*'s unthinking and ritualistic rejection of anything even remotely 'normal'. *Honi*'s objectivity is on a par with that of the Murdoch press it regularly lambasts. The political economy articles in last week's issue opened with nice-sounding and broadminded phrases about giving 'both sides equal representation' only to degenerate into an attack on professors Hogan and Simkin.

The blatant bias evident throughout the year 'climaxed' with the Homo *Honi* of several weeks ago. Without making any comments on homosexuality as such, I merely say that if Mr Harrison ['a gay Christian'] knew his Christianity as well as he would have us believe, he would realise that it is quite possible to hate the sin and love the sinner. By my somewhat less than wholehearted support for homosexuality, I am, of course, displaying my seduction by the evil establishment and my unnatural conformity to the unreal concepts of the past. In fact, *Honi* would no doubt have me believe that I am some sort of queer. The entire 'Homo Honi' was appallingly unfunny. The choice of the Queen as 'Honigirl' showed *Honi*'s total insensitivity, although 'Queen' was an apt description of the contents.

However, ignoring the relative virtues of homosexuality, with what justification did *Honi* devote a whole issue to it? Why should one pressure group be so privileged ahead of all the others? If the rationale behind the decision was thrust home to its logical conclusion, then issues should be devoted to every group of crackpots on campus. Yet again, the insidious control of student politics by a group of committed ideologues is manifest. One wonders what they hope to achieve by their blind support for subversive trendy or way-out ideas. They must certainly succeed in further alienating the bulk of students.'

The aggression had gone up a few notches, though remaining controlled. Abbott's well-known wit, irony and sarcasm were already developed in the 18-year-old. His verbal thrusts, pokes and prods infuriated his political adversaries. There was a good reason he had a swipe at *Honi* and its coverage of the political economy issue. In June, PE Movement militants, with the unwavering support of *Honi*, were gearing up for a full-on assault on those standing in the way of establishing a separate Political Economy Department. The first attempt in the early issues of *Honi* had petered out. By April, the Movement had regrouped to begin a period of skirmishing. Readers of *Honi* might have thought something was brewing because the editorial collective was suddenly buzzing in reaction to the Vice-Chancellor's warning he would call in the police if students resorted to 'disruption' on the campus.

Six weeks later, *Honi* came up with another bumper PE issue that risked causing casualties of boredom on campus (H11, 8 June). Far-left Economics Representative Martin Hirst announced in an 'open letter to all students' the time was up for the Vice-Chancellor (H12, 15 Jun). Williams must approve the third and fourth-year courses in political economy pronto. Hirst reminded the Vice-Chancellor that his procrastination of the previous year had culminated in the occupation of his office. 'Unless students take this into their own hands this year', he warned, 'we may not...have

[3rd-year PE] next year. Can we afford the time to let the VC procrastinate?' He urged students to attend 'a front lawn meeting on Wednesday, 6 June, to call on the VC to split the Department of Economics and let discussion of 3rd year Political Economy courses go on in an atmosphere of harmony, not conflict'. As it turned out, the last thing on Hirst's mind was harmony.

On Wednesday, 7 July, around 100 students angered and frustrated 'over the fucking around that this administration has done in relation to the [political economy] unit' marched from their front lawn meeting to the Vice-Chancellor's office. There they 'spontaneously' pushed their way in and occupied the Registrar's office and the vestibule. The Australian reported that the students 'broke down a grille door blocking the stairs to the administration offices [and] once inside, they forced a door lock and entered the office of the Registrar, Dr K. W. Knight. Six staff members watching the demonstration from the hall were asked to leave and, when they did not, were bustled down the stairs'. *The Sydney Morning Herald* added that later in the day, the radicals painted 'slogans ... over the university's historic stone cottage at Hunters Hill ... and the home of the Vice-Chancellor, Professor Bruce Williams'.

The students claimed (H11A, 7 July) the 'damage to property was still very limited (1 metal grille, 2 locks broken, 3 panels knocked in)'. I suppose that's limited compared to earlier occupations when the offices were trashed and set alight. The *Australian* also reported that the Vice-Chancellor said 'in a statement later, he had made it clear to the students before the meeting that he would publish it as soon as he made a decision. "By their violence, the people involved have cast a very bad light on the movement for political economy and raised grave doubts about the integrity of members of that movement"'. Indeed.

The front page of H11A roared the collective's outrage under the headline 'The VC Defies Academic Board and Suspends Three Students'. Those students were Martin Hirst, Rod O'Donnell and Lance Baker. They were charged with 'assaulting a member of staff' and 'impeding members of staff in their proper pursuits'. No surprise that the Vice-Chancellor announced 'there would be no autonomous Political Economy Unit'. This, said the indignant editorial collective, was 'a double-barrel attack [on] Political Economy and anyone trying to reform this University'. Charges of injustice, authoritarianism, and victimisation would flow without letup in the coming weeks. Student support for the Vice-Chancellor was not lacking. The editorial collective was decent enough to print some dissenting letters.

Jenny K. (Arts II) wondered, 'just how much longer do we have to tolerate the irresponsible actions of the Political Economy mob? Just how much do we have to take from this radical "show off" minority? 200 people are agitating for a Political Economy Dept. There are 17,500 students attending Sydney University. Must we all get lumped into the same bucket of shit? Just who gave those dickheads the right to kick down the VC's door?' V. Schabinsky BSC on the same page wrote that 'the decision by the Vice-Chancellor has the support of the bulk of the university, both staff and students, and under NO circumstances should he submit to ignorant minority pressure groups with nothing better to do than to disrupt lectures and cause trouble'. But it took Tony Abbott in his third public intervention to analyse the state of play and outline objections a thoughtful conservative would have to introducing political economy in the Department of Economics:

'Recently we have once again been treated to hysterical PE agitations. For a relative newcomer to this campus the sight of more than 100 supposedly intelligent students stomping around the place like zombies, is slightly ludicrous. The mechanical chants of 'Strike, Strike, Williams out' reveal the mindlessness with which many people take up the 'cause'. But what is all the fuss about? PE claims the VC has overruled Academic Board recommendations. In fact, of the 27 staff members of the Dept. of Economics, only 2 felt that setting up of a unit of PE would definitely ease tension. 6 felt it may improve the situation, while 17 said it would definitely not help. Since such a unit already exists in all but name, why the need for violent demonstrations? Since the 'traditional' course is far more relevant to a mixed capitalist society, I feel the contemplated 'unit of PE should be within the Depts of Government or General Philosophy rather than that of economics.

'It seems that there has been a long history in this university of student discontent over one issue or another. As moratorium faded, conveniently, PE arose phoenix-like from the ashes. It appears that some elements, unaware that attending uni is a privilege denied to many, have a vested interest in maintaining unrest at as high a level as possible. These professional students – agitators of the left – criticise the social order, not to improve it, but to destroy it. Before supporting them or their causes, consider carefully whether you can afford the destruction of contemporary principles and the society they uphold.'

Abbott was right to say political economy belonged in the Department of Government or General Philosophy. Since Marxism rests on the materialist dialectic borrowed substantially from Hegelian metaphysics, political economy belonged in the Department of General Philosophy, where the 'dialectic' could be analysed, rather than in a department that prepared students for work in Australia's economic, social and political conditions. It was an astounding, high-level critique from a student in his first year of university.

The issue of political economy raged on with the same tedious repetition of the radicals' case supported by their abuse. The Vice-Chancellor would continue to outrage them by refusing to give in. Bravo. But I will leave the close-hand combat and return to the machinations of the SRC under the leadership of the scheming David Patch, whose regime was coming to an end. Like the Borgia court, Patch's junta had, by this time, become entangled in its Machiavellian manoeuvres to eliminate its enemies. Already in April, Warren Gardiner, Patch's replacement SRC Vice-President, found it necessary to defend the SRC's 'El Presidente' against the charge of being the grand manipulator of the right-wing purge. It was a wobbly unsure defence, at which the conservatives scoffed. Valdis Berzins (Arts III) thrashed Patch and his junta (H12A, 22 Jun).

The 'putsch', he said, eliminated 16 of the 29 elected members of the 48th SRC by the 'perverted use of a left-constructed Constitution', leaving the junta with 'a dictatorial stranglehold on the Council and its monies'. If student democracy could be so easily perverted, he asked, what hope was there for the future? SRC monies would continue to flow into the pockets of 'radical movements' instead of going to 'essential campus and student services'. He demanded that 'all politics on campus be confined to the political clubs ... which are allocated sufficient grants to finance their favourite minority causes'. He finished by saying that 'minutes and financial statements of the SRC should be a regular feature of the *Honi Soit* so its members, over 14,000 students, can keep a tab on its operations'. Patch would not allow such scurrilousness go unanswered.

He wrote (H14, 29 Jun) that Berzins' accusations were 'a totally unwarranted and unscrupulous mass of distortions, clearly written by someone with a highly conservative perspective'. The charges issued exclusively from the far-right 'who oppose myself and the other progressive people now on the SRC for reasons that are clearly political in nature ... Not a single allegation of improper practices has been proved, nor is there any foundation for such allegations'. Those sacked were sacked because they weren't doing their jobs. Yet Patch's faction had eliminated all elected opposition. Patch was not without support. The feverish far-left Martin Hirst rushed to support his dear leader (H14, 29 June). 'What the fuck is Valdis Berzins talking about?' he exclaimed. 'The present SRC has done a lot of shit-work for students, especially since it became "left-wing"'. Then in an almost unbelievable ingenuousness, he listed some of those far-left campaigns (e.g.

democratisation, political economy) whose aim was 'a decent education for everybody, free from financial hassle and in the service of and for people'. Was Hirst so brainwashed he could not see it was precisely those campaigns the conservative criticised?

In the same issue, John Cozijn expressed vigorous support for the 'rightful and constitutional sacking of right-wing extremists from Council' but went on to pursue the inconvenient logic of the direct democracy Patch espoused. If the SRC was no more than 'the internal wranglings of 28 "representatives" and the actions of the President between meetings', he wrote, 'then the SRC is no more democratic than our illustrious, bourgeois Parliament'. A true democracy is an 'open-committee system, whereby the functions of the SRC are carried out by committees open to ALL students in areas'. If the SRC were to be a true democracy, it would 'restructure, the official bureaucratic (President's and Council's) functions of the SRC in favour of the open-committee system, which directly involves students without the mystification of elections, executives and councils'. Cozijn finished by criticising the 'continued predominance of Presidential decision-making rather than the devolution of power to the real centre of SRC activity, the open-committees'. Patch did not comment.

Criticism of *Honi* continued. T.J. Gates wondered why nobody seemed to complain about the 'uninterrupted stream of bull-shit to which we've become accustomed in "*Honi*"'. He was sick to death of 'the same ideological crap and trivia [produced] by a bunch of humourless demagogues who insist on pursuing a narrow, bigoted section viewpoint which is piss-weak entertainment, uninformative shit and a complete waste of time'. Why could *Honi* not commission 'guest writers'? There were surely enough weirdos on campus to scribble something entertaining. Patch and the editorial collective remained silent. Perhaps El Presidente had more important things on his mind.

Around this time, 'two spirited young men' set out one evening with posters, a brush and a bucket of glue (H11A). They had pasted a poster about a planned university-wide strike on the notice board in Science Road when a late model Holden skidded to a stop in front of them. One of the three men inside jumped out and attempted to relieve David Patch of his bucket of glue. Patch and the grey security man grappled with each other until Patch 'demanded that the men identify themselves, informing them...he was a fellow of the University Senate'. You've got to laugh. Here's the dear leader of the SRC junta identifying himself as a member of the university's administration, which bourgeois body he was doing his best to subvert. Patch kept the bucket, and the security men left.

Skirmishes between the far left and the conservatives continued. When the editorial collective announced (H11A, 8 Jun) that the General Elections for Sydney University's 49th Students' Representative Council and the editor of *Honi Soit* would take place between 27 and 29 July, the action took itself into the highways and byways of campus. The editorial collective seemed to relish announcing the coming contest. 'It's that time of year again folks', they wrote, '[when] the campus erupts with chalking [and] opposing factions improve each other's slogans'. 'Chalking' was the revered SU tradition of scrawling political messages in chalk over whatever surface came to hand. Extreme far-left John Cozijn secured space in *Honi* to whinge about the chalkings.

He wasn't promoting his policies, he assured the *Honi* collective (H11A), but replying 'to some of the scurrilous slander and misrepresentations that have appeared in chalkings around campus'. He objected to being called a '"Colonel in the KGB' a supporter of the "Moscow line", a "professional Communist Party organiser" sent to campus to gain "agitation training". Nor do I "fuck dogs", etc. Nor does left-wing politics on this campus, despite what the Democratic Club and Valdis Berzins would have us believe, follow some conspiratorial dynamic of manipulation and secrecy'. He held members of the hated Democratic Club responsible for the slander, people infected by some 'brand of neo-fascism' reflecting 'a deep-seated paranoia' that saw anyone left of [Catholic] B.A. Santamaria as ... agents of Russian Communism'. He appealed to all political actors to defend their policies 'in an open and honest manner' and not to sink 'to the level of clandestine machination'. His opponents surely wondered whether he was not speaking from the moon.

As nominations were to be submitted by 16 July, the candidates for the SRC presidency, *Honi* editor, and faculty representatives were announced in H17A (20 Jul). Those for the presidency split into conservatives and various shades of the far left with the expected policies. The conservatives were Valdis Berzins, Jeff Phillips, and Tony Rogers. Their policies were similar. They highlighted the flagrant undemocratic action of the Patch regime as an example of what the student body would get if they elected candidates of the far left. They wanted the SRC to work as a true democracy that represented all students' interests instead of a minority pursuing their narrow political aims. There would be far more responsible financial management, and they would seek a cooperative relationship with the university's administration, which was the traditional role of the Students' Representative Council. They also undertook to keep and strengthen the existing student services.

The other four candidates included two of the far left, John Cozijn and David Patch, one left of centre, Peter Mitch, who until then had not featured in student politics, and Stephen Scholem, who thought the others were a pack of useless bastards and should be ignored. He need not be considered. With John Cozijn and David Patch, it was more of the same. Cozijn distinguished himself from Patch by following the logic of the hard left to its impossible bitter end. His extreme left program of open committees and the destruction of any and all constituted authority would have collapsed the SRC within months. Patch, nominated by the permanently feverish Martin Hirst, and seconded by Barbara Ramjan, bored the *Honi* reader with a long list of his accomplishments and his unchanged political goals whose attempted implementation in 1976 had been a complete failure. Peter Byrnes proclaimed a pox on both houses who, he charged, were only interested in their own political goals.

The 1976 SRC had been a 'ridiculous circus', Byrnes wrote. 'The radical left has been singularly unsuccessful in gaining real reform in the faculties ... They have "activated" themselves over Political Economy, but even on that issue, broken doors and windows have been the main accomplishment'. On the other hand, the far right 'adopted a policy of blind negativism and obstructionism'. They did not represent the students and were given to 'the worn-out tirades of fortunately discredited national morons such as [Catholic] Gair and Santamaria'. Byrnes, who boasted he was beholden to nobody, would change all that. He promised to oversee the finances, remedy 'the antiquated system of exams and staff control in various Arts Departments', pressure the state government to 'curtail the near-autocratic powers of the Vice-Chancellor', and support the 'establishment of a unit of Political Economy'. It must have occurred to Patch he hadn't much to change there. As it turned out, Byrnes convinced enough students to vote him into the SRC presidency. It remained for the tangle of writhing scheming worms to work out how best to manipulate him.

It might have been no surprise to see Abbott have a go. He put himself forward for one of the two positions for Representative Economics Men. In contrast to the *curriculum vitae* of some candidates, Abbott could only list 'enthusiastic member of Rugby Club'. His 'Policy Statement' in full:

'Comrades, in seeking your support, I offer two points for your consideration: - By section 5 of the SRC constitution, 'the object of the Council shall be to promote the interest and maintain the traditions of the University and student body'. – This SRC has promoted nothing but division among the students, and by its sackings and ballot-riggings, maintained only itself in office. The present left-wing SRC, by its encouragement and support for various trendy causes has besmirched the image of all students. Because they have no significant effect, I strenuously oppose the granting of student money to off-campus activities. The money can be far better spent on tangible benefits for students. More campus-wide social functions could be organised by the SRC, and faculty societies and clubs could receive greater financial [support]. More telephones and extended information services on jobs, for instance, could be provided. One important area to which I would devote attention is the setting up of effective machinery for consultation between the administration and the SRC. Lack of such machinery is partly responsible for the PE row. This dispute, which has violently racked the university for several years, could have been avoided. Above all, I will work for achieving a consensus among students.'

This is a conservative statement. In contrast to the far left who think state and society are to begin over again each day, Tony Abbott looked back over the history of the establishment of Sydney University and the particular traditions, conventions and institutions that had grown over the years. These things gave it its character. Tony wanted to conserve that character. Essential was the close cooperation between the administration and the students. That cooperation had prevailed until a small minority were brainwashed into thinking nothing of the past was worth conserving. He then provided the detail of his program within that conservative framework. His primary opponent was Stephen Rixon, who aimed to pull down the achievements of the past and replace it with something of his own imagining. He was in the Patch camp. He was elected with Abbott.

Abbott was not the only one to put himself forward for the first time. Barbara Ramjan entered the fray. She was on a joint ticket with far-left Mary Bolt and Faye Westwood for the three Arts Women Full-Time representative positions. Their policy statement was merely a repetition of the Patchian democratic fantasy with special attention given to female students who 'have always held a unique position as a group'. The statement was modest without the heat and flint of such as the feverish Martin

Hirst. Indeed, Hirst had held himself aside from the faculty representative positions. Instead, he had his eye on the *Honi* editorship. He and Marian Kearney were one of four groups who offered their services.

From their submission, you would think them sensible, moderate, and willing to produce a newspaper balanced in politics and catering to the broad interest of the student body. They promised *Honi* would be a 'forum for all student opinion, and not a propaganda sheet for any one group or clique ... would not be apolitical, but it would be open. It would be critical and questioning without being dogmatic or doctrinaire'. What? Is this the eye-rolling slavering fanatic who barged his way into the administrative block, bashed down a door, broke a couple of locks and scared the staff witless before pushing them out of the building? Indeed, it was. Hirst and Kearney devoted more than half of their submission to telling *Honi* readers how clever and professional they were. It worked. They bagged *Honi* for 1977. Time would tell how well they lived up to their spiel.

Barbara Ramjan missed out, but her colleagues Mary Bolt and Faye Westwood got up. Barbara would be compensated in the election for SRC Officers, scoring the Welfare Officer's position – to her delight, as her activities testified. Patch's coddling tutelage had borne ripe fruit. Far-left Garry Bennett grabbed one of the two Arts Men Full-Time representative positions, with moderate leftist Damian Furlong taking the other spot. The election results showed the far left had again triumphed. There would be no need for a Patchian intervention to get rid of the elected undesirables. Added to the hard-left triumph was Patch's re-election to the Senate, the position he cherished most – and held the most authority and prestige. Abbott had also put himself forward for one of the three Senate positions, but in vain – to Patch's gloating thirty-five years later. The other two Senate positions went to the hard left. The triumph was a clear signal to the conservatives to review their tactics. When it came to tactics, the far left steamrolled the conservatives every time. Would Abbott make a difference?

The final election for the year on 21 October was for the delegation to the Australian Union of Students (AUS) Annual Conference in Melbourne in January 1977. The delegation consisted of the local AUS secretary plus four elected delegates. Candidates had to submit a policy statement. Chris Mackinolty, now parading as Electoral Officer, urge all students to vote and to 'read carefully' the policy statements, meaning those of the far right. Despite the far left's victory in the SRC and Senate elections, the *Honi* collective found it necessary to back Mackinolty's exhortation by printing Local AUS Secretary Steve Bolt's dire warning about the far-right subversives who were (allegedly) formulating sinister plans to blow it all up. In a piece matching Patch's prolixity, Bolt wrote, 'the existence of AUS is being threatened'. It's happened before, but 'the current attacks are much better organised, and thus much more serious'. The right-wing plan was to bring about the secession of individual campuses from AUS. The press, particularly *The Australian*, were running 'AUS bashing' pieces that were 'a mixture of lies, misrepresentations and totally unsubstantiated accusations against AUS and individuals within AUS'. It was a preposterous lie that AUS was 'an organisation of highly trained political agitators who spend their lives trying to brainwash "ordinary students"'.

Leading the push, said Bolt, was 'right-wing Melbourne Uni SRC president Michael Danby'. His moves had failed, but he would strike again with help from his far-right mates at Sydney University. He named 'a petition (yes, Frank Lane-Mullins is around again) against compulsory payment of SRC and AUS fees'. This was nothing but a 'not too subtly disguised ... petition against compulsory unionism'. Voluntary unionism would 'destroy both the SRC and AUS because both bodies cannot exist without compulsory fees'. The way to defeat the sinister hard right was for all students to avail themselves of AUS's democratic processes. 'The democratic structures are there', he said. 'The way to improve AUS (and the SRC) is not to destroy it, but to become more active in it'. Tony Abbott, Valdis Berzins and Greg San Miguel, who submitted their candidatures and policy statements (H25), had grave doubts about CPA Steve Bolt's ideas on democracy.

Those in the Sydney University's delegation to the AUS conference must represent all students, Berzins said in his policy statement. The previous year's delegation was anything but representative consisting of 'well-known members of the Communist Party of Australia (i.e. Cozijn, Press and Sheehan) along with fellow ideological travellers, Angela Nanson and Rick Kuhn'. CPA members, including SU's very own Sarah Sheehan, dominated the AUS executive. Abbotsleigh girl had come from Comrade Dave's tutelage to scaling the heights of student radicalism. It was deplorable, wrote Berzins, that the two main parties (Liberal and Labor) 'had no influence at all'. As a member of the Liberal Party, Berzins would promote 'issues genuinely of the centre and of progressive reform'. Greg San Miguel enunciated a similar platform charging that the present AUS was unrepresentative and squandering money on 'idiotic non-representative activities'. He would ensure proper financial management. But it was left to Tony Abbott to press home the conservatives' position in his none-too-subtle policy statement:

'In recent years AUS has been little more than a front for undemocratic subversion. This year AUS was the small-m mastermind of the idiotic 'Smash Rockefeller' campaign and is influential in arranging 'spontaneous rage' against the Governor-General. AUS has consistently supported world-wide terror, notably the Palestine Liberation Organisation. This support for the PLO contradicts the stated wishes of the majority of Australian students and is indicative of what AUS really thinks of democracy.

'AUS will never gather student support, nor will it ever be democratic while its bureaucracy is controlled by communists. These elements exploit AUS finance for their own sordid political ends, merely fobbing off students with limited welfare schemes. The present AUS hierarchy is not interested in the real needs of students and never will be. The allocation of only $1000 to the TEAS [Tertiary Education Assistance Scheme] campaign is proof of this.

'This laughable situation is the sad result of the unshakeable apathy of most students. Last year only 200 voted in AUS elections at Sydney [University]. To reform AUS and to ensure its dedication to the interests of students and not to a mythical communist Utopia, please vote in these elections.

'Moreover, to substantially undermine the extremism of AUS, it is essential that delegates be proven anti-communists. Nothing will be achieved by the election of delegates lacking the commitment and stuffing to fight extremism. On these grounds, I commend my candidacy to you. If elected conference delegate,

'I will strive

- to dissociate AUS from the lunatic left.
- to channel all AUS funds into welfare.
- to expand AUS travel and insurance
- to investigate AUS interest-free loans to students.
- apart from that, I wouldn't mind a trip to Melbourne.'

Abbott again showed his forthrightness, even to the point of hinting at some irregularity in AUS loans dealing and making fun of the whole AUS enterprise. Most students would see his quip about a free trip to Melbourne for what it was – a bit of fun. It would be used against him for the next forty years. Note that all three conservatives did not mention a plan to introduce voluntary membership of AUS.

If the conservatives repeated their platform for membership of the AUS delegation, the far left served up the same dish stale with age and repetition. They were Barbara Ramjan and Mary Bolt jointly, Anne Talve, Garry Bennett and Steve Lewis jointly, and David Patch. There was little difference in their policy statements – the far left's rhetoric about the democratisation of everything mixed with undigested Marxist ideas about bourgeois society and 'the oppression and exploitation of women, migrants, blacks, [and] homosexuals'. They would resist the 'political right's cynical attempts to 'depoliticise' the AUS, which was a 'smokescreen ... to hide their real intentions of rendering AUS ineffectual'.

As it turned out, the four elected included two on the far left and two on the right, which was somewhat surprising given the far left's dominance in the other two elections. Perhaps more surprising (and dismaying) was Tony Abbott's election. What an outrage that a far-right first-year student was elected to represent the student body at such an important political happening. By this time, the left hated Abbott's guts. It was bad enough that he resisted the immovable campus hegemony of the far left. It was intolerable he remained undaunted by the bullying of the leftist heavies. But it was beyond all established limits that the rebel could articulate the conservative vision, tear apart the ideology of the far left, and satirise and make ridiculous those in the far left's frontline. In 1976, no student writing in *Honi* could better Abbott's style and articulation. The first effort to destroy him came in the last issue of *Honi* (H27, 26 Oct).

In a sloppy, poorly argued letter, Abbott's fellow economics representatives, far-left Steve Rixon and Debbie Mitchell, tried to prove that Abbott 'misrepresented his position as Economics Men Rep and has consistently run counter to the platform on which he was elected'. The first item of inconsistency was that while Abbott claimed the SRC promoted 'nothing but divisions among the students, [he] circulat[ed] a petition aimed at smashing the SRC and AUS ... [and] stood for the SRC, and stood as a delegate to the AUS Conference'. Presumably, Abbott was inconsistent in accusing the SRC of creating division, while his 'actions' (allegedly) created division in the SRC and AUS. There's no inconsistency in charging the left-dominated SRC with causing division by locking out all those in disagreement but at the same time taking action to reform the SRC and AUS so that both bodies represented all students. That was always his stated purpose. Even if he promoted a policy of voluntary unionism, he was still not inconsistent in his actions. Rixon and Mitchell's conclusion that he used his position to misrepresent the SRC does not follow. Indeed, there is no demonstrated connection. If there was any misrepresentation, it was by Rixon and Mitchell.

Rixon and Mitchell ran several other dodgy arguments to show Abbott's inconsistency and misrepresentation of the SRC, but it is unnecessary to rehearse them, the point having been adequately made. They were a coarse prelude to the central action which was the formal censure of Abbott instigated by none other than budding lawyer Patch. He moved a censure motion got up by him and Cozijn at a meeting of the SRC:

'MOTION: That the SRC censure Tony Abbott, an Economics Men Representative, who has been circulating a petition seeking to have the SRC fee not collected by the University, contrary to the interests of students.'

'The motion was carried by the narrowest of margins 11 votes to 10. Patch later treated *Honi* readers to another tedious explanation which he termed 'arguments in favour of a censure motion'. They included the same wobbly arguments as the Rixon/Mitchell effort and though more clearly expressed, hardly stood up better. The essentials are in the following:

'The censure motion was moved in order to bring to the attention of all members of the SRC to the actions of the Economics Men representative in circulating a petition aimed, ultimately at destroying AUS, and misrepresenting the SRC in informing a television interviewer that he was representing the SRC with the petition.

'Arguments by Abbott that the motion was merely an example of the political victimisation that many right-wingers often shout about, were merely weak attempts to gloss over the fact that Abbott is part of a concerted right-wing effort to destroy AUS. Having found it impossible to gain control democratically of AUS, these people have set about a campaign to emasculate one of the most active unions in Australia...

'At the SRC meeting in question, the opinion was expressed that, due to the opposition by Abbott to all AUS services and activities and to Political Economy he was incapable of representing the true interests of students. In view of this fact, the other Economics representatives said they would begin a campaign to inform students of Abbott's real position and, if enough opposition to him was expressed, that moves would be made to have him recalled. Such an action would only occur after this opposition was expressed by a large number of students.

'The SRC is the representative of AUS on campus. Attacks on either constitute an attack on both and are a direct affront to the intelligence and an attack on the interests of all students. In view of this, it was seen as a necessary move to publicise Abbott's position and to enforce the policy stand of the SRC in favour of an active students' union and against attempts by DLP ideologues to smash anything they can't control.'

Abbott's reply was succinct and covered the pertinent points of Patch's explanation:

'I stand condemned by resident communist Cozijn and self-styled Laborite Patch apparently on two grounds.

'Cozijn alleges that on the day of the TEAS Strike I told the press I represented the SU Students' Representative Council. In fact, I merely mentioned that I am SRC Economics Rep. If the press inferred that I spoke for the SRC, their credulity equals Cozijn's malice.

'Patch claims my taking up a petition calling for voluntary SRC fees is an attempt to destroy the SRC. On the contrary, it calls the present regime to account. They have squandered money secure in the unshakeable apathy of students. If membership is voluntary, most students would still join for the undoubted benefits the SRC confers. Moreover, voluntary membership ensures a far higher percentage would actually vote.

'My intention is the ongoing reform for which I was elected. Was Patch elected to sack his opponents?

'The SRC voted to censure me 11/10. When I refused to resign, Steve Rix (Economics Men) and Debbie Mitchell (Economics Women), indicated they would circulate a petition demanding my removal. Of these two worthies, one was elected unopposed, and the other trailed me when the poll was declared—so much for the people's choice.

'Why are they so anxious to remove me? They have a huge majority on Council. Are they frightened of what I may do or say?

'My only crime is political opposition to the Cozijn/Patch junta. The elimination of opposition is expected of communists. For how long will this be tolerated by students?'

Abbott rightly highlighted Patch's penchant for manipulating constitutional processes to eliminate his opponents. What he does not mention is Patch's sectarian allusions in his reference to the DLP – read Catholic. Nor does he address Patch's incoherent discussion of the AUS fee, which takes up almost a third of his explanation. 'Demands to end the automatic collection of the AUS fee', Patch wrote, 'can be seen as the patently ridiculous notions they are when the facts are examined'. The 'facts' are first that the fee is a measly $2.50 paid by the student for AUS services. The remaining facts are the '$100 Miscellaneous Allowances' the student gets to 'cover compulsory fees' and 'other compulsory fees such as the Union and Sports Union fees' of $40.

Patch's argument seems to be that because the AUS fee of $2.50 is small and virtually subsidised by the government, and the Sports fee provided many you-beaut bargain benefits, the $2.50 is of no account. The students should be grateful it was not more. The conclusion does not follow, and more to the point, it had nothing to do with Abbott's contention about the misuse of the fee, which totalled around an enormous $750,000 in the hands of the radicals. That amount of money was the motivation for some tricky self-serving reasoning.

Patch's engineering of an SRC censure of Abbott was unprecedented. Let's get clear on what's going on here. A 19-year-old student at the end of his first year at Sydney University was thought so inimical, so dangerous, to the radical cause that the leftist elites did their best to rub him out. You could call it unfair, unjust, and bullying. In essence, it was a recognition that a powerful conservative force had arrived on campus, a force that represented around 1,500 students from the same background (North Shore private schools). The attempt to destroy Tony Abbott would be unrelenting and employ whatever tactic outside the reach of the law.

Chapter 8

The 1977 AUS Conference and other violence

ALTHOUGH THE far left ended 1976 in control of the Students' Representative Council, the year had not been an unalloyed success. For a start, it was not as if they triumphed because of their electoral appeal. Students didn't have to vote. And most didn't. The cynical elimination of elected representatives was a turn-off. Why vote when the result was subjected to political manipulation? An embarrassing minority of students propped up the radicals' triumph. The election of two conservatives to attend the AUS Conference indicated a Tony Abbott effect.

The quality of *Honi Soit* had deteriorated. The paper was scrappy, depending much on outside articles. The conservative opposition rarely appeared in *Honi* letters, though the attacks on the 'extremists' of the Democratic Club and their newsletter were constant. People concluded submissions from conservatives found the wastepaper bin. The 'parliamentary' tussle in *Honi* attracted a student readership, far more so than the far-left articles often above most students' heads (and interest). The lack of contest resulted in piles of *Honi* lying around unread on campus.

Disproportionate coverage was given to the political economy campaign, even for an utterly biased student newspaper. Several letters testified to the torturous harping on behalf of the PE Movement. Despite the constant railing about the fascist authoritarian Vice-Chancellor, Bruce Williams ended the year by suspending not three but six students and refusing to introduce a unit of political economy within the Economics Department. The occupation seemed to have backfired. The editorial collective was often not collective. The lack of editorial cooperation was one explanation for the layout's scrappiness and the paper's varying size. *Honi* was sometimes down to 12 pages. One week, the editors had to excuse themselves from producing an edition.

The dissension broke the surface when far-left Gary Nicholls, long-term student, attacked the editors for their lack of support for the AUS-organised nationwide student strike on 30 September. Nicholls had surveyed the newspapers of Sydney's universities and found *Honi* pathetic in comparison. A student newspaper should 'reflect some editorial competence in political propaganda and analysis', he wrote (H25, 12 October). He meant, of course, that the propaganda and analysis were expected to be right behind the far-left cause. All the editors could manage was 'two articles and a back cover two weeks before the event'. Instead of concentrating on this momentous event, the editors produced a 'filth issue' which served 'to debase student activism'. The editors were fixated on 'boring, inane and non-descript covers, headlines, and content'. Nicholls warned that 'many students will look to the incoming *Honi* editors to greatly improve the consistency and value of Honi in 1977 so that this kind of serious fault does not occur again'. Savage criticism, indeed. It is something when a *Honi* 'filth issue' can debase student activism.

Faye Westwood, always displaying a selfless devotion to the far-left cause, was seriously displeased. She did not direct her answer entirely to Nicholls. It took, she said, a lot of work – including 'shit work' – and 'a tremendous amount of energy' to put together an edition of *Honi*. She and Michael Gormly did not operate in an authoritarian manner but let the collective work 'democratically'. She then made an astonishing admission. Producing *Honi* on a democratic basis 'points to serious weaknesses in the paper's role of producing good political journalism'. Any conservative would say the same about all that collectivist nonsense. It doesn't work. You need a management hierarchy headed by proven competent in the job. Take David Patch. For all Patch's rhetoric about direct democracy and collective decisions, he had worked himself to the boss position in the far-left rabble that ran the SRC in 1976. At the elite position of student senator, he had burnt off the university's security when caught in the act of vandalism. Democracy was not for the guiding vanguard elite.

Given the weakness of the democratic structure, Faye was 'disappointed that those who criticise have not contributed to building a sound basis for such a [democratic] role'. She meant people like Nicholls. She then turned on fellow editor Michael Gormly. 'It is well known in the SRC corridors', she wrote, 'that Michael Gormly and I have widely different political perspectives'. Furthermore, *Honi* may be produced democratically, but 'the editors, the DSP [the Director of Student Publications] and the Advertising Manager' oversaw the final product. They had political and legal responsibility. Next, she got something off her chest that had been bugging her. 'I would like to add that I disclaim editorial responsibility for the cartoon on page 3 [of the filth issue H23] and the incidents surrounding it'. The cartoon was of a McDonald's clown sitting atop a McDonald's store masturbating. Beside the cartoon was a description of the 'wet the biscuit' game, which consisted of the players masturbating on a biscuit in turn and then ... well, I will leave the rest to the reader's imagination. Faye was rightly disgusted with this creepy juvenile game. Looking back, it seems Faye's political perspective lost out.

The dissension in *Honi* also explained the lack of election coverage. The warring editors did not provide the breakdown of votes cast in the SRC elections. Nor did they give the names of the SRC officers for 1977, or those elected to the AUS conference delegation for 1977. The reader had to find out from chance mentions of them. *Honi* 1976 ended the year paralysed, serving up the same stale leftist menu. It was significant the highlight of the last edition was the Stalinist effort to smash Tony Abbott – all in defence of the democratic order. At least, that would have entertained the student readership, whatever they thought of the naked political action.

It was just this interest that the far-left editors of *Honi* missed. If you are an editor of a student newspaper, your objective is to secure a readership. You get a readership by making the newspaper appealing to the varied student community. That does not mean compromising the political out-look the editors defend. But it does mean providing light, shade, and opposition – and not an endless regurgitation of the same unexamined political dogma. For Tony Abbott, this sales and marketing problem was all too obvious. So he went to outside news platforms where he could get his message across. In *Battlelines*, he explained:

'As a conservative in 1970s campus politics, the only way to avoid being howled down was to put your arguments in writing. Unlike a speech, a let-ter in *Honi Soit*, the Sydney University newspaper, could not be drowned out by hecklers. I soon discovered that it was harder to take intellectual short cuts or to get away with debating tricks if your case had to stand up in print rather than just to sound plausible in a melee of voices. From the start, though, I was less interested in reporting events than in shaping them. That's hardly unusual for a politician, even a student one. Often enough, through lack of interest or political bias, the student paper wouldn't print conservative arguments, so, even as a student politician, I became a con-tributor to metropolitan and even national newspapers and magazines ... What mattered to me, then and now, was the impact of ideas on events and the critical importance of a written argument in shaping people's ideas.'[84]

Tony had committed the unforgivable sin of approaching the outside press to air his concerns about the leftist monopoly of student politics and the money that came their way. Within a few months of the 1977 academic year, he would do more to intensify the hatred the perceived betrayal had aroused. First, as a stark contrast, I want to balance that hatred with a few words on how others on campus saw him.

Greg Sheridan, Tony's closest friend during this period, provides the best-written source for Tony, the student politician. He and Tony collaborated in writing for the *Democrat*, and they planned political action together. From the beginning of their acquaintance, Sheridan wrote, he observed something unique about his friend, both in character and in thinking. Tony was outgoing and gregarious. He had 'a vigour and a force-of-nature quality about [him] that was irresistible ... [he] was a ball of energy and action, a good-natured and very friendly alpha-male ... He had the remarkable constitution of healthy young men and loved the drinking, singing, rugby-playing side of undergraduate life'.

In contrast with this outgoing physical nature, Tony had a mind that dwelt on the wide-ranging questions of life. Men of ideas and men of achievement attracted him. It was not an attraction that caused a slavish parroting of their ideas. The ideas and experience of great men were milled and sifted and adjusted to Tony's own thinking and experience. During this time, he acquired many friends from what Edmund Burke had called different 'platoons' of society. He never abandoned his school friends. To them, he added friends from politics and rugby.[85] These different groups would sometimes end up at the Abbott house in Killara, where Mrs Abbott served up food amid the drinking, raucousness, and sometimes the laughter and splash of someone landing in the pool.

Abbott and Sheridan's activity often brought them to the NCC (National Civic Council) office in Kent Street, where there was much social activity.[86] Young men and women from the different Democratic Clubs in the state attended the meetings at Kent Street. 'Lots of strong women,' Sheridan wrote, 'emerged as leaders' from the Democratic Club. Despite the malicious slander of people like Susan Mitchell, the Democratic Clubs drew together young men and women who shared a similar political philosophy. Not only people of faith were members. After the meetings, they 'would all repair to a nearby pub, generally the Windsor Tavern'. Only once was there a 'real moment of discord' between Abbott and Sheridan. 'Tony didn't get abusive,' Sheridan wrote. 'I never saw him get abusive with anyone'. That is certainly a jaw-dropping claim considering the image scribblers like Susan Mitchell and David Marr have conjured of him. The following is an example of the way Mitchell manufactured her portrayal of Abbott. Instead of using information from research that a writer would pursue with such a book, she delved almost exclusively into Michael Duffy's book that was complimentary of Abbott rather than the opposite. She wrote:

'[Abbott] spent most of his time playing football and drinking in pubs ... Duffy claimed that Abbott seemed to prefer the company of men because he 'got on better with them than women'. He loved the male rituals, the sanctioned aggression, the respect for fixed rules, and the closed society of the team. As if that wasn't enough to keep his aggression and testosterone in overdrive, he also took up boxing to counteract the damage from foul play in the scrums.'[87]

Most, if not all, readers would swallow this as an accurate reproduction of Duffy's meaning. Here are the passages on which she draws:

'[Abbott] had the confidence and the hearty, effusive manner that characterises him today – it was not uncommon to see him dancing on a table in one of his favourite pubs late in the evening. Everyone, male or female, was called mate ... With his highly competitive nature and strong views, Abbott got on better with men than women ... Tony had a girlfriend but he seemed to prefer being part of a group than a couple ... And, of course, there was the football, which he played whenever he could ... He loved the practice, the discipline of playing to rules, the legitimised aggression, and being part of the small society of the team.'[88]

Mitchell shamelessly takes slabs from Duffy's book, often without referencing and with minimal effort to paraphrase, but leaves out crucial
sentences or phrases to suit her hatchet job or adds material not there.
For example, when she writes quoting Duffy that Abbott seemed to prefer
men to women, her meaning is that Abbott preferred men because he
disliked women, a major theme of her book. That is not at all Duffy's
meaning. Duffy said nothing about Abbott preferring men to women, and
he implies nothing about Abbott's (alleged) dislike of women. He simply
claimed that because of particular character traits, Abbott made a better
connection with men. Abbott may have adored every woman he met, and
fallen at their feet, but he would fail to connect with them because of those
traits. No contradiction. Duffy does not offer any evidence for his claim,
I should add. It's merely his opinion. Besides, it would be a rare man that
got on with every woman he met. Finally, men and women gravitate to a
group of their own sex. If it were true that Abbott got on better with men,
it would be a marginal difference with other men.

Next comes another theme she thrashes: the badness of maleness. 'He
loved male rituals' is not even a paraphrasing of 'he loved the practice
[of football]'. Mitchell likely hasn't a clue what's involved in practising
football, but I am here to tell her it's not about men running around in
loincloths waving spears and shouting, 'we hate women!' I must also tell
Mitchell, who (astoundingly) has a PhD in 'creative writing', that 'sanctioned' does not have the same meaning as 'legitimised', and that a 'small
society' is not necessarily a 'closed society', meaning a closed society of the
accursed male. If one reads these passages of Duffy's attentively, then one
would understand he is describing Abbott in the same terms as Sheridan.
They both recognise Abbott as outgoing, friendly, and gregarious. Duffy
emphasises Abbott's liking for the friendship and solidarity of the group.
He also highlights Abbott's tendency to qualities one would describe as a

conservative outlook. That outlook comprises a liking for rule-based activities, self-discipline, cooperation and the solidarity of the group. Above all, the conservative – certainly in the Burkean mould – cherishes order in human society. Mitchell sees nothing of this because she wanders blindly in her ideological fantasy.

Having distorted Duffy's meaning about Abbott's love of football, Mitchell sneers about Abbott's out-of-control testosterone. But in the effort, she gets herself into an embarrassing tangle. Abbott's taking up boxing, she says, 'is to keep his aggression and testosterone in overdrive', but then adds (correctly) it was 'to counteract the damage from foul play in the scrums'. Well, what was it? Pumping himself full of (woman-hating) testosterone or taking action to deal with the bigger, older and tougher opponents he encountered in first-grade football? Duffy says it was the second. It goes to show how easily a writer can trash her writing when ideology overcomes the pen. A self-respecting writer would be embarrassed about the publication of such trash. Scribe Publications should be embarrassed about publishing it.

Louise Adler, the respected former CEO of Melbourne University Press and publisher of Abbott's *Battlelines*, found it 'disappointing that Mitchell's book provides little new insight', that it 'relies heavily on Michael Duffy's study of Abbott and Mark Latham', and as a result was a 'reploughing of old ground'. In her dealings with Abbott, feminist Adler, who differs from Abbott on most political issues, found him 'unfailingly gracious'.[89] All these textual problems are apart from the long list of Mitchell's factual howlers Gerard Henderson noted in his Media Watch Dog blog (No.115, Oct 2011). If Abbott had a wide group of friends and admirers, then why did the Left harbour such a devilish hatred for him? The reasons Sheridan gives concur with my own findings:

'It was impossible to intimidate him. He was politically incorrect and took positions, mild enough in mainstream Australia but completely outra-

geous in the world of student politics, which they hated. They also understood that he had formidable skills as a publicist, stupendous energy and
a strong capacity to win. Therefore every argument and accusation that
could be made against Tony was made. He was constantly denigrated in
Honi Soit and all the Left's publications. Anyone reading the back issues
of *Honi* today would get a completely false idea of who Tony was.'
90

The first characteristic Sheridan names is Abbott's fearlessness, often fearlessness when he was the only one who had ventured onto the field of
battle. Of course, Abbott was not the only conservative to suffer the vilification and violence of the Left. They all copped it. When the far Left did
not achieve their aims, they often resorted to violence. As an eyewitness
to the events of 1976, Sheridan confirms my account of the constitutional
manipulation that bounced the elected conservatives from the SRC. He
also speaks of the far left's intolerance. 'Control,' he writes, 'was viciously
held by an amalgam of communist, Trotskyist and other far-left groups
and individuals who were constantly at war not only with us but with each
other over points of far-left doctrinal purity'.[91] Both Sheridan and Abbott
were to suffer a severe dose of the far left's manipulation and violence
during the AUS Annual Conference in January 1977.

The Australian Union of Students (AUS) was established in 1971 as an
affiliation of the student representative bodies of Australia's universities.
The pretext was the welfare and general interest of Australia's tertiary students, but AUS quickly developed into an organisation that ran campaigns
on such leftist issues as racism, sexism, homosexual rights, education and
international questions. Students paid a fee for the university's membership (included in the general student fee). By 1974, the AUS executive
had a whopping $667,000 at its disposal. At first, 'aspiring Labor Party
politicians of the moderate Left had dominated' the proceedings, but by
1973 they had lost control. Barcan:

'In 1973 a radical Left alliance of the Communist Party of Australia, the Maoist Worker/Student Alliance and the Trotskyist Socialist Youth Alliance took over. In August that year, the AUS Council committed itself to building a socialist Australia and recognised the need for 'groups and nations' fighting for social justice to resort to violence when peaceful means had been exhausted.' [92]

The following year, AUS 'passed a series of motions supporting the Palestine Liberation Organisation and the elimination of the State of Israel ... the first of which informed the National Union of Israeli Students that it did not recognise the existence of Israel nor the Israeli National Union'. The voting down of the motions by ninety-five per cent of the students after The Australian Union of Jewish Students campaigned against them reflected the consternation caused. The AUS Council was undeterred. Showing the far left could not give a damn about majority feeling, they again tried the following year (1975), but the motions again got the boot. The message had sunk in by the following year, and at the 1976 Conference, the AUS Council voted not to have a policy on the Middle East. For as much as the far left could be pragmatic and back away from their rigid ideology, this was a pragmatic decision. It must have caused much psychological pain. It was into this atmosphere that our two intrepid 19-year-old politicians stepped after just one year in the brutality of student politics.

Sheridan devotes a chapter to the events of the 1977 Conference. He and Abbott drove to Melbourne in Abbott's Leyland P76. Without having booked accommodation, they managed to cadge sleeping quarters at a Catholic college across the road from Monash University, where the conference was held. Their entrance into the conference hall the next day was like, as Sheridan put it, being in 'the famous bar scene in Star Wars'. Slogans, flags and colourful posters representing the full range of far-left causes were everywhere, and the air reeked of the haze of marijuana. What happened after the conference got going was consistent with the 'gaudy' decorated madhouse they walked into. Sheridan wrote a lengthy account of their experiences and observations, but it is Abbott we're interested in. *The Weekend Australian* of 29 January gave young Tony half a broadsheet page to report on the conference under the headline 'J'ACCUSE' (I Accuse). The report provides an excellent case study of Abbott's sharp political perception, his understanding of the conflicting ideologies, and his ability to express the conclusions of his analysis, besides the description of the conference and its demented attendees. Here it is in full:

J'ACCUSE

'The Australian Union of Students, AUS, which represents a quarter of a million students, has in recent years been plagued with the unfortunate image of unrepresentative extremism. Genuinely liberal initiatives and sentiments, particularly in the field of black affairs, have been obscured by the disruptive violence of the moratorium campaign, its support for left-wing subversion, and its connection with radical politicians, such as Bill Hartley.

'At this year's conference, I hoped it would be different. AUS would cease acting as a mini world parliament and return to the needs and aspirations of the average student. This year, I hoped, rational argument, reasoned evidence, and a willingness to compromise would prevail. As a delegate, I hope to contribute to this process.

'I will not deal at length with the actual policy of AUS, for this is substantially unaltered and isn't central to my story. Rather, I will attend to the methods employed and my personal path from hopeful idealism to disillusioned realism. That path began even before I arrived in Melbourne for the conference last week.

'Everything at the council is done by delegates. Each tertiary institution sends a five-man delegation. At my campus, Sydney, two ultra-left and two non-left delegates were elected by student vote. The automatic addition of the AUS Secretary [far-left Steve Bolt] gave the Left a 3:2 majority. The left-dominated Students' Representative Council then insisted that the delegation vote as a bloc and that the leader, the AUS Secretary, should decide the speakers.

'Thus, while about half the Sydney students voted for moderate delegates, their representatives were outnumbered in the delegation and consequently were accorded neither vote nor voice. I was never allowed to speak on behalf of the University of Sydney, although I had received the highest personal vote in the election. This cynical manipulation of democratic forms to undemocratically deny expression to a large body of opinion typified the machinations that followed.

'It was an unpleasant start to an unpleasant conference. Generally, the air was heavy with the not-unpleasant odour of marijuana. The conference hall was gaily decked with gaudy Maoist flags and communist slogans. Some delegates wore badges cheerfully urging the 'smashing' of Fraser and the shooting of Kerr. Books on sale covered everything one wanted to know about abortion, street fighting, subverting universities, indoctrinating the young, and homosexuality. I did not see one heterosexual couple, although everywhere lesbians and homosexuals were clasped in fond embrace. It was almost as if heterosexuality had become the 'fascist perversion'.

'In the hall, one was bombarded with left-wing rhetoric; all the tired clichés about class war and capitalist oppression – and this from allegedly intelligent people. One was confronted with a microcosm of contemporary communism; the level-headed, almost rational CPA, the amorphous Trotskyites, and the increasingly ascendant Maoists. A number of Maoists, though delegates, were not students and later proved a little better than thugs. Not surprisingly, their presence caused considerable tension. I make no apologies for the personal account that follows. As a participant in the tragic farce, I vouch for its accuracy, though two weeks ago I could scarcely credit such daily insanity.

'For some time now, AUS has been preoccupied with the Palestinian question. Films on Palestine were shown – films distributed by the PLO that take a blatantly pro-terrorist stance. When four delegates, including myself, went to the film and expressed opposition to the film's sentiments, heated argument developed and one of the delegates was struck on the head. The arrival of pro-PLO heavies forced us to leave. Outside the hall, we were abused and threatened.

'But the vital election of union officers to positions which mean great power within AUS triggered the worst excesses of the extremists, to the point where it appeared some delegates were afraid to speak. The ever-present tension increased during a series of penetrating and provocative questions to the left-wing candidates. After one question, a furious Maoist delegate accused several anti-communists, notably Herzog of Queensland and Blandthorn of Victoria, of being 'agents'. Herzog was asked to leave the hall, and outside, his files were searched. Because of the violence-tinged atmosphere, he would have been foolish to resist. Maoist ire was aroused by complete lists of intending candidates for AUS office discovered in his files – especially when he sarcastically implied the lists were for ASIO and the CIA.

'As many Maoists and Aboriginals (for some obscure reason) were turning ugly, the then president Tasma Ockenden, informed one group that should Blankdthorn remain, she could not guarantee his safety. He had earlier been told by someone else: 'You'll bleed tonight'. During a lull, he was escorted to his car and managed to leave safely. As I was leaving the hall with Anne McCosker, a prominent anti-communist from Newcastle, she was told by two Maoists she might be safe that night but not in the future. A few minutes later, in the corridor outside the room she'd been allocated on campus, I was attacked when the two returned with four or five friends, one armed with a beer bottle. A fight started, and I was expecting to end up in hospital when McCosker came out and very bravely pushed herself between me and the assailants.

'Swearing horribly, having spat on her, having regaled her with the terrible fate awaiting anti-communists, and having told her never to return to the conference on pain of death, the heavies left. An executive committee before which McCosker and I appeared investigated the assault. Subsequently, an abortive attempt was made to have her expelled from the conference for circulating to the conference and the 'monopoly press' a statement containing the true story of what happened.

'McCosker, too, had been denied voting and speaking rights by some strange machinations – and as she'd been a DLP candidate (she's no longer a party member) for NSW in the Federal Senate elections, she was marked as an obvious target for the left wingers. Newcastle had sent an elected party of six – two delegates and four observers. But as the Left dominated the group, it was able, when it reached Monash, to vote out Adrian O'Connell, who'd won the most student votes, from his elected position of delegate. Neither O'Connell nor McCosker was allowed to speak for Newcastle.

'This is how she describes the incident reported above: "The Herzog affair took place at about one in the morning. A whole lot of Maoist thugs were among those who went out of the conference room when he was searched. They pushed one of the moderates into a woman, and a scuffle developed. Later when they came back, they claimed that he'd assaulted the woman. 'One black person came over to me and said, "We'll do you in tonight. You'll get yours". We stayed in the room for about three hours, hoping most of the thugs would go. Then Tony (Abbott) and Valdis (Berzins from Sydney) came with me to escort me back to my room in one of the Hall's Residence.

'"wo white Maoists came up to me outside and said I was lucky they hadn't got me that night, but there's another time. We headed off, and then we heard footsteps following us. By then there were more of them, and we ran like hell. I was very frightened. They caught up with Tony in the corridor and were kicking him. One of them had a beer bottle poised over his head, and fists were flying. They were all on to him, and I thought he was going to be badly injured.

"There were four of them – two blacks and two Maoists, one who seemed to be high on something. But eventually, other people heard the noise and came out, and that defused the situation. I'd been pushed about a bit and was slightly bruised. My neck had been put out, and I had a headache for a few days.

"About 4.30 am, we came back to the conference, which was still going, and demanded some sort of disciplinary action be taken. At first, they just laughed. Then some executive members took me into a private room. They grilled me in detail – I was shaken and crying at the time. I pointed out the two people who'd done it. They took evidence from one of them as a witness – a participant as a witness. He denied it all."

'That wasn't the only incident McCosker was involved in. Near the beginning of the two-day conference, after she'd complained to the press that she'd been denied speaking rights, she was accosted in the car park at night.

"There were about five people there – I couldn't see who they were. They called me a fascist right winger. One grabbed me by the arm – I was terrified. I managed to break away and ran for my room."

'McCosker says that although most of the conference was conducted in a relatively orderly manner inside the room, there was still intimidation. During a vote on the allocation of funds to Aboriginals, one Aboriginal went around the room, staring at the delegates likely to question it. Two heavies who weren't delegates stood near McCosker through another period of debate staring at her.

'On the surface, that may sound piffling – but in the context, it added up to a very obvious attempt at intimidation The allegations made about violence and intimidation were seen by some sections as a plot to discredit AUS. But the situation had, in fact, got so out of hand that one delegation

– from Queensland Agricultural College – withdrew, making this statement which I quote in part.

"The Queensland Agricultural Delegation gives notice of its intention to withdraw from the 1977 Annual Council in protest against the decision of this council to accept allegations that the incidents over the last few days were part of a plot to discredit council.

"While not in any way supporting the use of press statements on matters that have not been fully discussed by Council, we still condemn council for its failure to act to stamp out psychological and physical intimidation which is used to prevent a free flow of views in this chamber."

'So I am certainly not alone in my concern. There is no room for complacency in this matter. The Left have penetrated the universities to such an extent that their influence over those who will eventually lead society must be considerable. In the universities' artificial hothouse atmosphere, the radicalism of the Vietnam era has not died but changed from an emotional attack on an imperfect society into something far more systematic and dangerous. Realising the importance of the universities in the liberal democratic framework, the communist parties have made special efforts in this area, even to the point of placing trained agitators on campus.

'Denied a conference forum, I take this opportunity to present views which would never be published in the student media. Extremist control will not survive exposure of AUS activities by unflattering media – hence their exclusion. Greater knowledge of the methods and aims of AUS, presently denied, will stimulate greater involvement by the average student and thus democracy will be made to work.'

Abbott's contemporary report has the immediacy and freshness an account written years later cannot have. As a conservative, he was doing more than expressing his ideas and his judgements. He represented the thoughts of ordinary people who unconsciously lived the traditions, customs and moral principles of their society. He was applying those principles. He recognised that society always has social problems to deal with. Any society of fallible people needs reform. The task for the conservative is to reform where there is need, while conserving the essential nature and makeup. Continuity must be maintained to protect those benefits won over time. Abbott acknowledged there were social problems, 'particularly in the field of black affairs', but the political extremists had no healthy or enduring solution. They refused to deviate from their ideologies' rigid abstract prescriptions, so they abandoned all rational argument and compromise. Because of that abstract rigidity, they would not tolerate deviation and worked to silence the dissenters. Despite mouthing the rhetoric of democracy, all appearance of democracy sank beneath the rigidly controlled 'committees'. It is a recurring story of the extreme left – bashings, arrests, intimidation, and the searching of papers by darkly clad thugs.

Abbott's comments on homosexuality would now be taken as more evidence of his entrenched 'homophobia'. For Mitchell and Marr, such comments justified their depiction of Abbott. As with women, Abbott is 'fearful' of homosexuality and hates homosexuals. But again, Mitchell and Marr distort and misrepresent Abbott's views. Already in *Honi* in 1976, Abbott had cited the common attitude to sin and sinners in Catholic teaching about homosexuality. You hate the sin but love the sinner. In a more general sense, if Abbott did not approve of homosexuality, he reflected the views of most of the population. But the significant distinction he focused on was between a general community view of homosexuality and an extreme Marxist view. Most people, although believing homosexuality unnatural, were happy to leave homosexuals to live their private lives without harassment. The Marxist rejected this view as the outcome of bourgeois capitalist thinking, and such thinking was corrupt, oppressive, and evil. The homosexual, as the oppressed, must be rescued from the oppressor. In brief, naturalness and normalcy were switched around. Homosexuals and homosexuality were liberated, and the majority (white) bourgeois view, with its oppressive heterosexism disqualified. Praxis was to follow the theory, that is, the forcible imposition of the Marxist view on society. This is the background to Abbott's comment that 'it was almost as if heterosexuality had become the "fascist perversion"'. By 2016, with the imposition of the Safe Schools 'anti-bullying' program, it had.

Abbott asked where the far left's capture of the university would lead. It was a remarkable insight at the time to draw the distinction between a possible failure of policy about the Vietnam War (the result of an imperfect society) and the unrelenting dogged effort to subvert that society based on a systematic theory. It was the distinction that Edmund Burke drew about the French Revolution. The French Revolution was not an ordinary uprising of disaffected people. It was a revolution driven by 'theoretic dogma' that aimed to sweep away all French society. For a time, it did – until a dictator arose, as Edmund Burke had predicted.

Abbott and Sheridan could deal with the bullying, but Anne McCosker was another matter. The Maoists wouldn't leave her alone. So worried about her safety, Abbott and Sheridan rang Peter Westmore (the now retired head of the NCC in Melbourne) in the middle of the night. Westmore picked up McCosker and took her to his house, where he and his wife gave her shelter for the duration of the conference. He took her and picked her up each day. For further protection, he arranged a group of men to enrol as observers and accompany her to the conference.[93]

The threat of violence continued to stalk Abbott and Sheridan. Eventually, they decided they had had enough. Besides, there was nothing for them to do other than listen to the interminable Marxist rants. When they got into Abbott's Leyland P76 to drive back to Sydney, they had a lot to think about. Tony had come to the conference as a hopeful idealist. Now he was returning as a 'disillusioned realist'. He had undergone a significant reorientation of mind. The far left's behaviour had hardened them in the view that 'AUS was beyond reform and the best measure would be to get universities to disaffiliate from AUS altogether'. To succeed, each

student body at each university would have to vote for secession. There wa
s a difficult road ahead of them.

Chapter 9

1977 – The battle was on

TONY ABBOTT had risen to national notice with his report on the far-left fiasco at the AUS Annual Conference. The responses in the *Weekend Australian* reflected the interest his report had generated. How would his opponents at Sydney University react to the community attention aroused by a 'far-right' operative defending capitalist bourgeois society? Well, they reacted in the only way they knew how – in the time-honoured and effective tradition of pulling out all stops to destroy their opponent's character. No addressing the arguments. That took up far too much time. So, the first edition of Honi for 1977 (28 Feb) featured the headline 'AB-BOTT REVEALED' on the cover. And who was the man for the job? None other than big hitter Harry Moore, who had 'revealed' the sinister background of the 'far-right' on campus in a long melodramatic piece in *Honi* 1976. Now he was at it again.

Moore began by acknowledging the articles and letters in the 'downtown press' about the 'alleged' violence at the AUS Conference. Many of the allegations came from 'so-called moderate' Sydney University students, among whom were Abbott and Lane-Mullins. Now many students were asking, 'just who are these people?' He seemed to have forgotten he had named a whole bunch of them and their sinister connections in his earlier article – apart from Abbott. He would do the campus the valuable service of supplying the 'available facts'. The consistent link with the 'moderates', he wrote, was Sydney University Democratic Club which was the dark representative of the darker National Civic Council, behind which was the still darker Bob Santamaria. At this point, Moore's melodramatic fantasy is in overdrive. The Democratic Club 'has a long history of politically motivated violence – whether as vigilantes for vice-regals, smokebombers for Saigon, poster-pullers for political reaction, or bullies for by-elections'. Vividly put, but Vigilantes for vice-regals, smoke bombers and poster pullers? Is this the extent of the violence – granting Moore had not indulged in his penchant for Gothic embellishments? You call that violence? Compare it with the actions of a true professional like eye-rolling slavering Martin Hirst, the editor who has printed Moore's article.

Moore then boringly repeated what he had written about Frank Lane-Mullins in the earlier article with a few sneering comments about his mediocrity. We can skip over this because Tony Abbott was Moore's real target. He sneered that Abbott arrived on campus 'fresh from Riverview'. Get the sectarian poke? He sneered that Abbott set about 'revamping the Democratic Club in his own image – somewhat crass, blundering and stylistically simple'. On a roll, he quipped that Abbott 'seems to have polished up his style so much over the holidays – well, you would almost think the [newspaper] story had been written by someone else'. Mocking someone else's writing is always a risk. Abbott's determined expression and precise style were superior to Moore's.

Moore, who seemed to have taken on the role of sneerer-in-chief for *Honi*'s far-left collective, continued to sneer that Abbott was voted one of the delegates for the AUS Conference, 'after all, his one clear policy statement was his great desire for a "trip to Melbourne" (possibly to meet Bob and the boys)'. Is Abbott's waggish comment all that Moore has? After a 240-word policy statement, Abbott summarised his aims: 'to dissociate AUS from the lunatic left; to channel all AUS funds into welfare; to expand AUS travel and insurance; to investigate AUS interest-free loans to students'. He added, 'apart from that, I wouldn't mind a trip to Melbourne'. The student constituency understood. Abbott received, far and away, the most votes in a record turnout.

One other mocking dig is worth a mention because David Marr quotes it without referencing it in his essay Political Animal. Moore wrote, 'After a narrow defeat in the Senate elections', '[Abbott] came down to the SRC and kicked a glass panel on the front door in – not that he meant to mind you, things just seem to happen to Tony'. Taking the whole facetious sentence, one would think Abbott accidentally broke the glass panel – if he broke it all and it wasn't a concoction of Moore's. There was never a third-party confirmation of the event, and it never came up in later conflicts. If it wasn't an accident and deliberate, why would Moore add 'not that he meant to' and 'things just seem to happen to Tony?' Reading the sentence first up, however, the meaning is likely to come across as Abbott kicking in the door out of anger for his defeat in the Senate elections. Marr took this meaning in his book to support his manufactured picture of Abbott as violent and unruly. Moore finished with a barely coherent paragraph about the trials of 'multimedia personalities' at the end of which he urged, 'moderation Tony, moderation!' – no doubt putting himself forward as an example. There was nothing more to Moore's article than sneering, mockery, and false insinuations, as the student body undoubtedly saw it.

The same edition of *Honi* revealed that fine example of moderation, Martin Hirst, the office occupier with violence, had lost his elected fellow editor Marion Kearney. He and unelected Anne Talve were the editors for 1977. Talve, who had nominated with Jean Rhodes for the editorship, pledged 'to publish dissident, extreme or outrageous material that few other journals would consider'. She was an approved substitute. No explanation for the missing Kearney. No reason for the replacement without the democratic process so loudly promoted by the Left. In their first edition, Hirst and Talve assured their readers *Honi* would not be a 'vehicle' for their 'particular viewpoint' but would discuss 'certain issues ... of great importance to the well-being and interests of students, many of which are controversial'. But turn over the pages, and you find article after article, commentary after commentary, all pushing the far-left cause with the usual wonky Marxist analysis. I have said enough to show that the SRC and *Honi* were in the hands of the far left and that *Honi* was an instrument to proselytize, to shut down the conservative opposition, and to guard the power and ascendancy of the Left. From this point, I will focus on the conflict between the far Left and the conservatives who were increasingly falling in behind Abbott.

H2 (8 Mar) ran a letter from the presidential David Patch, taking *Honi*'s editors to task. He said, 'AUS has been the victim of a highly organized right-wing attack in the establishment media over the last month, based on an incredible series of lies and distortions about the events at AUS Council and AUS policy'. He did not bother to detail the lies and distortions of the supporting witnesses – like Anne McCosker. That might have been self-incriminating. That was bad enough, he complained. But it was so disappointing to read that the editors had added to the distortions by getting AUS's policy about the Middle East wrong. Didn't the editors know AUS had a 'no policy' on the Middle East? He signed as 'David Patch, AUS National Executive Member'. With this, we know that Patch had moved up to another boss position from which he could push around his campus underlings.

John Cozijn indignantly complained about the stupid editors of the *Democrat* who wrote nonsense about him that did not bear 'any resemblance to reality'. He named a string of mistakes like getting names wrong, the number of years he was at university, the places people lived, and other such trivial details which, it must be admitted, the Democrat should have got right. I rather doubt that he did not 'ram Marxism down students' throats', given his declared in-the-distance far-left position. Peter Rixon backed up Cozijn about the 'goons in the Sydney Uni DLP Club'. The context of his letter suggested he was writing about the same edition of

Democrat. Talk about the DLP and Santamaria had a preferable sectarian tinge to the blander reference to the Democrat. He lashed the newsletter's 'semi-illiterate ravings' and its inability to 'construct a coherent argument' showing 'their puerile political incompetence', in addition to 'indulgent raves consisting of distortions and lies'. The trouble was that Rixon did not offer one argument or any evidence to back up his claims. Cozijn and Rixon were targeting Abbott, so they had plenty of material from which to quote. Abbott's writing quality and sharp analysis were a good reason they avoided the task.

But all this was to lead up to major news in H3 (15 Mar). Beside a crude drawing representing Abbott as a beer-swilling ocker, Steve Bolt reported that Abbot had again suffered censure at the hands of the SRC. The censure was 'for his misrepresentation of the work and functioning of AUS nationally and AUS at Sydney University through the article in The Australian and other areas of the mass media'. The reprimand was necessary because of his 'ranting and raving...following AUS Annual Council'. Abbott's accusations about 'violence and intimidation' ranged 'from gross distortion to outright lies'. Bolt did not mention the other witnesses to the same happenings. Again, that might have undermined the campaign. All this was merely to serve Abbott's goal of destroying AUS and 'muzzling dissent', a task he revelled in. Abbott pretended that he represented 'average students', but this could only be so if all students were 'male heterosexual right-wingers'. Indeed, it is likely most female and male students then were heterosexual moderates or conscious conservatives who ignored the lunacy of the small group in control of the SRC and *Honi*, as is probably the case today.

Abbott was getting under their skins. His writing was anything but semi-illiterate ravings without a coherent argument. P. E. Donnelly (Ag III) asked, 'Is it possible that one student has managed to stir up so much concern amongst the members of the AUS and the SRC? Could Abbott be sprouting some truths? Is he stirring mud or shedding some light?'

Donnelly did not know. He had read nothing that had enlightened him at that stage. A 'complete analysis' and an 'unbiased assessment' were needed to resolve the Abbott phenomenon. It was a vain wish.

The editorial collective continued to receive a rubbishing for their biased one-track newspaper. Six students wrote a long letter detailing their frustration with *Honi*. They reminded the editors of Hirst's undertaking in his policy statement that *Honi* 'would be representative of the whole student body' and not be a vehicle for the editor's politics. The students cited H3 as an example. There should be less politics and more non-political subjects of interest to the general student body. Otherwise, 'our dear editors', they wrote, 'the paper leaves the average student utterly bored and thus defeats its (and your) purpose'. The one-sided political content may have defeated the purpose of *Honi* as a student newspaper, but it did not at all defeat Hirst's purpose. The editors devoted a whole editorial to slapping down the six students and others who entertained the same muddled ideas.

'How can any strident paper be representative of the whole student body?' they asked. Well, it can't. A 'strident' newspaper would not be representative of a diverse community but would run and defend a particular political view, as Hirst's *Honi* did unashamedly. The editors' wish to be as 'balanced as possible' was simply incompatible with their stridency and admitted status as communists. The distinction between political and non-political, Hirst continued, is false. 'As Communists, the editors feel that everything is political... To cut down on the number of pages of political copy, or to print none at all, is a political move favouring the status quo – so energetically defended by the Right-wingers'. Students are naturally concerned with politics. The university functions in the 'context of a Capitalist social order. In a Capitalist society, the university reproduces capitalist relations and politics. Again as Communists, we feel that this must be exposed and opposed'. Hirst and his editorial team would continue to utter the hollow wish to be balanced and representative of all but at the same time promote their communist worldview without letup. The principle of non-contradiction was a bourgeois construct.

Sydney's Easter Show featured in H6 (5 Apr). The cover was in the spirit of offending Christians as much as possible. The rest of the paper was mostly the same boring stuff. Note that we are already into April, and there has been no sign of the SRC president. When Patch ascended to the heights of the SRC presidency, the presidential proclamations in *Honi* were frequent. Things obviously weren't going well for 1977 SRC President Peter Byrnes. Indeed, how would Hirst have viewed a president who had spurned the radicals, saying that 'broken doors and windows have been [their] main accomplishment' and he was 'sick and tired of the radicals giving themselves "carte blanche" in the use of petty vandalism for supposed political purposes!' Things looked grim for him. By this time, *Honi* and not the president seemed to be determining the direction of student affairs. Hirst brought the focus back on Abbott to enliven the otherwise boring Honi.

Peter Rixon took on the task of answering the question of who Tony Abbott was. His question was a pretext to launch an internecine attack on his far-left enemies, the detail of which must have been somewhat obscure to most students. It was easy to see what Abbott was, said Rixon. His 'union bash' in the Australian and his favour with the 'screaming tabloids' branded him far right. If there was any further doubt, said Rixon, just look at his 'election statement which outlined 'a platform of "idiot power" plus "I want a free trip to Melbourne"'. He then focused on his real target. 'AUS-orientated left groups', he wrote, 'had only helped give such bullshit a ring of validity'. Apparently, Rixon's point was that they helped by reacting to Abbott's article. Abbott probably shook off this sort of obscure tirade, but oppositional lefty Harry Moore did not. He couldn't put a lid on his scorn. In H8 (26 Apr), Moore sneered, 'poor, poor Peter Rixon'. He had got his facts abysmally wrong and was 'so bitterly anti-organized left politics' that some notice may be taken of him. It seems the hair-pulling was between the 'organized left' and the unorganized 'grassroots' left. It is not necessary to go into such baffling internecine far-left strife. It merely illustrated what Abbott had to contend with. One wonders whether P.E. Donnelly was any the wiser after reading this exchange.

In H7 (19 Apr), Hirst and his team were back to whipping the ideological infidels. They put the heading 'Nationalism and Racism go Foot in Mouth' to a letter from J. Doyle (Arts III). It's worth reproducing this prophetic letter in full:

'While I fully recognize the contribution that migrants have made in the past 30 years to the Australian Commonwealth, I urge all Australians, especially students, to seriously re-evaluate the aims and circumstances of the question of immigration. It has been stated openly by Mr Grasby that Australia's official immigration policy is to fabricate a 'multiracial', 'multicultural' hybrid society in Australia. Surely such an ambition is not only self-destructive to our own Australian culture but is sheer folly considering the impossibility of administering such a nation, even if we only consider such minor problems of communication for example. Surely the aim of immigration is rather to assimilate as readily as possible by the second generation, at the latest, non-British migrants; a process which has worked well up to now. At a time when Australians need above all unity, Mr Grasby's projected plans of establishing massive Asian and Arabic communities with distinct geographical definitions seems in the least, sheer bloody madness. There will always be a Turkey, a Greece, and an Asia, but there can only ever be one Australia, and to destroy a way of life, a culture and a national identity in merely re-creating what exists elsewhere in the world is the saddest decision any group of politicians have ever made for Australia.'

As a postscript appeared, 'We print this letter as an example of middle-class racism and prejudice combined with White Australian Nationalism'. Hirst and his team would have been gratified if they could have seen into the future. Their opinion is now firmly and angrily held by Australia's dominant leftist class, who despise and condemn a majority of Australians alarmed at the runaway migration policy, the lack of integration, and the vilification of Australia's 'white' Anglo/Celtic character. Most Australians would be surprised that the leftist rhetoric of anti-white racism was already rife among the far left forty years ago. It shows how successful the Left's long-term campaigns have been. It also shows Tony Abbott's acuity in recognizing the implications of the soaring trajectory of far-left student activism way back in the 1970s.

The Hirst collective continued to receive letters condemning their editorial regime as pathologically biased and utterly irrelevant to most students. Gary Thompson (Arts II) wrote (H8, 26 Apr) that he had never seen 'so much bullshit and irrelevancy' in a student newspaper. Anyone not a 'Marxist revolutionary' did not feature. Students, he said, should have the option at the next SRC elections to vote 'no SRC at all'. He was confident most students would vote no. This would force the editors to cater to the student community. A second strategy to bring the editors into line would be to charge the students a nominal amount. As it was, piles of Honis were lying around, ignored.

At this time, two brawls were raging in *Honi*. The fiercer by far was the hair-pulling among the far-left factions, of which Moore vs Rixon was an illustration. The other conflict was between Christians and the materialists, who were not all Marxists. The Christians strove to explain Christian belief based on the Scriptures while the materialists abused and mocked them. Hirst added an editorial note to a letter trying to prove Christianity was a better choice than Marxism for 'curing' the ills of society. 'Once again', he wrote, 'why is it always the most oppressive people who are the most religious?' The communist gulags were a case of out of sight, out of mind. A notable absence from the religious exchanges was Tony Abbott. Mitchell's and Marr's religious fanatic rarely contributed to such debates, leaving the defence of Christianity to the 'evangelicals'. Duffy wrote that 'Tony and Greg [Sheridan], while faithful church-going Catholics, were more interested in the politics of the Church than theology, were more likely to discuss what the pope was doing about Eastern Europe than spirituality. They had almost nothing to do with the Catholic Chaplain on campus'.[94] Odd behaviour for a Catholic fanatic. Mitchell, who depended on Duffy (short of plagiarism) for her warped account of student Abbott had nothing to say about such passages.

While Hirst and the collective were busy mocking Christians and railing about White Australian nationalism, Abbott was putting into operation his first significant political action. It would come out of left field, so to speak, and have a stunned Harry Moore muttering about the unconscionable Right. Moore, with all his slimy verbal talent, was caught short. For a full understanding of the action, we need to go back to 1974.

In the lead-up to the 1974 SRC elections, the Sydney University Liberal Club (SULC) was accused of 'perverting' their liberal principles by dealing with the 'ALP', in this case, meaning the likes of far-left David Patch. The leadership of the SULC treated the accusation with scorn but, at the same time, foreswore any ideological connection with the Young Liberals and the Liberal Party. They told their accusers that a genuinely progressive liberal group would dialogue with all parties to test where there was a common interest. The Liberal Party could 'learn something from those propounding different ideologies and even occasionally agree with them'. Aavo Karulin summarised the Democratic Club's view of such a disgusting collaboration. 'Weak, weak liberal minds', he wrote, 'fearing to go against the "grain" of the university built by the vocal pro-Communist left-wing, have decided to go AP or ALP and become uncontroversial, fitting into fashion'. He claimed the collapse of liberalism in the SU Liberal Club was reflected in the federal Liberal Party with their adoption of Labor policies. It was the same disease. The clash raged over *Honi* Nos.14-25. It ended with the incendiary accusation that the SULC had come to an agreement with Patch. If Patch gave specific commitments to the SULC, they would support him for the presidency. Patch and the SULC leadership were outraged. Patch's explanation for the SULC support was that they recognized his superior abilities for the position of SRC president. A year later, the clash was still working itself out.

In H6 (1975), a comment appeared under the heading 'Reactionaries Rock the Boat – Tory takeover'. The occasion was the election of the new SULC president. As was often the case, the commentator, showing scorn for the forces of the Right, remained anonymous, signing as 'IIB'. 'The SU. Liberal Club', IIB gleefully wrote, 'found itself buffeted by the waves of the Democratic Club'. Among the buffeters were the notorious Frank X. Mullins and Jeff Phillips. The election of 'dubious legality' need not concern us. Of interest was IIB's facetious account of the election's 'foreplay'. The previous year's president Ian Wisken had, in the meantime, resigned. Some wanted his resignation letter read:

'Apparently, unauthorized support had been given last year [1974] to candidates of the Left... Horrors! Patch and the *Honi* Editors 3 were given the nod at last year's SRC ... The Wisken-Culey liaison and the 'Dean (ex-Pundit Editor) Affair' was labelled a period of traitorous flirtation with the sinister socialist cause. All three are now in political oblivion, licking their big 'L' inflicted sores.'

Some candidates declared the 'Club needs revitalization after last year ... the Socialist forces must be crushed ...' etc. etc. The election's outcome, however, was the choice of 'progressive' liberal Katrina Penrose for president, just beating out 'champion of the right' McWilliam, who won the vice-president position. McWilliam's win was followed by '20 odd Democrats' taking out membership of the SULC. Clearly, the Democratic Club already had designs on the SULC.

Several weeks later, the editor of *Pundit* (the SULC newsletter) deplored (H12) the forgery of *Pundit*, produced 'at the behest of the less than scrupulous opponents of "political economy", academic freedom, and freedom in general'. This undisguised rhetoric of the Left explains, at least in part, the interest conservatives would have had for what was meant to be, and should have been, an arm of the Liberal Party. *Pundit* editor Richard Waddell wished to 'disassociate us all from that particular document, a fraudulent and dishonest piece of work'. SULC President Katrina Penrose took up the same themes (H13). The forged *Pundit* was an underhanded, deceitful way of pursuing the right-wing's agenda. 'None of the points of view which were represented in this badly written, incoherent piece of nonsense', she wrote, 'are to be associated with the Liberal Club'. She did not give examples. The SULC was a democratic group 'run on democratic principles'. It refused to be 'pushed into a right-wing position'. They wanted to 'retain a flexible position; a position which can enable us to support or, in some cases, not to support certain people on certain policies'.

That position was the same as that of past-president Ian Wisken, which kept 'alive that fundamental tenet of liberalism: the freedom of the individual to speak and act as he pleases'. Katrina Penrose seemed not to understand that (so stated) the SULC's brand of liberalism was libertarian, which was far from Menzies' conception of the Liberal Party. In showing support for the Marxist based political economy movement, Penrose and the SULC leadership were trapped in a diabolical confusion, the sort of confusion that led to the 'fellow-traveller' phenomenon. The SULC was crying out for intervention. The successful intervention came under the leadership of Tony Abbott. Why had it not come before Abbott's action when already attempts by conservatives were underway to take over the SULC? Perhaps the reason was Abbott himself. The accounts of the takeover disagree on some points. First, Abbott in *Battlelines* gives a broader context for his motivations:

'[In] 1977, I joined the Sydney University Liberal Club, not because I was then much of a Liberal but because I wanted the Liberals to support Democratic Club candidates in student council elections. The first Liberal Club meeting I attended was a rowdy AGM where the old executive was replaced... In any event, it was an early lesson in the realities of politics. The arguments in favour of student Liberals taking a more robust political stance hadn't changed, but, at least at Sydney University, the numbers certainly had. Elsewhere, though, the argument seemed to have become more compelling. Right around the country at that time, Liberal students were becoming more involved in university politics. The Australian Liberal Students Federation was formed, with Michael Kroger, Eric Abetz and Michael Yabsley prominently involved.'[95]

Susan Mitchell quoted the first sentence and bizarrely added an unwarranted deduction. 'In other words,' she commented on his plan, 'his real political interest was in using the Liberals as a stalking-horse for DLP candidates. The religious aim took first place over the political'.[96] Mitchell is so obsessed with her lurid conception of Abbott's imagined religious beliefs that all rationality flies out her ears. She is too busy obsessing to see the broader context of the growing political activism among student Liberals in the conservative tradition of the Liberal Party. It had nothing to do with Abbott's religious belief nor with that of the Catholics supporting him. If she had done any research at all on Abbott's student period and not relied on a selective interpretation of Michael Duffy's book, she may have learned the conservatives had targeted the SULC two years before Abbott appeared on campus.

Duffy seems to give little importance to the action. He wrote no more than that 'Tony Abbott and Greg Sheridan took over the Liberal Club, then a wine and cheese group with no great interest in politics. They stacked its membership with all their friends and had themselves appointed to its executive positions so they could run as Liberals in the next election'. Mitchell ignored Duffy's book on this point. Otherwise, she couldn't stick it to Abbott alone for the stalking-horse plan. Duffy's description of the SULC is not accurate on the evidence in *Honi*. David Marr offered a different version in *Political Animal*. He wrote that Joe Bullock claimed it was his idea 'to knock off the Liberal Club'. He quotes Bullock:

'I said [to Tony] we need a banner to fight under. We've got to have some-thing that can draw people to us. The Labor Club was extreme Left. There was no chance of knocking it off. But the Liberal Club was a dreadful bunch of dilettantes and social climbers. And there were not many of them. So I said: 'Let's knock off the Liberal Club'. But Tony was really reluctant. 'Oh, no, I don't want to join the Liberal Club'. He made it clear his loyalties were to Labor. Eventually, I persuaded him against his better judgment to join.'[97]

This is an embarrassing claim for Marr and Mitchell – that Abbott, the political animal, saw himself aligned with the Labor Party. If true, it would diminish the strength of the right-wing DLP case against Abbott. There is, however, a reason for Mitchell and Marr to doubt Abbott's alleged allegiance to the Labor Party in 1976. How could Abbott be attracted to the policies of the conservative Democratic Labour Party and feel any allegiance to a Labor Party under the control of the Left? It does not seem reasonable. Greg Sheridan challenged Bullock's account of the action. The idea of taking over the SULC, he wrote, was 'Tony's initiative'. Sheridan was against it. He thought they would be better off concentrating on making the Democratic Club more appealing to the students. He and

Tony 'weren't particularly committed to the Liberal Party', and he 'didn't think that the brand of the Liberal Party would help [them] particularly in student elections'.

Abbott saw things differently. What was missing in student politics, he said, 'was the presence of the mainstream political parties' through which political groups could work. It seems clear looking back that the SULC was just the club for conservatives to work through. Sheridan fell in with Abbott, and they launched their takeover. 'Taking over the Liberal Club was easy and entirely democratic', wrote Sheridan. 'We just enrolled sufficient new members into the club before the annual general meeting, stood for all the positions and won them'. At this point, according to Sheridan, he and Abbott were operating 'completely independently of the NCC office', which was a source of friction because the NCC had refused to work with the Liberal Party.[98] Their working independently of the NCC contradicts a central theme of both Marr and Mitchell – that Abbott was slavishly devoted to Santamaria and the NCC, and they were telling him what to do. It's also worth noting that the same slavishness could be attributed to Sheridan and the other Democratic Club members involved in the takeover if Marr's and Mitchell's arguments were sound. But they weren't.

Abbott and Sheridan's successful takeover operation was completed in May 1977 in the run-up to the July SRC elections announced in H14 (28 Jun). The takeover didn't go unnoticed. As usual, one of the Right's critics had a letter in H14 under the heading 'A Springtime Coup?' Its author, the hitherto unknown Jamie Carey, noted the appearance of (election) chalkings around the university grounds, but this year with a 'most interesting variation'. There had been a 'renaissance' of the SULC under the leadership of Tony Abbott 'well-known rightist leader of the National Civic Council backed Democrat Club ... definitely one of Santamaria's golden boys ... the Liberal Club hope to take over the SRC, it would seem, as a gift, no doubt, to their beloved leader, Malcolm (or is it John?) Fraser'.

The fantasy that Abbott, the NCC, the Liberal Party and Prime Minister Fraser were in cahoots, despite the evidence, was unshakeable.

Unfortunately, several issues of *Honi* (Nos. 18 & 19) are missing from the archive, preventing the full tracking of the takeover. However, we know that there was at least one other comment. John Diddington, signing himself as 'President of Sydney University Liberal Club' (1975), referred to an article in H19 under the heading 'Extremists Take over Liberal Club' (H20, 28 Jul). Barring a couple of points, the article, he said, was 'substantially correct'. Diddington's letter is interesting for its parallels with the conflict within the Liberal Party during the last ten years, certainly since the shock rise of Abbott in 2009. Indeed, the clash between the so-called 'moderates' and the conservatives likely has its origins in the years immediately after Menzies' resignation in 1966. Diddington's letter is worth reproducing in full because it relates the course of events and delineates the issues between the 'progressive' liberals and what he calls the forces of reaction:

'In late 1975 a group of people associated with the Democratic Club attempted to join the Liberal Club. Some were successful, and they mounted an attempt to win control of the Club's Executive. However, in this, they failed, albeit narrowly. But in 1976, and again this year, the National Civic Council succeeded in infiltrating many of its people into Liberal Party branches, particularly in the Western Suburbs. This has been used to move, at University of Sydney, into the Liberal Club, resulting in its 'take-over'. Hence the fact that people such as Tony Abbott, Richard Waddell, and Joe Bullock are able to pose as 'Liberal' candidates for the SRC. The Liberal Club no longer represents what I regard as the essence of Liberalism that is progressive, constructive proposals for change [*sic*]. It is nothing but another victim of the attempt by extremists to move into the NSW Branch of the Party. Accordingly, the candidates of the 'Liberal Club' must be opposed by all students who believe, as I do, that Liberalism is a force for progress, not reaction.'

It is a sheer fantasy that the Liberal Party was always liberal in the liberal-left sense. Menzies may have made oblique references to J.S. Mill, but the more frequent references were to Edmund Burke. 'Reactionaries' weren't infiltrating the Liberal Party. It was likely the other way around. Any attentive observer could have seen that materialist liberal-left ideas began appearing in the Liberal Party after the departure of its founder, the 'simple Protestant', as Robert Gordon Menzies described himself. Menzies was the President of Melbourne's University Student's Christian Union in 1916, hardly the credentials for a member of the materialist left. As for the accusation of 'reaction', it is nothing more than name-calling, signalling the user doesn't know what he is talking about when it comes to conservatism as a political philosophy. The Burkean conservative is not against change. The essence of SULC's liberalism may be 'progressive, [offering] constructive proposals for change', but it was never the essence of Menzies' liberalism.

Harry Moore, his sneering somewhat curbed by alarm, took up the SULC's accusations (H20A, 28 Jul). It was now rather with an air of resigned foreboding that he spoke about right-wing extremists like Tony Abbott, Valdis Berzins, and Joe Bullock attempting to gain 'respectability' in the electorate by subverting the SULC. Abbott and his 'hysterical, cold war NCC/DLP warriors' were using the 'Liberal cover to maximum advantage'. And to show that the extreme left never shy away from even the most outrageous hypocrisy, Moore accused Abbott and his extremist mates of resorting to their well-known white-anting activities. 'The "white-anting" activities of these people', he wrote, 'are well known to those who study the history of the ALP and the trade union movement'. The history of communist movements (including that in Australia) is one of disinformation, infiltration, sabotage and subversion. My account of SRC politics over seven years (1973-1979) is to demonstrate just that.

Far-left Moore, in his concern for right-wing enemies less pernicious than Tony Abbott, wondered what 'genuine supporters of the Liberal Party at Sydney University [thought] of all this?' I wonder whether Diddington was comforted by Moore's worry for the welfare of genuine Liberal Party supporters. But who is this Diddington claiming to have been the 1975 SULC President? Have we not seen that Katrina Penrose was elected SULC President for 1975?

FOUR WEEKS before Moore's and Diddington's letters, Hirst and his collective announced that SRC President Peter Byrnes had resigned. No explanation for this dramatic turn of events, no information, no discussion, no regrets – nothing. Hirst merely stated the constitutional provisions for a new election and the appointment of a temporary officer. The appointment had already taken place because the announcement was signed by 'John Cozijn, interim Acting President, On behalf of the SRC Executive'. It was not hard to guess the reasons for the resignation. Byrnes would never be an effective president after he condemned the far left in his policy statement. His demise was like Chris Sidoti's, Bret Mattes' and the 1976 conservative officers'. In Byrnes' case, it appears he was ignored.

By July, annual election activity was in full swing, but *Honi* only had eyes for the (alleged) excesses of the Right. The viciousness of 'an aggressive and intimidating push … to take control of the SRC' outraged Garry Bennett. In a long post-election letter (H22, 2 Aug), he catalogued the abuse to which homosexuals and women were allegedly subjected. You would have thought hordes of knuckle-dragging right-wing fanatics roamed the campus picking on the poor defenceless candidates of the Left. Bennett and his team for *Honi* editors and Barbara Ramjan for SRC President were, he charged, the object of 'extremely sexist and heterosexist chalkings' boasting that their candidate (Tony Abbott) would piss on 'commie poofters'. Left chalkings were changed to 'Ramjan for Prostitute (20c)' and 'Ram Jan? Yes, ram her'. Yet after cataloguing the extensive abuse and intimidation, Bennett had to admit that 'by the end of the campaign no one had been seriously attacked or hurt by the Right-wingers'. A point, crucial for later, was that Bennett, or anyone else, never accused Tony Abbott of taking part in the alleged violence or abuse.

It must have surprised many on campus that Barbara Ramjan popped up as a candidate for SRC President. Most students had probably never heard of her. She was in her fourth year of Social Work and took her role as Welfare Officer seriously. But her direct political experience was narrow, mainly in leftist committees, particularly those related to women's issues. David Patch could have written her policy statement. After all, Patch was Ramjan's campaign manager. Her undertaking was 'to improve our cours-es, reform methods of assessment and achieve control of decision-making' to make 'the SRC ... a genuinely democratic organization and not entan-gled in bureaucracy' to 'support open committees of the SRC' to arrange 'regular general meetings for students to air their views' and to establish 'direct election of SRC Officers'. All line and verse according to the Patch political manual. A sound case could be made for Ramjam acting as Patch's proxy in his battle with Abbott.

Abbott's policy statement for the SRC presidency can be summarised in a few points. First, the SRC should not engage in outside 'partisan political causes'. This is not the task of the SRC, apart from the misdirection of funds. Second, the SRC must be 'active within university life' catering to students in need and providing facilities for the student body. Third, the quorum should be raised to '5% of the student body' to prevent any political group from controlling front-lawn meetings. Fourth, he would do all he could to stop communist fanatics' posing as representatives. His policy for economics representative included the same points and added others all of which he would continue to promote:

'The excesses of recent SRCs have led many students to believe (quite rightly) that unless the SRC can be made genuinely representative, it no longer deserves to exist ...

'To eliminate the possibility of ballot-rigging, SRC elections should be conducted by an independent party and not by a former *Honi* editor and communist partisan, however eminently impartial.

'Political bias is sometimes evident in humanities subjects. But I believe the best teaching is that which presents all the facts and a range of interpretations while leaving the student to decide. Thus I oppose the establishment of a Department of Political Economy based on one dominant ideology. Moreover, students in the Government Department who feel they have received low marks for reasons other than merit should have the opportunity of reassessment.

'On the last SRC, I opposed motions vitriolically condemning the Vice Chancellor and paying the fines of students 'victimized' for smashing his office. I consistently opposed motions supporting extremism and sought instead to promote a consensus among students. I hope these efforts receive your continuing support.'

This is the platform of Tony Abbott everywhere broadcast as an extreme right-wing religious fanatic. If one takes the meaning of his words and not the imaginings of his far-left opponents, Abbott is against extremism and for an outlook on life shared by the general community. He is not so much against people with different social and political visions as against extremists and those naïve enough to help them. It was reasonable for Abbott to insist on voluntary membership for the irreformable far-left AUS and the disbandment of the SRC so long as it remained year after year captive of the extreme Left.

It is unnecessary to survey the policy statements of the other presidential candidates and the faculty representatives. They are divided into moderate-left, far-left and conservative (conservatives in the minority), whose ideas and motivations I have already covered. The great contest was between Ramjan, the far-left puppet, and Abbott representing the conservatives. There was one interesting detail, though. Moderate Ron Grunstein was a candidate for the Men's Medicine representative. To his undertakings, he facetiously added that he supported 'giving the Richard Nixon Honesty Award to those SRC politicians who forced this year's SRC President to "resign"'. The allusion to the dishonesty and trickery of the dominating Left was unmistakable. The outcome of the SRC elections was a clear defeat for the conservatives but not by any stretch an unqualified victory for the radicals. They would have to resort to their well-tried tactics to maintain ascendancy.

A rather smug and self-satisfied report of the election appeared (H24, 13 Sep) under the heading, '9% Swing to the Left in SRC Elections – Rightist push on SRC Fails'. The report was unattributed but had the detail, tone and style of David Patch, with the usual distortions. The record turnout, allegedly 24% of students, showed that student politics was not irrelevant to the mass of students. The conservative claim was not that student politics was irrelevant, but the Left's overwhelming dominance made actual student politics at Sydney University irrelevant. The outcome, said the report's author, was a 'major rebuff to the National Civic Council/Liberal Party-backed candidates of Tony Abbott, the Joe Bullock *Honi Soit* "team", and the right-wing faculty tickets'. Abbott's failure to win was also a defeat on a 'national level' for the NCC/Liberal Party Coalition, who saw an Abbott victory 'as an all-important step in their takeover of student organizations in this country'.

Even more satisfying, the author gushed, was the stunning victory of Barbara Ramjan as President in the face of 'a concerted campaign of hysteria, reminiscent of the red-baiting of the McCarthy era'. Patch would know all about political baiting. Most satisfying of all, though, was that Ramjan's campaign, under Patch's management, maintained 'the progressive political role of the SRC at Sydney [University], in direct opposition to the cynical effort to grab power by Tony Abbott and his gang'. There is a critical point to be made here about Abbott and his gang. The author of this report did not mention anything about events surrounding the declaration of the election results. The declaration was most likely on the evening of Thursday, 28 July, after the close of polls. I will come back to this critical point in the last chapter. The final paragraph of the report struck an ominous note for conservatives, especially given the alleged 'distortions':

The composition of the Council itself is at this stage unclear and won't resolve itself until after the first meeting of Council and the election of officers. Certainly, because of the distortions produced through Faculty representation, the Council appears likely to have at least a third of its membership comprising National Civic Council-backed representatives. However, the rest of the Council representatives appear likely to support and maintain student interests in the welfare and political arenas. [*my emphasis*]:

If I am right about the far-left rushing in Ramjan as an appealing but easily manipulated puppet to defeat Abbott, then it is reasonable to wonder how much trauma they were subjecting her to. What was the cost of her election victory to her state of mind? Student politics was a tough, brutal game, and nothing in the years leading up to the 1977 SRC elections suggested Ramjan was a toughened operator. It was quite the opposite. She was now mixing it with fanatics like Hirst and Bennett and obsessed manipulators like Patch. It did not take long for Ramjan to feel the heat – and tell everyone about it. Her first letter as 50th SRC President appeared in H24 (13 Sept):

'On [Wednesday] 7 September 1977, the first meeting of the 50th SUSRC met to decide and elect officers of the SRC, the Executive, and the Finance

Committee. During the elections, two women – one a representative, the other an undergraduate standing for an officer position had to endure the most degrading sexist comments and actions I have yet heard of on this campus.

The first woman was confronted by John O'Mara, the Dentistry rep. Who decided to 'have a bit of fun', and exposed his genitalia to her as well as urinating against a tree. She was harassed and intimidated, all because Mr O'Mara wanted some fun. The other woman, a representative, was also outside Council Chambers waiting to make her election speech when Mr O'Mara decided to have more fun. After harassing and intimidating her with such phrases as 'fucking rag', he decided to re-enter Council Chambers to continue consuming his well-stocked beer provisions.

Not only did he physically intimidate two women outside council chambers, but verbally intimidated women inside chambers as well.

I am disgusted and disturbed that Mr O'Mara, a person elected by Dentistry students, should stoop to such actions at a meeting of Council.

If this is the person that Dentistry students wanted as their representative, then I am left with no alternative but to move a motion at the next council meeting censuring and demanding disciplinary action against Mr O'Mara by Council.'

It is vitally important to note that Ramjan was talking about the meeting for the election of the SRC officers on 7 September and not about the annual election results declared on 28 July, five weeks earlier. Crucially, she did not mention Tony Abbott. The focus was solidly on O'Mara, who (allegedly) verbally brutalized Ramjan's friends. As expected, Ramjan had rousing support from the far-left collective. Michelle Martin, Anne Woods, Garry Bennett, and Rose Vines wrote in the same issue of *Honi*:'

'The first meeting of the 50th Sydney University SRC was characterized by an unending stream of sexist incidents and attacks by right-wing representatives and their cohorts. However, in addition, I would like to draw attention to the racist attack against the newly elected Ethnic Relations Officer, Takis Constantopedos. Snide comments referring to the candidate's name, such as 'is that one person or two', were heard to emanate from a group including Tony Abbott, John O'Mara and others. Comments like this, directed in a mocking and denigratory manner, are a reflection of the racist attitudes of reactionaries. Such intimidations must be condemned and rejected by students, particularly when engaged in by their own 'representatives'.'

Abbott now had a mention but only as belonging to a group accused of racist comments. He was not singled out for any specific action. The criteria here for racist comments would make everyone racist at some time or another. Most pertinently, Abbott's 'punch' alleged by Ramjan in Marr's *Political Animal*, and the trauma it caused, is not mentioned in either of these two letters. Why? Why was not such a traumatic event that caused media uproar for weeks on end thirty-five years later not screamed out by Ramjan in her letter complaining of the far less serious actions of someone else? So that we know the detail we're dealing with, here is the critical passage from Marr's book. The 'punches' came just after the announcement that Ramjan had won the vote for SRC President:

'[Abbott] approached Ramjan. She thought he was coming over to congratulate her. "But no, that's not what he wanted. He came up to within an inch of my nose and punched the wall on either side of my head." Thirty-five years later, she recalls with cold disdain what he did. "It was done to intimidate."

Is it credible that in her first comment as SRC President Ramjan's mind was on the hectoring comments of John O'Mara (7 Sep) and not on the far more serious (alleged) physical assault of Abbott (28 Jul)? It doesn't make sense. Abbott struck back hard (H26, 29 Sep) under the heading 'Politics of Deceit'.

'It was Goebbels' theory that if you say something often enough, people will believe it, and, certainly, the Nazis' branding of all opponents, communist or conservative, as 'enemies of the fatherland' is echoed, not very surprisingly, by *Honi*'s attacks on 'enemies of student interests'.

'*Honi Soit* has been remarkable for its consistent and absolute disregard for the truth. Articles have been uniformly from the left, while those few critical letters have been derisively titled or ridiculed in postscript.

'But I refer particularly to the letters of Miss Ramjan and Miss Martin et al in the *Honi* of 13.9.77. Not only are the motives attributed to John O'Mara and myself false and malicious, but they are justified with 'facts' that are bare-faced lies or gross distortions. I really don't think urinating against a tree is such a terrible crime. It was quite late at night, the nearest toilet was several hundred yards away, and there was no one of delicate sensibilities about—or so it seemed. It seems strange that O'Mara's actions should so offend those who now proclaim 'Sexuality Week'.

'The woman passer-by referred to by Miss Ramjan must have been several yards away, and O'Mara, after all, was facing the tree. Her eyesight is exceptional! The claim that O'Mara 'exposed his genitalia' is a deliberate lie.

'Inside the meeting room, O'Mara and other opponents of the Left were subjected to continual abuse particularly from one Jenny Ryan, who is not a member of Council but was allowed to rave in the foulest language without rebuke or caution from the chair. Her remarks to O'Mara were particularly insulting. Miss Ramjan's claim that O'Mara was drunkenly insulting women is malicious and untrue.

'This sort of cheap smear has been a feature of this year's *Honi* and, under normal circumstances, would hardly merit a reply. But most people are incapable of a brazen and outright lie and accept most of what they read and hear as approximate truth—so some of the mud sticks.

'The extreme Left's constant exploitation of what they see as the 'gullibility of the masses' is further evidence of their fundamental contempt for ordinary people.'

My account of the far left's political activity corresponds with Abbott's accusations. He was vigorously denouncing not only Ramjan as a barefaced liar and hypocrite but the whole bunch of those carrying her forward. Hypocrisy, double standards, 'bare-faced lies and gross distortions' were never an issue for the Left – unless it concerned their perceived disadvantage. Overwrought Ramjan could hardly contain her anger. She and two (far-left) friends returned fire in a rambling piece (H27, mid-Oct) whose ridicule ran to the edge of coherence. They signed themselves Barbara Ramjan, (SRC President), Michelle Martin, (SRC Welfare Officer), Anne Woods. Again, no mention of the punches:

'It is with exasperation that we refer to an article in *Honi* of 27.9.77 ambiguously entitled 'Politics of Deceit' by one of Sydney Uni's 'resident-extremist-right-wing-moderates', Tony Abbott. This article represents just one more episode in Abbott's championing of 'truth and justice – the Democrat way'.

'The letters in *Honi* of 13.9.77 to which Abbott refers were not interested in the personal motives or intentions of O'Mara and Abbott and their cohorts but were political accusations of sexism and racism.

'At the risk of boring readers by filling in some details, we repeat that O'Mara, the SRC Dentistry Rep. did indeed expose his genitalia: O'Mara was facing the tree while urinating (as Abbott points out), but he turned right around, directly towards the woman as she passed then back to the tree. However, Abbott's vision may have been obscured since, as O'Mara turned, his back was facing him. Shortly later, as the woman returned to the SRC meeting, O'Mara dropped his pants (perhaps for Abbott's entertainment, he seemed highly amused) and bowed in Abbott's direction, flashing his bum towards the woman. Such events are not a question of 'delicate sensibilities' but of deliberate, harassing and intimidating, sexist acts.

'Throughout the evening, Abbott and O'Mara continued to harass and insult women standing for election. This sort of manipulative politicking by the Right is an unjustifiable misuse of their positions on Council. A person is elected to represent the views of their Faculty; they are not elected to cause chaos or engage in destructive, petty actions because they might find them amusing.

'Given Abbott's concern for the 'bare facts', one is nevertheless hard-pressed to find anything of substance in his article. Tony merely slanders and hypothesises, and exhausts his word-space with repeatedly unsubstantiated, self-righteous accusations of 'disregard for the truth'. Tony's brand of journalistic expertise may well please such publications as *The Australian* or *The Bulletin*, however, were it not for *Honi*'s tolerant policy, we might be spared such twisting mendacity and mangled garble, posing as critical and political comment!

'We stand by our statements. We suggest Abbott if he believes them to be false and malicious ... barefaced lies, to take legal action against us. We shall be delighted to see him in court.'

No doubt supported by her political director, David Patch. But there was another reason for the confident legal challenge besides trainee lawyer Patch, which I will come to. 'Snowflake' now has common currency to describe brittle thin-skinned university students who can't cope with the pressure of political debate when the focus is turned on them. It's okay against others but not them. Ramjan had a sensitive ear for Abbott's robust, unyielding discourse. She was deaf to the abuse and foul language of her far-left faction. But she had arms enough to comfort her. Her far-left feminist friends continued to rally around with their denunciation of the sexist opposition. Leslie Podesta of SU (extremist) Feminist Group and General Philosophy Feminist Collective, now SRC Women's Officer, spoke of O'Mara's boorish behaviour during the meeting but did not support Ramjan's accusation of mooning and urinating (H28, late Oct). Again, the far left's talk in *Honi* in the aftermath of the SRC elections focused on the boorish behaviour of Dentistry Rep John O'Mara. In Podesta's case, Abbott, though present, was not even grouped with O'Mara. If Abbott had been guilty of boorish drunken behaviour, you can be sure it would not have escaped overheated comment in *Honi* by Hirst and his collective.

In the same issue, Abbott rejected physical violence in politics, rightly highlighting the double standards and hypocrisy of the Left during the visit of world-famous psychologist Professor Eysenck:

'At last Wednesday's SRC meeting [the 4th], a number of people, who were not members of Council, pelted those present with eggs, two of which struck myself. To forestall any slanderous imputations or allegations from the extreme Left, I want to state quite clearly my attitude to this sort of activity. The essence of a democratic society is the right to free speech. However, disagreeable certain views may be, such activity is a deliberate and unacceptable attempt to harass SRC members. However, there is an obvious parallel between the SRC incident and the recent Eysenck demonstrations. Extreme left SRC members were adamant that Eysenck was a racist and thus 'must not be allowed to speak on campus'. Yet the same SRC members were outraged at this apparent attempt to disrupt their meeting – at which were stated views equally repugnant to many students.

'But they are not content merely with double standards. Professor Eysenck, a world-famous psychologist, was unable to utter a single word; the SRC was interrupted for only a matter of minutes. The demonstrators hurled smoke bombs, and there were several scuffles; Wednesday night's intruders threw a few harmless eggs. Most importantly, the Eysenck lecture was a solemn occasion for debate on scientific matters, but there is nothing dignified about the extreme left ideological cant heard at the SRC.

'SRC heavies have been quick to justify the Eysenck incidents. But imagine the feelings of those who realise the effect university political activity can have on society as a whole, and who are appalled at the domination of campus politics by unrepresentative extreme left and communist elements with no respect for the values of the overwhelming majority – who have never voted in any student election.

'There are a number of reasons why students are consistently deceived by the fine words of the communist left, but that doesn't make their lies any easier to stomach.

'When money is refused to a faculty society and granted instead to the Lidcombe Workers' Health Centre, when those who campaigned as 'broad-left' announce themselves as communist after the election, when those who claim to be 'independent' and 'non-partisan' show a quite contradictory obsession with Palestine and a disregard for all but their own rather cowardly group – then intense anger and frustration may be generated.

'The Left are quick to justify violence when a group feels itself oppressed or disadvantaged, and to laud the deeds of these 'freedom fighters'. Without in any way seeking to excuse the egg-throwing incident, surely it is the eminently understandable response of those who feel the SRC does not represent them and never will.

'This incident and the Eysenck affair are both deplorable though they differ in degree. I fail to see how even our SRC could distinguish the principle.'

The clarity of this comment on the far left's double standards, unrestrained violence, and subversive action to undermine Western Society relieves me of further explication. The 'egg-throwing' incident to which Abbott referred was done to death in their accusations about the (alleged) right-wing violence. In brief, four masked students burst in on the 4th meeting of the 50th SRC and threw eggs around until someone made a grab at them, after which the four decamped from the egg-spattered meeting. The incident thus could not have been more than a matter of seconds. It was alleged that John O'Mara was behind the stunt. I will return to this incident later but will suffice here with noting that in Irving Wallace's satirical send-up of the event, he alluded to the presence of 'Patch, Ramjan, Bolt & Co'. Patch was always there pulling the strings with his co-puppeteers Steve Bolt and Gary Nicholls.

Abbott had made his final contribution to 1977 *Honi*. He may have submitted other letters, but if so, they were not printed. I have included all his contributions bar one, which was not relevant. My purpose has been to show the character of Abbott's writing in contradiction of the accusations to which the left subjected him. In his arguments, he was considered, analytical, and concise without the abuse and ridicule he had to swallow from others. Although he was tough and determined, never retreating, he remained, for the most part, respectful of his opposition. His enemies accused him of loud, sexist comments during SRC meetings. The evidence suggests he was no different from the bulk of students in the outspokenness of their debate and a lot more constrained than most. I have offered ample proof of the Left's style of debate. I have also included all Barbara Ramjan's contributions about Abbott and his conservative colleagues relating to her claim Abbott 'came up to within an inch of my nose and punched the wall on either side of my head'.[99]

I have done this to show that a dramatic suspension of reason and leap of faith are required to reconcile the contemporary evidence with Ramjan's accusations after thirty-five years of silence. We are to believe it was just coincidence it became public when David Marr interviewed her for a book whose aim was to destroy the detestable Abbott. I will look more closely at the coherence of the allegations of violence in the final chapter. There is, however, another aspect of Ramjan's accusations that is pertinent to the affair. If Ramjan aimed to complete the work of fatally wounding Abbott, a task she could not finish as a student, then she might have given more away about herself than she intended. She told Marr:

'He was the most in your face. That's what set him apart. There were, of course, other Liberal Party and DLP types on campus, but they weren't offensive, and they weren't rude. They were people you could talk to. You could sit down and have a cup of tea with them. I would never do that with Tony Abbott. He's not that sort of person. I don't care what your politics are, you can still engage with another person. You don't have to be threatening. You don't have to be just that awful person. I have no doubt Tony was a most charming man when he wanted to be. It was a very conscious choice he made.' She called the year that followed – with her as president and Abbott on the SRC executive – the worst of her life. 'I doubt there would have been any moment in that year that he would have been charming towards me.'

Ramjan as a far-left scheming activist sitting down to have a cup of tea with the despised far-right enemy? More suspension of reason. And what far-right person did she ever sit down with for a cuppa and a cosy chat? She claims the SRC presidency was the worst year of her life and blames Abbott for it. But is it not more the case that Ramjan was not up to the fierce brawling of student politics? Running to mummy in the courts because a bad boy said bad things about her was not promising. Was she not far too nervy and thin-skinned? Moreover, she had to contend with more than Abbott, as the above letters show. If she had a miserable time (and that will be tested in the next chapter), the evidence is that others besides Abbott played on her nerviness. Marr ignored such possibilities because, like Ramjan, he was only interested in trashing Abbott's character. There was more evidence of her 'delicate sensibilities' and lack of experience and the suggestion she was dangling at the end of puppet strings.

On 7 September, during or after the same meeting for the election of SRC officers, the election for the delegates to the Special AUS Council the following week took place. Two delegates were allocated to represent Sydney University, but the SRC decided to send a caucus of five, including the two delegates. The results of the election were Ramjan 10, Abbott 7, Jones 5, [Marianna] Shaw 3, Wallach 2, Fine 1. That seemed to be a result beyond contention. It wasn't. Third-year medical students Rosemary Fine and Ron Grunstein described (H24) what happened next:

'At this stage, there was considerable discussion as to the method of counting the votes and this was satisfactorily resolved. At this stage, there was no mention of the possibility that Ramjan and Abbott were not properly elected.

'By midnight many representatives including Abbott and his 6 close supporters had left the meeting. At 12.30 am, a protest was registered by Barbara Ramjan as to the result, suggesting the method of selecting the 2 delegates should have involved full distribution of the preferences as though no caucus was being elected ... The 2 Returning Officers and the Chairperson of the Standing Legal Committee upheld Barbara's protest... The distribution of preferences changed the vote so that Ramjan and Jones were elected delegates.

'One can question whether a declared result can be invalidated and, once invalidated, can it be recounted by any method. Though the election of Jones from a political point of view was preferable to us rather than that of Abbott, we are still concerned about the events of the evening.'

Not everyone by far was happy with Ramjan's suspicious manoeuvre. Jeremy Jones wrote, 'I was one of the not unsubstantial number of reps who thought that, even though the final interpretation of the rules was probably correct, it was very dubious that the moment the person most adversely affected walked out the door the "mistake" of earlier was discovered' (H26, 29 Sep). But was the manoeuvre initiated by Ramjan alone? Or was her campaign manager behind her, pulling the strings? As it turned out, biffing Abbott off the formal delegation to the Special AUS Council meeting did not prevent Ramjan's neutralisation at the conference. And it was not Abbott who disempowered her.

Two delegates from other universities were so indignant about Ramjan's treatment they just had to poke their noses into SU's affairs. Ted Murphy, Latrobe Senior Delegate, claimed Jeremy Jones and Irving Wallach consulted with delegates from other universities and made decisions without consulting Ramjan and Marianna Shaw (H27). 'This undemocratic procedure continued', wrote Murphy, 'despite the frequent protests of Barbara Ramjan and Marianna Shaw'. Poor helpless Barbara and Marianna, distressed damsels in need of protection. Murphy did not mention Tony Abbott. Presumably, on Murphy's account, he was also a victim of Jones's and Wallach's high-handed behaviour – which does not suit the manufactured image.

The second intervention came from Don Gibbons, Education and Politics Convenor, Rusden State College Victoria. In his more detailed account, Jones and Wallach were the primary culprits whose undemocratic behaviour – 'standing over' Ramjan and Shaw – 'amazed and disgusted' him, though he did not excuse Abbott of associated complicity. Gang leaders Jones and Wallach, he wrote, ran roughshod over Ramjan and Shaw and conferred with delegates of other campuses before making decisions independently of Ramjan. But he added an accusation that had not occurred to Murphy. Abbott and Wallach, as non-delegate caucus members, he complained, on five occasions 'exercised Sydney's voting rights whilst a delegate [Ramjan] was present. The delegate was not given the chance to vote – more standover tactics'.

What a frightened, timid operator Ramjan's far-left colleagues made her out to be without the protection of Patch & Co. How would she handle her presidential duties in 1978? Sometime during the Christmas break, Ramjan married top-gun criminal lawyer Greg James, one of the youngest barristers ever appointed Queen's Counsel. James was thirty-three and had a brilliant career ahead of him in our bourgeois capitalist society. Patch must have cried an ocean. Ramjan would become an active member of the society she execrated and schemed to undermine when a student at Sydney University. How's that for false and hypocritical behaviour?

IN THE last issue of *Honi* for the year (H29, Oct), an article 'Violence on Campus' appeared. There was no name to it, but it was almost certainly from someone in the Women's Collective. The article's two fundamental claims were that all men were innately violent and 'potential rapists'. As a concrete example of male violence, the author cited the egg-throwing incident during the 4th meeting of the 50th SRC. Abbott condemned such 'violent' tactics, and the author relieved him of complicity. But if the Women's Collective wanted a genuine example of unrefined male violence, they could have taken Ramjan's and Patch's testimony. Why didn't Ramjan and Patch give it, and why would the Women's Collective take the irrational decision to ignore such a wonderful example of Abbott's (alleged) innately violent character?

Chapter 10

The Ramjan puppet presidency

IN HER POLICY statement for the SRC presidency, Barbara Ramjan reeled off the rhetoric about staff-student democratisation and subject assessment in which Patch and the far-left gang had tutored her. To this, she added her undertaking to defend women against 'the general anti-woman attitudes held by most men at this campus'. I wonder whether her far-left male mates were free from the Nevillism that allegedly infected such squalid male dens as (Catholic) St John's College (see below). With my observations of the attitudes and preoccupations of the male left during those times, I hardly think so. Such considerations, though, were of no account when it came to Ramjan's undertaking to establish the left's scheme of democracy in the SRC. She was focused. 'I support open committees of the SRC, regular general meetings for students to air their views, direct election of SRC Officers', she had declared, 'and I will report on what I am doing through a column in *Honi Soit*'. But it was Tony Abbott who was first to rise in the student parliament. As a preamble, he generously complimented centre-left Paul Brereton and Law Representative Chris Dummer for 'the recent allocation of nearly $8,000 for a no-fault insurance scheme' for students. He continued:

'But as usual, those who most loudly trumpet their concern for students were horrified that SRC money might be diverted from such 'progressive' issues as black land rights, feminism, and the uranium moratorium.

'It seems neither Barbara Ramjan's recent marriage nor Gary Nicholls' switch to Sydney Teachers College have cooled their ardour for the revolution at Sydney Uni.

'I suppose it would be unfair to recall Barbara's election claim that she alone was genuinely interested in students. Fine sounding phrases fall so easily from left-wing lips — if only they were true. The tardy introduction of this scheme illustrates two points. The first is that the careerists and extremists who have dominated the SRC for so long are really interested only in its exploitation. The second is that only the so-called right is willing to forsake ideological grandstanding and mob manipulation for the unspectacular task of actually benefiting all students.'

Abbott again raised an ongoing indictment of far-left activities – the syphoning off student monies to far-left causes – to which they only ever returned abuse. He had a mild dig at Ramjan considering the seriousness of the accusation – scarcely what you would call 'in your face'. More interesting were the reappearance of CPA Gary Nicholls in SRC activities and the coupling of Ramjan with Nicholls. Nicholls was now in his postgraduate year and the only CPA member of the 1978 AUS Executive. As it turned out, Ramjan's first contribution to *Honi* was in H4 (4 April), and it was not about student affairs. And it was not about Tony Abbott being 'in her face'. Indeed, it was not Ramjan's utterance but the reproduction of a press release from IMAGINUS, a Toronto-based company promoting a 'travelling art show' which Ramjan supported. It appeared she thought it a good idea for Sydney University to help make IMAGINUS's art product available to the students. 'For additional details', interested parties were invited to contact 'Barbara Ramjan, President, Student Representative

Council University of Sydney, New South Wales 2006'. What was she – Imaginus's Sydney (commission) agent?

Between Ramjan's election as SRC President and her promotion of a Canadian travelling art show, she had spoken twice in *Honi*. Both times were to complain about the boorish behaviour of someone other than Tony Abbott. She had not published the faculty representatives or the SRC Officers as was customary. She had not reported on SRC meetings. Most students would have only known about them from references in *Honi*. There was no welcome for new students. It seems she was leaving the president's responsibilities to others, or those others were determining her actions as president. I suppose being freshly married to a hot-shot lawyer caused some distractions from her undertakings and SRC responsibilities. James's influence loomed in Ramjan's next contribution to *Honi* (H5, 11 April). She had raised her sights from Abbott to no less a figure than the Vice-Chancellor. And it was on legal points. Ramjan had acquired a hitherto undeclared interest in the law. The trouble with her over-confident piece – apart from its muddled expression – was a lack of context for her legal points.

The issue was over a report in 'The University of Sydney News' that 'the Vice-Chancellor lent his office and name to various statements of law in commenting on a student meeting'. Whether she had a legal point against the Vice-Chancellor in paragraphs 2 and 4 of his statement, which she did not detail, no one could tell without further explanation. Of as much interest was her ignorant Patch-like arrogance in speaking about the Vice-Chancellor, a feature of the far left's behaviour that Abbott condemned.

First, she attacked the Vice-Chancellor's knowledge of the law. 'It must be appreciated the Vice-Chancellor's discipline is economics', she sniffed. 'His views as to the law are those of a layperson, well or informed [*sic*], depending upon the ability and skill of his informant'. Then she ridiculed him for his estimation of the numbers attending the meeting in question. 'The Vice-Chancellor's attempt at a meaningful statistics [*sic*] would not have gained him a pass in any first-year course except Propaganda I'. Like her tutor Patch, Ramjan would know all about propaganda – and contempt. No one in later issues of *Honi* thought her legal objections interesting enough to comment on. Someone, though, had something to say about her new-found legal status. Ted Marr, the President of Sydney University Union, commented: 'I am amused that within one month of commencing Law I, Barbara Ranjam has appointed herself legal advisor to the Vice-Chancellor'.

Ramjan's next appearance in *Honi* would be at the end of June. It appeared Abbott's distance from her face during the first half of the academic year was not serious enough for her to resort to *Honi* for a whinge. Nor did Abbott write anything about her after the mild dig. Nor was there any reported SRC meeting during which Abbott could come close to her face. Ted Marr's letter (H7, 26 April), of which the above was the opening paragraph, clarified Ramjan's attempted legal correction of the Vice-Chancellor. The context was the university's proceedings against those responsible for the violence during the demonstration against Professor Hans Eysenck in September of the previous year.

To the hearty cheer of most people in the general community, Vice-Chancellor Bruce Williams refused to be cowed by slavering fanatics like Martin Hirst. He took decisive action and slapped two-year suspensions on Hirst and Jean Pender 'during which time they [were] not permitted on any part of the university grounds'. Hirst was already under suspension for his role in occupying the Registrar's office. Greg Schofield of the SU Communist Group received a one-year suspension and a $100 fine. 'Twelve other students received fines ranging from $25 to $100'.[100]

Stella Brown leapt to the radicals' defence in H2 (14 March). Eysenck and his former pupil Arthur Jensen, she wrote, were 'well known for their belief that intelligence based on the scoring from IQ tests is governed chiefly by genetic factors (about 80% of human intelligence) and only minimally affected by environmental factors (about 20% of the quotient)'. Their theories, she alleged, gave aid to racists and their political programs. The students had cause to demonstrate. They were allowed their right to free speech, weren't they? Besides, there was no violence, was there? No, they were just 'shouting, clapping, chanting, and blowing whistles!' – no reason to single out anyone to be charged. Paul Brereton, SRC Executive member, said Stella Brown's letter amazed him 'because of the number of lies, half-truths, and distortions it included' (H4, 4 April):

'There were no violent acts', says Stella. You've got to be kidding! Unless you think, Ms Brown, that punches, water bombs, smoke bombs, attempts to break down doors, and kneeing attendants in the crutch, aren't violent. At least tell the truth when you try to defend your inexcusable denial of a person's right to speak ... I would remind her that the tactics that she and her friends and allies use to suppress Eysenk are exactly the same as the National Front uses in England today to suppress opposition, the same as Hitler used in the early 1930s to impose racism and eliminate all dissent. The demonstrators' behaviour links them with the forces that they profess to oppose.'

Tony Abbott was not the only one condemning the far left's routine lies and violence. However, in a thoughtful piece in the same issue, free of the aggressive inflammatory comments of which he was often accused, he broadened the implications of the far left's justification of violent demonstrations:

'There has recently been a feeble attempt by the forces of coercion and misrepresentation on this campus to turn a group of violent malcontents into heroes of the longed-for revolution. I refer to those 'victimised' for their disruption of lectures given last year by the distinguished psychologist Professor Hans Eysenck. Allegations that Eysenck is a 'racist' do not presently concern me, though their flimsy 'proof' that he believes genetic factors may influence intelligence is thoroughly unconvincing. Likewise, I do not wish to comment on charges that the Senate procedure was unfair, only to point out that none of the tedious justifications for refusing free speech have actually denied that actions taken prevented Eysenk's talk.

In left-wing eyes, it seems that Eysenk's crime was to be a 'racist' and to speak at a closed symposium of staff. On both counts, all means of disruption were legitimised. To deny the occasional necessity of closed meetings and the subsequent entitlement of any group to hold them is patently absurd. The transparent hypocrisy of the left is amply demonstrated by their outrage over the SRC egg-throwing incident last year.

But the idea that only 'free speech', which is 'non-racist, non-sexist etc.', is permitted is far more dangerous. It threatens a totally unacceptable tyranny of one concept over others on the whim and caprice of a particular group. Such monstrous inhumanities as the slaughter of the Jews and the psychiatric imprisonment of Russian dissidents have stemmed from the similar subjective qualification of fundamental human rights. It would be nice to think that the purveyors of such pernicious dogma (who, of course, should be allowed expression) would be exposed as the soul-mates of Hitler and Stalin they are. Quite the opposite – for years, they have dominated student politics at this university.

Unfortunately, the ignorant believe their fine words, while the better informed and more fully disillusioned rarely bother to vote.'

Martin Hirst rushed to respond. In brief, the radicals were not violent, there was no proof of their violence, and, anyhow, the psychology department people started the violence. And what about other occasions when the left were (allegedly) subject to violence? He gave a string of examples. The mangled analogies were meant to demonstrate the hypocrisy of those vilifying Hirst. And what about Hirst's free speech? Wasn't he denied his right to free speech by being shut out of the Eysenck seminar? Besides, free speech was a capitalist myth. This is just what Abbott and Brereton missed:

'Eysenk is a political figure, as are all people in his position – those who cre-ate the ideological justifications for capitalism. What Brereton and Abbott don't point out is that Eysenk's 'right to free speech' is GUARANTEED by his position as a privileged academic. Further, they refuse to admit that by defending Eysenk's right to free speech, they are in fact, denying these rights to economically and politically oppressed groups, who have not the position or privilege to hold closed seminars for the dissemination of their views. The right to express any opinion in our society is dependent on the support of the forces of control and repression.'

It would have been useless to point out that Abbott had scorn for Hirst's Marxist analysis of capitalist society and its notion of free speech. There were long-established problems with Marx's socio-analysis – not to mention the overwhelming concrete evidence of Marxism's failure. Hirst signed off as, 'Yours in suppressed anger and expressed contempt, Martin Hirst, Suspended Student'. Hirst appeared in urgent need of bourgeois anger management therapy. CPA Nicholls ran the same mangled analogi-cal arguments but spared us the Marxist rant.

He attacked the Vice-Chancellor's 'ill-considered and inflammatory re-marks in the University of Sydney News'. Wasn't it the top point of in-justice and hypocrisy that a small group of inoffensive left-wing students 'who merely attend or shout at a Psychology Staff Colloquium' are charged 'whilst [the] much more abhorrent but nominally apolitical behaviour' of some right-wing brutes go unpunished? Nicholls was talking about the egg-throwing at a rowdy SRC meeting. He reeled off a series of such ex-amples. He ended by saying, 'What has been woefully absent from the uni-versity's actions against the anti-Eysenck demonstrators has been any sense of perspective. Look at what else was happening last year; the constant harassment of progressive students on campus, the provocative nature of the Eysenck "closed" meetings, the lack of any effort at conciliation by the University and/or Psychology Department authorities'. Don't look on us as 'jackbooted stormtroopers of the left', he appealed.

Union President Ted Marr greeted Nicholls' fantasy with contempt. 'The university', he continued from above, was 'indeed under attack by "jackbooted stormtroopers of the left"'. Hirst and his mates had no intention of going along to the seminar to express their opinion. Days before, they had signs proclaiming, 'KEEP EYSENCK OFF CAMPUS' and 'NO RACISTS ON CAMPUS'. No way would they let Eysenck speak. The meeting was closed for sound reasons. Their actions 'are in the tradition of the Inquisition, of the Calvinist zealots, of Hitler and the Nazis, or of the Ku Klux Klan. They have in common with these a conviction of absolute right, a belief that they have discovered a magic formula for the cure of all ills, and a sense of purpose which permits, if persuasion is not effective, attempts at destruction of opposition, in short, the "Correct line" favoured by the Maoists ... The university and the Vice-Chancellor are quite right in denying such people the privilege of membership of this community, and they deserve the support of all of us who believe in a free society'.

Unperturbed, Nicholls continued to expound his fantasy about the dark forces of the administration harassing his inoffensive comrades (H12, 20 June). After acknowledging the last of those fined were forced to pay up or suffer expulsion, he appealed to those same dark capitalist forces to donate the money to the Aboriginal Legal Services, which amounted to tipping the money into the far-left coffers, as Abbott pointed out in such cases. This was the last of the exchanges in this affair. I have tracked these exchanges to show that Abbott was not alone in his assessment of the far left and their cynical activities. His piece on the Eysenck affair was less charged and more measured than those of his moderate colleagues. And he did not give Barbara Ramjan even a mention, which indicated he was still at an inoffensive distance from her face.

Another surprising reappearance on campus in 1978 was Abbotsleigh girl Sarah Sheehan enrolled in Arts II. What had happened? Sarah had risen high in the hierarchy of the AUS. As Services Vice-President overseeing AUS Student Travel, she was one of the five CPA members who were AUS full-time officers in 1977. Her words to apply for this position in the capitalist business world were not about the tried and proven measures of a market economy. No, none of that nonsense. She wrote: 'First and foremost, the position of SVP should be seen as a political position. In the context of the mobilisation of conservative forces, both on and off campus, AUS needs a militant leadership to defend the rights and interests of the membership against the Nareen Squattocracy and the interests [Prime Minister] Fraser represents'.[101]

By August 1977, the $22 million AUS travel empire had collapsed, leaving $3.5 million owing and the business in administration. AUS was bleeding memberships and money. After the fiasco and violence of the 1977 AUS Annual Conference, moves by the moderates to defeat the entrenched Marxist hierarchy bore fruit. The 1978 AUS Annual Conference was a moderates' rout of the far left, leaving only CPA Gary Nicholls on the AUS Executive. So, Sarah Sheehan was back on campus pursuing the destruction of bourgeois capitalist society with flair and taste only Abbotsleigh, an Anglican private school for girls, could cultivate. Was she embarrassed about her part in the crippling AUS had suffered? If she was, her interventions in *Honi* did not reveal it. With her far-left colleagues Gary Nicholls and Steve Bolt, she carried on the campaign to control the SRC and its funds and render the opposition impotent – not just Abbott and the *Democrat*.

Moderate Jeremy Jones was now the Local AUS Secretary and member of the AUS Executive. In a chatty piece (H2, 14 March), he encouraged new students to learn more about their union. There was much to learn and get involved in. There was the 'travel debate', AUS delegation elections, and 'extraordinary resolutions' to deal with. He was available to answer all enquiries. Quite a reasonable approach early in the year, you would think. He was back in H6 (18 April) bemoaning the lack of response in the same friendly manner. Was it because everyone was 'fully aware of the structure and functions of AUS?' Was the AUS office too far from the 'deodorised Old Union?' Or was it because nobody cared? He enlarged upon the vital work AUS did. There was no mention, though, of the previous year's crippling under the Marxist hierarchy, the collapse of AUS Travel, the legal actions, and the secession movements. Clearly, he meant to be upbeat about AUS's prospects, even if it seemed a lost cause.

This was all very 'slack' for Ms Sheehan, former AUS Services Vice-President and now in her sixth year of university and student affairs. Jeremy and 'his surrogate AUS Secretary, Paul Brereton', had done nothing to promote AUS matters (H7, 19 April)). Oh yes, there had been a few meetings devoted to 'boring bits of necessary, but trivial, bureaucracy'. There had been 'one scratchy leaflet produced on the morning of the meeting and badly distributed'. A totally unproductive waste. Two meetings were cancelled because of Jones's slackness. 'Jeremy/Paul', lectured Sheehan, was 'interested only in holding the formal power of being AUS Secretary and not seeking to improve the lot of students by any constructive political action ... Only a massive change in orientation, to an activist orientation which involved students in a real way by publicity, promotion and action will solve students' very real problems'. You must admire Sheehan's blind, unswerving adherence to the party line. The directors of Abbotsleigh's board must have wept in despair.

Jeremy Jones was too smart to apply the antidote of 'Abbotsleigh's most famous communist' to the problem of student disinterest in the AUS. No one could take her criticism seriously 'after [her] term as AUS Services Vice-President in 1977', about which she 'was the constant recipient of equally justified criticism' (H10, 6 June). With an overload of sarcasm, Jones said he must plead guilty to cancelling one meeting because a postal strike prevented sending the letter of advice. He should have gone to the 'strikers, explained that the letter was ideologically pure, and asked them to get back to work'. The second meeting was cancelled because there was not enough for a quorum. 'I did not stand for election on an "activist orientation" platform', he wrote, 'but rather on one of trying to represent mainstream student opinion, which I have consistently adhered to ... I have a more egalitarian ideal, and I suppose therefore I must accept criticism from Comrade Sheehan and her ilk'.

Her ilk, in the form of Steve Bolt and Gary Nicholls, tumbled over each other to come to her defence, gallantly putting down all criticisms of Sheehan and the far left's action in AUS. Their opponents among the students and the administration behaved like the most frightful hypocrites in their attempts to eliminate the far left's stranglehold on student affairs, whether it was the SRC or AUS. Mangled analogical arguments were thrown about. Whatever accusation the authorities levelled at the far left to justify their interventions, Bolt and Nicholls could accuse them of the same fault. If the authorities penalised students because of their violence, Bolt and Nicholls had examples of the authorities overlooking the violence of the non-left – e.g. egg-throwing in an SRC meeting vs the violent demonstration against the Eysenck lecture. If the authorities imposed voluntary student unionism on the SRC, Bolt and Nicholls had examples of organisations where membership was compulsory, e.g. the sports union.

It would be boring to show where most of Bolt's and Nicholl's analogical arguments collapse in the disparity of the comparisons. Besides, it is evident in most cases. A bit of egg-throwing in a rowdy student meeting is not the same as a violent demonstration thoroughly planned in its detail and aimed at disrupting the university's administration. The egg-throwing incident during the 4th meeting of the 50th SRC was just one of those occasions the far left could endlessly manipulate, as the unnamed female author of the article on campus violence did in the last issue of *Honi* 1977 (H29). I spoke about her claim that males were innately violent and potential rapists, but her piece went far beyond males as males. The 'question of violence', she wrote, 'cannot be separated from the issue of power'. Our author from the Women's Collective then degenerated into Marxist rhetoric. 'Men exercise power, women are oppressed', she continued. 'The values of capitalism with all its inequalities are all pervasive and those who would oppose them have no institutional power to wield'. Male power as the driver of the capitalist order was her focus. Here male power, society and rape came together. At this point, the article bordered on incoherence:

'Violence against women may be seen in two senses; the obvious acts of beating and rape, and the political implications of such instances. Women are accused of provoking violence, thus denying the seriousness of bashings. If men are to be disciplined, other men can benefit from the incident by saying, 'it wasn't me' – another way of denying the seriousness of violence against women.'

She then recounted the (alleged) incidence of rape and violence on campus that portrayed Sydney University as the rape capital of Australia, a fantasy only the deluded could swallow. You would expect such criminal acts, if true, to be reported to the authorities, and news of them splashed across the front pages of Australia's newspapers. They weren't. She continued, 'humiliation has been culturally created so that women feel shame at having been forcibly violated and feel reluctance to "admit" or report it'. The final paragraph is a challenge to one's comprehension:

"There also exists the appalling situation where men and conservatives can get away with isolating a few men as examples – perpetuating the idea that 'some men are bad, and, therefore, others are good." The same thing happens with rape – rapists are maniacs, they should be disciplined, whilst all other men are O.K., or only "having a bit of fun". All men are potential rapists and violent, and will be if they want to. And, as long as men get away with disciplining the so-called 'undesirables', all other men benefit from women being bashed and raped, because all other men are then seen by default to be "goodies".

The lack of coherence in such ideological passages results from the effort to squeeze the round observable facts into the square hole of rigid Marxist ideology. It is observable that a minority of men are guilty of rape, and the majority aren't. It is a true statement that 'all men are potential rapists'. There's no contradiction. Abstractly considered, all persons with a penis are potential rapists, just in the same way all women are potential child killers. But the question is not an abstract one. It is a matter of empirical evidence. The evidence is that a small minority of men rape women and that most men find the crime of rape abhorrent, a crime requiring severe punishment. Just as most women do not kill their children and find the idea nightmarish. If we go to the bottom line, the Women's Collective asserted that men were rapists essentially, that is, essentially bad, and as essentially bad warranted disqualification, if not elimination. It's the same proposition that governs Susan Mitchell's book about Abbott.

The 1977 article on campus violence was a prelude to the third issue of debate in the pages of *Honi* during 1978 that would draw a contribution – in part controversial – from Tony Abbott. A fictional piece of sadistic pornography under the rubric 'Chicken Grawp' sparked the debate. Lesley Podesta's response to it 'on behalf of the Women's Collective' told the story. Here are the opening paragraphs:

'Chickenfoot Grawp is degrading to women. It is a classic example of male fantasy, where a woman is physically abused, exploited and finally murdered.

Basically, the article describes an encounter on a street, where the 'hero' meets a woman who is crying and has obviously just been beaten. They go to her room (after he slaps her face), she strips, suggests that they fuck, and he shoots her through the vagina. His justification for such violence? She was a 'tramp', she swore, and her genitals were 'revolting'.

This article strengthens and justifies the male ethic that men can direct their potency and aggression towards women, and women shall passively submit to them (in fact, even enjoy it). For, such works effectively 'punishes' a woman who steps outside her role, or sexually threatens a male.'

This male ethic is a fiction of Podesta's and the Women's Collective, conjured to suit their ideology. 'The power relationship between men and women in our society', charged Podesta, made all women vulnerable. Such writing contravened SRC policy. The Women's Collective demanded 'an apology and explanation from the editors' and insisted 'no similar material be published'. Apart from the made-up male ethic, Podesta had a point, you would think. It was a pretty nasty story.

Alice Clarke (Ed. I) did not think so. She was full of contempt for Podesta. 'Poor Leslie Podesta!' she wrote (H4, 4 April). 'It appears she has no sense at all – of humour, literary appreciation, or the right of free speech'. Grawp was a pseudonym for an 'attractive sensitive girl' (Ed. II) who wrote her stories 'to relieve her boredom in psychology lectures'. Clarke said *Honi* editor Pat Lane thought Grawp's stories had literary merit. They were 'fine satires on the very subject of sexism and discrimination that Leslie is complaining of ... Leslie, somewhere along the road to hard-nosed narrow (marrow) minded feminism, has traded her sense of humour for a dog-eared copy of Kate Millet misread'. Well put. As for the ban by *Honi* of such literary pieces, did Podesta think the student newspaper was 'merely a mouthpiece of SRC propaganda?' Abbott was not alone in criticising the extremists of the Women's Collective.

Podesta did not have to worry about support. A letter in H5 loudly attested to her sense of humour and her intervention 'on behalf of the Women's Collective, which has over twenty members'. No prizes for guessing the colour of the signatories. Among the thirteen were Sarah

Sheehan, Steve Bolt, Chips Mackinolty, Garry Bennett, Martin Hirst, and Michelle Martin. In the same *Honi*, Podesta had other support that might not have been entirely to her taste. A group of senior students, males and females, including members of the Sydney Uni. Newman Catholic Society (SUNCS), bitterly protested about the advertising for the St Andrew's and St John's College balls. 'How could anyone, within six months of a woman being raped and murdered in the University grounds', they wrote, 'conceive of calling a social function a root [fuck] ball or a roman orgy?' People who associated St John's College with such functions were representing Catholicism. The group wanted to make the point 'forcefully ... that we are revolted by this advertising and wish to dissociate all ordinary Christians and Catholics from this repressive and insulting attitude to women'. They accused the student organisers of a 'third form mentality', which was to insult third formers. Rather than insult third-formers, they should have spoken about the pervasive influence of Nevillism to which the male left-wing mind particularly was in thrall.

The St John's College criticism did not affect the overheated spirits of the Women's Collective. Penelope Pether (Arts/Law II) heartily congratulated the feminists for their 'productive, creatively vengeful, an inspired and inspiring protest' in the St John's car park on the evening of 11 April (H6, 18 April). It was 'the perpetration of an act as animal as the Andrew's advertisements'. She cheered 'tasteful slogans' smeared on the university's walls 'advocating mutilation' of male genitalia, the picketing of St John's ball, a bomb scare, slashing of tyres, filling petrol tanks with sugar, and painting 'rape in red enamel paint' on cars. That was the feminist way of dealing with tasteless advertising. The Women's Collective were unrepentant.

In what can be considered an ongoing conservative manifesto, Tony Abbott responded to the ideas the Women's Collective relentlessly propagated (H13, 27 June).

'The world of student politics is generally one of bitter contention between rigid ideological certainties while most students could unflatteringly analyse the average student politician's compulsive need to strut and fret his hour upon the stage. And the more extreme the ideology, the more dogmatic its truths, the more unbalanced are the members of this crew of misfits it attracts.

'In the world beyond the narrow confines of tertiary study, a feminist is one who believes that women are as equally capable as men but have in the past been restrained by strict sex roles, and hence, is one who believes in equal opportunity for all. The occasional strident excesses of these people do not obscure the validity of their cause. But the ultra-militant women associated with the women's collective are altogether different.

"Feminist" is a misnomer – they would deny everything that is feminine. They are consumed with spite and malice; obsessed with imagined oppressions and insults; and introverted to an extraordinary degree. They publicly proclaim the fatuous notion of the exact equality of men and women and advocate drastic steps (such as not allowing men into law courses) to achieve this arithmetic equality. They completely fail to recognise the different aptitudes, though equal talents of men and women. Even denying the female form, their dress and mannerisms ape the worst excesses of 'ocker' or exhibitionist males.

'Their outspoken encouragement of lesbianism is insulting to heterosexual women. And what 'strength' or 'independence' is there in pretending that the basic human need for companionship of the opposite sex doesn't exist?

'University feminists are violent – the vandalism at St John's earlier this year is only their most spectacular transgression – the delight some of them take in kicking or spitting on opponents usually goes unreported. But ironically, they are not averse to using the privileged position of women in certain aspects of the law and the respect society still has for women when it suits them.

'But their own demands at the last AUS Council for 'positive discrimination' in favour of women, for the 'compulsory re-education' of men, for the availability of 'feminist doctors' and the condemnation of rape as a 'political crime, executed by men against all women (in which) all men are complicit' throw more light on their attitudes than anything I can say.

'Such is the voice of women on campus!

'Their fantastic delusions would be regrettable in any event, but they are being utilised for political purposes. Campus feminism requires the abolition of liberal democracy and its replacement by 'socialism'. The fact that the communist bloc is no women's only nirvana is immaterial; the feminists think it is, and they labour for its advent with all the unbalanced zeal of their monomania.

'At the SRC meetings, ten or so unkempt, dishevelled and overalled members of the women's collective disport with each other in slovenly embrace. Those who disagree with them are intelligently refuted with a stream of obscenities while all speakers are regularly interrupted by their inane giggling. Surprise, surprise, few students would recognise them as the well-meaning eccentrics who stand for election!

'It is a great pity that such fanatics have become the banner bearers of women's rights on campus. Their strutting arrogance and exaggerated hysteria certainly inflames the prickly attitude of most men towards women's issues. Similarly, I think they confuse and dismay most women.

'Yet I suppose the vast influence of these fanatics on student politics is revealing of its nature. The SRC has chosen to ignore the role of a service body and organiser of social and educational functions and sought instead that of a political pressure group. But this is a role of dubious necessity. 'Student rights' is quite rightly a big yawn to most, but their disinterest allows groups like the feminists to take over by default. It is ironic that as students become more conservative — and disinterested — their representatives become more committed and radical.

'Feminist-inspired AUS motions condemned liberal democracy because 'the definition of sexuality under capitalism is designed to perpetuate the dominance of men', the acceptance of sexuality as primarily 'penis-vagina oriented', and demanded the elimination of discrimination based on 'sex, class, race, religion, sexuality, marital status, and age' – on a basis so broad, in fact, that society could not function.

'What has happened to free speech, pluralism, and even mother nature? We are to become vengeful humanoids free to indulge our bodies but not our minds; obsessed with pleasure as a means to happiness; jealously competitive in nothing save uniformity and mediocrity so as to curry favour with the all forceful state, where equality springs from the barrel of a gun.

'The degree to which students apparently don't care about such aims in their purported representatives is profoundly disturbing.'

The editors headed this contribution with 'Some Outrageous Thoughts on Feminism'. They made no effort to explain why Abbott's thoughts were outrageous. It was enough that he displayed a monstrous deviation from the Marxist dogma, blindly motivating the extremists. Far worse, though, was that Abbott articulated as few people could the ideas of most of the community inside and outside the university. Again, he was lucid, measured, and analytical but determined in his expression. There was none of the heated sexist abuse his opponents accused him of. In no way was he against the idea of the basic equality of men and women and the justice of equal opportunity. His unflinching criticism was of the far-left feminists and the ultimate danger they represented to traditional Western Society. His criticism arose from a clearly defined conservatism.

BESIDES ABBOTT'S contributions, other letters periodically criticised the left. They were individual contributions. Abbott was the only conservative to publish regularly. There seemed to be a tacit recognition of Abbott's ascendancy and leadership. And why wouldn't the conservatives leave it to the person without equal on campus in understanding the ideology of the left and could so lucidly articulate a response? One new development was the emergence of Jeremy Jones and Paul Le Gay Brereton, who distinguished themselves from the far left and 'far right' as 'centrists'. Jones and Brereton were in my view centre left. Their criticisms of Abbott and their efforts to avoid being tainted by any association with the 'far-right' (conservatives) wrapped them in political saintliness. In H7 (26 April), the fragrance of their saintliness wafted from the letters section.

The 'good old left/right battle just doesn't happen anymore', they announced. The 'present SRC is unpopular both with the extreme left and right' while they, as small 'm' moderates, avoided being 'negative or unconstructive', making the SRC a more effective organisation. As examples of the balance, they listed calling for *'a student no/fault insurance scheme, proportional representation to allow minority views to be heard and represented, bringing all motions which ask for financial allocations to* off/campus organisations to student general meetings, and increasing provision for allocations to University Clubs and Societies' [their emphasis]. But weren't these just the sort of measures Abbott called for? Two weeks later (H9, 9 May), not Abbott but 'centrist' Brereton got into Barbara Ramjan's face:

'It is with some regret that I must depart from my previous policy of not attacking SRC President Barbara Ramjan in public. Until now, despite our political differences, I have been able to refrain from this. Now, however, her highhanded and despotic treatment of the St John's College Motion Affair must, in the interests of students and the SRC, be publicised.'

Three weeks before, a petition had called for a general SRC meeting about a motion to condemn the vandalism to the St John's College car park and to pay $300 to compensate for the damage. Ramjan refused to call a meeting, saying she did not have to call a meeting if the motion was invalid. She thought the motion invalid. She paid $80 for legal advice about the general principle of validity but not about her particular decision. Brereton was too polite in characterising Ramjan's wasting $80 on legal advice as 'capricious'. Ramjan dug in, refusing to allow her decision to be legally tested. She squibbed attending an SRC meeting to determine whether the motion was valid. The meeting overruled her, but she still refused to 'put the motion to a General Meeting'. Understandably exasperated, Brereton ended his letter:

'Ramjan and her think-alikes of the lunatic left have always made much of the provision for general meetings by petition as evidence of 'grass roots democracy in the workings of the SRC'. Why then, when a motion with which she apparently disagrees and which she is afraid might be carried is put forward, does she REFUSE TO ALLOW THIS 'GRASS ROOTS DEMOCRACY' TO OPERATE?'

The plain answer was that the far left's idea of democracy was anything but democratic. A more interesting question was why it was not Brereton's policy to attack Ramjan in public. Other than she was not up to the public challenge, what other reason could there be? Brereton should have known the lunatic left would never support a motion condemning the vandalism of the Women's Collective extremists. Ramjan's obduracy and her resort to legal strategies had the smell of the puppet master pulling the strings. She did not reply until six weeks later (H12, 20 June) which is no surprise considering a response that showed once again the left have no shame.

People misconstrued her actions, she complained. They even accused her of impropriety! The motion 'makes very serious accusations against the

SRC, claiming that the SRC is ultimately responsible for the damage done to the St. John's Students property'. That is not what Brereton said the motion 'claimed'. According to Brereton, the motion wanted to condemn the vandalism and contribute $300 as compensation for the damage. A free contribution does not infer responsibility, legal or otherwise. Ramjan said she had a grave duty to ensure 'that a motion is both constitutional and legal, in order to protect the SRC from legal action in the future'. Brereton should be 'aware of the consequences of illegal payments'. Then came the muddled *ad hominem* argument. Those 'responsible for maintaining and overseeing the running of the SRC [must] do so with utmost compunction and are not ruled by their "future" [ALP] political aspirations'. She then tormented her critics with a labyrinthine explanation of the reasons for consulting legal opinion. All very clever, as if other minds were messing around in there.

I imagine Brereton succumbed to 'Ramjan and her think-alikes of the lunatic left' and gave up pursuing the petition. There was no further mention of it. It must have been a bitter lesson in tactics and legal manipulation for Brereton. In the meantime, he had Abbott to deal with. He congratulated the *Democrat*, 'Tony Abbott's mouthpiece, [for] praising the moderates on the SRC. Because Abbott, certainly, is neither moderate nor is deserving of praise' (H12). Abbott and his NCC-backed representatives, Brereton alleged, had not contributed anything constructive to the SRC that year. They had attended few SRC meetings. Abbott himself was more concerned with his football than helping to 'make the SRC more representative and relevant to students'. Worse, he colluded with the extreme left in voting down pressing budgetary measures. He quoted Abbott's words about the far left against him: 'Fine sounding phrases fall so easily from Tony's lips – if only they were true'. He accused Abbott of the most cynical of motives – of keeping 'the SRC as extreme as possible, so he can justify destroying it'. If this was not bad enough, Brereton attributed even darker motives to his political action.

Abbott had a new tactic up his sleeve, Brereton warned. Because Brereton and his centre-left pals rejected 'both the lunatic left and the ideological emptiness of Abbott's reactionary right', Abbott realised he was 'no longer the only force' to oppose the radicals. Abbott saw his 'doom' in this new development and was trying to 'envelop them [the centrists] in the right'. The attempt was doomed to fail because the centre's reform plans and the 'defence of Student Unions' meant their beliefs were 'diametrically opposed' to his. Abbott's effort 'to include such dedicated centrists as Peter Costello and Michael Danby under the umbrella of the Democratic (DLP) Clubs' is an insult to people 'who have spent as much of their efforts in attacking the reactionary schemes of himself as they have in rebutting the lunacy of the many and varied sects of the left'. If Abbott persisted with these tactics, he deserved 'to be treated with the same contempt he displays for those very people that he pretends, in his cynical way, to praise'.

This borderline rant was uncharacteristic of Brereton. So much was unsustainable on the evidence. Brereton's position was centre left. Costello, a committed Christian, was much closer to the conservative position than Brereton. Much of Abbott's policies and aims were as 'moderate' as Brereton's. The accusation of reactionary is leftist name-calling. Rarely is the accusation of 'reactionary' explained. Brereton and his mates were at a loss to explain because they had little idea of what conservatism was as a political philosophy. Or was 'reactionary' a cover for an anti-religious prejudice? The lack of sustained argument gave the impression he was more worried about Abbott than Abbott about him. Abbott, in any case, was more than capable of refuting the inaccuracies. He returned Brereton's belligerence with a conciliatory approach (H13, 27 June):

'It is with some reluctance that I reply to Paul Brereton's recent accusations. I do not wish to criticise his industry or diligence in performing the role he has chosen for himself, which is prodigious. Nor do I wish to disparage the admirable stand he has taken against extremism. But his mendacious innuendo in the last Honi should not pass without comment.

'Paul is fortunate that nothing else prevents his total involvement with the SRC. I think, however, that to expect SRC duty to always override one's other responsibilities, is just a little self-righteous.

'Due to sporting commitments, I have missed one SRC meeting which was set down for Tuesday instead of the usual Wednesday. I missed two meetings over the Christmas vacation because I was working. That is all.

'I did not vote against the budget, nor have I ever voted for communist candidates. I have always advised that preferences be given to other moderate candidates.

'Now, undeviating consistency is too much to expect from most politicians. But I do object to implied virtue where none exists. Brereton and his supporters elected a vice-president from the far left. Brereton and his ilk consistently refuse to allocate election preferences for fear of jeopardising their previous 'redibility'. Please, Paul, your moral outrage is somewhat selective.

'Brereton has shown particular dislike for the Democratic Club, which has fought campus extremism for ten years – long before it was an almost fashionable cause. The club has consistently supported generous tertiary assistance to those in need, staff-student consultation, a range of assessment methods, and the revision of all courses which present dogma rather than seek the truth. We have never advocated the abolition of the means test, which would favour students at the expense of the underprivileged, student-staff control, which would result in academic anarchy, self-assessment or the abolition of exams, which would render degrees worthless scraps of paper, or the interference of student representative bodies in issues beyond their mandate, which are the proper concern of the parliament of all the people. The Club believes in God and in man.

'I don't think these aims justify the epithets bandied about so easily. Do you Paul?

'There has been nothing extremist or reactionary in most of Brereton's proposals on the SRC this year. Yet why does he so excoriate the only other group on council – The Democratic Club – which has supported them? Nor has he, in turn, offered the slightest shred of support to equally moderate measures that are not his own.

'The inevitable conclusion is that his actions are designed simply to ingratiate himself with certain sections of the ALP on whom he may one day depend for pre-selection. Or alternatively, by attacking the left and the "right" he wishes to become, by definition as it were, a "centrist" worthy of support at the elections, which he knows are only weeks away. Such careerism is hardly praiseworthy.'

Brereton did not respond. Perhaps it was enough to distance the centre left from any association with Abbott. He wanted to be free to give the far left a comprehensive whacking. And this he did in the same issue (H12). The centre-left faction had been trying to arrange 'no-fault accident insurance policy for students' since August the previous year. At every turn, they were obstructed not by Abbott but by the far left in the persons of Gary Nicholls and Steve Bolt. Brereton finally blew his top:

'The barefaced duplicity and hypocrisy, and utter contempt for students of the local Communist Party junta, under the leadership of Puppeteer Gary Nicholls, who pulls their strings, and Steve Bolt, was blatantly displayed at last Wednesday's SRC Meeting.

Nicholls was there with the apparent purpose of drawing out the meeting as long as possible and obstructing his allies' opponents when they could not be outvoted. At the meeting, he spoke more frequently and at greater length than all the members of Council put together: yet Nicholls is not on the SRC and has not been elected to any position by students. This reveals that, in trying to run the meeting while not a member of the Council, his CPA has not forgotten its Stalinist heritage.'

No mention of Ramjan. She was likely there saying nothing, happy to dangle this way and that at the end of the strings while her protectors ensured she was not put under undue strain by the terrible Tony Abbott, who, to that point, showed no interest in her. Ramjan might as well have been in Siberia, such was her distance from his thoughts. Brereton then gave an account of the slippery tactics used to stop a decision on the non-political insurance policy and to make sure 'the SRC's capacity to support political causes was not harmed'. He ended with a brief description of the leftist copybook manipulation that puppeteer and *de facto* president Nicholls applied to undo a democratic vote:

'The trouble with the SRC this year has largely been that, although these extremists have not always had the numbers on the SRC itself, they have been able to perpetrate the rule of the far left through their control of the 'OPEN' committees, the Officers, and the Presidential powers, to frustrate and circumvent the SRC itself.

When the motion to take out the insurance from next month was put to the vote, it was carried. However, one of the left's reps had left the room before the vote was taken, with the result that there was no quorum, and the result was therefore invalid. 'God-father' Nicholls won the day, without being able to defeat the motion, through the tactic of obstruction.'

Sarah Sheehan came to Nicholls' defence (H13, 27 June). She indulged in a whole lot of sneering about 'Hi, I'm Paul Brereton, and I'm running for SRC President', but had nothing substantial to say as an answer. Steve Bolt, Nicholls' pardner in their SRC duumvirate, also indulged in a bout of sneering with stock-of-mill leftist tactics (H14, 4 July). David Patch, Electoral Officer, announced the Annual General Elections for the 51st Students' Representative Council to take place on 2-4 August 1978 (H16,18 Jul). Barbara Ramjan's presidency was nearly at an end – to the extent you could call it a presidency. Not only did she not fulfil her undertaking to report regularly on SRC affairs, but she scarcely said anything in *Honi*. The evidence suggests she was a puppet and a figurehead behind the *de facto* operating president Gary Nicholls and Vice-President Steve Bolt. At all points, interfering Nicholls was in immediate charge, not always with Ramjan as his dutiful support. His main task was to block whatever moves the centre left, and the conservatives made to restrict the far-left control and their syphoning off money to their causes.

There was one 'positive' task, though, that kept both Nicholls and Bolt submitting long repetitive pieces to *Honi*. State Liberal governments were investigating legislation to take control of student affairs away from the grip of the far left. Despite the frequency and length of their submissions, Nicholls' and Bolt's arguments boiled down to a few simple propositions. Outside intervention would deny student organisations' autonomy, their right to organise, and the right to use student money how they saw fit. In a word, such legislation would overthrow the democratic processes to which they were so passionately devoted. Without people like Nicholls and Bolt, there would be no one to counter the reactionaries! Tony Abbott answered the radicals' assertions in an article that took a fitting place in his ongoing conservative manifesto (H7):

'Under no circumstances should anyone be absolutely compelled to join a particular organisation. There are a few occasions, however, when the benefits won by a body are such that exemption from membership is on serious personal ground alone. It is argued that trade unions are such bodies and on this basis compulsory membership of the Australian Union of Students and the various Student Representative Councils is justified.

'But this categorisation of student political associations with trade unions is a most serious error of logic [a bad analogical argument]. The relationship between employees and employer is one of necessity and economic survival; that of student-administration is one of choice and privilege. Students, unlike workers, are a favoured elite generously endowed and financially rewarded for a lifetime. Thus students associations never have and never will be trade unions.

'Student associations cannot properly behave like trade unions to gain benefits which can only be at the expense of the poor and underprivileged. The legitimate and perennial complaints of students – poor lecturing, unjust assessment etc. – are better dealt with by departmental consultative committees. They certainly don't require large expensive bureaucracies.

'The inevitable result of this lack of a strict vocational role is that student associations devote the bulk of their resources to purely peripheral political issues. There is no question of compulsory unionism here. The only AUS office remotely concerned with student welfare, the services vice presidency, receives approximately 10 per cent of the budget. The demand of AUS that all students be paid 120 per cent of the Henderson poverty line approximately $65 per week, would cost the Government something like $900 million annually. Seemingly motivated by concern for members, this is actually the typical irresponsible demand of a body interested only in compounding our economic problems.

'Nor does AUS limit its radicalism to attacks on the Government. Among its 'education' policies are demands that course content be decided by mass meetings of students, and that courses reject the 'racist', 'sexist', and 'anti-working class' bias in present teaching. These are not the aims of a body genuinely concerned with the conditions of members. When AUS champions the women's movement, homosexual liberation, the anti-uranium mining campaign, it is moving beyond the scope of unionism.

'That a union should express opinion on such matters is arguable: but it is clearly wrong for the union to devote substantial resources to these matters. Moreover, unions are sectional bodies. When they use their muscle to influence areas of general politics, they are usurping the function of the elected Government and foisting their will upon the people.

'It is sometimes objected that voluntary membership will destroy student services. Cheap travel is the result of a government provided monopoly. It owes nothing to mass compulsory membership. Travel and insurance schemes could function without compulsory membership, along the lines of university co-operative bookshops. Students, on joining the scheme, would qualify for cheap travel and insurance, or receive a rebate.

'Other student services where they exist ought to be taken over by services and amenities bodies such as the union. Voluntary membership establishes freedom of choice. Only voluntary membership will ensure that student associations are truly responsible and accountable. The ability of dissatisfied students to withdraw their financial support would ensure that they catered for their real needs.

'Under a voluntary system, those 'opting-in' would take far greater interest in their union's activities than those who currently join automatically – voluntary membership would produce more democratic student movement.

'It is often claimed that if students wanted voluntary membership they would obtain it through the 'Democratic process'. But students never asked for an SRC or AUS. The SRC was lumbered on them 50 years ago by the senate. Why should they then be responsible for altering a situation they didn't want and is, in any rate, wrong in principle? It is absurd to expect the bulk of students who are interested in passing exams to assume the same activism as a dedicated minority with a vested interest in the status-quo.

'The complete disinterest of students in 'unions' is indicated by the minuscule proportion voting in elections. And on those occasions when students have expressed an opinion it is overwhelmingly in favour of voluntary membership. Only 40% have paid fees at Melbourne University this year while on the morning of the first National Student 'strike' more than 700 at this university petitioned for voluntary AUS and SRC membership.

'Those who most loudly tout the 'People's will' are terrified students will vote with their feet if given the chance.'

The reason that obsessed radicals like Nicholls and Bolt mocked and sneered at Abbott, made up claims about him, and attributed views to him he did not hold was because they could not answer the calm, analytical, non-abusive statement of policy like the one above. You could not have a more comprehensible analysis of voluntary fees. They had no answer to Abbott's coherent set of policies.

As the 50th SRC drew to a close, there was increased activity in granting funds to student associations. Alex Naple (Ecs/Law III) claimed that in an SRC Finance Committee meeting, 'Gary Nicholls wore two hats by being a member of the Finance Committee and representing the Communist Group' (H16). The meeting was to decide to whom grants should be given. Finance Committee meetings required a quorum of four. But three remained after Nicholls and Ramjan had pushed Naple and a fellow student out the door and shut it. The cosy meeting allocated the 'maximum amount [to the CPA] which could be granted without a general meeting of the Student Body'. Naple expressed the optimistic hope regulations would be followed in future. He might have applied to David Patch, a stickler for SRC regulations, to correct Nicholls' acrobatic 'interpretations of SRC regulations'.

Nicholls arranged another Finance Committee to ratify the grants, which, Naple concluded, showed the earlier meeting was 'improper'. Naple noted that Barbara Ramjan, a member of the quorum, was 'in a corridor' while the others were in the meeting room. Ramjan's presence was not needed. Puppeteer Nicholls could manage on his own. Paul Baram covered the same meeting (H16) in a far more heated manner, referring to 'Comrades Ramjan and "Rent-A-Speech" Nicholls' as 'CPA hacks'. Abbott dealt with the far left's manipulation of the regulations less heatedly. He wrote (H16):

'This year's SRC is an improvement on its predecessor. At least it has remembered to appoint someone to conduct the coming elections and will not have to rush out a special quarto broadsheet edition of *Honi* to ensure their validity!

'Nevertheless, we have an SRC which is unable to produce minutes (to me, at any rate!) for more than one-third of its meetings, and which, at some meetings, does not receive a report from a single one of its officers (there are twelve).

'Do you know that not once has a "detailed statement of monies received and expended" been presented to council as required by regulations 5 (7) and 2 (4d), which can perhaps be excused on the grounds of pressure of work or forgetfulness. But is it not disturbing that the elected SRC Secretary Treasurer was for several weeks categorically denied access to all the SRC financial records, for which he is legally answerable, by the appointed office staff?

'In fact, according to a recent SRC executive decision, representatives have no right to inspect the books of the body for whose actions they are legally responsible. The extreme reluctance of office secretary Di Holdway to let me examine the books, contrasting with their ready availability to others of a different political persuasion, is entirely consistent with the ramshackle hillbilly operation the SRC has become.

'Yet remarkably, the SRC, which has generally continued as a resource centre for ultra-militant feminists and hard-line Marxists, has always had a moderate majority.

'There are a number of reasons for this seeming paradox. The first is the fact that extremists still populate the various SRC 'open committees' on woman's issues, AUS Aboriginal Affairs, Ethnic relations etc, which annually spend more than $5000, about which council is left completely in the dark.

'The second is the skill of people like Gary Nicholls in manipulating procedures to confuse and divide their faction-ridden opponents. Meetings are effectively jammed. Standing orders are invariably suspended, so granting $99 to the Radical Education Group or the Spartacist Club can be debated and their representatives leave early. Then Nicholls, who until last week held no SRC position or Bolt, who has held the education position for little longer, speak interminably on every subject.

'Anyone who noticed Nicholl's turgid controversies with the Spartacists and Trotskyists, which filled the pages of *Honi* last year, over who was the purer Marxist, will realise his unique and endlessly boring mixture of hysteria and ideology.

'After several hours of shouting, points or order, and submissions to the chair, most people leave, quorum is broken, and nothing has been achieved.

'But here we get to the nub of the problem. The game of the communist group activists is clear to all but the most naive, but few are prepared to use legitimate and proper means to prevent their filibustering. Representatives will not vote that the question be now put for fear of 'stifling debate'; they will not vote that the speaker no longer be heard for fear of 'refusing legitimate opinion'; they are always willing to send matters to stacked front lawn meetings lest they be accused of 'denying the will of the people'; they are reluctant to support in any way measures associated with the Democratic Club for fear of being labelled 'Right-wing'.

'Quite simply, many genuinely moderate representatives, for instance, Brereton, Kefford, Jones, Paget and others, in their desire for 'credibility', in their efforts to be fair and conciliatory, allow the left to push around them, council, and ultimately all the students. Too many SRC reps regard Nicholls, Podesta, and the like as people of reason and goodwill. They are not. Unpalatable though this sounds, they are completely impervious to reason, except that which supports their own preconceptions.

'One can only guess at what impels their political passions. It is certainly incomprehensible to me. Witness their slippery manoeuvrings over the insurance scheme, which is the SRC's single significant achievement. Originally it was opposed because of the cost, then because it would restrict more worthwhile political activities, and finally because it was not sufficiently comprehensive!

'The small numbers who vote in SRC elections (a record 24% last year) are only a part of the problem. Unfortunately, apart from left-wing zealots, the SRC tends to attract would-be prime ministers or do-gooders who think they know best for other people. And it will continue to do so while it is an overstated, over-funded, political pressure group with policies on everything from uranium mining to the theories (unread) of the unfortunate Prof Eysenck.

'If students generally are to take an interest and participate in the SRC, it must be of some meaning and relevance. This means involvement in the ordinary, mundane concerns of students, such as parking, library facilities, organising social functions, sponsoring speakers, and organising concessions. Then we will really have a representative Council of students.'

This is a sound analysis of the manipulative tactics of the far left that, again, hardly needs explicating. It is worth, however, summarising the two ways the radicals subverted the democratic process they pretended to guarantee. The primary way was the open committee, which sounds fine in theory. If all the people concerned attended meetings, the open committee should work. The majority vote would be decisive. But in practice, a small number of those possessing voting rights turned up to SRC meetings. Most students were uninterested. Others stayed away because the radicals alienated them by physical or psychological intimidation or by making their contribution appear fruitless when it opposed their plans. The small number made it easy for the radicals to stack the meeting. The second way was by jamming a meeting with endless speeches or frustrating it by abuse of procedures when the numbers were not favourable. Tireless fanatics like Gary Nicholls showed how easily the open committees could be manipulated or meetings jammed with useless discussion.

The concrete example Abbott gave of the Left's frustrating tactics was the unelected office staff blocking access to the administration. The refusal to allow those responsible for overseeing the SRC's finances access to the books reflected a politically captured administration. But such moves seemed more than a political tactic. Could there be another reason the radicals refused Abbott access to the financial records? This is not an irrelevant question, as may be seen in the final phases of the Ramjan presidency.

Nicholls replied in H19 (1 August). It was a typical evasive reply, indulging in a whole lot of repetitive sneering and ridicule of Naple and Abbott. In response to Abbott's thoughtful, analytical writings, Nicholls spoke of 'the positively idiotic in the ramblings of Abbott. Stream of consciousness writing is not Tony's forte – neither is any other style, it's true – but Tony keeps on trying'. A pitiful response. But there was no other way for Nicholls to take Abbott on. He was no match for Abbott's intellect and powers of articulation. The urgency to destroy Tony Abbott was high because, by this time, it was clear his series of powerful manifesto writings were a prelude to his campaign to capture the SRC presidency. Abbott's final piece (H17, 25 July) was a philosophical defence of his political platform:

'In the last eighteen months, there has been quite a campaign of vilification waged through the letters page of *Honi* directed at the Democratic Club in general and perhaps myself in particular. Epithets such as extremist, fascist, careerist, and most recently parasite, have been freely bandied about. Thank you for this opportunity to reply.

'The NCC tag is a hoary old favourite. That the club sympathises with many of the aims of the National Civic Council has never been any secret.

The extent of the slur is the degree to which that body's policies are obnoxious, which is minimal.

'A more damaging criticism sometimes made by thoughtful people is that we blindly support the status quo. The vast bureaucratic ramifications of modern government, which unnecessarily affect everyone in so many ways; the crushing size of so many institutions; the abandonment of the country for impersonal cities; the glorification of materialism and the senses, and the widespread denial of God and the family are abhorrent to us.

'However, the alternative – Marxism – which is often espoused by the club's critics is no panacea. Marxism elevates petty control of people's lives from an occasionally necessary vice to a positive virtue of government. The 'peoples' democracies' regard huge armed forces not as a necessary defence against external enemies but as an essential instrument in ordering their own citizens. Theoretical communism is admirably concerned with the freedom and brotherhood of man. But practically, it shackles his spirit to an ideology which has evolved into something more fantastic than most fairy tales and anchors his body to the grinding poverty of every communist system.

'Communism subordinates the individual to the state just as surely as medieval man was a prisoner of the church and his lord.

'Now it seems to me there is no virtue in partially opposing something which is altogether wrong, provided, of course, that opposition does not submerge one's positive philosophy. We are not blindly opposed to communism but to the complete subservience of man that it, or any other totalitarian system, entails.

'There are two broad types of issues pushed by totalitarians, those that actually tend to increase the subordination of the individual and those which are intended merely to alienate people from liberal democracy by exposing its abuses.

'It is indeed, essential for sincere democrats to intelligently support the second category, which includes such matters as environmental protection; racial equality: equality of opportunity, etc., which have all, in recent years, prominently involved communist party members.

'But to support their primary aims is quite indefensible. Thus, it is wrong to support the extension of government power simply for its own sake or the extension of union or corporate power to the extent where it reduces human beings to the level of machines without compelling reasons.

'Determining which is which is the great dilemma of contemporary liberals. But how often in their bickering of degree, in their arguments over who is 'right' or 'left', do they forget the absolutely fundamental qualitative difference between themselves and the advocates of force?

'On a campus level, campaigns to subvert teaching from a means of the dissemination of knowledge to an instrument of propaganda cannot be tolerated. It is perfectly clear where this is currently happening at this university. Similarly, campaigns to extend TEAS [Tertiary Education Assistance Scheme] must be supported but only to the extent that benefits actually increase individual welfare without unduly sacrificing that of non-students or unnecessarily expanding the tentacles of the state.

'The restrictions on a student's freedom that compulsory membership of the SRC, AUS, the Union, and the Sports Union entail, can only be justified if these bodies provided benefits producing freedoms commensurate with what was lost. Their activities must be rigidly directed at improving the well-being of students. No such benefits presently accrue from AUS and SRC membership, and until they do, their membership should be voluntary.

'I hope you'll forgive my somewhat involved explanation of the club's position in terms of this underlying philosophy.

'Western civilisation has gross flaws – its selfish disregard of the wake of unfashionable, and its transcending crass materialism. Nor is its exact form suitable for every country. Nevertheless, its considerable successes – the general elimination of physical want; an unprecedented degree of personal freedom, and the waning influence of unnatural taboos and inhibitions – are the achievement of many generations of wisdom and courage and constitute what is hitherto man's greatest product.

'The unbroken development of civilisation since the renaissance, distinguished from earlier periods by the further freedom of the ordinary man, is the tradition which the Democratic Club seeks to uphold. It is the tradition which is under threat from rapidly expanding tyranny which now dominates more than one-third of the world's population.

'I know of no more noble aspiration than the fullest possible individual liberty consistent with the freedom of others. That is the genuine idealism of the Democratic Club.'

It was proper for Abbott to end the series of manifestos with an outline of his political philosophy. The outspoken defence of Western Civilisation, the result of centuries of growth and development in traditions, customs and a liberal form of government, was straightforwardly Burkean. His implicitly placing a transcendent intelligence – God – as the author of a morally ordered world added the natural law to his conservatism. His emphasis was on the empirical orientation of Burkean conservatism, that is, on the priority to deal with the concrete circumstances of life to which principles determined by the natural law were to be applied. He stood his philosophy against the totalitarian mindset exhibited by the Sydney University radicals. He contrasted the empirical orientation of his conservatism with the abstract theory of Marxism. He warned about falling for the totalitarian traps clothed in the language of the freedom and brotherhood of man. About Marxism as a totalitarian collectivist theory that excused barbarity never before witnessed in human history, he was unambiguous.

But he conceded too much, needlessly in my view, both about the sincerity and goodwill of his opponents (they weren't sincere and showed not a jot of goodwill) and the 'flaws' of Western Civilisation. For the far left, there's a strict prohibition against giving an ideological sucker an even break. A month or so later, the far left would show just how pitiless, unjust, and ideologically driven they were. Although Abbott's concessions were tactically counterproductive, they were motivated by the best intentions – to be honest and fair to everyone, including his opponents.

A week later (31 July), *Honi* published the policy statements of the candidates for the Annual General Elections (H18). Throughout the year, there had been no full-frontal attack on Abbott in Honi. There were frequent sneers and ridicule, but nothing sustained about his politics. Nor were there any denunciations of the general 'thuggish' behaviour his enemies accused him of 35 years later, for which they offered no proof. Barbara Ramjan had nothing to say about him at all, forget about Abbott being constantly in her face. If Abbott had worried her, one could be sure that thin-skinned Ramjan would have whined about it in *Honi*, and her far-left protectors would have rushed to her support. But she didn't. And they didn't. Abbott only mentioned her when it related to specific political issues.

In his policy statement for president, Abbott said he did not want to talk about labels. He wanted to concentrate his policy on what the SRC failed to do. Among other failures, it could not 'supervise the spending of $5,000 plus by the open committees', it did not insist on the right of the Hon. Secretary-Treasurer to examine the financial records, and it could not push through an insurance scheme favourable to students. There were front lawn meetings that were 'rigged by raising the quorum'. The SRC, via the Arts society, made 'clandestine payments (e.g. to the Victorian Power Workers). Finally, 'the SRC refused to ensure the honesty of student elections by having these conducted under a lawyer's supervision'. He concluded,

'Essentially, an SRC which caters for politicians will always be dominated by them — at students' expense. So it needs fundamental reform. Its wide objects make it a target for manipulators seeking to abuse its funds. One solution – voluntary membership – would weaken the SRC's potentially constructive role. A better answer is to confine its activities to those where a broad consensus of members operates. I propose constitutional amendments limiting the SRC's attention to the vocationally oriented educational and welfare interests for which it is elected.'

Abbott had been arguing for voluntary membership because the evidence suggested the SRC could not be reformed. The far left had always successfully manoeuvred to keep control of it, whether the radicals were in a minority or majority. Only a plan of voluntary membership could break the far left's political control and their misuse of the SRC monies fleeced from students' pockets. Abbott now appeared ready to give compulsory membership another chance. But his proposal included constitutional amendments that would just as effectively wrest financial and political control from the radicals. Whichever plan Abbott promoted, the destruction of a body representing the students was not part of it. That did not stop the far left and the centre left under Paul Brereton from pretending it was. Abbott generously urged students to give their second preference to Brereton. Brereton presented a detailed centre-left 'moderate' program but did not return Tony's generosity.

A record turnout of 4,000 voted Abbott and his platform in as President of the 51st Students' Representative Council 1978/79. The previous record cited by David Patch as a justification of the Ramjan mandate was 2,400. Abbott drew the unambiguous message:

'Most of the 4,000 who voted in the annual elections ... would have been aware that for some years, a group had controlled the SRC who were interested in little but pushing a particular political barrow. The SRC was important to them because it was worth $150,000 annually and cloaked their extremism with respectability. They would thus presumably be anxious to hang on to such a valuable political resource. And as you know, in the elections they were resoundingly rebuffed by students.'

Chapter 11

Stop Abbott by hook or by crook

I COVERED Five SRC General Elections before the 1978 elections. In each case, the new Students' Representative Council took office within two or three weeks of the declaration of the winners, and the first meeting was held after three to five weeks. The 1977 election, during which Barbara Ramjan was elected SRC President, was in the final days of July. The declaration was on 28 July, and the first SRC meeting was on 7 September 1977. No problems. Just as it had always been. The SRC constitution prescribed the routine. But, as with all written constitutions, convention and unwritten rules supported the smooth changeover of office. Considering the far left's propensity for scheming and manipulation, it might not come as a surprise that Tony Abbott faced an army of resistance to his official assumption of the office of SRC President. The breathtaking cynicism, spite, lies, violence, and shameless manipulation that worked to stop him from legitimately taking office forced some extreme measures.

Abbott and Brereton sent a jointly signed letter to *Honi* (H24) on 19 September. They pointed out that the counting was completed by 3 August, showing a catastrophic defeat for the 'left collective'. Besides Abbott's election as president, a 'moderate team was elected to edit *Honi Soit*', and the council seemed centrist. Despite the clear results, there was 'a concerted attempt by the left collective to prevent the new council from taking office'. Now step forward the master manipulator. Electoral Officer David Patch either 'lodged' or 'instigated' protests about the positions of President, Economics Men, and Engineering Men. The President's and Engineering Men's results were contested because a candidate had spent his own money campaigning. That candidate was disqualified, which meant, it was asserted, the elections should be declared invalid. The Economics Men's election was disputed because women had allegedly voted. When Patch was asked to give evidence, he produced six statements from women, 'each of them identically worded'. 'What is clearly happening', wrote Abbott and Brereton, 'is that through the Electoral Officer [David Patch], the left collective is attempting to have elections declared invalid in the hope that they might win back several positions in a re-election'. A month and a half had passed, and Patch had not presented the Electoral Officer's report, which was needed for the new council to take office. Patch gave no sign it would happen soon.

At the same time, *de facto* president Gary Nicholls and Ramjan opened another front. Ramjan appointed Nicholls, who had never been elected to any office, as 'acting president' while she flew off on a jaunt to Darwin, where she could witness her hotshot lawyer husband in action. As 'Acting Honorary-Secretary', Nicholls had already dismissed elected representatives that year on concocted charges. Now he was pulling the same trick 'to give himself virtual complete control of the council'. He ignored the constitution and all the accepted conventions and 'declared the elected executive positions vacant'. Nothing now restrained him except the council, which he had 'purged' of all non-left resistance.

I have cited this letter of 19 September to make clear the charges of subversion came from centre-left Brereton as well as from Abbott. As Brereton was the *de facto* leader of the moderates/centre left, it was again a small group opposing the wishes of the majority, not only of the electorate but the elected representatives. There were several commentaries on Abbott's bruising battle with the far-left forces before he took office as SRC President. They were from those opposing the far left, the most extensive being Abbott's report to the first meeting of the 51st SRC on 4 October (H26, 18 October). Patch and Nicholls, and their goons did not comment since their sole purpose was to bomb the SRC and force Abbott to take office in the shambles. Patch and Nicholls, driving the agitation and obstruction, featured in the reports of the action. Little mention of Ramjan. Why? Because Ramjan was always a puppet and figurehead to be manipulated. I combine those accounts into a timeline to give a complete picture of the bastardry. Unless stated otherwise, the account and quotes are from Abbott's report delivered on 3 October.

2-3 August

The vote count was completed showing Abbott as the runaway winner of the vote for president. There was a record turnout of around 4,000 student voters. 'This triggered a cold-blooded attempt to unreasonably delay the taking of office of the new council (which had previously always occurred within the first two weeks of third term) and hence to effectively stall much needed reform till next March when fresh elections would be only five months away ...' As Abbott admitted, the obstruction was 'largely successful'.

ca. 15 August

David Patch lodged his protests against the Economics, Engineering and Presidential results. The basis of the protests was that a candidate spent his own money campaigning, and women voted in a men's election.

10 September Sunday

In the case of the candidate Jeffery's spending his own money, the Electoral Legal Arbiter (ELA) John Hickey announced his decisions on 10 September. Hickey declared the election (of the two representative positions in engineering) void, so (remarked Abbott suggestively) 'the new council has lost two moderates. After the distribution of preferences, [Abbott] had beaten Thornton by more than Jeffery's total vote, so the presidential result was upheld'. Hickey 'asked Patch to produce evidence to back up his claim that women had voted in the Economics Men election resulting in the victory of two Liberal Club members'.

20 September Wednesday

Patch finally produced several statements and two statutory declarations. Some of the signatories were noticeably active in the Political Economy campaign … Hickey rejected Patch's contention that the election be declared void because to do so could have involved accepting that female students knowingly voted in a men's election or signed a false statement.

21 September Thursday

Seeing he couldn't take the protests any further, Patch posted a notice advising the Economics and Presidential results. Until now, Patch had maintained the show of keeping to the constitutional provisions, no matter how much he stretched them. With nowhere to go, this preacher of direct democracy dropped all appearance and leapt into totalitarian mode. Abbott thought with all results published, Patch could present his electoral report at the meeting of 27 September, 'enabling the new council to take over'. According to the regulations, Patch had to do this. But no, Patch found another regulation which said he had to publish the poll in two issues of *Honi*. But this had never been regarded as necessary to present the report. And it had never been complied with. The regulation to publish the results in two editions of *Honi* was unconnected with the electoral report's presentation. On Patch's reasoning, a question over the validity of Ramjan's 50th SRC arose. And over all those SRCs before. But this 'interpretation had been specifically rejected earlier by the council of the 50th SRC'.

Pushed into a corner and showing that ideological advantage was far more important than decency and consistent reasoning, Patch 'airily replied that he would not repeat past errors', meaning the error of not publishing the results correctly of the Ramjan victory. Patch continued withholding the results and thus the electoral report, elevating inconsistency and unfairness to shameless heights. 'When confronted with the contradiction of relying on the same publication requirements for a declaration that he had so blissfully ignored concerning the announcement of the results, Patch again replied that he did not wish to repeat his own mistakes!' In the meantime, the Vice-Chancellor, Paul Brereton and Abbott had received legal advice that publishing the results in *Honi* was simply publishing a result or a declaration that had already taken place.

Around this time, Ramjan, finding more pressing things to do, flew to Darwin to watch her lawyer husband in action. She did not appoint the Vice-President as Acting President, as was normal, but the 'Acting Honorary Secretary/Treasurer' Gary Nicholls. Abbott commented that 'Nicholls has graced this campus since 1970 and is now enrolled in 3rd year of General Philosophy'. Twenty-seven-year-old puppeteer Nicholls was in his ninth year as a student.

'As Secretary/Treasurer,' Abbott continued, 'Nicholls had the power to dismiss councillors for non-attendance at two consecutive SRC meetings unless explanations he considered satisfactory had been offered. Deeming all "Broad Left" explanations satisfactory and all others inadequate, he had progressively reduced council from 28 to 12 representatives, ensuring it was dominated by his cronies. As Acting President, he dismissed the elected members of the executive, relying on a section of the regulations which, according to Paul Brereton's legal advice, conflicted with the constitution and was thus invalid. There were now no fetters on his exercise of authority.

'The Left's plan was now obvious and audacious. Patch would not present a report to the SRC meeting of 27 September, and Nicholls would not call another until the end of October. If Patch presented a report, it could be accepted or rejected at Nicholls' whim. The prospect of indefinitely extended control by Nicholls' hand-picked council was now very real'.

Finally, Electoral Legal Arbiter John Hickey, Barrister Renshaw, and the Administration declared that Abbott had been President 'from at least 21 September'.

22 September Friday

Abbott 'felt it was important to assume the position immediately so [he] could call a meeting of the old council and instruct Patch to present his report'. He wanted to prevent giving Patch and Nicholls the time to think up more tricks. He continued: 'Armed with a letter of recognition from the Vice-Chancellor, I entered the SRC offices at 4.45 pm on Friday, 22 September, and told those present I was taking over and having the locks changed and that if they attempted to interfere, I would ask them to leave. Nicholls said I had no authority to do so and ordered me out. He made it clear he would not allow the locks to be changed or hand over any keys.

'In a very short time, a large and rowdy group of his supporters had gathered. The police were called but did not want to take any action that might have resulted in violence. After being harassed and abused for a considerable time, Alex Naple, Chairman of the Standing Legal Committee and I were forced to leave at about 5.30 pm

'Later that evening, the administration instructed the police that they regarded me as the legitimate president and informed me they would co-operate with reasonable steps to secure access and authority over the SRC offices'.

John Stroud (Ecs. III) later challenged 'a number of scurrilous slander-sheets containing an amazing collection of lies and misguided accusations circulated on campus by the far left'. He noted some of the slander sheets were anonymous, indicating the authors did not have 'sufficient faith in the truthfulness of their rags to have their names associated with them'. His account (H23, 12 October) corresponded with Abbott's but in more vigorous language. When Abbott tried to take office as the legitimate president, 'Gary Nicholls (the illegally appointed acting-president of the SRC)' and his far-left goons blocked access, 'and even went so far as to have [Abbott] thrown out of the office altogether!' But Stroud added a detail not included in Abbott's account. 'The question that arose in Tony's mind (and in the minds of many others) was why the far left were so intent on keeping him away from Level One Wentworth [the SRC offices]. Could it be they had something to hide?' Abbott suspected an issue with the accounts.

23 September Saturday

The Union Manager, Peter Edwards, let Abbott, Alex Naple, the Associate Registrar and a group of SRC members into the offices. Again, Stroud adds information not included in Abbott's report. He claimed the purpose for entering the office was to check the 'files and financial books'. It looked like 'certain of these may not have been in order'. To prevent 'a large-scale lifting of files and financial books, Tony immediately had the locks changed'. That would not stop Nicholls. Accompanied by his goons, he broke in and changed the locks. Stroud added that 'the place was apparently ransacked quite thoroughly and purposefully'. The far-left publications 'tried to make out that Tony Abbott, Alex Naple, and Paul Brereton were guilty of breaking and entering and theft. Yet Gary Nicholls admitted in court on Wednesday, 27 September, that he was responsible for the Saturday night burglary!' One must admit that Nicholls had all the required qualities.

24 September Sunday

On Sunday morning, Abbott had the locks changed for the third time. In the afternoon, a group of far-left goons, including suspended Martin Hirst, began prowling around outside the SRC offices. Stroud said they were 'hammering on doors and windows and vandalising at least two cars'. To prevent another break-in, Abbott camped overnight in the SRC offices.

25 September Monday

On Monday morning, Abbott fought off attempts to gain entry. He had to allow entry to 'bash-'em-down' Hirst and 'all-men-are-rapists' Leslie Podesta, who passed for 'SRC Officers'. One wonders how the suspended Hirst could pass himself off as an SRC Officer. Podesta and Hirst spent their time delivering 'diatribes regarding [Abbott's] alleged non-entitlement to act as President'. Those with genuine business were allowed access. The doors were locked to the disrupters. On the pretext of having business with Honi, Peter Woof gained entry and then tried to keep the door open to his mates. Abbott had to restrain Woof in reaction to which 'he flung himself to the ground and grabbed anything that was bolted down' [Stroud]. He 'also had to restrain David Patch from closing the front office in [his] face'.

Abbott decided the situation was getting out of hand and called the police and the Registrar. The Registrar closed the building. John Stroud's account of Monday morning corresponded with Abbott's except for one point. Abbott barred entry to SRC offices 'to ensure that nothing more could be taken from the files until a thorough check could be made on their state'.

26 September Tuesday

In the meantime, Barbara Ramjan had arrived back in Melbourne, images of her swashbuckling lawyer husband energising her mind. The lingering visions raised her to a high state of legal aggression – evidently to the delight of her grinning puppet master. According to an unattributed report (H23, 12 October), 'Barbara Ramjan ... and Gary Nicholls ... applied to the [Equity] Court for orders to the effect that Ramjan was still President and that Abbott was not and could not be until the election results had been published in two issues of *Honi Soit*'. In a move designed to fetter all Abbott supporters, they served summonses on Abbott, the university, the Vice-Chancellor, and the University Union. Whose legal direction gave Ramjan the boldness to carry out such outrageous subversion of accepted SRC conventions – without speaking about fairness and everyday decency? Likely a legal mind, still in honeymoon mode. During this process, Nicholls 'wore his perennial Cheshire Cat grin'. And why wouldn't he? The summonses were delivered during Tuesday.

27 September Wednesday

The case was heard in the Equity Court under Mr Justice Kearney at 2 pm Wednesday the following day. 'Almost immediately', wrote Abbott, 'barrister Madgwick [for the plaintiffs] conceded nearly every issue and sought unsuccessfully to withdraw Nicholls and Ramjan from the case'. Abbott and the university 'filed a cross-claim for a declaration that [Abbott] had been president since at least 21 September'. Madgwick did not argue the claim. Justice Kearney judged that Abbott had been president since the declaration of the poll results on 4 August and that 'the requirement for publication in two issues of *Honi* was purely for informing the student body of the results of the election and was not a prerequisite for taking office'. In short, he pricked the bubble of Ramjan's legal hubris. Despite the defeat, Nicholls' 'grin did not disappear'. And why would it? Pulling Ramjan's strings, he had created enormous mischief for Abbott and 'illegally' delayed his taking office 'for seven weeks'.

Abbott's far-left enemies took the judgement as a mere phase in their dirty tricks campaign to subvert his election. David Patch, soon to graduate in law, continued to show what a lot of cynical rhetoric he spouted about 'democratisation'. At the SRC meeting of 27 September, Patch ignored Justice Kearney's judgement that Abbott was president from 4 August. He declared he 'refused to present a report', repeating that 'he would present a report to any SRC meeting held after the declarations [were] published in two issues of *Honi Soit*, i.e. on or after Wednesday 11 October, given the regular appearance of *Honi*'.

That meant that 'officers of the retiring SRC including Nicholls and his obnoxious crew would remain in office for a further two weeks, provided, of course, Patch [did] not discover some further prevaricating trick'. Considering Patch's talent, it was on the cards. It was unacceptable, said Abbott, that the 'new Council can remain in limbo 10 weeks after elections for a fifty-two-week term ... Further court action may be necessary to overcome the continued bloody-minded obstruction of Patch and Nicholls'. Abbott's frustration was understandable. On the evidence, one could hardly dispute his summary of the events:

'The events of the last few Weeks illustrate a complete absence of good faith on the part of the Broad Left. They have manipulated the rules when it suited their purposes, otherwise completely ignoring them. The susceptibility of rules designed for well-intentioned parties to complete breakdown when one party relentlessly pursues its own ends beyond all reason, ethics or good sense is also amply demonstrated.

'Yet I suspect that some of you who abhor the tactics of the 'Broad Left' may still consider some of my actions precipitate. The lesson of repeated bitter experience is that the 'Broad Left' is possessed not of reasonableness but consumed with malice and ill-will and prepared to go to almost any length to secure political advantage. I felt that desperate and unusual circumstances justified my actions.'

Abbott's justification for his radical action against those trying to nullify his lawful presidency mirrored (in a small way) Edmund Burke's justification for the 1688 Glorious Revolution. In brief, a conservative works to maintain the integrity, stability and continuity of his community or organisation developed over a long period. Faults, incoherence, decay, external and internal attacks that arise need different degrees of correction, often without undue disturbance to its members. Sometimes an attack requires extreme measures to conserve the community or organisation. The British Parliament in 1688 thought it had no other choice to preserve the British Constitution and its freedoms than to replace James II with William of Orange as the British Monarch. In the same way, Abbott thought there was no other remedy to the wholesale subversion of the SRC constitution and its conventions than to call on the administration and police.

Patch and Nicholls had run their tactics of subversion to the bitter end. They had to face the inevitable – the confirmation of Abbott's election as SRC President. They could pat themselves on the back for creating so much nuisance before they laid down their arms, Patch to graduate and pursue a career in the law and Nicholls to ... well, to take up one of the many options available to an unconscionable far-left agent. In H26 (26 October), Abbott reported that it took 'a ruling by the Supreme Court, receipt of Summons threatening further court action, an afternoon's conference with lawyers, and the printing of a Special *Honi* Supplement' to force Patch 'to finally present an electoral officer's report to an emergency meeting of the SRC on Wednesday 4 October'. What an inglorious final act for this insufferable sanctimonious bag of radical wind. During that same meeting, the election of the officers and the executive of the 51st SRC took place.

The council on balance was moderate/centre left. Tanya Coleman, as a member of the executive, would be the only one to prove a staunch ally to Abbott. But despite Coleman's support, Abbott would find himself on the battlefield as Tony Abbott *contra mundum*. Three motions condemning him reflected the unrelenting animosity: for calling in the police (passed); condemning the administration for interfering in SRC affairs (passed) and upholding the right of student access to the SRC and condemning Abbott for closing it for three days (passed).

Abbott's final contribution to 1978 *Honi* was in H26 (26 October). It was on the second last page of a 26-page edition devoted almost entirely to extreme left causes and the childish mockery of the bourgeois capitalist world. There was a particularly offensive double-page spread mocking and slandering Christians. Abbott rarely responded to the unbroken stream of anti-Christian bigotry in *Honi*. And so it was in this piece from the 51st SRC President. Above the article, with an illustration of an obese man vomiting, they posted the heading 'Fearless Leaders Inc. Present: Technicolour yawning with President (watch out for the moderates) Tony!!' Abbott spoke of a debilitating problem he had in waging an effective battle against the far left:

'The first meeting of the new SRC, also held on the 4 October, once again highlighted the lack of cooperation [with the right] and obsession with image which has plagued moderate elements for so long and allowed extremists effective control.

'The problem is that the middle-ground, those aligned with Paul Brereton, allow tactical differences [with the right] to obscure not only their unit of goal with the Liberal/Democratic group – an SRC that works for students – but also their fundamental differences with the Broad Left who believe the SRC is fair game for all sorts of peculiar political preoccupations.

'The campus left manipulates the rules when it suits them. Otherwise, they are ignored. The centre and the right believe the rules are for the good of all. Yet the apparent inability of the centre to distinguish between fundamental and superficial disagreement has bedevilled the SRC for as long as I can remember.'

Abbott gave several examples of the Brereton faction's lack of consistency. He devoted the second half of his article to the extreme prejudice and the violence to which the far left resorted to quash their opposition. Mary Whitehouse, an ordinary English woman who fearlessly campaigned for all the traditional decencies, had addressed a front lawn crowd. Most of the 'huge' crowd, said Abbott, appeared interested in what she had to say. The far left didn't care a fig. They responded in their usual mindless way by 'by pelting her with oranges, cheesecakes etc., which ... they hurled at anyone else who aroused their ire'. Such a response was 'especially abominable in an alleged centre of learning'. Abbott then targeted the double standards while defending Western Civilisation's right to free speech:

'But the plain fact is that similar activity [as the Whitehouse protest] has been condoned by student representatives for a long time. The violent disruption of Professor Eysenck's lectures last year involved the previous SRC Honorary Secretary/ Treasurer [Gary Nicholls] and the current AUS officer [David Patch]. The Immediate Past President [Barbara Ramjan] was also present in support.

'Their indignant and superficially appealing defence that racists are not to speak on campus entailed a glib and totally unsupported claim that Eysenck was, in fact, a racist. Yet, distasteful though they be, racists have as much right to free speech as communists, fascists, animal liberationists, prime ministers, and vice-chancellors. There are methods more meet for the rejection of intolerable views than street brawling.

'Most members of the broad left are not hopeful idealists, occasionally overreacting in defence of passionate beliefs. They cleverly play on the better instincts of students to lend some respectability to brazen political stunts. Eysenck is a dedicated opponent of communism and fascism, which he fled in the thirties. Whitehouse is a sincere, if perhaps over-zealous, defender of the Christian family values the left is pledged to destroy. The left has no monopoly of virtue. Instead, its more skilful operators are possessed of cunning, subtlety, and malice to an unusual degree.'

The cunning, subtlety and malice of Patch and Nicholls pulling the strings of their puppet Ramjan may have succeeded in bombing Abbott's presidency for the last term of 1978, making him eat ash among the shambles. What Abbott did achieve besides presenting his conservative vision in a measured analytical manner was the unmasking of David Patch. Gary Nicholls didn't care who saw him for what he was. A self-satisfied Cheshire cat grin accompanied his knavish tricks while he gave the finger to those challenging him. But David Patch hid behind the manipulation of procedures and regulations until the last months of 1978 when it ceased to be effective. Then he showed that he, too, would resort to any dirty trick to stop Abbott. Abbott hardly mentioned Ramjan throughout 1978, and then it was only about political issues. Ramjan never mentioned Abbott. The evidence in *Honi* contradicts Ramjan's claims he was continually in her face, worrying her to death. Indeed, she seemed to have an excellent time of it, surrendering her duties as president to Nicholls or flying to Darwin to be with her smitten hotshot 34-year-old husband.

The last edition of *Honi* (H27, 2 November) was nothing more than the continued mindless mockery and name-calling of Abbott. There was, however, a curious letter from Tim Walshaw, 'SRC Representative', about the SRC finances in H25 (18 October). In a postscript, Walshaw said,

'Peter Mickey, Legal Officer, says this letter is not defamatory'. The letter was about 'the state of the SRC Bank Account when the new [51st] Council took over'. The pertinent passages were:

'On the day of the first SRC meeting (Wednesday, 4 October), the Account was overdrawn, and the Bank was busily bouncing cheques!

'Now it is well known that the SRC receives an income of $150,000 a year from us students. Indeed, a Statement published by Gary Nicholls, the previous Acting President-Hon Sec/Treasurer, shows that the Bank Balance stood at $45,044 on 31 August 1978. (A little over a month later, it was zero. Excepting $8,000 in the Book Store A/C.)

'The new SRC administration was forced to rush to the university, who agreed to pay the final $20,000 they owe us, $5,600 now, and the rest in instalments later! This has to pay all staff wages and SRC expenses until we receive next year's subscriptions next March.

'Now I am sure the SRC has a lot of justifiable expenses. However, I strongly object to this largely unauthorised 'spending-spree' entered into by the previous SRC administration in the period between when the results of the election became known and when the new council was finally installed (under threat of Court Order), unauthorised because the previous council did not meet during this period and the executive (to my knowledge) authorised no major expenditures.'

There was not a word about these claims in *Honi*, suggesting someone or some persons went on a wild 'spending spree' in the closing weeks of the 50th SRC. In 1979, Paul Brereton spoke about the financial problems held over from 1978 but refrained from explaining. The financial delinquency of the left was well-known, but this was well over the top. Why the silence?

Chapter 12

1979 – Tony Abbott contra mundum

IN PREVIOUS Years it had taken one of two issues of *Honi* for the student debate (or abuse) to get going. In 1979, it was on from the start. Indeed, it was on even before the start of term. Education Officer Tanya Coleman found it necessary to apologise (H1, late Feb) 'on behalf of the Students' Representative Council' to the Italian Department for an article in *The Flipside*, 'the counter-course handbook'. The article 'Don't enrol in the Italian Department' attacked a staff member 'in a most malicious and un-deserved way'. Coleman promised to make up for the insult by publishing 'a more representative assessment' in a following edition of *Honi*. Coleman was far too polite.

Kim R. Turner, President SU Liberal Club, provided the fire. 'Once again', wrote Turner, 'an unrepresentative minority group have organised to swamp a committee and subvert its aim to use it as a device to peddle their own peculiar political beliefs'. Coleman was the only elected person on that committee. The rest were blow-ins intended to swell the committee to bring the handbook 'to the level of a cheap propaganda sheet'. Far-left Mark Thornton moved Coleman's editorial from page one to page three and substituted an article critical of her. That and other changes were made without consulting her, the editor. To stop a repeat of this tactic, Turner suggested giving complete control to the editor in such cases or 'abolish the Open Committee System, which is no more than a ploy by the left to ensure their control over SRC monies and materials'.

The hitherto unknown E. Carpenter cranked up the far-left rhetoric to manufacture a glowing picture of the 'broad left' as a body of altruistic inoffensive students fighting the spoilers and fascists of the far right. The ascendancy of 'extreme conservative' Tony Abbott had introduced 'a major change in the functioning of the SRC' – for the worse. A picture followed of an idyllic SRC in which students could blissfully come and go, accessing the abundant resources 'to use in organising social activities, educational work, and political campaigns'. Then there were the free concerts sponsored or organised by the SRC, as well as the help given to groups hosting dances and parties and other social functions. In this pre-Abbott idyll, the SRC 'helped small groups of students in numerous departments, etc. try to get a fair deal when faced with what they see as discriminatory treatment'. Students had to thank the broad left for this wonderful haven of altruism. But supporting students as students, having the general welfare of students in mind, was precisely the conservative platform run against the extreme political activity of Comrade Carpenter and his mates manoeuvring to gain control of SRC monies.

The 'radical and progressive officers and staff of the SRC' did all the work, Carpenter continued. The progressives had produced a bonzer Orientation Week with the publications of the Women's and Welfare Collectives, the *Orientation Handbook* and *Honi Soit*. Abbott's SRC had done nothing. Abbott, he charged, spent his time making 'life difficult for the more active people', meaning the radicals. The deception was transparent. If the radicals 'did all the work', as he claimed, it was because they controlled the activities either directly through the far-left officer involved or indirectly by 'open committees'. Conservatives did not stand in the way of activities they supported. The measures Abbott introduced to make life difficult were efforts to bring order to the work of the SRC, to make it more professional and efficient, and to guard against the constant attempts of the weasels and ferrets to gain control. Comrade Carpenter ended by warning, 'If Abbott gets his way, there will soon be no SRC at all'. This was an allusion to what would become the great contest of 1979, a contest between centre-left Brereton, who rejected voluntary SRC membership and conservative Abbott, who wanted an end to forced membership.

In a sense, Carpenter was right about Abbott being an 'extreme conservative', but not in the sense of the right-wing extremist or fascist whose idea of government (like the radicals) was collectivist and dictatorial. Abbott took his lead from the thought of Edmund Burke. Nations and communities, according to Burke, were not established on the basis of the provisions of an abstract theory. There was no agreement by an 'aggregate' of individuals to come together out of the state of nature to establish state and society. He rejected the abstract contract theories of Hobbes and Rousseau. No, a particular community or nation arose over time out of people already in community, however basic. Man's original nature was to be in community. At some stage, the conventions, customs and traditions cohered to make them a particular society with a particular form of government. The constitution of that society was to be found in a group of foundational arrangements, some written and some unwritten – conventions, customs and traditions. The foundational arrangements did not preclude change, but it must be change that maintained character and continuity.

Many associations and social organisation form in an analogical manner. There is a foundation document accompanied by implied conventions from the society in which the association is formed. Even without knowing Tony Abbott's philosophical outlook, one can see from his actions and contributions in *Honi* that these ideas about the origins of communities and association were his chief motivations in his battle with the far left. Abbott wanted to bring the contemporary operation of the SRC into line with its foundational constitution. He allowed change or reform as long as the character and purpose, according to its constitution, remained intact. Abbott agreed with Brereton that the SRC 'should limit its activities to working for those students who fund it'. But he rejected what he saw as Brereton's inconsistent support of some of the far left's anti-liberal, destructive campaigns. He did not mince words in his first contribution in 1979 *Honi* (H1). He heartily welcomed newcomers to the university, encouraged them to 'become involved in as many activities' as they could, gave his contact numbers if they needed help, and then turned to things 'more dismal.'

'In 4 months as president, my strictly necessary functions have been signing cheques, authorising loans, and answering enquiries. About the only presidential endeavours of any worth have been representations made to the administration on behalf of students with academic difficulties.

'In the 3½ months since the inauguration of the new council, useful initiatives amount only to one fairly reasonable resolution on the determination of course content and a number of long overdue but rather bureaucratic changes to the regulations. This is despite 3 meetings, all of which lasted until the small hours of the morning. In the same period, about $35,000 of student money has been spent.

'Some of this has paid the lawyer's salary, various grants to faculty societies, and emergency loans to straitened students. So far, so good.

'But what else have we to show for it? Students have paid the wages of two secretaries. We have paid over $15,000 in AUS fees and sent 9 delegates to AUS annual council, which was as usual, a Marxist-dominated farce. We have printed several issues of *Honi Soit,* which last year, as everyone will remember, was a disreputable rag. Large amounts have been spent purchasing stencils, ink and other equipment to keep the propaganda factory operating.

'Finally, there is the education counter course handbook. This scurrilous document slanders the Vice-Chancellor and most of the teaching departments and spouts all the familiar Marxist cliches, *education serves the capitalist class etc.* This everlasting rubbish was produced by an open committee (i.e. anyone can join) despite the opposition of the elected Education officer.

'In fact, apart from the legal aid service and the faculty grants and loans, which are administered separately from the SRC's other activities, the SRC's spending has achieved nothing beyond soothing the edges and obsessions of a few left-wing fanatics. The useful work of the SRC has not involved the spending of any money at all.

'Late this term, I shall seek to end compulsory subsidisation of the SRC. I will keep you informed of further developments.'

At the end of 1978, Abbott still entertained introducing reforms to bring the SRC in line with its foundational arrangements. The cussed determination of the far left and their success with the open committees paralysing all efforts to preserve the democratic structure prescribed by the constitution had changed his mind. Now he had no alternative but to make the SRC a voluntary organisation. The left were unteachable, entirely impervious to notions of fairness and straight dealing. In the meantime, he gave a President's Address to New Students and their Parents (H2, 5 March) in which he broadened his philosophical vision. He could have supported parts of his address with quotations from Edmund Burke's writings:

'Ladies and gentlemen, the basic problem of our age, it seems, is this: not IGNORANCE of the truth but rather FEAR of the truth. It is not that we do not know the truth but that we will not face it. Nowhere is this more evident than in our universities.

We respect excellence in sport never achieved without sweat and effort; isn't the same true of intellectual excellence? 'Knowledge makes a bloody entrance'. Yet some educators, ostrich-like, continue to defend 'progressive' education long after its disastrous results are clear to all with eyes and ears to learn.

'That a university should seek the truth is beyond question. To those who would say it is about knowledge I would reply, what is knowledge if it does not lead to truth. A university can nourish many human ideologies, but while taking the good from each, it must ultimately reject them all because no model can ever fully explain emotional, irrational and inconsistent human behaviour.

'Yet one cannot say then that the only truth is that there is no truth if for no other reason than to establish anything requires some frame of reference.

'And so the question arises – what is truth? Existentialist philosophers say that as nothing is immutable, there is no truth, and given their assumptions, their logic is undeniable. All physical objects, all human works are quite insubstantial in the parade of eternity – only God endures. In all ages, progressive thinkers have announced the death of God. My friends, He has made more comebacks than Mohammed Ali. For most of us, He refuses to die.

'This is the FUNDAMENTAL TRUTH that has been forgotten by the university in its rush to be fashionable. There is another related matter, and that is the universities' failure to build character.

'Today's graduates may be brilliant – but what is brilliance without character. Look at the selfishness that pervades every level of society especially the top – as Prof. Messel said, it's the 'Big me' complex. But if there is no end higher than oneself, personal indulgence or selfish aggrandisement becomes man's highest duty.

'Our universities have renounced all responsibility for the personal growth of students, claiming such an interest would mean the imposition of a particular moral code. But the practical difference between this attitude and a deliberate espousal of amorality is minimal.

'A human being is an entity, not a series of segments. It is not enough to inculcate scientific or historical facts yet to ignore appreciation of the human spirit. It's like building a car without wheels. The Christian ethic or at least some moral code must permeate education in every field if we are to develop the whole man as we should.

'And so, my friends, the adventure of university with all its pitfalls and potential is where many of you now find yourselves. I have told you what I believe. But perhaps it is not so important to grasp the truth – we may never find it – as to seek it humbly and consistently. In these challenging times, I think we do well to remember this. You get from university what you put in – nothing more, nothing less. Never underestimate your potential. Inevitably you will be discouraged but don't be deterred. You will be rebuffed but still persevere. Our society is far from perfect. Nevertheless, it rewards courage and determination with ultimate success.'

The parents and students listening must have found this pastiche of philosophical ideas encouraging, even if it was not all quite comprehensible. Abbott had attempted much in a short space. Truth exists in the world, even if somewhat hidden by those with a political investment in obscurity. The task of us all is to seek it out. The struggle will be rewarding, and it will build character. Abbott touched on the challenging question of what human reasoning is about. The Enlightenment philosophers treated reason as a linear mathematical process. They reasoned from fundamental premises to build a theoretical structure. That theoretical structure was then held to be prescriptive in moral and political matters. Marxism is a great case in point, with its roots in German philosophy. Burke argued that moral reasoning and reasoning about politics were not like that. Individual human reasoning had its limits, which it is foolish to exceed. *A priori* abstract theories would never be adequate for arranging and securing state and society. Also, Burke thought one could find wisdom outside the individual mind in the form of enduring social arrangements, as a sort of third-person reasoning.

These are complex epistemological (knowledge) issues, and I can only give a notion of them in a short space to show the conservative direction of Abbott's thought. The final important point is the moral one. Abbott brings God into it to provide an objective reference and framework for human behaviour. Without such a reference, there would be no restraint on human behaviour except arbitrary government, elected or unelected. The people would be at the whim of those with the power to usurp government constituted within the framework of Western Civilisation. The restraining framework in Western Society has, until recently, been the natural law, which I have briefly discussed. The natural law arises out of the observable order of the universe, and that order for Burke presupposed a transcendent intelligence whose prescriptions were discernible. I suggest these notions of the natural law were present in Abbott's short address. There is also the notion of *pietas* in the background, even if he may not have been conscious of it. *Pietas* was the essential Roman virtue of paying honour and respect to the gods, to family (especially parents), and to country. *Pietas* incorporated a humble acknowledgement of one's duties and debts.

The student body had to wait until the third edition of *Honi* (12 March) to find Abbott cast as a nasty fascist. It came in a letter by far-left Greg Schofield, notorious for mindless violence on campus (he was suspended) and who boasted his communist credentials with an undertaking not to compromise a jot with bourgeois capitalist society. In a feverish paranoid letter, he warned of the rise of the 'National Alliance', a fascist group insinuating its disgusting propaganda into schools and tertiary institutions and setting up cells. Schofield did not directly accuse Abbot of being a National Alliance fascist but just as effectively smeared him by association. National Alliance propaganda, Schofield wrote, was 'a skilful blend of the nationalism of BOB SANTAMARIA' using 'many of the concepts TONY ABBOTT has gained electoral success by' and is merely 'a stronger version of the same sought [*sic*] of politics that TONY ABBOTT typifies'. Enough said. Schofield ended his letter with a frantic call for the National Alliance to 'BE SMASHED'. He urged 'the formation on campus of an ANTI FASCIST LEAGUE of all who wish to oppose the threat of Fascism'. I detected no further reference to the National Alliance in *Honi*, or anywhere else. Immune to this sort of far-left paranoid rant, Abbott ignored Schofield, leaving him to his far-left delirium.

In 1979, Mark Thornton stepped forward to fill the unfillable shoes of Gary Nicholls. In his response (H3, 3 March) to Kim Turner's charges about the Counter-Course Handbook *Flipside*, he said that Turner's lack of context meant 'hardly anybody knows what the hell he/she is talking about.' On the contrary, the context was clear, if one bothered to read Turner's letter with a minimum of attention. The accusation of lack of context was a pretext to lasso Abbott into the dispute. 'Both Tony Abbott (our nasty right-wing President) and now, it would seem, Paul Brereton (our little less nasty little less right-wing Hon/Sec-Treasurer)', he wrote, 'are making every attempt, both legal and political, to bring about the demise of the Open Committee System'. Open committees were 'an extremely democratic system of organisation that gives each and every student on this campus the opportunity to get involved and make the decisions'. That does not answer the obvious complaint that the far-left, people like him, manipulated the open committees to secure far-left control. The 'open committees' were, in practice, closed committees. He was at least right about Abbott's intention of doing away with open committees. In the same *Honi* edition, Abbott listed the services the SRC provides, paid from the compulsory $10 student fee. He continued:

'However, this sort of activity requires less than one-third of the SRC's budget of $150,000. Moreover, it is true that what is presently done by the SRC could be both performed either by non-political bodies or a non-financial SRC. Legal Aid would be more effective if the officer were not constantly sorting out the SRC's own legal tangles. The Bursary & Assistance Fund would be more efficiently administered as part of the Registrar's loans scheme. Faculty societies would be better off if grants were paid directly rather than through a muddled intermediary.

'The fact remains that the vast bulk of the SRC's money provides a political infrastructure still devoted to the Marxist hobby horses of ultra-militant feminism, homosexual proselytism, and environmentalism gone to crazy lengths. This is because SRC activities and publications are generally controlled by open committees (i.e. committees which anyone can join), which have for years been composed of General Philosophy, Political Economy and ADHOC [homosexual] activists with nothing better to do than hang around the SRC playing lefty politics ...

'Surely it is not necessary to tolerate an expensive and obnoxious political bureaucracy in order to obtain Legal Aid and other services. It would be infinitely preferable if SRC services were assumed by non-political bodies while the SRC is reorganised on a non-financial basis. The SRC would still be the representative body of students, but it will no longer be able to throw student money after every cause which takes its passing fancy.

'There will be a referendum after Easter on the question of voluntary financing of the SRC. I hope all of you will take the trouble to vote.'

The SRC, under the left's hegemony, had been wrenched from its foundation and become a monetarised weapon in furthering the Marxist project. If the SRC could not return to a state showing a strong continuity with its foundation, then it must be submitted to the knife so that the diseased parts could be excised, and the remainder serve the students in the manner intended. Abbott showed here he had a sharp down-to-earth mind for organisation. His difficult task was to convince most students of his vision. He did not want to destroy the SRC. He wanted to reform it or remodel it according to an established pattern.

There was, however, an area in which Abbott overstepped the (conservative) mark – the mark of what was possible. If the far left were not always negligent of personal hygiene, they were generally a pack of grubs. It would have been useless to put rubbish bins around the SRC headquarters. As one student put it during Comrade McKnight's presidency, the SRC was a pigsty of swirling paperwork and fast food wrappings dropped wherever the food was consumed. Abbott's conservative sense of order impelled him to clean up the SRC headquarters and make it correspond to the expectations of those with a modicum of education in manners and self-respect. But all that was a bunch of bourgeois rubbish for the radicals. The more mess and dirt, the better to break down the capitalist's sense of order. There was another equally important motivation. Property. Private property was one of the bulwarks of a capitalist society. It must be eliminated. An essential part of the process of elimination was disrespecting all property not belonging to the radicals personally. They scrawled graffiti over the walls of the SRC offices. The graffiti consisted of semi-literate slogans supporting the favourite far-left causes. With the Abbott presidency, they now had a fascist target that provided endless scope for their scrawls and scribblings. Abbott wanted to clean it away.

His program of clean-up was far too optimistic. As he has often said, politics is about the possible in the concrete circumstances. Getting the far-left grubs to clean up would be impossible. In H3 (12 March), he deplored his lack of success in an article the editorial collective obscured with great blobs of black printing forming the letters 'SRC' Patterns of dense dotting obscured other parts. The SRC collective was proud of their mess and filth, and they would not be deprived of it. In some frustration, he said in a legible passage, 'These scribblings indicate the attitude and obsessions and utter disregard for student property of their authors'. He submitted a quote for $800 to the meeting on 28 February to have the SRC repainted. It was knocked back, and to rub his nose in it, the meeting voted to allocate the money to 'boosting the open committee bodies and employing a part-time research officer to act as a "contact service"'. With justification, he commented, 'the walls of the SRC remain a monument to irresponsibility and paranoia'.

To Abbott's single column on a full page devoted to the subject, the editorial collective gave the rest (three columns) to Eliza Chidiac for a Marxist rant and ridicule of Abbott. *Honi* 1979 was Chidiac's first appearance, but she showed she was full to the brim with the rhetoric. The blobs of black ink and the dense pattern of dots also obscured her long piece, but the drift was evident in the legible parts. Abbott and his mates, she said, should stop pretending they were 'acting in the interests of the students and admit they're out to completely destroy the SRC'. She rejected the charge that the left stacked meetings. It was all democratic, didn't you know? Then from Abbott's proposal to clean up the SRC surroundings, she took flight.

Abbott's urge to cleanse the SRC offices was part of a far bigger bourgeois scheme to protect their ugly concrete structures, reflecting their fetish for private property. The people are trained to 'value property over people ... Respect for property is ingrained – but how can we respect it if we do not have some part in its operating, democratically determining how it affects our lives?' Well, capitalist society gave privileged university students like Chidiac an education that opened up far more opportunity to enter the 'operation' (acquisition) of property than most her age. It could be that working to secure property might instil respect for what one's own efforts gain and add to feelings of community and solidarity.

But that was all bourgeois nonsense – just as it was nonsense to say that property is universally valued above people in bourgeois society, one of the many myths Marxists peddle to justify their trashing of the society that gives them such an indulged life. But the real point is that Chidiac, like all her half-baked Marxist mates, assumed Marxism. They held Marxism as a set of dogma. She went on about graffiti as the only expression of the downtrodden, that it was 'humorous and aesthetically appropriate etc. etc. It is the most effective way for powerless students to get their message across to other students'. Yes, it was so difficult for Chidiac and her mates to get their message across in every single issue of *Honi* without scrawling barely literate abuse over the university walls. She topped it all off with an extraordinary flourish, giving a peek into the unhinged mind of the leftist:

Bureaucratic bodies such as governments, councils and even Sydney University administration, spend so much money each year erasing what people write up. Abbott follows in their footsteps because he is part of them and united with them in their repressive actions. It reminds me of '1984', how the State, and all its intricately functioning parts, continually erase history - that is, what people are saying, doing and needing, etc.'

You've got to have sympathy for Tony Abbott. He gets mocked, abused, and slandered, he wins the SRC presidency but is prevented from taking office, his submissions are misrepresented, distorted or ignored, and there is no lie too big if it could do him damage. And then to be painted as a purveyor of state oppression by the representatives of a real nightmarish world of tyranny and oppression, it would be too much for most people to endure. But Tony stuck to his task. He would not flinch. He replied to Chidiac's piece (H5, 27 March), giving an insight into the tactics he had to endure. The editors gave it the heading 'A Day in the Life of the SRC President' clothing it with an irony they had scarcely intended. But, then, I suppose they had never heard of Aleksandr Solzhenitsyn's *A Day in the Life of Ivan Denisovich:*

'I arrive at the SRC to be immediately confronted by a garbage can on its side, and papers scattered all along the SRC corridor. However, this does not seem as dirty as one might think, as the walls themselves have been painted with obscenities. A clean floor would seem almost incongruous.

'I notice that the front office wall has been decorated with homosexual posters by one of the front office staff who stares sullenly and unco-operatively, especially when I take them down and ask him not to replace them with others of a partisan politico, socio, sexual bent. He complains to the Hon. Sec./Treasurer, the *HONI* editors and anyone else who will listen.

'I walk down the corridor to my 'office'. It is finally time, I decide, to remove the condom which has been pinned on my door. It rather clashes with the lesbian posters that have been plastered there. A notice I had placed on the door reads, 'Tony (confidentially), you are a fuckwit'. It has now been slashed for good measure.

'My first phone call is to someone who has been trying to ring me for days. Messages are often strangely mislaid at 'our' SRC.

'Finding a copy of *HONI,* I check on a feature I had suggested containing photos of SRC graffiti, an article of mine condemning such vandalism, with one defending it as 'art'. Photos and articles are almost indistinguishable on a blurred grey-spotted background, and the page is dominated by a daubed slogan. It seems the paintbrush is at work, even on the pages of *Honi*. Perhaps it is just as well – the pro-graffiti article is three times as long as mine. The *HONI* editors apologise profusely, but no, they will not reprint the feature.

'Returning to my office, I am troubled by the thought of the SRC's utter irrelevance to the daily academic grind of most students. These thoughts are not dissipated while I remain for several hours, receiving not a single call, letter, or visit from any student, except occasional abuse from the 'welfare' officers across the corridor [far-left Rogley and Schaeffar].

'I console myself with the thought that at least I haven't had to remove candles, placed so as to jut obscenely from the front office wall or try to stop payment on cheques disappearing from the front office.

'WHY DO WE ALL CONTINUE TO TOLERATE PAYING FEES TO THIS ORGANISATION? I HOPE YOU WILL HELP RESOLVE THIS QUESTION BY VOTING IN THE FORTHCOMING REFER-ENDUM ON THE SUBJECT.'

The issue of compulsory fees was now foremost among activists on both sides. Chris Grainger, President of the Democratic Club, summarised the problems for the conservatives (H5, 27 March). Compulsory fees to subsidise the SRC amounted to 'highway robbery', with the thief demanding the 'right to represent you'. Worse, no payment, no student card, and with no student card, you could not enrol. 'You pay under duress – and that is theft'. The apparent justification was that all must pay because all students benefit. He listed the benefits and provided a counter-response. In brief, they were that students benefited by being represented. But that representation was a travesty, with most students boycotting the elections. Second, the SRC sponsored cultural activities. But the choice was the arbitrary decision of student bureaucrats. Third, providing money to political clubs amounted to a gift to leftist clubs. Fourth, the student newspaper *Honi* Soit was subsidised. But *Honi*'s far-left content interested a small minority of students. 'Compulsory fees', he ended, 'cannot be justified on the grounds that all or even a third of students benefit. And if these cannot be the reasons for maintaining a system of blatant coercion, then what can be?'

Mark Thornton appearing to see himself as a leading Marxist theorist for his group, took up the cudgel (H6, 2 April). Would he explain the difficult points of the theory to enlighten his ignorant fellow students? Alas, no. At all critical points, he copped out, either through evasion or because he was not on top of the theory. Before he got down to the nitty-gritty of the 'voluntarist' position, he wanted 'to spend a little time in drawing out and appealing against its implicit assumptions' because 'the "voluntarists" are actually working with a theory of the relation of the individual and society that is in their interests to leave unstated'. Would he explain that social theory? Well, no. There was 'insufficient space' for him to do so. But students should 'keep in mind the way which people like Grainger and Abbott circumscribe the debate'. How do they do that? They make an 'emotional appeal that plays upon our often unconscious prejudices'.

What are the emotional appeal and unconscious prejudices? The answer seems to be 'the rights of the individual' and 'freedom of choice'. On why individual rights and freedom of choice appeal to emotions and unconscious prejudices, Thornton remained silent.

He then devoted much space to saying the students have interests and concerns, and the best way of defending or promoting those interests and concerns was to 'act together collectively' and to 'organise in autonomous student unions'. And how does the collective decide what are the collective views? 'Democratically! According to majority vote'. On the face of it, dark and sinister Abbott could not take exception. But the issue for Abbott was not about democracy and representation of students. Thornton and his mates subverted the democratic process with their open committees, which resulted in a leftist hegemony in the SRC and *Honi Soit*.

After explaining the need for democratically elected representation, Thornton tackled compulsory unionism. On this, he agreed with Paul Brereton that '"voluntary" unionism would mean, in reality, no unionism at all', which was a debatable proposition. To show how debatable, Thornton merely said students opting out of responsibilities would diminish resources. That may be so, but it did not follow that diminished resources meant 'no unionism at all'. His central argument was an argument from an analogy which he admitted was not 'direct'. That did not stop him from running it as if it were. It was the comparison of student unionism with trade unionism. The critical difference, namely that students were a group not dependent on the SRC for a living and trade unions were dependent on their employer, made it a weak analogy. In the long run, all Thornton could do was give dire warnings that 'extreme right-wing' Abbott, with his 'repressive policies', was bent on 'destroying unionism as a whole'. It was left to Paul Brereton to offer some coherent argument against Abbott's determined, articulate campaign to make student unionism voluntary. Instead of a Marxist-motivated harangue, Brereton offered compelling reasons for maintaining compulsory unionism, reasons

Abbott had to respond to. The core of Bereton's case was in the first two paragraphs of his defence:

'The opponents of compulsory subscriptions to the SRC put forward two distinct lines of argument. The first is that there should be no compulsion in any form: a general opposition to any compulsory fees. The second is that it is the SRC, specifically, which does not justify having its subscriptions compulsory for all undergraduates: a specific opposition to subsidising the SRC.

In the first place, it is important to realise that the proposal being put forward by Mr Abbott is not for voluntary MEMBERSHIP of the SRC, but for voluntary FUNDING. All students will still be able to vote, and to receive the benefits of membership of the SRC. But only those who have the conscience to pay the Annual Fee will have to, and their fees will subsidise the services and facilities available to all students, including those who do not pay. A more iniquitous proposal could hardly have been devised.

The proponents of voluntaryism argue that the SRC does nothing to justify compelling all students to pay the Annual Fee – a mere $10. This hardly bears serious examination. The first function of the SRC is precisely what its name suggests: to represent its student members.'

One cannot conclude from what Abbott had said thus far that he was against 'compulsion in any form'. He was certainly not against the university charging tuition fees. Second, on the specific issue of subsidising the SRC, he was in the concrete circumstances against it. This was the practical reasoning of the Burkean conservative. Had the SRC lived up to its foundational arrangements, he would not have objected. It was only after failing to break the dominance of the far left that he changed his mind. If the far-left could not be budged from the control of the SRC, then students should decide about funding. Brereton was on sounder ground with his second objection that non-paying students would enjoy the same benefits as paying students, but it was hardly as iniquitous as he claimed. In the abstract, the proposal appears inequitable. In the concrete circumstances, it was less so because most students did not want any association with the mad left and their activities. Furthermore, there were other ways, as Abbott would suggest, to deal with those welfare services. Brereton then produced a lengthy list of legitimate services that would be threatened if funds decreased substantially. Abbott had to cater to their possible loss in his plans.

Brereton responded to Abbott's claim elsewhere (not in *Honi*) that 'the University will take over all the SRC services'. The administration, he claimed, was unwilling to take such responsibility. Second, student affairs should be in the hands of the students. They should generally be, but circumstances were exceptional. On Abbott's suggestion that the administration would 'pay fees direct to Faculty societies', he queried how they would collect the fees. A fair point, but I wonder whether Brereton had reproduced Abbott's full proposal. To muddy the waters, Bereton fell into a logical fallacy. To allocate monies from fees in that scheme would require making fees compulsory. 'So much for the principle of voluntaryism,' said Brereton, claiming an inconsistency in Abbott's reasoning. But it does not follow that having made fees compulsory in one organisation, you have to make fees compulsory in all organisations. It is an empirical matter to be decided on the varying circumstances. Brereton's final point was reasonable. The SRC, in his view, was working well in 1979. Why spoil it? Abbott obviously had another view. In the same issue (H6, 2 April), Abbott produced a detailed proposal 'to end compulsory SRC & AUS funding', which included eight amendments and insertions in the constitution and the demonstration that an unfunded SRC would work. It was his final student manifesto and a genuine conservative document in the Burkean mould. It is not necessary to go into the detail. It is an expanded repetition of the points he had already argued.

The key philosophical points were that the SRC had broken irre-
deemably away from its foundational arrangements. For that reason, exceptional measures were required to bring it out of its corrupted state
back to circumstances that at least resembled the original intentions of its
founders. Second, on a general level, it conformed to ideas of individual
freedom in Western Society, ideas that had roots in Athens, Rome, and
Jerusalem. Third, and most important, Abbott justified his stand on 'principled and pragmatic grounds'. The notion that the practising politician
must apply enduring principles to the endlessly varied concrete political
circumstances is at the heart of Edmund Burke's political philosophy.
Finally, as with all of Abbott's interventions, this document was measured,
thoughtful, and without the abuse, ridicule and vilification he continually
suffered at the hands of his opposition. Would those opponents this time
treat his proposals on their merits? Of course not. It inflamed them, making them all the more determined to destroy him.

In the meantime, those for voluntary fees circulated a petition which
gained 450 signatories. It was presented to a special meeting of the SRC.
The meeting acted on the advice of the SRC's Standing Legal Committee
(H8, 23 April) and 'resolved by eleven votes to nil, with two abstentions, that it could not lawfully submit a petition calling for voluntary
funding of the SRC to a referendum'. The two abstentions were Abbott
and Tanya Coleman. The detailed explanation of the decision centred on
the (alleged) conflict of one of Abbott's amendment clauses (e) with the
AUS Constitution, which bound the SRC. An examination of the detail
is unnecessary. The effective point is that the provisions of an external
document defeated Abbott's proposal. There was no discussion of Abbott's political points. This was a common tactic of the left. The Standing
Legal Committee was made up of ten members, of which only two were
conservatives – Abbott and Coleman. The rest were far left and centre left.
The committee thus ruled the 'petition out of order', which decision the
special SRC meeting duly accepted. Abbott forcefully responded in the

same edition (H8), the thrust of which was in the opening paragraph:

'More than 550 students have signed a petition requesting that a referendum be held to abolish compulsory SRC fees. Now the SRC has refused to put the issue to vote. Invoking legalisms of dubious validity, the SRC has denied students the chance to decide whether they want the present SRC structure to continue.'

He then gave a point-by-point refutation of the committee's legal interpretation, raising the obvious question of how the SRC constitution could be 'subject to the AUS regulations'. Equally obvious was that the committee's legal objections could be resolved by 'deleting the offending clause' – if they were truly devoted to democratic processes. It was the same old political tactic of manipulating the constitution:

'What the SRC is doing is forcing the proponents of voluntary funding to start all over again with a fresh petition, go through all the rigour and tedium of collecting another 450 signatures, only to be exposed once more to the same sort of nitpicking legalistic malice, and bloody-minded obstruction from the SRC ... If further proof were needed, these devious machinations are sure evidence that the SRC is utterly impervious to change; that it has become quite indifferent to student feeling which does not accord with its own preferences...'

'After the meeting, Brereton was heard to quip, 'Thank God for the AUS', which indicated what a near thing Abbott's victory had been. The cynical manipulation of quasi-legal provisions triumphed. In forty years, not much had changed. If the opposition thought Abbott, defeated, would crawl back into his far-right hole, they were dead wrong. Abbott came out swinging. An 'open letter' addressed to Paul Brereton appeared in H10 (4 June). With more than a hint of irony, Abbott praised Brereton for his 'diligence' and 'industry' in student affairs and his 'admirable denunciation of extremism'. Nevertheless, no one should ignore Brereton's reluctance 'to slaughter any of the Marxists' sacred cows or to support a single significant measure proposed by moderates other than [him]self'.

'Certainly, you have not been guilty of harbouring gratitude towards those whose votes gained your office. You even refused to support the innocuous step of restoring to the president his right to preside over SRC meetings. You led council to refuse to put the issue of compulsory fees to a referendum, even though this had been requested by more than 500 students as required by the constitution.

'Later you admitted to solicitors that your grounds for refusal, breach of contract with AUS, were quite spurious. I can appreciate why you would only reverse your emphatic opinion, which happily coincided with your political tactic, in the face of potentially embarrassing court action.

'But it cannot be encouraging to realise that one needs the Supreme Court's help to obtain rights which must have been clear to you from the start.

'You have rightly justified secession from the Australian Union of Students, yet try to prevent students from determining the future of the SRC – wherein you hold office. You have pointed out the gross defects in the SRC committee system – which has always frustrated your purposes – yet fail to accept that the same ills afflict the SRC itself.

'Political ambition is not at all unworthy. But if one has no larger, idealistic vision of any sort, it invariably degenerates into cynical self-aggrandisement. Too often, you have confused the advancement of Paul le Gay Brereton with the good of the student body.

'Even in the narrow world of student politics, you are somewhat larger than life. In another context, talk of 'historic compromise' between social democrats and communists could be inspiring. But when applied by you to a sordid deal between yourself and the 'broad left' on AUS elections, it rings a little pompous.

'All your considerable gifts of energy and determination are being vitiated by obvious personal ambition and a seemingly inflated self-importance. There is sometimes political mileage in boring one's opponents, but I fail to see the objective need to hear from you at repetitive length on every issue.

'It would be nice to have an SRC which worked self-sacrificingly and wholeheartedly for the benefit of students. But it seems that in politics, which is simply a more stylised form of naked aggression and conflict, one man's gain is another's loss.

'Perhaps inevitably, students are subsidising, not a lobby for the common good but an instrument for conflicting ambitions.'

Abbott explained his reference to the Supreme Court's 'help to obtain rights' (H11, 11 June). Brereton and the Council had breached the constitution by refusing to go to a referendum on voluntary fees prescribed when a petition signed by 450 students had been presented. Abbott had called their bluff by appealing to the Supreme Court, which decided in favour of a referendum and ordered the SRC to pay the costs. Brereton's legal manoeuvre, said Abbott, was a tactic to delay a decision on the referendum until after the looming SRC elections. Then it would no longer be relevant. Abbott had succeeded in forcing a vote after all.

In the same president's report, he gave details of the draft report of the 1978 SRC finances. There was an embarrassing deficit of $20,000 signalling 'a degree of irresponsibility on the part of SRC administrations'. That would be an understatement. Echoes of the wild spending spree in the last months of Barbara Ramjan's presidency were surely heard. Still, there was no explanation. People were treading carefully. Not even Abbott ventured an explanation. Elections for Economics Men representative together with the delegation to the special AUS Council, were announced for 15 June. Frank Kristian, the candidate for Economics Men Representative, let loose about the deficit. The stranglehold the left had on the SRC and the syphoning of money to 'unrepresentative and extremist groups' were an outrage. Abuse of funds had to stop. As an example of the abuse, he named 'the unresolved matter of the missing money, in which (1977-78) [*sic*] showed that $20,000 IS missing and unaccounted for'. He, too, was silent about the possible destination of the missing funds.

Paul Brereton found it distasteful (H12, 18 June) that Abbott had resorted to 'poison pen letters of abuse' to advance his cause. Brereton obviously did not know what a poison pen letter was (unsigned, libellous, abusive). Abbott's letter was tough and wounding, but it was not what you would call abuse. Not much correspondence in *Honi* would pass that sort of measure. Mindless abuse would be calling Abbott 'dickhead', 'fuhrer', and such names that flowed from the lips of his opponents. Brereton would maintain his dignity and not 'indulge in self-justification' but did just that. His excuse for collaborating with the far left was that it was 'possible to see some merit in a few of their causes'. Which causes? Abbott's point was that Brereton fell in with the far-left causes, and he often did it for political purposes. Brereton then suggested the centre left did not support Abbott's 'moderate' causes because he (Abbott) 'failed to put forward a single significant measure other than those designed to destroy the SRC'. The reduction of Abbott's determined campaigning and detailed argument to an attempt to destroy the SRC was a cop-out. Brereton's excuses for collaboration on other far-left causes were no more compelling. He wriggled out of the accusation of cynically manipulating the SRC constitution to block the referendum by claiming he made his decision (in good faith) on legal grounds. When apprised of his error, he gave in. Besides, he claimed, Abbott 'never presented any advice to the contrary of the reasons for initially refusing the petition'. Abbott's correspondence in *Honi* could not justify that claim.

Brereton was on sounder ground when he objected to the accusation that his unprincipled ambition motivated all his decisions. That was untrue, and Abbott must have known it. But let's allow Abbott a little exaggeration for effect when he was the object of endless abuse and misrepresentation. Brereton concluded that the 51st SRC had 'done much for students'. He listed achievements that were indisputable and about which Abbott would not have argued. But he went further. He attributed all the success to the 'initiatives of Centre Unity [centre left]'. Abbott would know this, he claimed. 'You fear that the SRC is fulfilling its role of representing and working for the benefit of students. You decry us because we threaten your plans to destroy it'. Again, Brereton could not justify that claim by what Abbott said and did. He evaded the real differences between him and Abbott by dismissing many of his policies as 'crazy'. It was another cop-out. Abbott defended Western Civilization from the philosophical framework of Burkean natural law conservatism, about which Paul Brereton seemed to have little idea. In any case, the fight would continue.

You could not have had more formidable opponents than Abbott and Brereton, who, together with Comrade Dave McKnight, were the most articulate students during the years I have surveyed. While Brereton kept his head down, avoiding direct conflict, Abbott was indefatigable. He presented his case repeatedly in different ways and with different emphases. He went outside to the regular media. He had articles in the *Australian*, the *Bulletin* and the *Catholic Weekly* and even appeared on ABC/TV Nationwide. He turned the coterie of his enemies into a buzzing hornets' nest. Their glowering hatred was volcanic. Abbott had his supporters, but no one appeared in *Honi* to defend him – except Tanya Coleman, Education Officer (H16, 16 July). 'Has anyone a kind word to say about Tony Abbott?' she asked. 'The campaign of vilification waged against him as President' upset her:

'Abbott has been painted in *Honi* as a scheming, lying, brutish and oafish extremist. He has done little really to deserve all this. He has been consistently attacked by other SRC Officers; some of whom have scrawled highly distasteful slogans about him on the walls of the SRC, and others of whom petulantly refuse even to speak to him. Is it any wonder that they sometimes receive a waspish tongue in reply?

Unfortunately, student politics is a hard game. It is perhaps inevitable that to achieve anything one must tread on the ambitions of others. Abbott is the only president for years who has actually tried to implement fundamental reform of the SRC, and not simply bask in glory. For this, he deserves praise and not denigration. I think we should all be thankful that despite ceaseless hostility from some quarters, he has the tenacity to keep on fighting for us. Answer: Yes, there are lots of us [who have a kind word to say about him].'

It was generous support and a true description of the conflict's circumstances. Abbott did not for a moment back down. He ratcheted up his campaign. He was the white knight alone on the battlefield, in full regalia, with rearing steed, facing the enemy, prepared to defend his culture to the death.

During this time, *Honi Soit* interviewed him (H14, 25 June). It was a wide-ranging interview with sensible pertinent questions during which he repeated much of his case for voluntary fees. There were a few crucial passages that gave an insight into Abbott's thinking, one of which now has legendary status. The aim of the questions was clearly to get Abbott to hang himself. The connected questions about the purposes of the university, for example, were to drive him into a position that conflicted with a critical Marxist view of bourgeois education. Abbott appeared to be onto it, but it was enough for him to answer the questions honestly. We must assume that not one person conducted the interview but a committee of males and females because of the expected questions about Abbott's 'attitude' to women:

HONI: Your article in the *Australian* expressed your views on the university and its purposes and how it relates to the rest of society. What do you think is the function of the university, and what kind of people is it trying to produce?

ABBOTT: The university's prime role is the pursuit of excellence and truth in the context of vocational learning. The university ought to be trying to maintain the highest standards of scholarship and excellence in learning in every discipline. It has certainly a most essential research function, but then it ought to be bringing in students, basically in the areas where there are jobs for them . . . The purpose of a university education is twofold: it is (a) to educate, and (b) to get people jobs – educational and vocational purposes – and I don't think you can really divide them terribly simplistically. I think they go hand in hand. But I certainly think it's wrong for the university to be turning out ever more Arts graduates and economics graduates who simply can't get a job commensurate with their education.

HONI: Do you think it has a function to produce people that are constructively critical of society?
ABBOTT: At the moment, unis. are being funded by the tax-payer – the community; and so basically they have to pursue the roles of the propagation of truth and excellence in the context of the wider community needs. I think community service has got to be one of the overriding aims of the university.

HONI: At such a time as this, when there's high unemployment and so on, then surely at least part of the university's duty to the community is to produce people with ideas that will possibly ease these problems of that community.
ABBOTT: I would certainly agree that I think university academics have

a right ... I won't say they have a duty to offer alternatives, to present methods of doing things and solutions to current problems ... But I think that while the university academics can do this, I don't think that they should try and encourage students themselves, who are still in the learning process, to take matters into their own hands. I think what's happening in a number of areas at the moment, for instance, general philosophy and political economy ... is not so much a search for solutions to current problems of society, but people are simply denouncing the liberal-democratic society and advocating rather simplistic solutions, and they're doing that for their own ulterior political purposes ... you understand the distinction I'm making between research academics making constructive solutions to problems and alternatives to the present way we're doing things ... and the situation where politically motivated academics try and indoctrinate their classes that the present society isn't perfect, and that some specific alternative is to be preferred.

HONI: Do you agree, though, that the university does produce people to fit into a certain ideological system, which is the current one, this society, and that possibly by giving people a different perspective such as a Marxist perspective, then they're giving them another way of looking at the problems of the current liberal democratic system? Can you see the value in giving people another perspective on how to solve those problems when they come out of uni?
ABBOTT: There's no point in substituting a grossly imperfect system, that is Marxism ...

HONI: No, this isn't suggesting a substitution, but using the ideology to get a perspective on this system of ours ...
ABBOTT: Mind you, all my comments about bias in the universities refer generally to the faculties of arts and economics and specifically to a few departments.

The interviewers appeared to think they weren't getting anywhere with that line of questioning and turned to funding.

HONI: In your article in the *Australian*, you said you thought Federal education funding should be cut, and thus 'by stringency force the academics to decide what, in the final analysis, they want the university to be'.
ABBOTT: Well, most academics believe the university should be, as I said, a centre for excellence and learning. At the moment, because of the system that we have now, with the government handing over a whole lot of money and telling the academics to go to it ... I mean courses on aesthetics which are simply devoted to a study of punk rock, this sort of nonsense. If the universities actually had to go out into the marketplace and attract funds, they would have to cut out this sort of trivia.

HONI: So you think, notwithstanding the education cuts in the previous two Federal budgets, there should be much more savage cuts?
ABBOTT: I think too much money is spent on education at the moment. I think if the amount of money available to the universities was cut, the academics would then have to seriously think about whether they are going to allow departments like General Philosophy, Political Economy, and what have you, to survive at the expense of far more useful and relevant departments, such as Engineering, Medicine or Science. I think they would then start to really analyse exactly what departments were necessary, and exactly what is the quality of the scholarship in the various departments, and I think General Philosophy and Political Economy would be the first to go, and I think that would be a very good thing.

The interviewers appeared to think Abbott had said enough about the departments of General Philosophy and Political Economy to hang himself. They turned to women's issues, where their expectations were more than realised.

HONI: Do you think that there is a need for a feminist organisation on campus?

ABBOTT: One of the things I abhor in present society is this growing trend for people to see themselves not as members of the community, but as a particular section. I fail to see why all the groups which make up a society can't be adequately represented in the body that represents society as a whole.

HONI: Do you see that women are in a disadvantaged position?

ABBOTT: Well, I don't think that they are advantaged or disadvantaged. I think that women and men are simply, and always, going to be different.

HONI: Well, do you think then, that there's a place for women to participate in a male-dominated society?

ABBOTT: Of course, of course. I think that if an individual woman has the particular aptitudes and abilities to rise to the highest position in society, then sure, she should have every opportunity to do it. But I think it's a biological, physiological fact that we can't get around that women and men are basically going to always be doing different things.

HONI: You don't see the changes in the last fifty years or so mean that the things preventing women from becoming involved were social/ cultural?

ABBOTT: Oh, well, I would certainly agree with you that women have been discriminated against in the past.

HONI: They are discriminated against in this university.

ABBOTT: Well, I'm not aware of it, to be quite honest. If people are prepared to bring up examples, I would be only too happy to consider them, but I personally believe that there are few areas in society now where women are discriminated against. I think it's a laudable thing that women are much more able today to go into a whole range of activities. *But I think it would be folly to expect that women will ever dominate, or even approach equal representation in a large number of areas, simply because their aptitudes, abilities and interests are different for physiological reasons. That's my opinion.* [my emphasis]

The interviewers' heads must have nearly exploded with joy and satisfaction. Despite lauding the opportunities available to women and firmly supporting the principle of equal opportunity, Abbott, in the eyes of the far left, had politically annihilated himself. To suggest there were innate differences between men and women – a fact for which there is overwhelming empirical evidence – was high heresy in the church of political correctness and cancel-culture. To hell with the scientifically testable evidence.[102] It was the never-to-be questioned dogma that counted. Abbott's heresy is the feature quotation in Susan Mitchell's book. Did Abbott worry about challenging a sacred dogma of the left? Not one bit. Fact derived from observation of life's concrete circumstances was paramount. He wasn't budging from it. The issues of the purpose and funding of tertiary education have not changed since Abbott's defended his views in 1979. They are more urgent now, having narrowed to freedom of speech on campus. It is astonishing that Abbott had such a lucid understanding of identity politics years before anyone had ever heard of it.

Would Abbott ease off on the run-up to the SRC annual elections? Not on your life. On the eve of the polls (19 July), Tony led a contingent of Channel Ten news people on a guided tour of the pigsty that served as the SRC offices. He brought them to a stop in the women's room where the lurid posters and semi-literate graffiti of Sydney University's fanatical feminists confronted young Mike Munro and his camera crew. No one could doubt his purpose to show the general community the corrupt state of student politics in general and the quality of student leadership in particular. The community had a right to know what motivated student leaders in their universities. After all, the government was paying bucket loads of their money to universities to molly-coddle privileged middle-class youth to an even more privileged level where they had access to the best professions. The mountain of money was not earmarked for the destruction of their community and the benefits that had accrued over the centuries. To get the message of decay across, it was worth bringing a television crew into the dirt and corruption.

Honi's editorial committee were beside themselves (H17, 23 July). In bringing the eyes of the community into student affairs, Tony had 'invaded' the sacred precincts of the SRC, showing once more his 'autocratic attitude towards the SRC'. In a moment of truly ingenuous reflection, the editorial charged Abbott with trying 'to shock the public by showing them an alienating perspective of the university, and of students'. Most people watching the Channel Ten report 'have never had access to a university education [and] would not understand the issues presented in graffiti and poster form on the walls of the women's room'. One must smile at the ease with which the patronage and condescension of the far left reveal themselves towards the oppressed people of the bourgeois state. The invasion of the SRC offices motivated by a 'godlike authority' was a fitting flourish to end Tony's campaign to restore the SRC to its original foundation.

SRC PRESIDENT Paul Le Gay Brereton chaired the first meeting of the 52nd Students' Representative Council in late July (H18). *Honi* did not report by what margin Brereton was elected president. In a buoyant mood, Brereton presided over the meeting during which the SRC Officers were elected. One of the items briefly reported was that there would be 'some liquidity problems for the rest of this year ... because of a large deficit inherited from 1978'. Once again, the reasons for the 'large deficit' escaped mention. Why? The next issue of *Honi* (H19) was not until 23 September, which pointed to the SRC's liquidity problems. In his president's report, Brereton thanked all those 'who voted for myself and other Centre Unity candidates'. He announced that 'the referendum to secede [from AUS] gained a simple majority although not the two-thirds required to bind the SRC'. Nevertheless, the SRC had given AUS notice that secession would take place on 7 November. This was as much a victory for Abbott. Most notable was that the 'referendum for voluntary funding was decisively defeated'. That should have been the end of it. Not for Tony Abbott. 'Mr Abbott, however, has announced in the *Herald* that he intends to ask Senate to do his dirty work and introduce voluntary funding'. While there were legitimate means, Tony would fight on.

The avenue of the Senate proved fruitless. *Honi* stayed silent about him. Paul Brereton was elected SRC President for the second time in July 1980 – a rare achievement in student politics. Centre left was as far to the right as most *voting* students appeared to want to go – or perhaps have the appearance of going. Tony Abbott was not so much defeated as forced fighting from the battlefield by a collaboration of the opposition groups, some of whom had more in common with him than with the far left. Had the Marxist influence already so penetrated the youth that many simply did not understand what motivated him? The conservative champion departed from the battlefield, his knightly robes soiled and white steed bruised. Like Cincinnatus, Tony shook off the dirt of the contest and withdrew to contemplate. That contemplation would take place at Oxford University, where he studied philosophy on a Rhodes Scholarship. A Rhodes Scholarship was awarded to those with 'moral force of character and instincts to lead'.

Part Four

Abbott and the Media

Chapter 13

David Marr's helpless religious and political bigotry

IN 2013, THE John Button prize for writing on public policy and politics was awarded to David Marr for his Quarterly Essay on Tony Abbott, then Opposition Leader. The judges under the spell of Marr's writing lauded the essay as 'a powerful, nuanced and beautifully written account of a man who may be prime minister'. In this unblushing praise, there's a hint of a warning. One of the judges, Geoff Galop, former Labor premier of Western Australia, said the essay explored 'one of the great themes of our time – the quality of leadership'. No prizes for guessing the quality in this case. He and his fellow judges were right about the essay being powerful and beautifully written – perhaps not powerful in the way they imagined. But nuanced? Marr said he was 'delighted [the essay] has been recognised as a piece of analysis'.[103] Again, I have to say, don't make me laugh.

Nuanced writing would be writing that makes fine compelling distinctions within sustained argument, drawing on solid evidence to demonstrate an irresistible conclusion. That's analysis. Marr's writing is woefully tendentious, profoundly coloured by his ingrained political prejudices, full of misrepresentations and undemonstrated assertions, all in a haze of atmospherics and the literary tricks of an accomplished writer. Never before has there been so much biased nonsense purveyed in such an impressive style in Australian political writing. The essay qualifies David Marr as one of our foremost postmodernist writers. Let me illustrate. In that same *Guardian* report by Oliver Laughland (an appropriate name in the circumstances), Marr is reported as saying, 'Abbott is a most unpredictable leader, because what appears to matter most to him, he cannot do. The electorate won't let him pursue his religious convictions, and his party will fight like mad over his social justice convictions'.

If one wants to make a short, incisive comment, one must ensure the comment is comprehensible. The point of prejudice is obvious and enough for Marr's prejudiced constituency, but what precisely are Tony Abbott's religious convictions? And why wouldn't the electorate let him pursue them? And how does that make Abbott an unpredictable leader? The inquiring mind is left to guess. The difference between religious convictions and political convictions is clear to most people. Religious convictions are those essential faith beliefs whose adherence makes one a member of a particular faith. You can't be a Christian if you deny the doctrine of the Incarnation. You can't be a Catholic if you deny the primacy of the papacy. Political convictions are about how state and society are constituted and run. One can be a Catholic and, at the same time, a member of the Labor Party, or the Liberal Party, or the National Party. It's unnecessary to name names. Why, then, would the electorate prevent Tony Abbott from following his Catholic faith and allow other Catholics in the three major political parties to go their way unhindered?

I could go on deconstructing Marr's throwaway comment to highlight similar difficulties. But one may think it unfair to pick on Marr for impromptu remarks made to a journalist in a media scrum. Let's go, then, to the 'nuanced' work in question, *Political Animal: The Making of Tony Abbott*. On page 2, Marr tackles Abbott for his admission of past errors – his 'stuff-ups' – and his need to apologise for them. As a first comment, it is pertinent to ask how many politicians gratuitously admit their stuff-ups, leaving aside their need to apologise? A visible part of Tony Abbott's character is his humility – his preparedness to be honest about himself. Many recognise his unnecessary public self-flagellation and admire him for it. Not David Marr:

'Long practice makes him good at confession. It's in his blood. The most Catholic thing about this profoundly Catholic man is his faith in absolution. The slate can always be wiped clean. Over the years, he has said and done appalling things that might have sunk another politician. But charm and candour and promises to do better have seen him forgiven so much. The loudmouth bigot of his university days, the homophobe, the blinkered Vatican warrior, the rugger-bugger, the white Australian and the junkyard dog of parliament are all, he would have us believe, consigned to the past.[104]

Appalling and outrageously spun stuff but beautifully composed. You can pause over the passage, admiring the virtuosity of the writing. The meaning is crystal clear and compelling. Pity it is all invention motivated by a debilitating bigotry, a worthy product of the Protestant Ascendancy and the Orange Lodge, from which Marr is likely descended. The central point around which all else turns is Abbott's status as a Catholic. 'Catholic' for David Marr is the very worst of personal and social qualities, denoting a person possessed of irrational myth, bigoted, and unrelenting in his effort to chain society to that imagined myth and bigotry. If this passage is insufficient evidence, then I refer the reader to any of Marr's political writings. One does not have to read far to come across his feverish anti-Catholic sectarianism. Marr is unperturbed about the accusation of anti-Catholic bigotry because he thinks his views about Catholics and the Catholic Church are the full truth, the whole truth and nothing but the truth, so help him Karl Marx. Besides, he has an adoring supportive constituency, ever ready to reassure him.

Tony Abbott not only suffers the stain of being Catholic, which in Marr's eyes disenfranchises the citizen to the degree this social stigma strikes him down, but he is 'profoundly Catholic'. The sign of this profound Catholicism is Abbott's 'faith in absolution', absolution being the critical act performed by the priest during the Catholic sacrament of confession. Marr has merged the common social act of saying sorry for political mistakes, oversights or transgressions with a Catholic sacrament behind which stands a theological and scriptural justification. In confession, a Catholic confesses his sins to a priest who stands in the place of Christ. Political mistakes, even serious misjudgments, are not necessarily sins in the Catholic sense. If he were 'profoundly Catholic' (hotly disputed by some traditional Catholics), Abbott would have no trouble distinguishing between sin and political error. More important, he would be conscious his confession would only be valid if he had a firm resolve not to repeat those sins. To commit sins, airily confess them without that resolve, and go on to repeat them would not only entail an invalid but a bad confession. A bad confession is a serious (mortal) sin for a Catholic, whose seriousness would not be reduced no matter how charming and candid the penitent was. Marr is trying to run an analogical argument here. But it doesn't work. The dissimilarities between sin in the Catholic sense and political error, even grave error, are too great. If the knot of Marr's unreason could be unpicked to justify his charge, Abbott would be a bad Catholic, the opposite of what Marr wants. In the end, it is all nonsense, all fantasy, all invention.

The poignant irony in this spectacular, well-written rant of Marr's is that he draws attention to qualities in Tony Abbott that do indeed show him to be profoundly Catholic. Not far behind the Scriptures' commandment to love God and thy neighbour as thyself is the exhortation to humility. Uncompromising love of one's fellow man requires a degree of self-effacement –putting aside one's interests for the benefit of others. Jesus exhorted his apostles to be like himself, 'meek and humble of heart'. The humble person is honest about himself, about his failings as a person. The braggart, the person full of self-importance, fails the Christian ethos. The general community admires the sporting champion who shows humility in the glare of public attention. Despite his extraordinary achievements, he is just like the rest of us. Such humility is necessary when approaching the confessional. One doesn't rush to the confessional, reel off a list of sins, and expect to have satisfied the requirements of a good confession. To prepare for a good confession, one must undertake a careful, honest, humble examination of one's actions. It is just this sort of humility and honesty of feeling that drives Abbott's apologies and his public admissions of fault rather than the muddled perverted idea of confession Marr conjures for his prejudiced constituency.

There is a more fundamental question here than exposing Marr's prejudice, misapprehensions, and failure of reasoning. Where is the evidence for Abbott's alleged ideas about confession and its invocation to cleanse him of the 'appalling things' he has (allegedly) done? Nowhere have I read anything that Abbott has said or written about confession and absolution. Nor indeed does Marr offer stand-up-knock-down evidence for the 'appalling things', for Abbott's homophobia and his loudmouth bigotry at university. The snarling 'junkyard dog of parliament' is a terrific image, but its justification remains elusive. If one speaks of a parliamentary junkyard dog, people are more likely to think of that cheap guttersnipe Paul Keating than Tony Abbott. As for the 'blinkered Vatican warrior' and 'white Australian' smears, this is just unabashed prejudice, as if Marr is contesting with Susan Mitchell over the purity of their political and religious bigotries – particularly those against Catholics and white Anglo-Celtic men. I would like just one instance of Abbott's fighting for the Vatican against Australia's interests. Indeed, if Tony Abbott is a Vatican warrior, every other practising Catholic is a Vatican warrior. But that's just the point, isn't it, of the Ascendancy, of the Orange Lodge and the penal laws: Catholics are the enemy of the state? And what of 'rugger-bugger', a term unknown to many? In the context, it has a literary glow – its main purpose – but isn't it an example of Marr's blissful literary overreach?

IT WOULD be helpful for an understanding of Marr's mode of reasoning in *Political Animal* to look briefly at his manifesto work, *The High Price of Heaven*.[105] In this popular book, we go to the basement of Marr's motivations, where we find an explanation for the breakdown in reasoning that affects all he writes. In typical dramatic Marr style, he opens with, 'I was a Christian. It's best I confess this right from the start'. He was not a cradle Christian. He 'took Christ into his life' in 1960 at the age of thirteen years, which seems to have been a born-again experience. But in this brief 'Christian' period during which he found the 'same sweet and sour port' at Anglican parishes, was bored to tears with Saint Augustine's *City of God* (one of the great works of Christian Civilisation) and 'fought masturbation and temptations too terrible to name', he seems rather to have had a still-born experience. His faith suffered an intellectual crisis, the sort all philosophical schools force on their adherents, but the real cause of dumping the faith he never had was sensual and emotional:

'I'd fallen in love. It was fraught, unfulfilled and extremely heady. All the Christian teaching I'd clung to about the who, the when and the how of sex now seemed arbitrary and cruel. If this was sin, I wanted to sin. The sooner the better.'[106]

Considering the evidence that the homosexual drive comes with rocket boosters, he could have added, 'and the more, the better'. Marr had not fallen at the first hurdle; he did not even get to the first hurdle. On the start line, he found Christian sexual ethics 'arbitrary and cruel'. But did

Marr justify this claim with argument and evidence? Of course not. That would be too wearisome. Better to invent a scenario with an appeal to the anti-Christian mind and then build a rickety edifice on that foundation. That foundation was pleasure. The enemies of pleasure are Christians. They are the 'enemies of films and books and magazines, of sex and music and drugs and television, of drink and dancing'. The reason they are the enemies of all these things is that such pleasures shut the gate to the locomotive heading for heaven. Christians campaign for what's in the next life, not what's in our earthly life. Not only has Marr jumped off the heavenly express, but he wants the train drivers to desist from imposing their painful puritanical views on the rest of society.

Most of this scenario is pure rubbish. The abundant evidence says so. I come from a typical 1950s Catholic family. My parents were devout Catholics. My mother was an insatiable reader. Books were her preferred present for birthdays, Christmas, and other important occasions. My love of reading came from thousands of comics, the Christmas boys' annuals, the Famous Five, the Mystery Series and many others in primary school, and from Charles Dickens and Jane Austen in secondary school. Dad loved the 'pictures'. As a family, we saw the *Court Jester*, *Knock on Wood*, *Hans Christian Anderson*, the *Merry Andrews*, the *Student Prince*, *Tammy*, and *Seven Brides for Seven Brothers*, to name some that come directly to mind. We wallowed in the pleasure books and films gave us. During my pre-school years, my mother had the radio on while she did her housework. A lot of forties and early fifties music takes me back to those early years of my life. My sister received Bill Haley and the Comets' *Rock around the Clock* album as a Christmas present. I received the 'Purple People Eater', my brother the 'Witch Doctor'. We wallowed in the pleasure popular music gave us. My parents organised a party for my elder sister in 1958, during which a whole lot of frantic jiving went on. I could go on. But I won't. The point is surely made.

Pleasure as such was not a problem for the typical 1950s Catholic family. Our love of books, music and film would not stop us from boarding the express for heaven. Nor did the television which came in the late fifties, or the wine and beer my teetotaller dad generously poured for friends and neighbours at Christmas time. The issue for Christians is where you can legitimately have pleasure, the same issue for non-Christians and society at large. It's about pain and harm prevention – not about restricting pleasure as such.

Marr's list of pleasure-giving activities illustrates one of his literary tricks. He presents his activities as one category, while the items form at least three categories. Films, books, magazines, music, television, and dancing usually are inoffensive activities that young and old, men and women, enjoy. They become an issue when perverted from their everyday use, for example, when books contain pornography or are used for subversive activities. Alcohol consumption and sexual activity are socially circumscribed. Societies have traditionally restricted them to adults with rules widely agreed on. Their pleasures are to be greedily enjoyed, but with a warning that abuse could cause great pain, instead of pleasure, and social disruption. On the other hand, drugs (of addiction) are way out there, forming a category on their own. There is no safe level of consumption. Addiction is likely and usual. Most people warn about the use of drugs precisely because the momentary pleasure often leads to degradation and destitution. Marr's trick is to reduce the malignancy of addictive drugs like heroin by associating them with the pleasures of books, music, and television – by sneaking them into categories where they do not belong.

Marr gravely warns that Christians are unrelenting in their campaigns to 'ban, censor and jail for our salvation'. What exactly they want to ban, censor and jail he does not say, nor explain how their banning, censoring and jailing differ from society's rules that ban, censor and jail. Not to worry about explanations, though. Having established to his satisfaction the false proposition that Christians ban pleasure to get us all to heaven, Marr goes into unrestrained fantasy mode. He whinges that 'the price we're expected to pay for getting us all to heaven is too high. Too much waste, too much cruelty, too much pain'. All beautifully written, of course. Whatever persuasiveness Marr possesses is due to his writing ability. His arguments don't bear scrutiny. He rounds off this introduction with another list of disparate issues and a statement of the book's purpose:

'Christians are engaged in an old crusade against sex, last-ditch battles with women inside and outside their congregations, guerrilla campaigns against homosexuals, harassment of AIDS- and HIV prevention programs, out-breaks of civil war in church schools, persecution of books and grim col-laboration with governments to pursue the War on Drugs. To understand what's going on here, the theology has to be disentangled from the politics. That's my purpose.'[107]

Marr has gone from the silly unverified claim Christians want to ban the pleasure of books, music and film to an emotionally charged list of social issues Christians meddle in. Let's take them one by one. First, it is patent nonsense to claim Christians are against sex. What about the long-held view of Marr's constituency that Catholics breed like rabbits? Any dispute about women in the Catholic Church is, by definition, restricted to the Catholic Church. One can leave the Catholic Church if one disagrees with its teaching. The same holds for the Church's teaching on homosexuality. Besides, many people of no faith share the Catholic view. What civil war in church schools? Without further explanation, always tedious for an ideologue and bigot, this looks like another Marr invention. Australia has very mild censorship laws. The breakthrough came, as I have written, in the 1970s. Any view the Catholic Church has about any particular book would be a matter of opinion, having little effect on the state's decision-making. The 'War on Drugs' is where Marr really gives himself away and displays his dodgy contradictory reasoning. Despite declaring his purpose of disentangling the theology from politics, he does nothing of the sort. He doesn't even bother to give a referable idea of what this theology entails. On the contrary, the critical reader is tasked with picking apart the tangle of his various assertions.

The first chapter, 'Leaving them to Drown', concerns the War on Drugs and Christians' 'grim collaboration with governments'. One wonders where the original proposition about pleasure went – that Christians were against pleasure. Depriving people of pleasure was the way to get everyone on board for the heaven express. Instead, the chapter heading and the 'grim collaboration' suggest the chapter is about how society deals with the terrible suffering drugs cause to the addict, the addict's relations, and society at large. And that's exactly what it is. Marr contrasts two strategies that should be familiar to most socially aware Australians. One is a 'soft' approach. Governments open safe injecting rooms to limit death from overdose. The other is the 'hard' option which is against safe injecting rooms and for taking an uncompromising stand against drugs and their supply.

It is not to my purpose to run the arguments for both sides except to say Marr takes the soft side and the then Archbishop Pell the hard side. He must, of course, rope in Cardinal Pell, who he wants to bash as hard and often as he can. The argument is not about suppressing drugs because of the pleasure they give, although Marr struggles to maintain the fiction in a disconnected way. The issue was about pain and damage. Second, Christians weren't only on one side – the hard side with Pell – and non-Christians on Marr's soft side. Both agreed about the malignancy of drugs but not about how to handle them. There are sound arguments on both sides. The sides weren't Christian vs the rest. In self-contradiction, Marr cites the disagreement between the Sisters of Charity, who supported safe injecting rooms and Archbishop Pell to show what a hard bastard Pell was to deprive addicts of their drugs. And just to show the mad depths to which he goes in prosecuting his case against the heartless, he invokes Christian charity to condemn those willing to let addicts die of an overdose. This is not a question of charging Christians with inconsistency. Marr's meaning is that it is unchristian per se to allow the risk of overdose.

The key to understanding David Marr's political discourse is that he deals in scenarios. He does not prosecute a position based on the empirical evidence argued according to the rules of reason. The persuasiveness of his scenarios is dependent on his considerable ability as a writer with all the literary tricks and atmospherics an accomplished writer possesses. He remains unperturbed about the criticism he receives as long as his scenarios succeed in persuading. In this, Marr is truly a postmodernist writer. For the postmodernist, there is no absolute truth. There is no 'privileged' worldview. All narratives possess their own truth. The successful political operative persuades people to his scenario, his narrative, to his worldview. The success of *Political Animal* and *The High Price of Heaven* is measured by the numbers his 'nuanced' writing brings to his side against Tony Abbott and hard bastard Cardinal George Pell – and there are legions.

⚜

MARR OPENS *Political Animal* with a Marrism. 'Australia doesn't want Tony Abbott. We never have', he asserts, identifying Australians with his political class while disqualifying the rest of us. As evidence, he presents the polls which are against Abbott. Later he admits Abbott proved an effective opposition leader. If he wins government, 'he will be remembered as the most successful Opposition leader of the last forty years, turning a rabble into government in four years'.[108] (Abbott won government with a handsome majority.) How does Marr explain the apparent contradiction? He doesn't. He is preoccupied with conjuring the image of Abbott as a political thug who 'slogs on with the ferocity that alarms the public' and is 'about destroying government'. No hard evidence for this. Let me suggest an explanation. Polls about individual politicians are often popularity polls. The polls claimed Abbott was not popular with a majority of people polled. People at election time are more discerning. They elect the government they think will do the job. They elected an Abbott Government, just as they elected a Howard Government. John Howard is Australia's second longest-serving prime minister. He had poll numbers similar to Abbott's. Abbott's and Howard's lack of popularity in the poll was at least in part due to the character attacks of Marr and his class. Marr's powerful scenarios showed the way for his less able scribblers.

The first section of *Political Animal*, from which I have drawn the quotations above, is titled 'Prince Hal', which should signal to readers the conjuring of another colourful scenario. The scenario is of Tony Abbott as the hopelessly romantic political knight jousting at windmills. The image of a knight is entirely appropriate. But instead of carrying on the image of a courageous Australian Prince Hal – the reference is to Shakespeare's Henry V – it is the deluded knight of Cervantes' *Don Quixote* that is worked up. Marr lists a mixture of qualities that (he asserts without evidence) belong to the quixotic knight of his imagination. Among those qualities is 'loneliness'. 'They tend to be lonely and see their loneliness as a mark of courage'. Where is the explanation backed by evidence for this singular assertion? A general quality like this is abstracted from several examples. There are none.

Marr concludes the scenario of the quixotic knight 'searching for windmills' by acknowledging there will always be such odd deluded figures in politics, but 'what's peculiar now is that one of them is leading the Opposition'. The impetus for this scenario was a passage in *Battlelines* in which Tony Abbott relates where his interest in public life began. I have already commented on this passage. I now take it from a slightly different angle in response to Marr's Quixote scenario. Abbott says his 'interest in public life first stirred as a child reading the junior Ladybird books' about such great men like Julius Caesar, Francis Drake and Henry V. He continues:

'The lesson, invariably, was that duty and honour carried the day. They were caricatures, of course, as I was to discover over time, but uplifting ones. In the real world, good doesn't always triumph and justice doesn't always prevail. Even the best turn out to have their flaws. Despite that, ideals don't cease to matter because they're never perfectly achieved or because their adherents are compromised.'[109]

The examples of the action of great men gave young Tony a sense of what the principled life entailed. The good life was one of adhering to enduring principles. One must recognise one's duty and carry it out no matter what marked the man of honour. At the same time, one must confront human fallibility and the possibility that the concrete circumstances do not work favourably. One passes from the idealism of childhood to the sober realisation of an imperfect world. The failure to come to grips with the concrete circumstances of life marks the man still carrying the jousting sticks of childhood. On his own saying, Abbott has left those jousting sticks with the Ladybird books in the nursery room. There are no windmills, no exercising the imagination, just the irresistible empirical data which adult Tony has absorbed about duty and honour.

If David Marr knew anything about conservatism, which he doesn't, he would know that the conservative mind is empirically oriented. The conservative begins with the concrete circumstances of political issues and applies enduring principles to those circumstances. This is Burkean (natural law) conservatism. In a famous passage in the *Reflections*, Burke wrote that the politician is not like the university professor sequestered in his academic office, abstractly discoursing on political matters. No, the politician is the 'philosopher in action' applying objective principles to the many and varied circumstances of political life. The politician denying this, and reaching for the provisions of an abstract theory, is not only mad but metaphysically insane. If the above passage on duty and honour are not explicit enough about the conservative cast of Abbott's mind, then we can go to the introduction in *Battlelines* where Abbott discusses what he sees as the Liberal Party's philosophical principles. In parts, he is paraphrasing Burke.

'To win elections', he wrote, 'a political party needs an agenda that appeals to voters' values and addresses voters' problems but is also faithful to the party's positions and principles'. About policy, he writes, 'The challenge is to express enduring ideals and aspirations in new policies that apply those age-old values to contemporary problems'.[110] To the accusation of 'backflipping' and inconsistency when changing his mind about 'some vexed questions such as multiculturalism and paid parental leave', he gives a copybook conservative explanation. The change was 'because I have reconsidered the application of principles, not changed them'.[111] It is nonsense to apply the Don Quixote image to Abbott. All the concrete evidence contradicts the invention. A final point, the most admired politician of principle is one who remains steadfast to long-established party principles while his colleagues surrender to the enemy's political pressure. The major unrequited enemy of Abbott's is the predominantly leftist media in Australia.

'FIGHTING THE Revolution' heads the second section of *Political Animal*. The title is ambiguous, but we can take it to mean that Tony Abbott was taking it up to the revolutionaries who controlled the SRC. Throughout this section, Marr builds two scenarios, both developing the thesis of *Political Animal*. Abbott is, on the one hand, a bullying, unconscionable political actor and, on the other, a Catholic fanatic under the spell of the even more extreme Catholic fanatic B.A. Santamaria. In earlier chapters, I argued that Tony Abbott was full of energy and exuberance, lapping up the pleasures of university life. Politically, he was tough, determined, and crystal clear about his political principles and who his enemies were. He was fearless, but he was measured and controlled in his political activities, even when he matched force with force. I have laid it all out in previous chapters. David Marr saw it differently.

He quotes an anonymous student who claimed Tony 'was wild even for a wild college boy'. Then running another of his disparate colourful lists, he added, 'Young Tony did things hard: drinking, writing, arguing, fucking and playing rugby'.[112] If Marr had limited the list to drinking, writing, arguing and playing rugby, we would have an image of Abbott no different from many of his fellow students. But the insertion of 'fucking' makes all the difference. It raises the drinking etc. to a new level, one well above the actions of the average hard-living male on campus. It's a verbal trick to conjure an image of Abbott out of control. In literary terms, well done. But does the image of 'hard fucking' match the evidence? It doesn't match the evidence and is at odds with the women-hating figure Marr and Mitchell strive to create. To fuck hard, meaning often and indiscriminately, a man would have to have appeal to women. A man thought to hate women, I suggest, would considerably narrow the odds of bedding women at will. Furthermore, according to Duffy, Abbott preferred the company of men, a claim Mitchell made much of. Such sexual promiscuity deviates from the image of Abbott as a devout Catholic and misogynist that Marr and Mitchell (particularly Mitchell) thrashed to death. Marr, however, does not limit his attack on Abbott to verbal tricks. He occasionally attempts to offer evidence for the image he is concocting.

From the moment Tony Abbott made his appearance on campus at Sydney University, 'he showed himself to be a muscular reactionary of extraordinary, boisterous energy'. Vividly put, and fair enough. Marr seems not to realise that in calling Abbott 'reactionary,' he contradicts the claims Abbott was of the far right. 'Reactionary' is usually an abusive word for conservative. Or perhaps Marr does realise it and uses it for the atmospherics. After all, conservative and reactionary amount to the same thing for many of the left. This boisterous muscular reactionary was a member of the Democratic Club, one of a campus network supported, not run, by the National Civic Council under the leadership of Bob Santamaria. Now follows a howler of breathtaking proportions.

Tony and his mates, Marr asserts, 'called themselves moderates, but their position was extreme: as far to the right as the Maoists and Trotskyists on campus were to the left'. This comparison should be too outlandish even for someone concocting a postmodernist narrative. It would have a writer with any self-respect blushing from head to toe. Marr has just called Abbott a reactionary, in the context, a conservative. Abbott cannot be a conservative and a fascist at the same time – if one follows the normal operations of reason. In this chapter and previous chapters, I have offered ample evidence and argument to support the claim Tony Abbott and the Democratic Club were a group of conservatives, not all Catholic, campaigning to defend Western Civilisation against a coterie of Marxists controlling the SRC. What support does Marr offer for his absurd claim?

He quotes far-left big hitter Harry Moore who provided his radical faction's fireworks when the circumstances called for it. 'This organisation [Democratic Club]', spun Moore, 'has a long history of politically motivated violence – whether as vigilantes for vice-regals, smoke-bombers for Saigon, poster pullers for political reaction, or bullies for by-elections'. Of course, Marr doesn't reference the quotation. That would spoil things. Apart from Moore's woeful credibility, one should note the vagueness and lack of evidence for the alleged 'far-right' violence. For example, what violence is there in pulling posters? Moore and his mates knew how to do political violence. Ripping down opposition posters or defending the Governor-General from the left's excesses weren't it. As for violence at by-elections, the boys and girls of the Democratic Club (there were girls, too) were kiddies compared with the far left, who beat down doors, terrified administrative staff and set fire to the academic offices. It's all there in *Honi Soit*, if Marr had taken the time to do some genuine research.

But Marr isn't finished invoking far-left guru Moore to boost the scenario of 'wild' out of control far-right Abbott. When Abbott failed to be elected as a student fellow on the University Senate, he, claims Marr, publicly lost his temper. He then quotes Moore as his only source, again without referencing him: 'He came down to the SRC and kicked a glass panel on the front door in. Not that he meant to mind you, things just seem to happen to Tony'. As I have already pointed out, this comment is oblique and facetious. It cannot be believed without qualification, especially as it comes from the mouth of someone who would say anything to harm Abbott. The charge was never repeated in *Honi Soit*.

The lack of hard evidence for his depiction of the Democratic Club as violent does not perturb Marr. It is enough to say the boys and girls 'were accused of rough-house tactics and wrecking what they couldn't control'. Who? What? Where? When? These fundamental journalistic questions continue to remain unanswered. Instead, Marr resorts to another of his disparate atmospheric lists:

'According to the roneoed flyers [Abbott] and his friends were handing around the campus, there was trouble brewing everywhere in universities: gays, strikes, sit-ins, the debauching of academic standards by Marxist lecturers, Palestine, abortion, the financial woes of AUS Travel and continued disrespect for the man who sacked Gough Whitlam. It had to stop.'[113]

Marr mocks the causes Abbott and the Democratic Club were fighting as if they were trivial or a right-wing fantasy. Let's do the list as the real substantial issues: radical homosexual proselytism; shutting down university departments; occupying academic offices and terrifying administrative staff; the debauching of academic standards by Marxist lecturers; AUS support for the terrorist organisation PLO; killing the unborn child; the collapse of AUS Travel caused by the left's delinquent financial management; and the persecution of Governor-General Kerr. The only item unchanged is the Marxists' debauching of academic standards. I have offered abundant evidence for the ongoing attempt to impose Marxism on the university as the default intellectual framework. Alan Barcan notes the continuing concern of the professorial board about the decline in academic standards.

I could go on taking apart Marr's hatchet job on Tony Abbott in the same way. For example, in response to the cynical crashing of SRC democratic processes in preventing Tony Abbott from taking office as SRC President, Marr could only comment that the episode turned into 'farce' involving 'police, rivalled teams of locksmiths, a mob of angry students, lawyers and university officials'. Nothing about the deceit, the unconscionable bastardry and trashing of the democratic principles the far-left leaders preached day in, day out, in season and out of season. Oh, no, it was Abbott's fault. 'Even those on the executive supporting his right to take office', Marr writes, 'thought his behaviour "senseless, futile and provocative"'. This time, at least, Marr references the quotation. It came from centre-left Paul Brereton and Jeremy Jones, whom Abbott accused of gutlessness in taking sides with the far left against their own interests, all to block Abbott. Interestingly, about Abbott's 'break-in' of the SRC offices, John Stroud wrote (H23, 12 October) the radicals 'tried to make out that Tony Abbott, Alex Naple, and Paul Brereton were guilty of breaking and entering and theft'. Why would the far-left group Brereton with Abbott?

If Marr is all invention about out-of-control far-right bully Tony Abbott – beautifully written, of course – then when it comes to B.A. Santamaria and his influence on young Tony, Marr's fancy and pen take a steep flight following Icarus to dizzying heights. He struggles to put a lid on his fiery hatred of this monster of religious fanaticism. Out came the lists. Santamaria was a 'bully', 'widely hated', 'his venom was phenomenal; his energy inextinguishable; and his fears legion', 'an alarmist', and so on, and so on *ad nauseam*. Not a skerrick of evidence to support this apocalyptic vision of the son of Sicilian peasants. This Catholic Rasputin cast a spell on young Tony, reducing him to a wide-eyed, staring automaton 'spouting pure Santamaria'. Tony could not but 'pledge his troth to Santamaria'.

Marr reduces the sway of Santamaria's toxic image somewhat by dragging inoffensive Jesuit Fr Emmet Costello into the field of dark influences on Abbott. Again, Marr pours out a list of unsupported claims: Fr Costello was 'a man of faith in the world of power', got 'around Sydney in a Bentley or BMW', 'heir to a gold-mining fortune', attended death beds in 'harbour mansions', considered 'forgiveness always available to the penitent', 'human rights [were never] Costello's bag', he was 'devoted to the papacy'. You get the picture. Taking his cue from Santamaria and Costello, Marr takes up the theme of male mentors unmercifully beaten up by Susan Mitchell. The difference is that Marr produces a passage of wonderful prose, one that belongs in a novel rather than a miserable, poorly argued hatchet job on a despised political enemy:

'Abbott is a man with mentors. Most were old men with embattled beliefs: true believers; relics of lost causes; men with a high view of their life and mission; men who believed in the magic of the crown, the church and old institutions. The chance to ride out with them to confront the zeitgeist touched something deep in young Tony. He was a kid with a powerful wish to serve.'[114]

It's a mark of a superior ability that a writer can so gloriously befoul someone's selfless ambition to serve the community. In any case, many a successful person has acknowledged the influence of a mentor on their life. Mark Latham, Duffy writes, paid tribute to the 'support and encouragement' he received from 'the older men in the [Green Valley Labor] branch', Frank Heyhoe and John Kerrin among them. Bob Hawke and Paul Keating have spoken about admired people who influenced them. Keating fell at the feet of that Labor brute Jack Lang. It is unexceptionable to pay tribute to the influence of successful people in one's life. Mentors *per se* are not the problem for Marr and Mitchell. It is the type of mentor who unleashes their deepest prejudices – aged, white, male, religious, and people who hold beliefs counter their own. Marr typically does not analyse the belief system. Instead, he resorts to creating a scenario that will appeal to his constituency, as he does in this vivid passage.

I will not linger over the nasty unsupported and unargued image of B.A. Santamaria. Santamaria was not flawless. Nobody is. He was not always right. And a few now take issue with his tactics to contain the Marxist juggernaut. Tony Abbott is among them. Those of us who admire Santamaria are in basic agreement with his warnings about and analysis of the dangers of Marxism to Western liberal-democratic society. Few had more insight and could articulate the issues as well as he could.

While he ponders the lasting influences of Santamaria's warnings about Marxism on Tony Abbott, Marr makes this astounding claim: 'Communism is utterly beaten, and only frantic nutters fear revolution these days'. Where is Marr's head to make this absurd claim? The attempts to establish Marxist societies (Communism in the Soviet Union, China, and Cambodia) crashed after the extermination of millions and the devastation of those societies. Marxists, however, have never given up – and never will. If you are not for Marxism, you are against it; those not gathering are scattering. Marr should get out a bit and read the many commentaries on Cultural Marxism and its long march through the West's institutions. That long march is far advanced. Marxist revolution does not only come in the form of naked violence. One of its many manifestations in Australia is the Safe Schools Coalition program, whose author is a fanatical self-declared Marxist. A lazy internet search will reveal the many groups advocating one or other form of Marxism, some of whom could not be more subversive in their plans. But it is outside my purpose to dwell on Cultural Marxism and other New Left theories still full of life. The evidence and the arguments I presented in the earlier chapters for the presence and unquenchable fervour of Marxists at Sydney University will suffice. As for Tony Abbott's recognition of the motivations and goals of the Marxists, Marr quotes from an interview on 'Nationwide' (20 March 1979) to justify his summation of Santamaria and his effect on Abbott. Abbott said:

'Marxists realised that the universities now play a crucial role in the education of the elite of modern society, and they understand if they destroy the academic standards, and perhaps even the moral standards of that elite, well then they have perhaps fundamentally and fatally undermined liberal democratic society.'[115]

Without for one moment considering the evidence for this accurate judgement Abbott offered in *Honi Soit*, Marr damned it by claiming Abbott 'was spouting pure Santamaria'. Abbott was not spouting pure Santamaria. Tony Abbott was spouting pure Tony Abbott. Abbott was a fearless, confident, independent thinker who did not always agree with Santamaria's opinions or his strategies.

It is significant that Marr does not offer any concrete evidence of Santamaria's direct influence on Abbott during his time at Sydney University. He claimed that 'from Santamaria [Abbott] took values rather than policies, values and attitudes beyond the ordinary reach of conservatism in this country'. Marr throws this in as a sort of conclusion. Not only is there no substantial argument leading to this assertion, but Marr has included evidence that contradicts it. Tony Abbott met Santamaria for the first time in January 1977 when he was twenty. Abbott's fundamental political and moral beliefs were already long formed by this time. He was expressing them outside the oversight of the local NCC office. And what Marr means exactly by 'values and attitudes beyond the ordinary reach of conservatism in this country' is anyone's guess. He doesn't explain. I don't wonder that Marr retreats from this bothersome task because he has given no sign he understands what conservatism is as a political philosophy with its pedigree going back to Plato and Aristotle.

I could go on taking issue with Marr's unsupported assertions and the scenarios he creates, but I will rest my case here. My case is not only that Marr conjures an unsupported image of Abbott, but he has not done the fundamental work of a journalist, that is, cover the evidence. The evidence is comprehensive in the editions of *Honi Soit* over four years. He hasn't read them. In his sections about Abbott on campus in *Political Animal*, Marr does not make his case for his distinction between values Abbott and political Abbott. My analysis in the preceding chapters has concluded there is no such meaningful distinction. The assessment of Tony Abbott's character and ideals lies elsewhere.

Chapter 14

Assault charges and the punches

LATE IN 1977, Tony Abbott was arrested and charged 'with indecent and common assault'. It seems significant the *Honi Soit* editorial collective never reported this incident, much less took advantage of it. Then, as now, Abbott's enemies seized on anything they could twist against him. It is a curious oversight.

Two detectives knocked on the door of his Killara house one morning while the unsuspecting second-year student was relaxing and minding his own business. After establishing his identity, they took him to the Chatswood police station, where they subjected him to the humiliating experience of being charged and fingerprinted. Abbott mentions the experience briefly in *Battlelines*:

'At the end of my second year at university, challenged at a public meeting by a fellow platform speaker about where I stood on an issue (I was standing behind her), I touched her on the back and made a facetious remark. She claimed that I'd indecently assaulted her, and a criminal charge went to court, where it failed.'[116]

Duffy wrote about that campus meeting of October 31 1977:

'Tony Abbott was campaigning for voluntary membership of AUS at the Ku-ring-gai College of Advanced Education. Before several hundred students, he waited behind and to the side of Helen Wilson, one of his opponents, who was addressing the crowd and demanding, to make some rhetorical point, 'Who is this Tony Abbott. Why is he here?' Tony reached across and tapped her on the lower back as if to say, I'm here, why not ask me ...? Helen Wilson had sworn a statement that Tony had groped her buttocks as she was speaking to the crowd.'[117]

David Marr was unusually restrained about the incident in front of a politically excited crowd of around 200 people. He tells it from Helen Wilson's point of view:

'After a meeting in August at Ku-ring-gai College of Advanced Education, Abbott was charged with indecent and common assault. Helen Wilson, a trainee teacher, was at the microphone defending AUS. She heard some- one shout, 'Why don't you smile, honey?' and says she then felt a hand groping between her legs. 'I jumped back, turned around, and saw Tony Abbott laughing about two feet away. The people in the audience began laughing and jeering'.[118]

Marr includes Abbott's response to the accusation:

'Abbott would give the court a different version and produce a number of witnesses to support him: 'She was speaking about me in a highly critical way, calling me an AUS basher and noted right-wing supporter. To let her know I was standing behind her, I leaned forward and tapped her on the back, about the level of her jeans belt'.[119]

The case went to court early in 1978. The judge dismissed it, citing the 'enormous conflict' in the evidence offered by the defence and prosecution. An impartial observer may remark that a sexual assault alleged to have been perpetrated in front of around 200 excitable students may have produced enough clear-sighted witnesses for the prosecution. After all, it was a meeting about the far-left AUS at which an AUS defender 'wearing jeans' was speaking. The meeting would have surely drawn every radical on campus. Marr typically places Wilson in the innocence of clothes of a 'trainee teacher' while no radical on campus could have been as hard-bitten as an AUS defender.

Long-time Fairfax journalist Michelle Grattan, an indefatigable rubbisher of Abbott, wrote about the incident in the *Sun-Herald* on July 18 2004 ('Abbott: I was charged with indecent assault'). She quotes Abbott as saying, 'it was a completely fictional incident', a put-up job staged by political opponents 'to be embarrassing. And it was embarrassing'. It was 'politically motivated'. Helen Wilson admitted she was 'the editor of two student newspapers' but 'denied she was a women's activist'. Pull the other one. You didn't defend the out-of-sight far-left AUS, and you didn't rise to the editorship of a student newspaper unless you were deeply of the faith. Grattan gives a slightly different account of what Wilson alleged. Helen Wilson's words:

'I had just commenced speaking when I felt a hand between my legs on my lower buttocks. I was wearing jeans. I jumped back, turned around, and saw Tony Abbott laughing about two feet away. The people in the audience began laughing and jeering.'

Marr says Wilson 'felt a hand groping between her legs' in contrast with feeling a hand between her legs on her lower buttocks. There is an unfavourable difference. Marr must exaggerate for his ideological purpose. Grattan noted that 'Ms Wilson declined to comment on the case when approached by *The Sun-Herald*'. I don't blame her. Considering the circumstances of the case, and the allegiances of the accuser, it requires a great leap of faith to swallow her version. Having the faith, however, is all-important, especially when the faithful have the pen and the microphone.

Kerry-Anne Walsh and Candace Sutton supported Grattan's piece with background material (July 18 2004) in their article 'Fellow students recall a champion of the right'. The champion of the right is Tony Abbott. With that prelude, and without knowing Walsh's current red-hot political bias, could the reader expect some balanced commentary? Not on your life. Tony Abbott, wrote Walsh and Sutton, 'burst like a snapping terrier into student politics'. He was at the centre of 'aggressive battles' with the left, 'a spear-carrier in a push to dissolve' the AUS' during 'an ugly and violent time'. Against this background, 'a sensational charge of sexual assault' landed Abbott 'in North Sydney court'. If the reader, twenty-seven years later, is not already thinking Abbott was the instigator of campus violence and guilty as charged, then there is extra incitement.

With hands over their innocent breasts, Walsh and Sutton write that 'an investigation by *The Sun-Herald* into Mr Abbott's controversial student days reveals that he spawned many more enemies than friends during those heady days'. Did he just? Well, where's the evidence? Nobody presented clear evidence of a ratio favouring either of the camps (radicals and conservatives). The empirical evidence, however, shows the radicals hated Abbott, and many shared Abbott's political platform. The conservatives constantly accused the far left of being a small minority. Abbott's overwhelming victory in the presidential elections of 1978, with a record turnout of voters (4,000), was proof of widespread support. So, Walsh and Sutton's claim is nonsense. But they did have witnesses for other charges. The first witness is one Barbie Schaffer, a fellow student now a teacher.

Schaffer claims Abbott 'was very offensive, a particularly obnoxious sort of guy' and 'very aggressive, particularly towards women and homosexuals'. How credible is Barbie's testimony? Here's the scoop. Barbie Schaffer was an active member of the extreme left group that agitated for control of the SRC and its funds. She was a member of AUS, the SU communist group, and the extreme Women's Collective. She was in the thick of the far left's campaigns for General Philosophy and Political Economy. Like all her far-left comrades, she hated conservative Tony Abbott with a pounding passion. It's all there in *Honi Soit* if Walsh and Sutton had bothered to do some genuine investigation.

The next few charges come with an appeal to 'published university reports'. Well, which ones? The unreferenced 'reports' 'show that after a narrow defeat in the university senate elections in 1976 ... [Abbott] kicked in a glass panel door'. If readers have paid attention, they would know far-left Harry Moore is the source – the only source – for this recycled claim about an alleged incident. There were no 'reports', and Harry Moore has no credibility. So much for the *Sun-Herald*'s investigation. The following unsupported claim has the same source – Harry Moore. Abbott, continue Walsh and Sutton, 'was repeatedly accused in the university paper of being a right-wing thug and bully who used sexist and racist tactics to intimidate his opponents'. No, there weren't any such accusations, no, he wasn't and, no, he didn't. If Walsh and Sutton, or anyone else for that matter, can provide the *Honi* references, I will retract. I won't hold my breath. Abbott was accused of being far-right – which was nonsense – and never directly of being a 'thug and bully'. And it was only in Harry Moore's mocking and facetious comments that an oblique unsupported charge of bullying is found. I refer the reader to my coverage of Moore's articles.

I will skip over Walsh and Sutton's appeal to David Patch's testimony that 'Tony used to stand outside the women's room with his right-wing mates and loudly tell sexist and homophobic jokes'. I have adequately demonstrated that Patch has little credibility when it comes to Tony Abbott. Walsh and Sutton are not finished yet. They quote the testimony of one Peter Murphy, who called Abbott 'a warrior of the right' (acceptable but needs qualification) and charged him with being 'the one most responsible for creating the atmosphere of terror that reigned on campus in

1977'. Utter nonsense. I refer the reader to the preceding chapters. All the violence reported in *Honi Soit* came from the left. Only members of the far left were suspended. All this false testimony is a prelude to Walsh and Sutton's (implicit) judgment of Abbott's guilt in the Helen Wilson Affair. They don't report that the judge dismissed the case or gave reasons for the dismissal. They write this:

'When it came to court the following January, Mr Abbott was flanked by his parents, a legal team including a QC, and seven witnesses. Advocates for Ms Wilson are to this day flabbergasted at the firepower Mr Abbott wheeled in, which left their under-represented side wilting.'

Oh, if only they had a QC and seven witnesses, it would have gone the other way. Walsh and Sutton should be so embarrassed by their brazen bias and unsupported claims that they should crawl away and hide in shame, as the ordinary person would be inclined to do. But they won't. And they're not finished yet. The rest of the article not only continues to show where their political allegiances lie, but it contains information of which they surely were not aware, information that has a bearing on Barbara Ramjan's 'punches' accusation. I learnt this crucial determining information in Gerard Henderson's popular Media Watch Dog blog.[120] Walsh and Sutton continue:

'The incident didn't seem to break Mr Abbott's stride, although his second tilt at election to the Student Representative Council (SRC) – which was happening at the same heady time – ended in tears. Barbara Ramjan, now a social worker, who defeated Mr Abbott for the SRC presidency that year, remembers the night of September 7, 1977, when [SRC] officer elections were held.'

First, note that the meeting of September 7 was to elect the SRC officers.

They got that right, at least. They seem to think, however, that the election of the officers and the declaration of the SRC election (July 28) were on the same night, showing they're hopelessly confused. Second, it was not Abbott's 'second tilt at election to' the SRC. It was Abbott's second year at university. In 1976, he campaigned for one of the two Economics Representative's positions, which he won. In 1977, he campaigned for the Economics position and the SRC presidency. He again won the Economics position but failed in his bid for the presidency. There is no indication anywhere that Tony was in tears over his loss. It's all there in chapters 7 and 8. More dishonest biased reporting. Walsh and Sutton have just made up what suits their narrative. Third, of critical importance, Walsh and Sutton in saying that Ramjan 'remembers the night of September 7' indicate they interviewed Ramjan for their article. Just to make my meaning clear, Ramjan provided the information to Walsh and Sutton about what happened on the evening of September 7 – not July 28. This is their account of the interview:

'Two letters [Ramjan] wrote then to *Honi Soit*, a student newspaper, outlined her version of the evening (September 7). One letter described how throughout the evening, Mr Abbott and his mates, including a dentistry student, harassed and insulted the women standing for election.

Outside the meeting, one woman 'was confronted by J [the dentistry student], who decided to "have a bit of fun" and exposed his genitalia to her as well as urinating against a tree', Ms Ramjan wrote.

'He dropped his pants [perhaps for Abbott's entertainment, he seemed highly amused] and bowed in Abbott's direction, flashing his bum towards the woman', the letter said.

In letters of reply, Mr Abbott compared the accusations to Nazi propaganda and said that the 'facts' presented were 'barefaced lies or gross distortions'.

Another letter by students Michelle Martin, Anne Woods, Garry Bennett and Ross [Rose] Vines complained the meeting had been "characterised by an unending stream of sexist incidents and attacks by right-wing representatives and their cohorts" as well as a "racist attack against the newly-elected ethnic relations officer Takis Constantopedos".'

Note that Walsh and Sutton put Abbott at the centre of the happenings of September 7. I commented extensively on Ramjan's letters in chapter 7, as well as on the support from far-left Michelle Martin, Anne Woods, Garry Bennett, and Rose Vines (Walsh and Sutton couldn't even get the names right). Ramjan's letter focused on dentistry student O'Mara. No mention of Abbott.

The appallingly biased and sloppy reporting, as obvious as it is, is not the main point. Barbara Ramjan supplied information to Walsh and Sutton that was designed to aid them in conjuring a picture of Tony Abbott as a 'right-wing thug and bully who used sexist and racist tactics to intimidate his opponents'. Why, then, did Ramjan omit to mention Abbott's (alleged) punches on either side of her head, actions far more serious than the rowdy behaviour Abbott and his friends were accused of? It doesn't make sense. At least, it makes sense if Ramjan's memory is playing her false. The literature on 'False Memory Syndrome' is extensive. That's one explanation, one that I don't accept. Another explanation, the obvious one, in my view, is more convincing. There are, however, more questions about Ramjan's silence. It has to do with the timing of the election and the first meeting of the 50th SRC on September 7 1977. We need a timeline.

Honi No.14, (late June) announced the elections for the 50th Students' Representative. Voting Tuesday July 26, Wednesday July 27 and Thursday July 28 closing 7 pm.

Honi No.21, before July 26 – The SRC Election edition provided the names of the candidates with their policy statements.

July 28 SRC annual election results declared after 7 pm

Honi No.22, August 2 – edition produced before the election results featuring Garry Bennett's complaints about 'the hostile campaign' (allegedly) 'due to an aggressive and intimidating push by the Right to take control of the SRC'.

Honi No.23, September 6 – Death of Elvis Presley edition – no mention of the results of SRC annual elections, nor anything about the elections.

September 7 – The first meeting of 50th SRC for (1) the election of SRC officers and (2) the election of the delegation for the AUS special council.

Honi No.24, September 13 – Ramjan's account of harassment before the meeting to elect SRC officers – nothing about the SRC annual election or the results declared July 28.

Honi No.25, September 20 – sexuality issue, no mention of the SRC annual elections.

Honi 26, September 27 – Abbott refutes and condemns Ramjan's accusations made about the September 7 meeting.

October 31 – Abbott accused of indecently assaulting Helen Wilson at Kuringai CAE.

At the risk of labouring the point, I stress there was no mention of the SRC annual elections or events, imagined or otherwise, on the evening of July 28. The editorial collective for H23 (Elvis Presley issue) six weeks later was a far-left stack under the leadership of Martin Hirst. If there was outrage about the 'aggressive and intimidating push' by the right as expressed by an indignant Garry Bennett and given prominence in H22, then why did Hirst not devote H23 to Tony Abbott's alleged violence committed on Barbara Ramjan? Two punches are far worse than some juvenile name-calling. Why the long lazy delay, and why the silence? Hirst and his far-left collective included wall-to-wall articles on a range of far-left issues in H23: East Timor, Israel, Uranium mining, Aboriginals, and more. But nothing about the unusual violence alleged by Ramjan against 'far-right' Abbott. Why was such singular far-right violence not the talk of the campus? Why was there no mention of Abbott's damaged fists? It is a mystery. David Marr and his research assistant either did not think this evidence important or did not get that far in their research. The second seems likely. As a prelude to his account of the Ramjan accusation, Marr continued from his restrained mention of the Helen Wilson affair with this:

'[Helen Wilson's] charges would be dismissed early in the new year, *but they were still hanging over him as he went into the university election season* and lost – to a woman – his campaign for the presidency of the SRC.

'Barbara Ramjan beat him hands down. She was of the left but her work as the SRC's welfare officer made her a popular figure on campus. The night her victory was declared, the SRC offices saw wild scenes of bad-boy behaviour: flashing, mooning, jeering and abuse. Abbott watched all this. His loss was a very public disappointment, one of the first defeats of his life that really mattered, one he would remember for a long time. [*my emphasis*]'

Once again, beautifully written, especially the evocative 'wild scenes of bad-boy behaviour: flashing, mooning, jeering and abuse'. Where is the evidence that Tony Abbott was so emotionally crushed by the loss to a woman that it was burned forever in his mind? And why give the impression the rowdiness was all by the right as if mad dog Hirst and his collective were cowering somewhere in a corner? All invention. But there's worse. Marr talks about the evening of September 7. He obviously thinks the declaration of the SRC annual election results was on September 7, and Ramjan's accusations about bad-boy behaviour followed the declaration of the results. His timeline supports this. He claimed that the Helen Wilson meeting at Macquarie University in August was *before* the declared results of the election (see above quotation). Not only has he got the time of the Macquarie University meeting wrong (it was October 31), but he has invented a scenario of flashing and mooning for which there is no contemporary evidence.

All this is an abject failure in basic research about the section most damaging to Tony Abbott, once again demonstrating Marr's pathological political bias. Understandably, Marr and his leftist publisher Morry Schwartz (Black Inc.) rushed out a revised edition (March 19 2013) less than a year later in which they tried to correct the timeline. Gerard Henderson hammered Marr through five issues of 'Media Watch Dog' in which he challenged him (among many other failings) over changes made without explanation.[121] After much evasion, Marr blithely made the pitiful admission that 'there are many revisions, editions and changes throughout the essay. That's what revised editions are for'. And that's all a fantasising religious and political bigot has to say about 'shoddy and unprofessional' writing (Henderson), not to mention dishonesty – for which his supportive class coughed up $20,000. So much for the prestige of the John Button award.

⁂

ON THE *Guardian* website, one finds a short biography of Richard Ackland linked to his article 'Andrew Bolt the latest to apologise over Tony Abbott's wall punch' (July 10 2014). Among other achievements, he publishes in law journals, is a Gold Walkley winner, a former host of ABC's Media Watch, a graduate in economics and law, and has been admitted as a legal practitioner to the supreme court of NSW. Impressive. You would expect commentary and analysis of the highest order. In his article, however, Ackland abandons the dignity one expects of a professional lawyer to indulge in some deep gloating at the (deserved) misfortunes of Tony Abbott and his supporters. The opening passages:

'As long as pundits keep questioning Barbara Ramjan's account of the Abbott university wall punch, they'll keep having to give grovelling apologies.

'Every time someone pops up and accuses Barbara Ramjan of lying over the infamous university incident when Tony Abbott flew his fists into a wall, there has been a handsome apology to her.'

First, a point Ackland is likely to think trivial. If Tony Abbott 'flew his fists into a wall', there is no way that he would have escaped serious injury to both fists requiring medical help. There is no report of Abbott wandering the campus with bandaged or plastered hands. Tony's (alleged) punches must have been no more than a tap if he had avoided injury from punching a gritty brick or cement wall. The lawyer has not only lost his dignity but his cognitive faculties. He names those who accused Ramjan of lying: Michael Kroger, Andrew Bolt, and Alan Jones. They withdrew their accusations and apologised. 'Where does this series of apologies to Ramjan leave Tony Abbott's denial of the incident?' he asks. To support his conclusion that it left Abbott nowhere to go, he quotes him as 'variously' saying that "it would be profoundly out of character had it occurred" and "it never happened". In the first, he leaves open the possibility it did happen, and in the second, he rules it out'. He could have added that Abbott also said he had no memory of the (alleged) event. We have two problems of logic in Ackland's analysis – for what it is.

Abstractly speaking, Ackland is right in saying that Abbott could have punched the wall even if such action was out of character. But it's not an abstract matter. In the abstract, everything's possible except a contradiction. All cases brought before the courts have a foundation in concrete circumstances, however tricky the abstract argument. In brief, if it can be established that the (alleged) punches were out of character, then it is information pertinent to a judgement about whether the circumstances were as Ramjan claimed. I will add that although Ackland refrained from this argument, it was not contradictory of Abbott to say he had no memory of the event and later to claim it never happened, as one long-time journalist charged. It is justifiable to claim that if you have no memory of an action someone accused you of, it never happened.

The second point of logic comes in the last paragraph of the article. 'If other players have apologised for imputing that Barbara Ramjan lied about the punches and intimidation', Ackland writes, 'Tony Abbott does seem out in the cold and alone with his "It never happened"'. Whether Abbott is alone out in the cold or not is not pertinent to the truth of his claims. The truth of Ramjan's accusation is the issue. Ackland seems to be saying that because Kroger, Bolt and Jones wilted in the face of expensive legal action, they admitted they were wrong. Is a man with degrees in law and economics and who writes for legal journals really so prone to basic errors of reasoning? Is he that naïve? Of course, he's not. It's political. He quotes Ramjan's legal case against Kroger:

'Among Kroger's claims was the allegation that she is a 'serial fabricator of false complaints'. Ramjan pleaded four imputations: she is a left-wing lunatic, she is a disgraceful nobody, she fabricated the Abbott allegation, and she told a vicious lie about Abbott as part of a campaign to damage him.'

'A disgraceful nobody'? I think this is the reaction of the nervy thin-skinned character for which I have argued rather than anyone holding that precise opinion of Ramjan. This is an issue among adults, not primary school children. The other 'imputations' are reasonable on the evidence I have offered in the previous chapters, apart from anything Kroger would bring forward if he were mad enough to go court. Kroger was a student activist around the same time as Ramjan. He had experience with the extreme left. It's my opinion that if the case had gone to court and the defence had employed all the evidence available in the student newspapers, not only *Honi Soit*, it's likely Ramjan's case would have been thrown out. I spent at least six months reading through the relevant editions of *Honi Soit* and making notes for this book. Did Kroger, Bolt and Jones want to subject themselves to the torment and money of such a drawn-out legal case? Their avoidance of a costly, time-sapping, relatively unimportant legal case (to them) was prudential. Few people would consider Mrs Greg James important in the scheme of things.

There is a final point of reasoning that Ackland completely ignores. He shows he is familiar with the accounts of two people he considers 'credible witnesses'. One is David Patch, who did not see the wall 'punches' but nevertheless claims to have been a witness. One assumes that if one is a witness to a happening, one saw that happening. Patch might have a different understanding of 'witness', of course, as he did with so much else during his wild days as an unconscionable radical student. The second is an anonymous witness who claims he saw the beginning of a punch but did not see it land. It's beyond me how anyone can be an eyewitness to something they did not see. This second witness provided an affidavit. The *Australian* reported the relevant parts of the 'redacted' affidavit (September 14 2015):

'I saw Tony Abbott raise his elbow and, with fist clenched, drive a punch downwards at Barbara Ramjan towards the end of the corridor where it opened into a bigger room, which had a table in the middle,' the affidavit reads.

'I saw Barbara Ramjan leaning against the wall, arising from a lower position (up from a kneeling position), obviously extremely shocked. I did not see the punch connect, only the sight of Tony Abbott punching down at her.

'I assumed he had hit her, and her visible shock afterwards only served to reinforce my impression.'

Before comparing this version of the incident with Ramjan's, I raise some serious questions:

* Why does the accuser want to remain anonymous?
* Why did it take 38 years for him to say something, and three years to confirm Ramjan's 2012 accusation?
* How was it possible that there was no witness to such a violent incident when the area was crowded with people awaiting the results of the elections?
* Why did Ramjan not crumple to the ground severely bruised after receiving one (not two) 'downward punch' from a fairly hefty first-grade footballer?
* Why did he not submit an account to *Honi* at the time when accusations were flying around about the boorish, sexist behaviour of the right?
* Why did he let the university's most hated right-winger off the hook when his witness could have silenced him forever?

Let me now compare Ramjan's version with that of Mr Anonymous:

'He approached Ramjan. She thought he was coming over to congratulate her. 'But no, that's not what he wanted. He came up to within an inch of my nose and punched the wall on either side of my head.'

These descriptions are so divergent that they cannot be held to be of the same event. The first has one punch driving downwards at a kneeling victim, with the imputation that the punch connected. The second speaks of two 'punches' against a wall with Ramjan standing upright. The punches were against the wall and not on Ramjan. Those who think both versions describe the same event are either consciously uttering a falsehood or delusional. The title of the *Australian* report by Jared Owens is 'Affidavit backs Barbara Ramjan's claims of Tony Abbott wall punch'. False. Was the

Australian's sub-editor stupid or simply willing Abbott's conviction like most of his colleagues in the mainstream media? But let's have a closer look at the description in the sworn statement.

Mr Anonymous saw 'Ramjan leaning against the wall'. This seems to be the initial sight of Ramjan after the alleged punch. How then did he know she had arisen from a kneeling position or that Abbott had punched down at her, let alone presume he had connected? These actions were before Ramjan was leaning against the wall. His own words defeat his description. But there's more. Two years before the affidavit, Mr Anonymous provided a version of the punch that did not correspond in all points with that of his affidavit. On September 13 2012, Mark Coultan produced this first version in the *Canberra Times* under the heading of 'Abbott's goon squad threw me against a wall':

'The man, a student at the time, said he was outside the Student Representative Council's offices photocopying when "Abbott's famous flying squad of goons crashed down the stairs, threw me against the wall, kicked in the doors of the SRC, and started creating havoc..."

"I saw Abbott throw a punch at Barbara Ramjan, but didn't see it land ... when next I saw her, she was in an extremely shocked condition, leaning against the wall ... I thought he had actually struck her, but I can see that was simply my assumption and rationalisation.

"If Ms Ramjan says the punches were aimed next to her head, I can't actually in fact contradict that ... simply I saw Abbott swinging punches, and certainly indulging in serious argy-bargy. I saw him swing a punch, I saw her in great distress."

Mr Anonymous corrected this version in the sworn statement. This one has Abbott not only 'throw a punch' at Ramjan but generally swinging punches aimed randomly at anyone in reach. He changed the thrown punch to swinging a punch at her. Where were his lawyers' heads with this rash of inconsistency? Finally, it is with loads of irony that Mr Anonymous saw what Coultan and Ackland did not see, or refused to see, that his version deviated from Ramjan's. On the other hand, he seems unaware his second reported version deviated from his first and Ramjan's. So we have three versions of the same incident. Perhaps someone will pop up anonymously and give a different and far more graphic version, with media sympathisers like Ackland and Coultan rushing to paper over any inconsistencies.

All the inconsistencies in these colourful damning descriptions aside, there is not a skerrick of contemporary evidence for any of it. Marr, in a rush of hatred for Tony Abbott, confused the election of the SRC officers on September 7 with the declaration of the results for the SRC annual election on July 28. The scenario of the 7th is the work of his powerful imagination. It demands a monumental suspension of disbelief for an impartial observer to accept Ramjan's and Mr Anonymous's version without contemporary evidence. The left would ordinarily have feasted on such 'far-right' violence for months. It is inconceivable that Ramjan and her far-left mates would whinge about flashing, mooning and sexist remarks, not about Tony Abbott but about another student, and fail to mention the violence she and Mr Anonymous alleges. It doesn't make sense – or only if one accepts where the evidence points.

Finally, why won't Mr Anonymous and his anonymous backers have the backbone to show themselves? What are they afraid of? Anonymous said he knew all about 'Abbott's famous flying squad of goons' yet knew nothing about David Patch and Barbara Ramjan's politics. How's that possible, given their high profile on campus? Was he blind to the chalkings around the campus? Was he not aware of Patch's celebrated coup? He had eyes for Abbott's goon squad but apparently not the excesses of the far left, assuring us he had 'no political affiliations to any formal party'. I suppose you can be excused from being selective in your attention if you want to rise to the heights of a 'biomedical professor'.

After 35 years, Barbara Ramjan entered the political fray to carry on her war against Tony Abbott, who represents everything most disgusting to her in a person. She could not bear the idea of Abbott becoming prime minister. The time frame shows the unappeasable bitterness of her feelings. But unlike most people engaging in political warfare, she does not have the courage to go head-to-head with her opponent. When things become too bruising, she runs to mummy. Then as now, she cannot stand on her own.

IN HIS *Sydney Morning Herald* piece, 'Then as now, you never knew what Abbott really stood for' (September 13 2012), barrister David Patch, as a prelude to his rubbishing of Abbott, entertains the reader with a little anecdote about being chummy with a 'DLP [Democratic Labour Party] candidate' who lost to him in the 1975 SRC annual elections. He writes, 'The DLP fellow, a decent bloke whom I now count as a friend, congratulated me, demanded a recount, and told me in a jovial fashion that he would win next time'.

That 'DLP candidate' was Jeff Phillips, for whom Patch expressed utter contempt and bounced out of the SRC as a good-for-nothing. Speaking about the elected SRC representatives Jeff Philips and Gary Philips, he said, 'I am implacably opposed to their kind of reactionary views, and it was a pleasure to move the motions that dismissed such irresponsible and lazy persons as SRC officers'. It's all there in chapters 6 and 7 about the ways and stories he concocted to get rid of political opponents. As I have shown, Patch had contempt for his political opponents and regarded them as dirt under his feet. We only have to recall the contempt with which he spoke to and about the Vice-Chancellor.

This little anecdote serves to contrast Phillips' (alleged) friendly reaction with Tony Abbott's, who was (allegedly) far from pleasant when he lost to

Barbara Ramjan in the 1977 SRC annual election. Yes, just as pleasant to Ramjan and Patch as they were to him. Think of all that Patch and Ramjan did to stop him from assuming the presidency, democratically won in a record turnout. Then as now, Patch must put his spin on things. Then as now, he must use the 'DLP' tag to colour his writing about his political opponents. In this case, it was falsely asserted because there was no DLP at the time. Tony Abbott and his conservative mates were members of the Democratic Club who had the support of the National Civic Council. Members of the Democratic Club were not all Catholic nor all religious. The DLP tag is an expression of Patch's insuperable anti-Catholic prejudice.[122]

The thrust of his article, though, is to overthrow the 'principle of non-contradiction', which says you can't assert one thing and its opposite in the same respect and at the same time. In this case, saying you were an eyewitness to something you did not see. This is Patch at his trickiest, as becomes a proficient lawyer and no longer the trainee student lawyer who continually flouted the rules of reason and common decency. He begins in an abstract mode. So, we will test him in that mode and not imagine we're in court where the lawyer's tricks are deployed. 'When someone complains about being assaulted', he writes, 'that complaint is accepted as evidence'. Wait a moment. To accuse someone of assault is evidence in itself? Are accusation and evidence the same thing in Australia's law courts? Indeed, you would think so when it comes to the legal abomination against Cardinal Pell, a legal process that caused dismay and scorn in legal circles around the world. But let me leave aside this counter-intuitive (at least for the average unaffected citizen) claim whose absurdity speaks for itself and examine Patch's abstract case.

He gives as an example a case where accusation is the same as evidence. 'In sexual assault cases ... when a victim complains to her mother about what a man has just done to her, that complaint itself is hard evidence that it happened'. Not necessarily. Keeping it in the abstract, the child might be an inveterate liar. She might want vengeance for something he did or not do. Abstractly speaking, there are infinite possibilities. He continues, 'This is because the law (and common sense) recognises that when victims complain immediately, it is very likely they are telling the truth'. Who says? Whose common sense? Now we have a qualification involving the same sort of slide Patch resorted to as a determined far-left student to pursue his political goals. It is 'very likely' the truth is being told. Well, that depends, too. Patch's example of a child accuser is self-serving. One would assess the degree of likelihood of truth-telling by going to the concrete circumstances of the incident, including the physical environment, the character of the accuser, what's at stake for the accuser, and how the accuser has always regarded the accused.

This abstract exposition is Patch's prelude to the particular case of Ramjan's accusation of the two punches against the wall. We're taking a gigantic leap from an uncomplicated abstract case of a child complaining to her mother of sexual assault to a vastly different set of concrete circumstances where we're dealing with (ostensibly) adults and where one's political and emotional investment could determine the assessment of claims. Viewed at its very best, Patch's claim to be a witness is only meaningful in an extremely attenuated meaning of 'witness', hardly to be compared with the abstract example he gives. After this dodgy exposition, Patch, as the bitter far-left student, returns to rubbishing Tony Abbott. He writes:

'Although he was an active member of a fundamentalist political movement with a religious base (the DLP and the National Civic Council led by Bob Santamaria), it was his personally offensive behaviour which stood out. He was always (verbally) attacking gays and feminists and lefties. You certainly knew what he was against – the trouble was that you couldn't figure out what he was in favour of!'

You would think by this time Patch would not have to rely on the Catholic fundamentalist smear, the falsehood of the DLP allegiance, and the mis-characterisation of the NCC and Bob Santamaria. That aside, Patch attributes a particular religious and political allegiance to Tony Abbott, but in woeful contradiction claims 'you couldn't figure out what he was in favour of'. Patch and his far-left mates never tired of trying to label Abbott as misogynistic and homophobic – all consistent with their imagined portrait of the conservative.

To make one's hair stand on end with astonishment, Patch goes on to say, 'Once again, the parallels with the way [Abbott] operates today are, to those who knew him then, quite remarkable'. That was just what I was thinking about Patch and Ramjan. And to top all this off, he says, 'I write not to land a blow on (or near) Mr Abbott, but to ensure that the debate about the character and suitability of a potential Prime Minister is fully and accurately informed'. Of course, that's what you're doing, David Patch, you unscrupulous far-left student radical. Your intentions could not be more transparent – to those familiar with the facts and not in a state of delusion. Like your carefully tutored nervy protégé, you could not stand the idea of Abbott becoming prime minister, and you would use the same sort of tactics you employed as a fanatical far-left student radical.

To finish, I will allow Tony Abbott to have his say. Abbott rarely showed anger in his writings. He was nearly always calm, measured, and analytical. His fiery response to Barbara Ramjan's description of the events surrounding the SRC meeting of September 7 1977, was an exception:

It was Goebbels' theory that if you say something often enough people will believe it, and certainly, the Nazis' branding of all opponents, communist or conservative, as 'enemies of the fatherland' is echoed, not very surprisingly, by *Honi*'s attacks on 'enemies of student interests'.

'Honi Soit has been remarkable for its consistent and absolute disregard for the truth. Articles have been uniformly from the left, while those few critical letters have been derisively titled or ridiculed in postscript.

'But I refer particularly to the letters of Miss Ramjan and Miss Martin *et al* in the *Honi* of 13.9.77. Not only are the motives attributed to John O'Mara and myself false and malicious, but they are justified with 'facts' that are barefaced lies or gross distortions ...

'This sort of cheap smear has been a feature of this year's *Honi* and, under normal circumstances, would hardly merit a reply. But most people are incapable of a brazen and outright lie and accept most of what they read and hear as approximate truth—so some of the mud sticks.

'The extreme left's constant exploitation of what they see as the 'gullibility of the masses' is further evidence of their fundamental contempt for ordinary people.'

❧

THERE WERE several combined aims in this book. I set out to refute the left's characterisation of Tony Abbott and his political beliefs by offering argument based on the hard evidence. In doing this, I outlined the rudiments of a Burkean conservatism. I proposed that Tony Abbott is the most Burkean conservative in Australia's history. Second, the book is about what it means to be conservative in a leftist world. The lesson for Australia's conservatives is that the mischaracterisation, often calumny, of Abbott's character and beliefs is what they should expect should they raise their voice in public debate. My book, however, was not only about Tony Abbott. A major purpose was to use Tony Abbott as a vehicle to express my criticism of the student rebellion of the 1960s and 1970s, a critical period of my youth and early adulthood. Having said this, one should not assume that the concrete expression of my Burkean conservatism is exactly that of Tony Abbott's.

THE END

APPENDIX I

Marxism: Its Basics

ONE OF CONSERVATIVE philosopher Roger Scruton's leading charges in his book *Fools, Frauds and Firebrands: Thinkers of the New Left* is that Marxist and neo-Marxists evade or seek to shield their theories from the objections raised against Marx's theories from the beginning. Ludwig von Mises raised many of those criticisms in a series of lectures in 1952 that later appeared in a book, *Marxism Unmasked: From Delusion to Destruction*, to which Scruton refers. What follows can be found in a variety of sources. I have, however, drawn much from Mises' and Scruton's books.

One can divide Marxism into three main areas. The first is a metaphysics that was taken and adapted from Georg Hegel's philosophy of history. The second is a theory of economics, and the third is about what it means to be a human person, reflecting on the ethics of the individual at work. For my purposes, I will look at the metaphysics and economic theory together and leave a more detailed discussion of the metaphysics to a separate paper.

Marx thought Georg Hegel had discovered an invariant law governing the evolution of nations through history. Hegel called it the dialectic. He had taken the term from Plato's dialogues, in which the dialectic was a progressive form of argument. In logical terms, it followed 'the method of the contrary'. If one defines one of the cardinal virtues – fortitude for example

– someone will likely offer a counter definition. If the speaker considers the objection serious enough, he will modify his definition to accommodate the objection. He then has a new definition. If there is another objection, a further modification results in a new definition. And so it could go on. The process of the dialectic, then, is thesis, antithesis and then synthesis which leads to a new thesis and so on. Hegel broadened the dialectic to explain the historical development of nations.

A nation does not remain static. It is always on the move. Its social, political, and economic structure will raise oppositions. Those oppositions will inevitably develop into conflict out of which a new structure emerges that accommodates the best features of each opposition. The new arrangements would be an improvement. It would not be too long, however, before oppositions arise which also develop into new conflicts. Out of the conflict, a new structure would emerge. One observes the dialectic in operation: *thesis*, *antithesis*, and *synthesis*. In the movement of the dialectic is found what Hegel called the 'Spirit' of the nation. The Spirit guides the nation to its perfection, its Idea or Absolute Idea. The process of the dialectic is clearly metaphysical – or spiritual. The dialectic is a necessary law of historical evolution. It will operate no matter what nations or individuals attempt.

Marx accepted this necessary law of historical development but added a correction to where he considered Hegel had failed. Instead of a metaphysical or spiritual process, Marx insisted the law was materialistic. It was not the spiritual but the material that was inherent in the necessary law of the evolution of states. That all-important material element was what Marx called the 'material forces of production' or the means of production. In other words, Marx's dialectic was about the nation's economic development. The materialist dialectic, a necessary law of development, decided the form the nation would take in every respect – government, law, customs, arts, and religion. The material forces of production, or the means of production, determined the production relations, which in turn decided the detail of the superstructure.

We can speak of an economic base from which rises a superstructure, a superstructure of laws, morality, government, property customs, religion, art and so on. Nations and peoples have no choice in what the superstructure consists. For Marx, Von Mises claimed, 'A person's consciousness is governed by place and role in historical evolution ... Every man's "class" position in society... is determined by his relationship to the ownership of the means of production ... [and the] owners in capitalist society by historical necessity exploit those offering labour.' The beliefs of the superstructure are its truth. Truth was relative to the superstructure. Beliefs are subjective. The materialist dialectic works itself out in the following way.

A nation's material forces of production and the production relations determined by them result in a conflict between those who benefit and those who are disadvantaged or exploited. A nation divides itself into classes. The concept of class is of the first importance in Marx's theory, although he is never explicit about what class is exactly. He says what it is not, but not what it is. Resentment and dissatisfaction arise between the classes until conflict arises. Specifically, the capitalist class will become ever more powerful, eliminating competition and impoverishing the working class – or the proletariat. The oppressed and barely subsisting proletariat will become conscious of their indigent state – become class conscious. They will begin their resistance.

The materialist dialectic is about the clash of class rather than the clash of nations. The course of history is an account of the clash of classes – of the oppressor and the oppressed. So we have the thesis in the economic state of affairs that prevails at a given point and the antithesis in the resentful exploited class. Conflict is inevitable. It develops and resolves itself into a new economic state of affairs in which the material forces of production are different – more advanced technologically. They determine a different set of production relations. The change in the material forces of production to a higher level is a crucial element in the resolution of the class conflict. We have the synthesis and the new economic order.

The materialist dialectic carries on relentlessly until it reaches a perfect state of affairs in which there are no classes and no conflict. The state will wither away, leaving a (materialist) paradise on earth – the state John Lennon so wistfully yearns for in his mega-hit *Imagine*, the 20th century's anthem of materialism. No heaven above, no hell below and no religion, too. Between the imploding of capitalism and the blissful state of communism, there will be the 'dictatorship of the proletariat'. 'It would prevent remnants of the old capitalist ruling class from trying to return to power and would "re-educate" the workers into a "higher consciousness" free from the residues of the prior bourgeois mentality.'

The concrete examples of clash conflict Marx gives are the ancient king states in which the king oppressed and exploited the slave population. That inevitable conflict resolved itself into the system of feudalism – the lords oppressed and exploited the serfs. The hand mill, a tool worked by the hand, characterised the means of production in feudalism. The conflict unleashed by the feudal system resolved itself into the capitalist system, today's economic system, in which the few own the means of production – represented in the beginning by the technologically advanced steam mill. Capitalists continue to maintain their position through technological advances. The capitalist class oppresses and exploits the immeasurably larger class of workers dependent on them for their livelihood.

In my summary, I have concentrated on the materialist dialectic, Marx's metaphysics. About Marxism as a commentary on economics, Marxists claim that he has offered a true economic description of the failings of the capitalist system. Included in this economic description are certain basic notions. There is the Labour Theory of Value, which in brief, says that economic value is decided by the cost of labour a commodity demands. There is also Marx's theory of Surplus Value. The employer pays a worker an amount estimated necessary to produce a commodity. However, the worker produces a product or commodity that is higher in exchange value than his wages. There is a surplus value that the worker has produced but does receive. It is shaved off as profit for the employer. Marx says this is the fundamental conflict between employer and employee or between the capitalist class and the working class. It is exploitation.

In addition to the injustice of capitalist exploitation, there is the degradation of the human person. The degradation is a consequence of the self-alienation the worker has to suffer in the capitalist system. This self-alienation and its causes form Marx's ethical theory. A worker on the factory production line loses a sense of who he is. He stands there, cut off from his fellow man performing partial repetitive work to produce a commodity. It is not even his. In his place on the production line, he does not even see the completed product. He is a sort of automaton separated from the person he is. His humanity disappears. He suffers self-alienation. At the same time, the capitalist system causes him to become an object and to attach life to the market forces and commodities. Hence, Marx speaks of commodity fetishism and reification. Fetishism is the attribution of life to material objects. Some of the neo-Marxists developed the notions of reification and commodity fetishism.

Suffice it to say that Marxism and neo-Marxism have been subjected to devastating criticism, not least by Roger Scruton, Ludwig Von Mises and Robert L. Heilbroner. It is not my purpose, however, to engage in a sustained analysis of the theory and its deficits, many of which would intuitively occur to most with a critical faculty. Instead, my aim was merely to state the basics to aid the reader in assessing the claims of the far-left students during Tony Abbott's time at Sydney University.

APPENDIX II

Some Reflections on the 1960s

MOST AUSTRALIANS born after 1970 could not be blamed for acquiring the impression that the 1960s was one long party of sexual abandonment, drunkenness, the defiance of authority, the Beatles and the Rolling Stones, British pop, anti-Vietnam protests, marijuana, hippies, flower-power and so on in that colourful style. One saying is that if you remember the 1960s, you were not there. A witty comment, but the small number abusing themselves to the state of memory loss are all long dead and in no position to make that boast. I can report first-hand, however, that this picture of widespread youthful abandonment is fanciful, designed to impress those who could not know better. In July 1960, I turned fourteen. I was in my second year of secondary school. My father carried his camera around with him, ever at the ready to shoot photos of his adored children. We have thus a pictorial record of those years when five of my parents' six children were in their teens.

Until I left school at the end of 1963, my dear mother, with her keen sense of decorum, forced me to wear my school suit to formal occasions. I was particularly peeved that at seventeen, I had to wear my St Ignatius Riverview suit to my sister's wedding in August 1963. On less formal occasions, my older brother and I wore a natty combination of navy blue blazer (which we called a reefer jacket), matching slacks, black shoes, and a white shirt with the indispensable thin black tie. Our hair was worn short, oiled and neatly parted, except for a brief period in 1960 when we tested my mother's sense of respectability by hacking away at our hair until we sported a close-cropped hairdo like Murray Rose's. Celebrated champion swimmer Murray Rose had again won gold at the Rome Olympics.

From memory, I stopped rubbing oil into my hair sometime in 1963, when the Beatles began making an impression on the Australian music scene. But it is more likely that my abandoning hair oil had more to do with the 'surfie' period that took hold until the Beatles and British pop became an overwhelming influence on Australian youth. I grew up on Sydney's North Shore and frequented Sydney's northern beaches like Manly, Harbord and Newport. So I was aligned with the surfies. It is significant that photos of the beach music group, the Chantays, show a foursome of suited oiled lads, a couple with pompadour-style hairdos. The Chantays produced 'Pipeline', the surfing number par excellence, which got them into the Rock and Roll Hall of Fame on that strength alone. The most popular television program for the youth was Brian Henderson's 'Bandstand', shown on TCN 9. During 1963, the performers on 'Bandstand', male and female, were dressed smartly, the boys oiled, some pompadoured, and in suit and tie, and the girls in brilliant frocks, which on viewing makes them look adorably female.

It might surprise some to learn that the first attempts to introduce the Beatles to an Australian audience in February and August 1963 failed. They scored their first number one in late December 1963 with 'I Want to Hold Your Hand'. The Rolling Stones' first number one was not until February 1965 ('Under the Boardwalk/Walking the Dog'). Their signature number (I can't get no) 'Satisfaction', made it to number one in August 1965. Until a critical moment in 1964, music, the great expression of youth culture, was a continuation of fifties music somewhat influenced by the Beach Boys and the surfing culture. Elvis Presley was still scoring hit after hit. Most of the music and popular performers were American: Bobby Rydell, Crash Craddock, Connie Francis, Bobby Vee, Del Shannon, Roy Orbison, and Ricky Nelson, to name a few of the chart-toppers. In Australia, we had the irrepressible Johnny O'Keefe, Col Joye, Johnny Delvin, Judy Stone, Vicki Forrest, Lana Cantwell and others that competed with the American stars. The style of music and dress was that of the fifties, as I have described it. All this fits the notion of the 'long fifties' spanning 1946 to 19 64.

The first time the mention of the Beatles made an impression on me was late winter in 1963, near the end of the schoolboy football season. After our match, a teammate and I were discussing the latest hits. I was a fan of Del Shannon's, his 'Run Away' one of my favourites. I mentioned his latest song, 'From Me to You', which was attracting attention. My teammate scoffed at it, declaring that Shannon's version was nowhere near as good as the Beatles' version. The Beatles' harmonies, he declared, no comparison! He then gave a horrible mocking imitation of Shannon's falsetto. It did not take me long to succumb to his musical authority. The entire youth of Australia succumbed. From a whiff of a breeze over calm waters, the Beatles' music whipped up and arrived in Australia with gale force, their UK hits released one after another. 'I Want to Hold Your Hand' was just the first number one. Beatles songs held the number one position on the music charts for the first half of 1964, only interrupted in the second half by Roy Orbison, Elvis Presley, Cilla Black, Mary Wells, The Honeycombs and Ray Columbus and the Invaders.

Apart from the Beatles' unoiled, silky clean 'mop-tops', the four boys dressed in a slightly modified fifties style of suits, white shirt and (thin) tie. It was not until around 1967, and the Sgt Pepper's Lonely Hearts Club album appeared, that the Beatles abandoned the suits and ties and dressed in a manner that reflected the cultural upheaval of the second half of the 1960s. Equally important from a cultural point of view was that their songs in their early period (say 1963-1965) were about the same issues that have ever preoccupied teenagers: love and heartbreak. The difference was that the Beatles, under the genius of John Lennon and Paul McCartney, plundered all the categories of popular music of the previous fifteen years to compose songs in which one can hear strains of Chuck Berry, Buddy Holly, Elvis Presley, The Everley Brothers, Fats Domino and so many other influential performers. Their lyrics were matched with engaging melodies and a performance of mesmerising harmonies.

Although I can admire the creative genius of the Beatles' 'mature' period, the songs of the first period have forever marked my late teenage years. Songs like 'All My Loving', 'P.S. I Love You', 'She Loves You', and 'Can't Buy Me Love' were the background music to all those buffeting emotions that plague or give joy to one's youth – and I was visited by plenty of them. The Beatles had brought their genre of popular music to its creative high point. Regarding the dramatic change in dress, it was the Rolling Stones who introduced the biggest change. At least, that's the way I remember it. When they first appeared on our television screen in our middle-class lounge room sometime in 1965, my parents were appalled by their slovenly dress and long hair. The Rolling Stones presented a picture of decadence to my parents' generation.

While photos of my brother and me at Christmas time from 1960 to 1964 show us in our smart slacks, navy blue reefer jackets and shirt and tie, I'm dressed in black stove-pipe slacks, black jumper, pointy black shoes and white skivvy at a family occasion in 1965. My hair in Beatles style gleams in now enviable silky blackness. The change in dress and style, a combination of Beatles and Surfie culture, was a glimpse of the cultural changes that were being unleashed. Others from a less conservative background went the whole hog and dressed as though they had just emerged from Carnaby Street.

Within a few years, the untidy look with long hair in the fashion of the Rolling Stones would be seen everywhere, especially with the youth coming up behind me. I did not venture further than my 1965 look in the following years. I was snapped after a niece's baptism in late 1967 in a splendid navy-blue suit, white shirt, black tie, and wrap-around sunglasses, with a cigarette elegantly dangling from the tip of two fingers. My shampooed hair, considered longish in 1965, was at the same length but now entirely unexceptional. Most of my friends and the groups I mixed in remained at the same stage of fashion development. I did not realise, and I don't think many of my peers realised, that the long hair and casual dress were an expression of the building youth rebellion. Until 1966, we weren't conscious of any significant social or political movement behind the changes in fashion. The social views of the great bulk of youth were still in the fifties.

Looking back, the girls I mixed with seemed as unconscious of any political cause behind the changing fashions as my friends and I were. To the extent I listened to their talk of fashion, it seemed just that. British fashion dominated. The aim was to stay abreast of developments and to maintain style and good taste. But one development in female fashion had a far greater impact, socially and politically, than the long hair and slovenly dress of the girls' boyfriends. It was the introduction of the miniskirt in 1966, the dress that raised the hemline above the knee to bare the female thigh. The miniskirt broke a rule and understanding about the relations between male and female that had existed for generations, indeed centuries, in Western Civilization. And it was intended not only to break that rule and understanding but to outlaw the rule and reverse the understanding.

Put simply, it was understood and accepted in the culture until that time that men and women responded to each other in different ways. Men initially responded more to appearance than women, while women sought an emotional connection over the physical. Men were taught to respect women and control their urges. Women were not to exploit what amounted to an advantage over men whose physical constitution made them easy prey to a woman consciously or unconsciously deploying her physical charms. While the rule for men was to control their urges and respect women, the rule for women was to act discreetly and dress modestly. Men who fell into the trap would sometimes be told to desist or stop acting the goat. More serious transgressions were treated seriously – some severely. The oversight of women was stricter. You see, women knew what women were up to (as they do today), and they knew what embarrassing fools men could be when they abandoned their self-control. The strict oversight of young women was the task of the older women, who usually had no stake in the mingling of young men and women – apart from seeing their relations well connected. I am talking about grandmothers, great-aunts, and senior aunts. My grandparents were born between the1875 and 1894, and my mother and father's generation was born between 1910 and 1925.

My irascible grandmother Wilson held court over the family females in her kitchen from which the men were banished or, if they passed through, were not to say anything other than give a meek greeting. As a child in infant school still allowed in the kitchen, I was exposed now and then to my grandmother holding forth over one or other social misdemeanour of a younger member of the court. That misdemeanour usually concerned the different degrees of the 'forward' unladylike behaviour I have just de-scribed. She did not restrict her judgement to family members, either, but cast her censorious net wide enough to include any failing female who happened to pass in her vision. And there were many.

Although it is right to ascribe the introduction of the miniskirt into Australia to 1966, the catalyst for its appearance was the year before, on Derby Day at Flemington Racecourse, Melbourne, on 30 October 1965. The spectacularly beautiful British model Jean Shrimpton appeared in a white Orlon fabric minidress whose hem was four inches above the knee. You could hardly have had a more powerful vehicle to force a radical fashion change through centuries of custom, a fashion that defied all social conventions and Derby Day protocols. Shrimpton said (and maintains) that it was all due to flukish circumstances. The dress was made short because the fabric manufacturer Dupont du Nemours International, who contracted Shrimpton to promote their product in Australia, supplied Shrimpton's dressmaker with too little material. A dress designed and planned for a top national sports occasion was made four inches above the knee because of a random mistake by the fabric manufacturer? Pull the other one. I don't believe a word of it. In 1969, Shrimpton was the girlfriend of one of the world's counterculture leaders.

The reaction on Derby Day was predictable. Men who had overcome their paralysis at the vision of an incomparable beauty – hatless, gloveless and stockingless – baring so much flesh in a formal public occasion and place began wolf-whistling and catcalling. The women, at first stunned into silence, gave voice to their outrage with scorn and jeers. The scorn and jeers would be in vain. Shrimpton's fashion coup, engineered behind the scenes, was not restricted to Australia. The revolution rippled worldwide. On Derby Day a year later in 1966, most hems were above the knee, if not as daring as four inches of bare flesh.

That exposed strip of bare flesh, however, was not any strip of bare flesh. It was bare flesh in the female erotic zone. Men do not view below the female knee in the same way as above. The attire of any prostitute or call girl testifies to that. A man sitting opposite a woman in a lounge chair in a public place may admire her shapely calves without being further distracted, but the moment the hem slides above the knee, the feelings provoked and the message conveyed are different. The miniskirt, the making public of the female erotic zone, proclaimed the message that it was acceptable for men to view women in general as sexual objects, there to satisfy their animal urges. It was just a matter of getting over a few obstacles. The miniskirt, whose invention is attributed to London fashion designer Mary Quant, was a principal weapon in the smashing of centuries-old moral codes and views about the natural relations between men and women.

If, in 2021, all this sounds more than a trifle weird, then I invite the reader to consider the logical continuation of the miniskirt breakthrough – if it were as uncontroversial as is popularly claimed. Shrimpton's dress was four inches above the knee. Why not six inches? Why not ten inches? Where do you stop? Today many 18-year-olds go out on a Saturday night in six-inch stilettos, wearing a skirt or dress whose hem is around the line of the crotch. They appear no different from the call girls conducting their trade in the venues they frequent. For those who don't get the point, a call girl sells her body to men who want to satisfy their animal urges. It is a business contract with no emotional commitment – certainly not on the man's part. As with any product, call girls present themselves to achieve maximum attraction to their product – they bare as much erotic flesh as permissible. It is not just teenage girls caught up in the Shrimpton breakthrough. It is now not uncommon to see 12-year-olds dressed as little call girls with their mothers looking proudly on.

It is either delusion or ideological pretence to dress in a way that strongly appeals to a man's animal nature and expect him to react as if he were walking among a group of women dressed in black Burkas. No feminist, however, should fear such regressive talk. The delusion, protected by such stunts as the SlutWalk, is now unshakable in our disintegrating Western culture. The endgame of the 1960s sexual revolution, where the miniskirt was seminal artillery, is today's Marxist-developed Safe Schools Coalition anti-bullying program. That program is primarily to rid society of all moral codes about sexuality and sexual behaviour.

Index of names according to chapters

Select Bibliography

Abbott, Tony. *Battlelines*, Melbourne University Press, Melbourne, 2009

Barcan, Alan, *From New Left to Factional Left: Fifty Years of Student Activism at Sydney University*, Australian Scholarly Publishing, North Melbourne, Australia, 2011

Duffy, Michael. *Latham and Abbott*, Random House Australia Pty Ltd, Milsons Point NSW, 2004

Franklin, James. Chapter 11, 'The Sydney Disturbances', *Corrupting the Youth*, Macleay Press, Sydney, 2003.

Gerster, Robin & Bassett, Jan. *Seizures of Youth: The Sixties and Australia*, Hyland House, Publishing Pty Ltd, Melbourne, 1991

Gillard, Julia. *My Story*, Random House Australia Py Ltd, North Sydney, p. 20.

Heilbroner, Robert L. *Marx: For and Against*, W.W. Norton & Company, New York, 1979.

Horne, Donald. *The Education of Young Donald*, Angus and Robertson, Sydney, 1967.

Martin, Malachi. *The Jesuits: The Society of Jesus and the Betrayal of the Roman Catholic Church*, The Linden Press, New York, 1987.

Marr, David. *Political Animal: The Making of Tony Abbott*, Quarterly Essay No.47, 2012, Black Inc., Collingwood.

Mises, Ludwig von, *Marxism Unmasked: From Delusion to Destruction*, Foundation for Economic Education, Irvington-on-Hudson, New York 10533, 2006

Neville, Richard. *Play Power*, Granada Publishing Ltd., London, 1971. Originally published by Jonathan Cape, London, 1970.

Neville, Richard. *Hippie Hippie Shake*, William Heinemann Australia, Melbourne, 1995.

O'Farrell, Patrick. *The Catholic Church and Community in Australia: A History*, Thomas Nelson (Australia) Ltd, West Melbourne, 1977.

Scruton, Roger. *Fools, Frauds and Firebrands: Thinkers of the New Left*, Bloomsbury, London, 2015.

Sheridan, Greg. *When We Were Young and Foolish*, Allen & Unwin, Crows Nest NSW, 2015

Wallace, Christine. *Greer Untamed Shrew*, Pan Macmillan Australia Pty Ltd., Sydney, 1997

Westmore, Peter. *The Strike at Sydney University: June-July 1973*, Quadrant, July-August 1973

Endnotes

1. Julia Gillard, *My Story*, Random House Australia Pty Ltd, North Sydney, p. 20.

2. The Liberal Party is the home for conservatives in Australia. The reasons are historical. In brief, the founder of the Liberal Party, the conservative Robert Gordon Menzies, wanted to establish a party that was anti-socialist but at the same time did not give an appearance of being reactionary. He wanted a non-Labour party that revered the country's traditions but looked to the future. The Liberal Party is said to be a 'broad church' for small 'l' liberals and conservatives.

3. Susan Mitchell, *Tony Abbott: A Man's Man*, Scribe Publications Pty Ltd., Brunswick, Australia, 2011.

4. See Chapter 4, 'What is Right', in Tony Abbott, *Battlelines*, Melbourne University Press, Melbourne, 2009.

5. David Marr. *Political Animal: The Making of Tony Abbott*, Quarterly Essay No.47, 2012, Black Inc., Collingwood, p. 16.

6. Alan Barcan, *From New Left to Factional Left: Fifty Years of Student Activism at Sydney University*, Australian Scholarly Publishing, North Melbourne, Australia, 2011.

7. Tony Abbott, *Battlelines*, Melbourne University Press, Melbourne, 2009.

8. Abbott, ibid., pp. 7-8.

9. Abbott, ibid., p. 6

10. Abbott, ibid., p. 7.

11. Abbott, ibid., p. 9.

12. Abbott, ibid., p.10.

13. Michael Duffy, *Latham and Abbott*, Random House Australia Pty Ltd, Milsons Point NSW, 2004. Duffy's book is the only biography of Abbott to date. It is useful for information about Abbott's early life, which I have already drawn on, but is more interesting for the orientation it gives of the philosophical framework of Abbott's thinking. Duffy does not discuss this philosophical framework in any depth.

14. Abbott, op. cit., p. 7

15. Duffy, op. cit., pp. 26/27

16. Abbott., op. cit., p. 10.

17. Abbott., ibid., pp. 10/11

18. Quoted in Robin Gerster & Jan Bassett, *Seizures of Youth: The Sixties and Australia*, Hyland House, Publishing Pty Ltd, Melbourne, 1991, p. 166.

19. Wikipedia entry on Richard Neville.

20. Jim Anderson in Drew Warne-Smith, 'The Story of Oz', Weekend Australian Magazine, 18 March 2006.

21. It is probable that the quotation came from Gerard Henderson's 2014 article in the *Australian*, 'Pro-pederasty past deserves an ABC apology'. Henderson drew the quotation from Neville's book Play Power, Cape, London, 1970. See Henderson references below.

22. 'Richard Neville, founder of Oz magazine, dies aged 74,' *The Australian*, 5 September 2016.

23. *The Australian*, 5 September 2016.

24. Richard Neville Obituary, *The Guardian*, Australian Edition, 5 September 2016.

25. 'The Story of Oz', *The Australian*, 5 September 2016.

26. Scruton, op. cit. Chapter 3, 'Disdain in America: Galbraith and Dworkin'.

27. Scruton, ibid. p. 58

28. Scruton, ibid. p. 63.

29. Scruton, ibid. p. 66

30. Gerard Henderson, 'ABC cannot deny the reprehensible actions of Richard Neville', *The Australian*, 10 September 2016. This articled followed and developed the content of a previously article: 'Pro-pederasty past deserves an ABC apology', *The Australian*, 15 March, 2014.

31. Richard Neville. *Play Power*, Granada Publishing Ltd., London, 1971. Originally published by Jonathan Cape, London, 1970, p. 60.

32. Neville, ibid., p. 58.

33. Neville, ibid., p. 60.

34. Neville, ibid., p. 14.

35. Neville, ibid., p. 56.

36. Neville, ibid., p. 207.

37. Neville, Ibid., p. 209.

38. Neville, ibid., pp. 212-214.

39. Neville, ibid., pp. 214-216.

40. Neville, ibid., p. 215.

41. Neville, ibid., p. 216.

42. Neville, ibid., pp. 223-224.

43. Barcan, ibid. p. 13.

44. Christine Wallace, *Greer Untamed Shrew*, Pan Macmillan Australia Pty Ltd., Sydney, 1997, p. 249

45. Wallace, ibid., p. 176.

46. Barcan, op. cit., p. viii.

47. Barcan, ibid. p. 2.

48. To explain the fundamental ideas of Marxism, I have drawn on the writings of Roger Scruton, Robert L. Heilbroner, and Ludwig von Mises: Roger Scruton, *Fools, Frauds and Firebrands: Thinkers of the New Left*, Bloomsbury, London, 2015; Robert L. Heilbroner, *Marx: For and Against*, W.W. Norton & Company, New York, 1979; and Ludwig von Mises, *Marxism Unmasked: From Delusion to Destruction*, Foundation for Economic Education, Irvington-on-Hudson, NY, 2006. All three are highly regarded experts.

49. Barcan, ibid., p. 49.

50. Barcan, ibid., p.25.

51. Barcan, ibid., p. 31.

52. Hall Greenland website: https://watermelongreenland.wordpress.com/

53. Hall Greenland blog: https://watermelongreenland.wordpress.com/2016/10/24/lbj-our-part-in-his-downfall/

54. Barcan, op. cit. p. 31.

55. Barcan, ibid. p. 33.

56. Barcan, ibid. p. 71.

57. Barcan, ibid. p. 45.

58. Barcan, ibid., p. 46.

59. Barcan, ibid., p. 58.

60. Barcan, ibid., pp. 80/81

61. Barcan, ibid. p. 67.

62. Bob Gould, *Desconstructing the 1960s and 1970s: An Open Letter to Keith and Liz Windshuttle*, A Self-Published Pamphlet, 30 June 2000.

63. Bob Gould, 'Hall Greenland Turns Sixty', *Ozleft*, 5 November 2004.

64. All this is easily found in an internet search.

65. Robin Gerster & Jan Bassett, *Seizures of Youth: The Sixties and Australia*, Hyland House, Publishing Pty Ltd, Melbourne, 1991, p. 54.

66. Gerster & Bassett, ibid., p. 54.

67. Gerster & Bassett, ibid., p. 102.

68. Gerster & Basset, op. cit., p. 183.

69. Gerster & Bassett, ibid., pp. 185/186.

70. Gerster & Bassett,ibid., p. 187.

71. Gerster & Bassett, p. cit., p. 189.

72. Barcan, op. cit., p. 93.

73. Because the editors of *Honi Soit* did not always date their edition, my references to *Honi Soit* will be according to the number of the issue. I will include the date where it is listed. I abbreviate '*Honi Soit*' to 'H' plus the edition number, e.g. H1, H2, H3, etc.

74. Students writing to *Honi* used the upper case for emphasis.

75. See chapters 1 & 2 in Robert L. Heilbroner, *Marx: For and Against*, W.W. Norton & Company, New York, 1979.

76. Quoted in Westmore, 'The Strike at Sydney University.'

77. See Franklin, Chapter 11, 'The Sydney Disturbances'.

78. Franklin, op. cit., p. 291

79. Franklin, o. cit., p. 298.

80. Mike Steketee, 'Fearless Advocate in Defence of Battlers', *The Sydney Morning Herald*, 4 May 2016.

81. Abbott, op. cit., pp. 10/11

82. Well-known journalist Greg Sheridan is a close friend of Abbott's. Their friendship formed during their time at Sydney University. In Sheridan's autobiographical book (*When We Were Young and Foolish*, Allen & Unwin, Crows Nest NSW, 2015) Abbott appears as his best friend with whom he shared many seminal political experiences. The book is interesting for the personal insight it gives of Abbott the person rather than the beaten-to-death persona peddled by his ideological enemies.

83. Greg Sheridan notes the external backing of leftist groups: 'Student politics was dominated by the far left. The campus left was an integrated part of the national left and received assistance from far-left unions and all the well-organised and well-funded communist parties'. Sheridan, op. cit., p. 135. p. 110.

84. Abbott, ibid., p. 12.

85. Sheridan, op. cit., p. 48.

86. Sheridan, op. cit., p. 153.

87. Mitchell, op. cit., p. 20.

88. Duffy, op. cit., p. 34.

89. *Sydney Morning Herald*, 5 November 2011.

90. Sheridan, op. cit., p. 188.

91. Sheridan, op. cit., p.151.

92. The information about AUS is taken mostly from Barcan, pp. 138-143.

93. Sheridan, op. cit., p. 169.

94. Duffy, op. cit., p. 41.

95. Abbott, op. cit., pp. 11/12.

96. Mitchell, op. cit., pp. 20/21.

97. Marr, op. cit., p. 16.

98. Sheridan, op. cit., pp. 184/186.

99. Gerard Henderson covers Barbara Ramjan's letters to *Honi Soit* 1977 (Nos. 24 & 27) in Media Watch Dog No.154, 14 Sept. 2012. I read all the relevant material in *Honi Soit* (and more) in the flow of the events and drew my own conclusions. They mostly correspond with Henderson's. I will provide acknowledgement where I draw information directly from his writings in the *Australian* and Media Watch Dog.

100. *News Weekly*, 4, 8 March 1978, p. 4.

101. *News Weekly*, August 1977, p. 3.

102. Jordan Peterson, clinical psychologist and Professor of Psychology at the University of Toronto is among the most quoted defenders of the position that there are undeniable differences between men and women. The scientific evidence is irrefutable. One of the specialists he quotes is Professor of Psychology Doreen Kimura who presents a case of overwhelming male superiority in mathematics in her book *Sex and Cognition*. Bradford, 2000.

103. 'David Marr wins prize for essay on Tony Abbott, political animal', *The Guardian Australia*, 23 August 2013.

104. Abbott, ibid., pp. 2/3.

105. David Marr, *The High Price of Heaven*, Allen & Unwin, Crows Nest, Australia, 1999, updated 2000.

106. Marr, *High Price of Heaven*, p. xi.

107. Marr, *High Price of Heaven*, p. xiv.

108. Marr, op. cit., p. 4.

109. Abbott, op. cit., p. 7.

110. Abbott, op. cit., p. x.

111. Abbott, updated edition, p. ix.

112. Marr, op. cit., p. 6.

113. Marr, op. cit., p. 15.

114. Marr, op. cit., p. 9.

115. Marr, op. cit., p. 21

116. Abbott, op. cit., p. 9.

117. Duffy, op. cit., p. 47.

118. Marr, op. cit., p. 16.

119. Marr, op. cit., p. 16.

120. Media Watch Dog No. 154, 14 September 2012.

121. Media Watch Dog Nos. 157, 172, 177, 178, 181, (October 2012 to May 2 013)

122. Gerard Henderson frequently corrected David Marr's claims about Tony Abbott's connection with the DLP (The Democratic Labour Party). In Media Watchdog No.154, 14 September 2012, he wrote, 'Abbott had no association with the DLP – which effectively went out of operation after the May 1974 double dissolution election (when Abbott was aged 16) and was formally wound up in early 1978. Moreover, the DLP was never a significant organisation in New South Wales – its base was in Victoria and Queensland. Abbott was associated with the National Civic Council which was headed by Bob Santamaria. Santamaria was never a member of the DLP'. The same applies to Jeff Phillips's alleged status as a 'DLP fellow'. There is more about Abbott's connection with Bob Santamaria and the National Civic Council in Henderson's definitive biography of Santamaria, *Santamaria: A Most Unusual Man*.

www.ingramcontent.com/pod-product-compliance
Lightning Source LLC
Chambersburg PA
CBHW021210090426
42740CB00006B/179